D1784179

BizTalk Server 2010 Cookbook

Over 50 recipes for developers and administrators looking to deliver well-built BizTalk solutions and environments

Steef-Jan Wiggers

[PACKT] enterprise
PUBLISHING
professional expertise distilled

BIRMINGHAM - MUMBAI

BizTalk Server 2010 Cookbook

Copyright © 2012 Packt Publishing

All rights reserved. No part of this book may be reproduced, stored in a retrieval system, or transmitted in any form or by any means, without the prior written permission of the publisher, except in the case of brief quotations embedded in critical articles or reviews.

Every effort has been made in the preparation of this book to ensure the accuracy of the information presented. However, the information contained in this book is sold without warranty, either express or implied. Neither the author, nor Packt Publishing, and its dealers and distributors will be held liable for any damages caused or alleged to be caused directly or indirectly by this book.

Packt Publishing has endeavored to provide trademark information about all of the companies and products mentioned in this book by the appropriate use of capitals. However, Packt Publishing cannot guarantee the accuracy of this information.

First published: April 2012

Production Reference: 1290312

Published by Packt Publishing Ltd.
Livery Place
35 Livery Street
Birmingham B3 2PB, UK.

ISBN 978-1-84968-434-7

www.packtpub.com

Cover Image by Artie Ng (artherng@yahoo.com.au)

Credits

Author

Steef-Jan Wiggers

Reviewers

Abdul Rafay

Randal van Splunteren

René Brauwers

Sandro Pereira

Acquisition Editor

Dhwani Devater

Lead Technical Editor

Chris Rodrigues

Technical Editor

Prasad Dalvi

Copy Editor

Laxmi Subramanian

Project Coordinator

Vishal Bodwani

Proofreader

Linda Morris

Indexer

Rekha Nair

Production Coordinators

Prachali Bhiwandkar

Alwin Roy

Cover Work

Alwin Roy

About the Author

Steef-Jan Wiggers is an IT architect with over 13 years of experience as a Consultant, Technical Lead Developer, and Application Architect, specializing in custom applications, enterprise application integration (BizTalk), Web services, and Windows Azure. He has experience in architecting, designing, developing, and supporting sophisticated and innovative software using many different Microsoft technologies and products. Steef-Jan is very active in the BizTalk community as a blogger, Wiki author/editor, MSDN forums writer, and public speaker. He has been awarded the Microsoft Most Valuable Professional (MVP) award in 2010 for his contributions to the world-wide BizTalk Server community and has been re-awarded in July 2011.

Steef-Jan lives in the Netherlands, is married to Lian, and has three lovely children, Stan, Ellis, and Cato. Last but not the least, they are accompanied by their English Cocker Spaniel, Barry. Steef-Jan is certified in MCDBA, MCSD, MCSD.NET, MCSA, MCAD, MCTS: BizTalk Server BizTalk Server 2006, BizTalk Server 2006 R2, and BizTalk Server 2010.

Steef-Jan works as a Specialist Knowledge Provider for Ordina, which lays the foundation of its clients' future success by offering a coherent proposition of Consulting, IT, and Outsourcing services. Within Ordina, Steef-Jan is responsible for BizTalk Expertise Group — sharing knowledge, exchanging experience, planning meetings, and facilitate courses. He manages the Line Of Buisness (LOB) BizTalk to create/maintain LOB year plans, coordinates contacts with the BizTalk community (BTUG) in the Netherlands and Sweden, and partners with Microsoft for BizTalk.

Steef-Jan has been a Technical Reviewer of the BizTalk 2010 Patterns book written by Dan Rosanova and is currently involved as a Technical Reviewer for the forthcoming book (MCTS): Microsoft BizTalk Server 2010 (70-595) Certification Guide. He is also a co-author of a series of BizTalk Server Administration books.

Acknowledgement

I started this endeavor at the beginning of the year 2011, when I was approached by Dhwani Devater, who is an Acquisition Editor at Packt Publishing. During the MVP Summit, I spoke to Richard Seroter about his experience with writing and talked it through with Randal van Splunteren. I then decided to go for it and asked Randal to help me as a Technical Reviewer. Through the whole process, Randal has provided me with a lot of valuable feedback and guidance. A few months later, he was joined by two other MVPs, Sandro Pereira and Abdul Rafay, together with my former colleague René Brauwers, who then started reviewing this book. They have put so much effort and time to increase the quality of the book. Thanks guys.

Besides this awesome crew of reviewers, there were others in the background, providing me with feedback for some of the content I wrote. So, I would like to thank Richard Seroter, Tord Glad Nordahl, Paul Gielens, Alex Thissen, Douglas Skirving, and Mikael Håkansson. I would also like to thank Saravana Kumar, as friend and contributor of content to the BizTalk monitoring chapter. During the process of writing, I was guided and supported by great people from Packt Publishing and I would like to especially thank Dhwani Devater, Chris Rodrigues, Prasad Dalvi, and Vishal Bodwani.

My employer, Ordina, has given me a lot of leverage to spend time writing this book, prepare for seminars, attend conferences, and write articles. I would like to thank Bert van den Belt and Marco Rutters in particular for their support in my efforts.

I missed some of my friends and family as they saw less of me, but kept me motivated. I would like to thank my dear friends and family members—Harco van Polen, Lisette Hofland, Ivo Brouwer, Anita van Eindhoven, Tom Backx, Stan Ketelaars, Dennis Leeman, Dennis van Oort, Jan van Thiel, Johan Muskens, Joost Smit, Walter Willems, Camilla Singh, Jeroen Peters, Diana Rigola, Tanja Ruijsenaars, Raymond te Beek, Ruud Vorster, Lucy Vorster, Sylvie Megens, John Megens, Evert Vorster, Julie Evans, Dick Perebolte, Annie Perebolte, Henk-Jan Perebolte, Monica Perebolte, Wim Perebolte, Keng Perebolte, Friso Wiggers, Maartje Wiggers, and my parents, Marijon Wiggers, Jan Wiggers, for their moral support.

Working on this book demanded a lot of effort and attention. My children and my wife supported me throughout the process by giving me space and room to work. Now that the book has been released, I will make it up to them.

About the Reviewers

Abdul Rafay (http://abdulrafaysbiztalk.wordpress.com) has been working on integration with BizTalk and other Microsoft technologies for more than 5 years. He works as an Integrator in a bank in Qatar, where he is involved in architecture, design, development, and testing of integration solutions built on Microsoft platforms, which mainly includes BizTalk, WCF, and Windows Server AppFabric.

He has vast experience with integration projects in the banking domain and has been involved in projects integrating banking applications with core banking systems and B2B partners. He has previously worked with the largest implementations of BizTalk in companies, such as United Bank Ltd. in Pakistan and SADAD in KSA.

He was awarded the Microsoft Most Valuable Professional (MVP) in BizTalk, thrice, and likes to share his knowledge and technical expertise on his blog, MSDN, and other forums.

Other than integration projects and BizTalk, Abdul has previously worked as a web developer with technologies such as ASP, ASP.NET, Sharepoint, and open source web applications.

I would like to thank my fantastic wife, Hira, for making this project, and my life successful. Thanks for your understanding, patience, and support, which lead me to success. I would like to thank God Almighty for giving me all what I have. I would like to thank all my friends who were there when I needed them and specially my in-laws. Thanks to all those who have contributed to my success and were part of my life.

Randal van Splunteren lives with his wife, daughter, and son in the Netherlands. He works as a consultant for a Dutch consulting company. His focus is on implementing integration scenarios, using Microsoft products and technologies. He has real-world experience with all versions of BizTalk Server and was awarded the Most Valuable Professional (MVP) for BizTalk Server by Microsoft, in 2010 and 2011. Randal is an active BizTalk community member and maintains a blog on BizTalk (`http://biztalkmessages.vansplunteren.net`). You can contact Randal at `randal.van.splunteren@hotmail.com`.

> I would like to thank Steef-Jan Wiggers for writing this great book and for giving me the opportunity to review it.

René Brauwers started his IT career at the end of the last century as a Web Developer/Designer and was primarily engaged with building websites using classic ASP. Soon, his focus got drawn more towards developing client/server applications, using the 3GL language, Centura/Gupta Team Developer. Around the end of 2002, he got involved with the EAI/B2B/B2C/BPM world, starting off with WebMethods and did this for the next three years with an occasional side step to .NET development. This occasional side step got him in touch with BizTalk Server in 2005, and since then, he has been involved with BizTalk Server and general .NET programming. Currently, he is employed as a senior BizTalk consultant for Motion10 (`http://www.motion10.com`) in the Netherlands and can be contacted via e-mail (`rene@brauwers.nl`), Twitter (@ReneBrauwers), LinkedIn (`http://nl.linkedin.com/in/brauwers`), or through his blog, "Me, .NET and BizTalk" (`http://blog.brauwers.nl`).

> One has to live one's life to the fullest extent possible; for me this includes sharing my life with the most wonderful woman in the world, Miranda. Thanks for being part of my life, being my friend, my soul mate, and my girlfriend. I can't wait to spend the rest of my life together with you.

Sandro Pereira lives in Portugal and works as a BizTalk consultant at DevScope (`www.devscope.net`). In the last few years, he has been implementing integration scenarios and Cloud Provisioning at a major telecommunications service provider in Portugal. His main focus is on Integration Technologies, for which he has been using .NET, BizTalk, and SOAP/XML/XSLT, since 2002.

He is an active blogger (`http://sandroaspbiztalkblog.wordpress.com/`), member and moderator on the MSDN BizTalk Server Forums, Code Gallery contributor, and was awarded the Most Valuable Professional (MVP) for BizTalk Server by Microsoft in 2011 (`https://mvp.support.microsoft.com/profile/Sandro.Pereira`). You can contact Sandro at `sandro-pereira@live.com.pt`.

www.PacktPub.com

Support files, eBooks, discount offers and more

You might want to visit www.PacktPub.com for support files and downloads related to your book.

Did you know that Packt offers eBook versions of every book published, with PDF and ePub files available? You can upgrade to the eBook version at www.PacktPub.com and as a print book customer, you are entitled to a discount on the eBook copy. Get in touch with us at service@packtpub.com for more details.

At www.PacktPub.com, you can also read a collection of free technical articles, sign up for a range of free newsletters and receive exclusive discounts and offers on Packt books and eBooks.

http://PacktLib.PacktPub.com

Do you need instant solutions to your IT questions? PacktLib is Packt's online digital book library. Here, you can access, read and search across Packt's entire library of books.

Why Subscribe?

- ▶ Fully searchable across every book published by Packt
- ▶ Copy and paste, print and bookmark content
- ▶ On demand and accessible via web browser

Free Access for Packt account holders

If you have an account with Packt at www.PacktPub.com, you can use this to access PacktLib today and view nine entirely free books. Simply use your login credentials for immediate access.

Instant Updates on New Packt Books

Get notified! Find out when new books are published by following @PacktEnterprise on Twitter, or the *Packt Enterprise* Facebook page.

This book is dedicated to my wife Lian, and my children Stan, Ellis, and Cato

Table of Contents

Preface

In your day-to-day job as a BizTalk developer, administrator, or consultant, you will face challenges when it comes to deploying a BizTalk Server environment, advising clients on integration with BizTalk, developing BizTalk solutions, working with its components such as Business Rules, or a feature such as AppFabric Connect. As an administrator, you will be responsible for keeping BizTalk healthy. The practical recipes in this book can strengthen your skills and knowledge. A developer can face challenges during implementation of functionality in an orchestration or while testing the solution. Having recipes in this book on how to deal with these challenges can be of tremendous value. Some of the recipes in this book will show you how to use other BizTalk-related tooling from Microsoft, the community, and third parties which can greatly improve your productivity as a developer or administrator. This book will provide you with guidance on using out of the box BizTalk capabilities combined with the capabilities offered by BizTalk tools found on CodePlex, and the Microsoft Download Center. BizTalk Server 2010 Cookbook is a practical guide for developers and administrators, which they can use as reference guide for their day-to-day job, making their lives easier.

What this book covers

Chapter 1, Setting up a BizTalk Server Environment, will provide the reader with guidance on setting up a robust and healthy BizTalk environment, from its inception to its deployment. Recipes in this chapter will show the reader how to use some of the community and Microsoft tools to validate, test, and tune the BizTalk environment and how to set up and configure critical components, such as MSDTC and SSO.

Chapter 2, BizTalk Server Automation: Patterns, gives an idea about patterns that can be applied to orchestrations. Recipes discussed in this chapter will show how to implement some of the common integration patterns with BizTalk Server 2010.

Chapter 3, BizTalk Server Instrumentation, Error Handling, and Deployment, introduces the reader to the concepts of instrumentation, error handling, and deployment of BizTalk solutions. Recipes discussed in this chapter will show how to implement instrumentation to BizTalk solutions, using logging and tracing, how to implement error handling, and how to deploy BizTalk solutions, using out of the box BizTalk features or the BizTalk deployment framework.

Chapter 4, Securing your Message Exchange, explains about security in BizTalk messaging context. It will show how to provide message security by using encryption and decryption, or signing and verifying. It will also touch transport security using SSL.

Chapter 5, WCF Services with BizTalk, introduces the concept of communicating with WCF Services through BizTalk Server. Recipes discussed in this chapter will show how to consume a WCF Service, expose schemas as a WCF Service, and other related possibilities.

Chapter 6, BizTalk AppFabric Connect, explains about the new BizTalk Server 2010, which shifts the boundaries of BizTalk to Windows Azure. Recipes discussed in this chapter will demonstrate how to expose orchestrations, and LOB systems through Window Azure Service Bus.

Chapter 7, Monitoring and Maintenance, will provide the reader with practical recipes on keeping BizTalk Server healthy and what monitoring solutions are best suitable in a given scenario. This chapter will demonstrate the capabilities found in community tooling, SCOM, and alternative monitoring product BizTalk360.

Chapter 8, Applying Rules, introduces the concepts of BizTalk Business Rules Engine. It will demonstrate how to use BRE with and without using the BizTalk Server runtime.

Chapter 9, Testing BizTalk Artifacts, will provide the reader with a couple of recipes to enable testing of the different BizTalk artifacts, such as schemas, pipelines, maps, and orchestrations. Testing can be done using the test capabilities of Visual Studio in conjunction with community test tooling.

What you need for this book

You need to install the following software:

- ▶ Windows 2008 (R2) Standard Edition
- ▶ Visual Studio 2010
- ▶ BizTalk Server 2010 Developer Edition
- ▶ SQL Server 2008 (R2) Standard Edition
- ▶ VMware Workstation or Player
- ▶ Windows Hyper-V

Who this book is for

This book is intended for BizTalk developers and administrators. It is provided with practical recipes that will help them enhance and strengthen their knowledge of BizTalk Server, its architecture, components, and infrastructure. The technical focus will make the book less applicable to managers unless they have a fairly deep technical background, but it will be useful to them in ensuring that their team stays on track with developing robust BizTalk solutions and to keeping BizTalk healthy.

This book expects a basic background knowledge of BizTalk Server, Visual Studio, and SQL Server. It is targeted towards the beginner or intermediate BizTalk developer and administrator, who has previous experience in developing on the Microsoft Platform in .NET or Visual Studio, or has administration experience with the Windows operating system and SQL Server. With lack of this experience, it will be challenging to work with BizTalk as a developer or administrator, or to provide advice as a consultant. Therefore, I recommend working with C# or Visual Studio a little on your own, ahead of time, to familiarize yourself with the IDE as a developer. An administrator will need to start working with the Windows operating system or with SQL Server to get to know the platform and the product.

The more seasoned, advanced BizTalk developers, administrators, consultants, or architects might learn some new tricks or can enhance their already extensive knowledge. They can gain some insight on how implementations can be carried out or use the recipes to enhance or compare with their own recipes. Finally, they can use this book as a reference guide for their day-to-day jobs.

Conventions

In this book, you will find a number of styles of text that distinguish between different kinds of information. Here are some examples of these styles, and an explanation of their meaning.

Code words in text are shown as follows: "During configuration of these BizTalk features, databases such as BizTalk MessageBox (`BizTalkMsgBoxDb`), BizTalk Management (`BizTalkMgmtDb`), BizTalk Tracking (`BizTalkDTADb`), BizTalk Rule Engine (`BizTalkRuleEngineDb`), BAM Primary Import (`BAMPrimaryImport`), and others (`BAMStarSchema`) are created on the database server."

A block of code is set as follows:

```
<sso>
  <globalnfo>
    <ssoAdminAccount>YourDomain\Accountname</ssoAdminAccount>
    <ssoAffiliateAdminAccount> YourDomain
    \Accountname</ssoAffiliateAdminAccount>
    <secretServer>ServerName</secretServer>
    <auditDeletedApps>1000</auditDeletedApps>
    <auditDeletedMappings>1000</auditDeletedMappings>
    <auditCredentialLookups>1000</auditCredentialLookups>
```

```
      <ticketTimeout>2</ticketTimeout>
      <credCacheTimeout>60</credCacheTimeout>
   </globalInfo>
</sso>
```

Any command-line input or output is written as follows:

```
cscript InstallHosts.vbs "BizTalk Application Users" "\MyUser" "My-
Password" "BtsServer1"
```

New terms and **important words** are shown in bold. Words that you see on the screen, in menus or dialog boxes for example, appear in the text like this: "Especially, the **Production Information** section provides detailed information on system requirements, roadmap, and the FAQs."

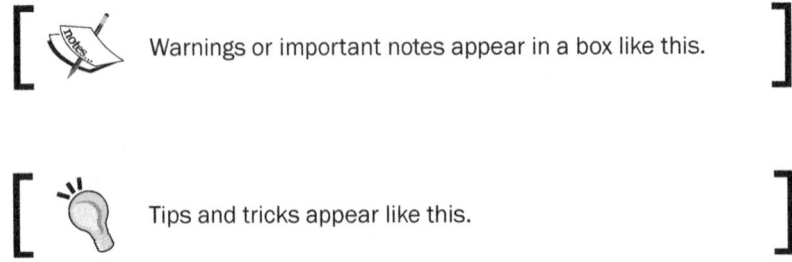

Warnings or important notes appear in a box like this.

Tips and tricks appear like this.

Reader feedback

Feedback from our readers is always welcome. Let us know what you think about this book—what you liked or may have disliked. Reader feedback is important for us to develop titles that you really get the most out of.

To send us general feedback, simply send an e-mail to feedback@packtpub.com, and mention the book title through the subject of your message.

If there is a topic that you have expertise in and you are interested in either writing or contributing to a book, see our author guide on www.packtpub.com/authors.

Customer support

Now that you are the proud owner of a Packt book, we have a number of things to help you to get the most from your purchase.

Downloading the example code

You can download the example code files for all Packt books you have purchased from your account at http://www.packtpub.com. If you purchased this book elsewhere, you can visit http://www.packtpub.com/support and register to have the files e-mailed directly to you.

Errata

Although we have taken every care to ensure the accuracy of our content, mistakes do happen. If you find a mistake in one of our books—maybe a mistake in the text or the code— we would be grateful if you would report this to us. By doing so, you can save other readers from frustration and help us improve subsequent versions of this book. If you find any errata, please report them by visiting http://www.packtpub.com/support, selecting your book, clicking on the **errata submission form** link, and entering the details of your errata. Once your errata are verified, your submission will be accepted and the errata will be uploaded to our website, or added to any list of existing errata, under the Errata section of that title.

Piracy

Piracy of copyright material on the Internet is an ongoing problem across all media. At Packt, we take the protection of our copyright and licenses very seriously. If you come across any illegal copies of our works, in any form, on the Internet, please provide us with the location address or website name immediately so that we can pursue a remedy.

Please contact us at copyright@packtpub.com with a link to the suspected pirated material.

We appreciate your help in protecting our authors, and our ability to bring you valuable content.

Questions

You can contact us at questions@packtpub.com if you are having a problem with any aspect of the book, and we will do our best to address it.

1
Setting up a BizTalk Server Environment

In this chapter, we will cover:

- Gathering requirements by asking the right questions
- Analyzing requirements and creating a design
- Installing and using the BizTak Best Practices Analyzer
- Validating BizTalk installation with the BizTalk Benchmark Wizard tool
- Automating performance analysis by using the PAL tool
- Managing the SSO system
- Configuring MSDTC for multi-server BizTalk platforms

Introduction

Having a stable, robust, (highly) available BizTalk environment is important. Many times BizTalk is installed, solutions are architected, and then the environment is not up to its task. System boundaries are reached fast and solutions do not perform well and make BizTalk throttle, as a result of excessive memory use or flooding of the system with messages. There are many ways to prevent this by using tools that are available, together with some best practices provided by Microsoft. They deliver a quite extensive BizTalk optimization guide (`http://www.microsoft.com/download/en/details.aspx?id=10855`) and operation guide (`http://www.microsoft.com/download/en/details.aspx?id=6282`).

Knowing your environment and its boundaries will provide insight on how to prevent your BizTalk environment from becoming a hotspot. For doing this, you have to go through the following steps:

- Process of setup
- Configure and test
- Adjust and test

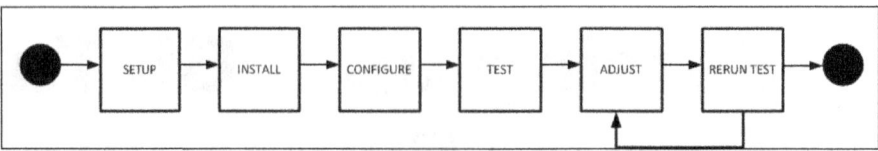

It starts with setting up your environment, but prior to that you will need to assess the requirements. You will only be able to do so by asking the right questions and analyzing them well. When you deploy BizTalk on the determined hardware and software, you will be able to validate, test, and tune it using the following:

- **BizTalk Best Practices Analyzer** (**BPA**)
- **BizTalk Benchmark Wizard** (**BBW**)
- **Performance Analysis of Logs** (**PAL**) tool

During assessing and analyzing the requirements, it is possible that you will end up with a design of a scaled out BizTalk configuration. This will affect some of the essential components in a BizTalk runtime, the **Microsoft Distributed Transaction Coordinator** (**MSDTC**) and the Master Secret Server. In a multi-server BizTalk environment, MSDTC is vital and needs to get set up and configured properly before one starts configuring BizTalk features, such as group, **Business Rule Engine** (**BRE**), or **Business Activity Monitoring** (**BAM**).

During configuration of these BizTalk features, databases such as the BizTalk MessageBox (`BizTalkMsgBoxDb`), BizTalk Management (`BizTalkMgmtDb`), BizTalk Tracking (`BizTalkDTADb`), BizTalk Rule Engine (`BizTalkRuleEngineDb`), BAM Primary Import (`BAMPrimaryImport`), and others (`BAMStarSchema`) are created on the database server.

The Master Secret Server plays an essential role in aiding the BizTalk runtime in securing information for the receive locations and send ports. Some cases in which high availability is required, SQL Server and the host instances, need to be clustered for certain adapters such as FTP, POP3, and MSMQ. The reason for clustering the adapters is to prevent message duplication. The FTP protocol, for instance, does not support file locking (`http://kentweare.blogspot.com/2009/04/clustering-biztalk-hosts.html`).

In this chapter, requirements gathering and assessment will be described in a manner that could aid you when undergoing this process at the client side. Once you have prepared the deployment of BizTalk, you can go through the *Analyzing requirements and creating a design*, *Configuring MSDTC for multi-server BizTalk platforms*, and *Managing the SSO system* recipe later in this chapter. To validate, test and tune your BizTalk environment; you can read the recipes mentioned earlier.

Gathering requirements by asking the right questions

Although, this is not an exact recipe, asking questions to obtain requirements for your BizTalk environment is important. Having a clear view and understanding of the requirements enables you to deploy the desired BizTalk environment that meets expectations of the customer. What are the right questions you may ask yourself? Well, there is quite a large area in general you basically need to cover with questions. These questions will be around the following topics:

- A BizTalk work load(s) that is functional
- Non-functional (high availability, scalability, and so on)
- Licensing (software)
- Hardware
- Virtualization
- **Development**, **Test**, **Acceptance**, and **Production** (**DTAP**) environment
- Tracking/Tracing
- Hosting
- Security
- Support

Getting ready

Organize the sessions, and/or the workshop(s) to discuss the BizTalk architecture (environment), functionality, and non-functional requirements, where you do a series of interviews with appropriate stakeholders. This way you will be able to retrieve the necessary requirements and information for a BizTalk environment. You will need to focus on business first and IT later. You will notice that each business will have a different set of requirements on integration of data and processes. Some of these are listed as follows:

- Business is able to have the access of information from anywhere any time
- Have the proper information to present to the proper people
- Have the necessary information available when needed

- Manage knowledge efficiently and be able to share it with the business
- Change the information when needed
- Automate the business process that is error-prone
- Automate the business process to reduce the processing time of orders, invoices, and so on

Regarding the business requirements, BizTalk will have certain workloads, and with the business you determine if you want BizTalk to aid in automating processes, exchange of information with partners, maintaining business rules, visibility of psychical events, and/or integration with different systems. One important factor to reckon with bringing BizTalk into an organization is risk-associated with transitioning to its platform. This risk can be of a technical, operational, political, and financial nature. BizTalk solutions have to operate correctly, meet the business requirements, and be accepted by stakeholders within the organization and should not be too expensive.

With IT, you focus more on the technical side of the BizTalk Environment such as, "What messages in size, format, and encoding are sent to the BizTalk system or what does it need to output?" You should consider security around it, when information going to or coming from trading partners is confidential. Encryption and decryption of data such as, "What processes that are automated need to interact with internal and external systems?" or "How are you going to monitor messages that are going in and out?" can come into play. Support needs to be set up properly to keep BizTalk and its solutions healthy. Solutions need to be developed and tested, preferably using different environments such as test and acceptance. For that, you will need an agreed deployment process with IT. These are factors to reckon with and need to be addressed when interviewing or talking to IT stakeholders within the organization.

How to do it...

Categorize your stakeholders into two categories—business and IT. Create a communication plan and list of questions related to areas mentioned earlier. With the list of questions you can assign each question to a person you think can answer it. This way you ask the right questions to the right people. The following table shows a sample of roles belonging to business and/or IT. It could be that you identify more roles depending on your situation:

Category	Role
Business	CEO, CIO, Security Officer, Business Analyst, Enterprise Architect, and Solution Architect.
IT	IT Manager, Enterprise Architect, Solution Architect, System/Application Architect, System Analyst, Developer, System Engineer, and DBA.

Having the roles clear belonging to either business, IT, or both, you will then need to have a list of questions and assign these to the appropriate role. You can find an example list of questions associated to a particular role in the following table:

Question	Role
Will BizTalk integrate with systems in the enterprise? Which consumers and host systems will it integrate with?	Enterprise Architect, Solution Architect
What are the applicable workloads?	Enterprise Architect
Is BizTalk going to be strategic for integration with internal/external systems?	CEO, CIO, Enterprise Architect, and Business Analyst
Number of messages a day/hour	Enterprise Architect
What are the candidate processes to automate with BizTalk?	Business Analyst, Solution Architect
What communication protocols are required?	Enterprise Architect, Solution Architect
Choice of Microsoft platform—Operating System, SQL Server Database	Enterprise Architect, Security Officer, Solution Architect, System Engineer, and DBA
Encryption algorithm for data	Enterprise Architect, Security Officer, Solution Architect, and System Engineer
Is Secure Socket Layer required for communication?	Enterprise Architect, Security Officer, Solution Architect, and System Engineer
What kind of certificate store is there?	Enterprise Architect, Security Officer, Solution Architect, and System Engineer
Is the support for BizTalk going to be outsourced	CEO, IT Manager

There's more...

The best approach to gather the requirements is to view it as a project or a part of the project. You can use a methodology such as PRINCE2.

PRINCE2

Projects in Controlled Environments (**PRINCE**) is a project management method. It covers the management, control, and organization of a project. PRINCE2 is the second major release of it. More information is available at `http://www.prince2.com/`.

Microsoft BizTalk Server website

The Microsoft BizTalk Server website provides a lot of information. Especially, the **Production Information** section provides detailed information on system requirements, roadmap, and the FAQs. The latter sections provide details on pricing, licensing, and so on. Go to `http://www.microsoft.com/biztalk/en/us/default.aspx`.

See also

- ▶ Refer to the *Analyzing requirements and creating a design* recipe later in this chapter
- ▶ Refer to *Chapter 4, Securing your Message Exchange*
- ▶ Refer to *Chapter 7, Monitoring and Maintenance*

Analyzing requirements and creating a design

Analyzing requirements and creating a design for the BizTalk landscape is the next step forward before planning and installing. With the gathered requirements, you can make decisions on how to design a BizTalk environment(s). If BizTalk is used for the first time in an enterprise environment capacity, planning and server allocation is something to focus on. Once you gather requirements and ask questions, you will have a clear picture of where the platform will be hosted and whether it needs to be scaled up or out. If everything gets placed on one big server, it will introduce a serious single point of failure. You should try to avoid this scenario. Therefore, separating BizTalk from the SQL Server is the first thing you will do in your design, each on a separate hardware preferably.

Depending on availability requirements, you will probably cluster the SQL Server. Besides that, you can choose to scale out BizTalk into a multiserver group, because of availability requirements and if the expected load cannot be handled by one BizTalk instance. You can opt for installing BizTalk and SQL separately first and then scale-out after performing benchmark tests. You can scale vertically (scaleup) by increasing the number of processors and the amount of memory each server uses, or you can scale horizontally (scaleout) by adding more servers to your BizTalk Server configuration. Other options you can consider during your design are as follows:

- ▶ Having multiple MessageBox databases
- ▶ Separate BizTalk databases

These options are best visualized by the scale-out poster from Microsoft (`http://www.microsoft.com/download/en/details.aspx?id=13103`).

Based on the requirements, you can consider isolating the BizTalk hosts to be able to manage BizTalk applications better and divide the load. By separating send, receive, and processing functionality in different hosts, you will benefit from better memory and thread management.

 If you expect a high load of large messages or orchestrations that would consume large amounts of resources, you should isolate send and/or receive adapters. Another consideration is to separate a host to handle tracking and relieve processing hosts from it.

So far we have discussed scalability and design decisions you could consider. There are some other design considerations for a BizTalk environment such as security, tracking, fault tolerance, load balancing, choice of license, and support for virtualization (`http://support.microsoft.com/kb/842301`). BizTalk security can be enhanced by deploying **Secure Socket Layer** (**SSL**), IPSec Tunneling, the **Inter Security and Acceleration** (**ISA**) server, and certificate services included with the Windows Server 2008. With the BizTalk Server, you can apply access control, implement least rights to limit access, and provide integrated security through Enterprise Single Sign-On (`http://msdn.microsoft.com/en-us/library/aa577802%28v=bts.70%29.aspx`). Furthermore, you can protect and secure applications and data by authenticating the sender of a message and authorizing the receiver of a message (refer to *Chapter 4, Securing your Message Exchange*).

Tracking messages in BizTalk messages can be useful to see what messages come in and out of the system, or for auditing, troubleshooting, or archiving purposes. Tracking of messages within BizTalk is a process by which parts of a message such as the body, properties, and metadata are stored in a database. These parts can be viewed by running queries from the Group Hub page in the BizTalk Server Administration console.

 It is important that you decide, or take up into the design, what needs to be tracked based on the requirements.

There are some considerations to make regarding tracking. Tracking everything is not the smart thing to do, as each time a message is touched in BizTalk; a copy is made and stored. Focus on scope by tracking only on a specific port, which is better for performance and keeps the database uncluttered. For the latter, it is important that the data purge and archive job is configured properly. As mentioned earlier, it is worth considering a dedicated host for tracking.

Fault tolerance and load balancing for BizTalk can be achieved through clustering, separating hosts as described earlier, implement a **Storage Area Network** (SAN) to house the BizTalk Server databases, cluster Enterprise **Single Sign-On** (**SSO**) Master Secret Server, and configuring the **Internet Information Services** (**IIS**) web server for isolated host instances and the BAM Portal web page to be highly available using **Network Load Balancing** (**NLB**) or other load balancing devices. The best way to implement this is to follow the steps in the *Checklist: Providing High Availability with Fault Tolerance or Load Balancing* document found on MSDN (`http://msdn.microsoft.com/en-us/library/gg634479%28v=bts.70%29.aspx`).

Another important topic regarding your BizTalk environment is costs and based on requirements you will choose the Branch, Standard, or Enterprise Edition. The editions differ not only in price, but also in functionality. As with the Standard Edition, it is not possible to support scenarios for high availability, fault tolerance, and is limited on CPU and applications. The Branch Edition is even more limited and is designed for hub and spoke deployment scenarios including **Radio Frequency Identification** (**RFID**). With any version, you probably want to consider whether or not to virtualize. With virtualization in mind, licensing can be difficult.

With the Standard Edition, you need a license for each virtual processor used by the virtual OS environment, regardless of whether the number of virtual processors is less than, or greater than, the number of physical processors on the server. With the Enterprise Edition, if you license all physical CPUs on the server you can run any number of instances in the physical or virtual OS environment. With both of these, a virtual processor is assumed to have the same number of cores as the physical processor. Using less than the number of cores available in the physical processor still counts as a full virtual processor (`http://www.microsoft.com/biztalk/en/us/editions.aspx`).

Last, but not least, you need to consider how to support your BizTalk environment. It is worth considering the System Center Operation Manager to monitor your BizTalk environment using management packs for the SQL Server, Windows Server, and BizTalk Server 2010. The management pack for the BizTalk Server 2010 provides two views, one for the enterprise IT administrator and one for the BizTalk Server administrator. The first will be monitoring the state and health of the various enterprise deployments, the machines hosting the SQL Server databases, machines hosting the Enterprise SSO service, host instance machines, IIS, network services, and is interested in the overall health of the "physical deployment" of a BizTalk Server setup. The BizTalk Server Administrator will be monitoring the state and health of various BizTalk Server application artifacts, such as orchestrations, send ports, receive locations, and is interested in monitoring and tracking the BizTalk Server's health. If necessary, he/she can carry out corrective measures to keep applications running as expected.

What you have read so far are considerations, which are useful while analyzing requirements and preparing your design. You need to take a considerable amount of time for analyzing requirements to be able to create a solid design for your BizTalk environment. There is a wealth of information provided by Microsoft in this book. It will be worth investing time now as you will lose a lot time and money if your applications do not perform or the system cripples under load while receiving the process.

How to do it...

To analyze the requirements, you will need to categorize them to certain topics mentioned in the *Gathering requirements by asking the right questions* recipe. You will then go over each requirement and decide how it can be met best. For each requirement, you will consider what the best option is and capture that in your design for the BizTalk setup. The BizTalk design will be a Word document, where you capture your design, considerations, and decisions.

How it works...

During analysis of each requirement, you will capture your considerations and decisions in a word document. Besides that, you will also describe the situation at the enterprise where the BizTalk environment will be deployed. You will find an example structure of a design document for a Development, Test, Acceptance, and Production (DTAP) environment, as follows, where you can place all the information:

1. **Introduction**
    - 1.1   Purpose
    - 1.2   Current situation
    - 1.3   IT landscape

2. **Design Decisions**
    - 2.1   Considerations/Issues

3. **Overview**
    - 3.1   DTAP landscape
    - 3.2   Scope
    - 3.3   MS BizTalk and SQL Server editions
    - 3.4   SQL Database Server

4. **ICT Policy**
    - 4.1   Operating systems
    - 4.2   Windows Server
    - 4.3   Backup
    - 4.4   Antivirus
    - 4.5   Windows update
    - 4.6   Security Settings

5. **Backup and Restore**

    5.1   Backup procedure

    5.2   Restore procedure

6. **Development**

    6.1   Development environment

    6.2   Development server

    6.3   Developer machine

7. **Test**

    7.1   Test server

8. **Acceptance**

    8.1   SQL Server clustering

    8.2   BizTalk group

    8.3   Acceptance server

9. **Production**

    9.1   SQL Server clustering

    9.2   BizTalk group (load balancing)

    9.3   Production server

10. **Management and security**

    10.1 Groups and accounts

    10.2 SCOM

    10.3 Single Sign-On

11. **Hosts**

    11.1 In process hosts

    11.2 Isolated hosts

    11.3 Trusted and untrusted hosts

    11.4 Hosts configuration DTAP

12. **Resources**

13. **Appendix A Redistributable CAB Files**

Design decisions are the important parts of your document. Here, you summarize all your design decisions and reference them to each corresponding chapter/section in the document, where a decision is described; you also note issues around your design.

There's more...

Analyzing requirements is an important task, which should not be taken lightly. Knowing architectural patterns, for instance, can help you choose the right technology and create the appropriate design. It can be that the BizTalk Server is not the right fit for the purpose. The following resources can aid you in analyzing the requirements:

- **Architectural Patterns**: Packt has published a book called *Applied Architecture Patterns on Microsoft Platform* that can aid you in analyzing the requirements by selecting the right technology.

- **Wiki TechNet article**: Refer to the *Recommendations for Installing, Sizing, Deploying, and Maintaining a BizTalk Server Solution* article at `http://social.technet.microsoft.com/wiki/contents/articles/666.aspx`.

- **Microsoft BizTalk Server 2010 Operations Guide**: Microsoft has created a BizTalk Server 2010 Operations Guide for anyone involved in the implementation and administration of a BizTalk solution, particularly IT professionals. You can find it online (`http://msdn.microsoft.com/en-us/library/gg634499%28v=bts.70%29.aspx`) or you can download it from `http://www.microsoft.com/downloads/en/details.aspx?FamilyID=4ef9eebb-b3f4-4534-b733-3eb2cb83d867&displaylang=en`.

- **Microsoft volume licensing brief**: *Licensing Microsoft Server Products in Virtual Environments* is an interesting white paper from Microsoft. It describes licensing models under virtual environments for the server operating systems and server applications. It can help you understand how to use Microsoft server products with virtualization technologies, such as Microsoft Hyper-V technology, Microsoft Virtual Server 2005 R2, or third-party virtualization solutions that are provided by VMWare and Parallels. You can download from the URL: `http://www.microsoft.com/downloads/en/details.aspx?FamilyID=9ef7fc47-c531-40f1-a4e9-9859e593a1f1&displaylang=en`.

- **Microsoft poster scale-out configurations**: Microsoft has published a poster (normal or interactive) that can be downloaded describing typical scenarios and commonly used options for scaling out the BizTalk Server 2010's physical configurations. This post clearly illustrates how to scale for achieving high availability through load balancing and fault tolerance. It also shows how to configure for high-throughput scenarios.

- A normal poster can be obtained from the URL: `http://www.microsoft.com/downloads/en/details.aspx?FamilyID=2b70cbfc-d158-45a6-8bbd-99782d6747dc`.

- An interactive poster created in Silverlight can be obtained from the URL: `http://www.microsoft.com/downloads/en/details.aspx?FamilyID=7ef9ae69-9cc8-442a-8193-831a414dfc30`.

See also

▸ Refer to the *Installing and using the BizTalk Best Practices Analyzer* recipe later in this chapter

Installing and using the BizTalk Best Practices Analyzer

The **Best Practices Analyzer** (**BPA**) examines a BizTalk Server 2010 deployment and generates a list of issues pertaining to best practice standards for BizTalk Server deployments. This tool is designed to assess the configuration of a BizTalk installation. The BPA performs configuration-level verification by gathering data from different information sources, such as **Windows Management Instrumentation** (**WMI**) classes, SQL Server databases, and registry entries and presents a report to the user. Under the hood, it uses the data to evaluate the deployment configuration. It does not modify any system settings and is not a self-tuning tool. The tool is there to deliver support in achieving the best suitable configuration and report issues or possible issues, that could potentially harm the BizTalk environment.

Getting ready

The latest version of the BPA tool (V1.2) can be obtained from the Microsoft download center (`http://www.microsoft.com/downloads/en/details.aspx?FamilyID=93d432fe-1370-4b6d-aaa8-a0c43c30f5ab&displaylang=en`) and must be installed on the BizTalk machine. As a user, you need an account that has local administrative rights, that is a member of the BizTalk Server Administrators group, and a member of the SSO Administrators group to be able to run the BPA.

You may need to explicitly set some WMI permissions before you can use the BPA in a distributed environment, where the SQL Server is not installed on the same computer as the BizTalk Server. This is because when the BPA tries to connect to a remote computer running the SQL Server, WMI may not have sufficient access to determine whether the SQL Server Agent is running. This may result in incorrect BPA evaluations.

How to do it...

To run the Best Practices Analyzer, perform one of the following:

- Start the BizTalk Server Best Practices Analyzer from the Start menu. Go to **Start | Programs | Microsoft BizTalk Server Best Practices Analyzer**.

- Open Windows Explorer and navigate to the Best Practices Analyzer installation directory (by default, `c:\Program Files\BizTalkBPA\`) and double-click on `BizTalkBPA.exe`.

- Open a command prompt, change to the installation directory, and then enter `BizTalkBPACmd.exe`.

The following steps need to be performed to do the analysis:

1. As soon as you start the BPA, it will check for updates. The user can decide whether or not to check for updates for newer versions of the configuration:

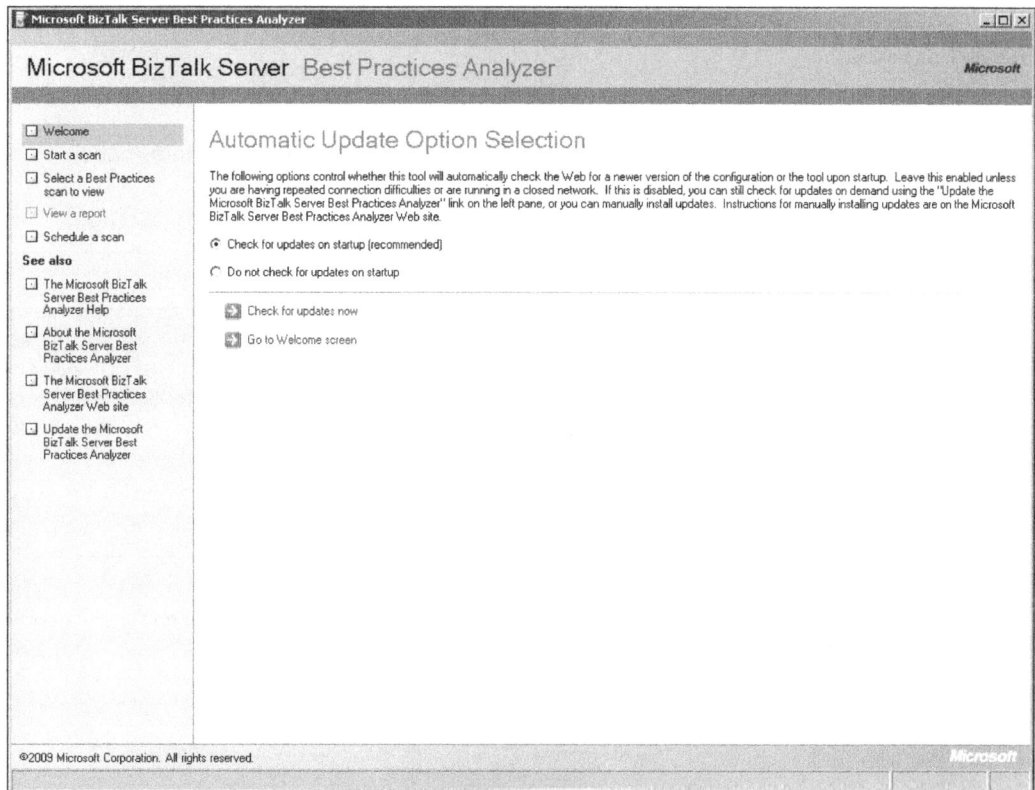

2. If a newer version is found, you are able to download the latest updates. The next step is to perform a scan by clicking on **Start a scan**:

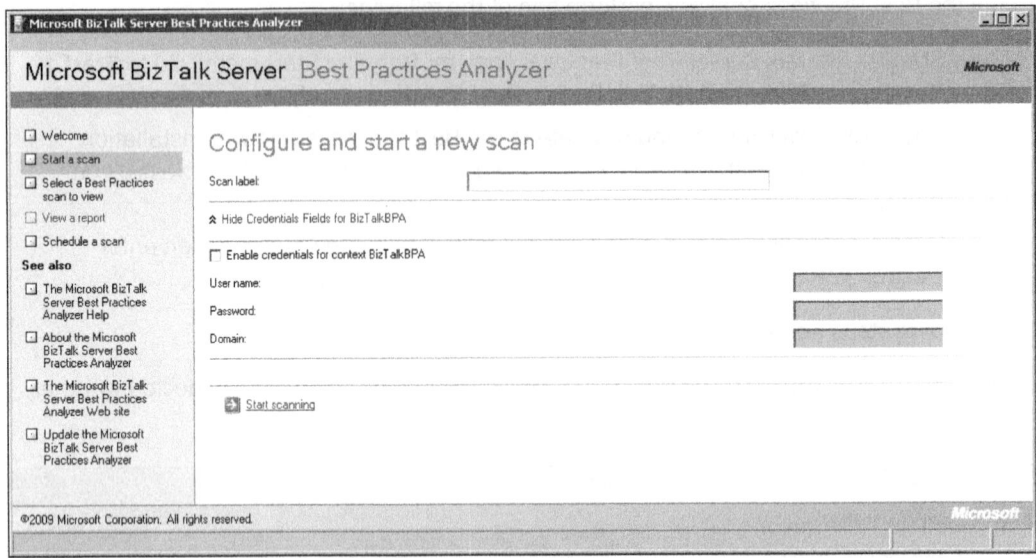

3. After starting the scan, `starts data` will be gathered from different information sources as described earlier.

4. After the scan has been completed, the user can decide to view the report of the performed scan:

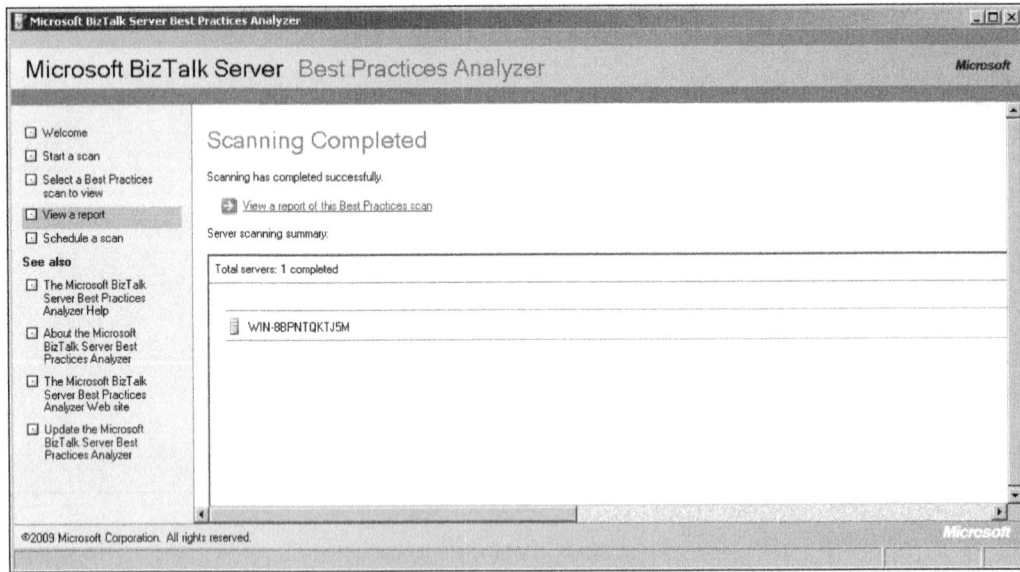

5. You can click **View a report of this Best Practices scan** and the report will be generated. After generation of the report, several tabs will appear:

- ❏ **Critical Issues**
- ❏ **All Issues**
- ❏ **Non-Default Settings**
- ❏ **Recent Changes**
- ❏ **Baseline**
- ❏ **Informational Items**

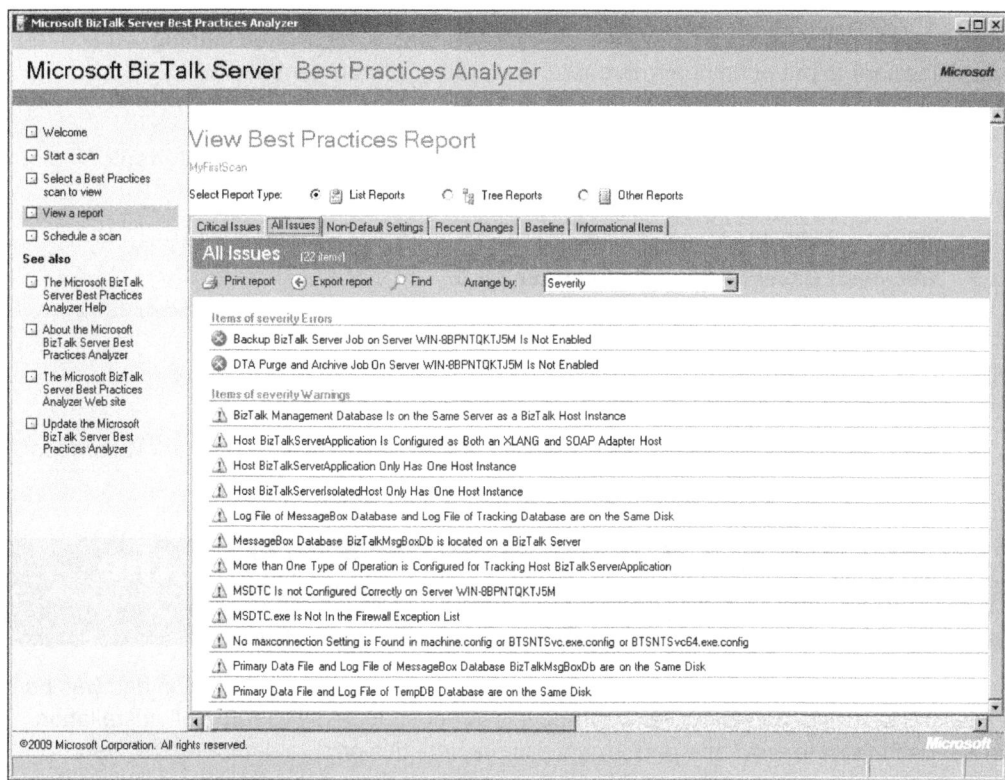

How it works...

When the BPA is running, it gathers information and evaluates them to best practice rules from the Microsoft product group and support. A report is presented to the user providing information on issues, non-default settings, changes, and so on. The report enables you to take action and apply the necessary changes to resolve identified issues. The BPA can be run again to verify that it adheres to all the necessary best practices. This shows the value of the tool when assessing the deployed BizTalk environment before it is operational. When BizTalk becomes operational, the **MessageBox Viewer** (**MBV**) has more value.

There's more...

The BPA is very useful and gives you information that helps you to tune BizTalk and to keep it healthy. There are more tools that can help in sustaining a healthy environment overall. The Microsoft SQL Server 2008 R2 BPA is a diagnostic tool that provides information about a server and a Microsoft SQL Server 2008 or Microsoft SQL Server 2008 R2 instance installed on that server.

The Microsoft SQL Server 2008 R2 Best Practices Analyzer can be downloaded from `http://www.microsoft.com/download/en/details.aspx?id=15289`.

There are a couple of analyzers provided by Microsoft that do a good job helping you and the system engineer to put out a healthy, robust, and stable environment:

- **Best Practices Analyzer**:
  `http://technet.microsoft.com/en-us/library/dd759260.aspx`

- **Microsoft Baseline Configuration Analyzer 2.0**:
  `http://www.microsoft.com/download/en/details.aspx?id=16475`

- **Microsoft Baseline Security Analyzer 2.1.1**:
  `http://www.microsoft.com/download/en/details.aspx?id=19892`

See also

- Refer to the *Validating a BizTalk installation with the BizTalk Benchmark Wizard tool* recipe later in this chapter

Validating a BizTalk installation with the BizTalk Benchmark Wizard tool

The **BizTalk Benchmark Wizard** (**BBW**) is a tool to validate a BizTalk installation and was built by Mikael Håkansson and Ewan Fairweather. It is intended to verify your BizTalk installation and is a useful tool to prove the performance characteristics prior to deploying the first solutions. You may also want to use it before you are about to scale out your environment, to make sure you are really using all resources, before investing in additional hardware and licenses. The BBW performs load to BizTalk Server in relation to specific scenarios. During the execution of the test, counter information is collected and benchmarked against collected statistics relevant to your BizTalk Server environment.

Microsoft provides guidance on performance optimization through the performance optimization guide that provides in-depth information for optimizing the performance of a BizTalk Server.

Even though the BizTalk Server 2010 Optimization Guide (http://www.microsoft.com/download/en/details.aspx?id=10855) is very useful while designing a BizTalk system, it does not provide any expected performance numbers related to specific environments.

This is where the BBW comes into the picture. After having configured the BizTalk group and applied some of the best practices by using the BPA, you can test your BizTalk configuration.

The tool is not a load or analyzing tool; it doesn't give advice or hints like the BPA. However, if the test fails, you can analyze the data using the PAL tool. You can run the tool on either a single-server or a multi-server installation. Regardless of the number of BizTalk Servers in your group, you should not run it with more than two "active" servers (http://www.microsoft.com/download/en/details.aspx?displaylang=en&id=2290), as it will otherwise not be covered by the benchmark values.

This tool should be used after the BizTalk Server has been installed and before any solutions are deployed to the environment. This will ensure that you are getting consistent and clean results from the BBW.

How to do it...

The latest version of the Benchmark Wizard tool can be obtained from CodePlex (http://bbw.codeplex.com/) and must be installed on the BizTalk machine. Follow the steps given next:

1. In a browser, such as Internet Explorer, navigate to the BBW download location (http://bbw.codeplex.com/).

2. On the BBW download page, download and run the self-extracting file.

3. Open a command prompt window and navigate to [installation folder]\Artefacts\BizTalk. By default, the installation folder is C:\Program Files\Blogical\BizTalk Benchmark Wizard.

4. In this folder, you will find the InstallHosts.vbs file. Execute it using the following parameters:

   ❑ NTGroupName: The name of the Windows NT group

   ❑ UserName: The name of the user account running the service instances

   ❑ Password: The password of the user account running the service instances

   ❑ Receive Host: The name of the server where you want to run the receive host instance

❏ Send Host: The name of the server where you want to run the send host instance

❏ Processing Host: The name of the server where you want to run the process host instance

5. If you have a single box installation, your script command might look similar to the following:

```
cscript InstallHosts.vbs "BizTalk Application Users" "\MyUser"
"MyPassword" "BtsServer1"
"BtsServer1" "BtsServer1"
```

6. The result will be as depicted in the following diagram:

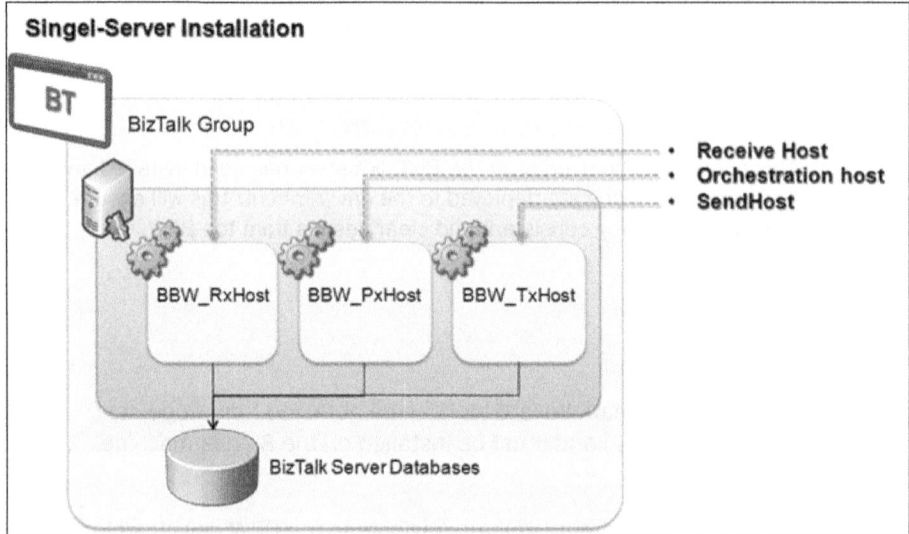

7. If you have a multi-server installation, your script command might look similar to the following:

```
cscript InstallHosts.vbs "MyDomain\BizTalk Application Users"
"MyDomain\MyUser"
MyPassword" "BtsServer1" "BtsServer2" "BtsServer2"
```

8. The result will be as depicted in the following diagram:

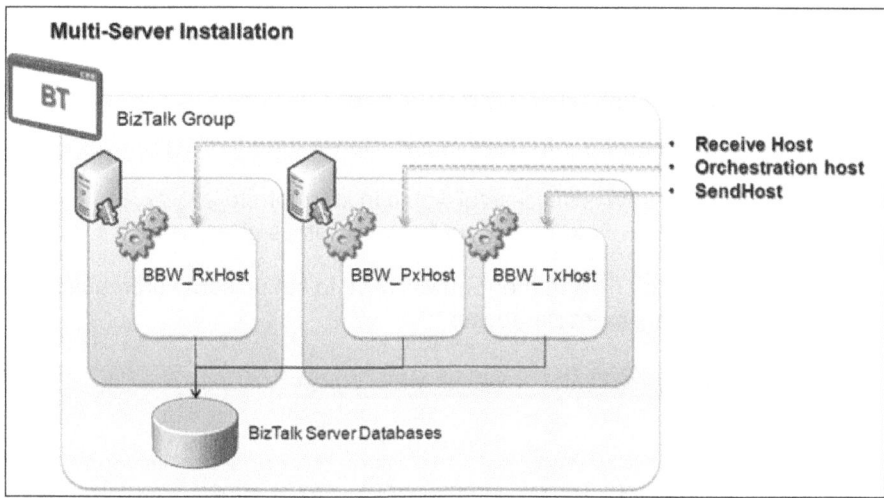

9. Execution of the script in a command line will result in creation of the hosts and the result of these actions is displayed in the following screenshot:

```
Microsoft (R) Windows Script Host Version 5.8
Copyright (C) Microsoft Corporation. All rights reserved.

NTGroupName = BizTalk Application Users
UserName = Administrator
Password = Administrator
Receive Host = WIN-8BPNTQKTJ5M
Send Host = WIN-8BPNTQKTJ5M
Processing Host = WIN-8BPNTQKTJ5M
************************************************************
Create BBW_RxHost
************************************************************
Host - BBW_RxHost - has been created successfully
Host - BBW_RxHost - has been mapped successfully - WIN-8BPNTQKTJ5M
HostInstance - BBW_RxHost - has been installed successfully - WIN-8BPNTQKTJ5M
MSBTS_ReceiveHandler for WCF-NetTcp BBW_RxHost - has been created successfully

************************************************************
Create BBW_TxHost
************************************************************
Host - BBW_TxHost - has been created successfully
Host - BBW_TxHost - has been mapped successfully - WIN-8BPNTQKTJ5M
HostInstance - BBW_TxHost - has been installed successfully - WIN-8BPNTQKTJ5M
MSBTS_SendHandler2 for WCF-NetTcp BBW_TxHost   has been created successfully

************************************************************
Create BBW_PxHost
************************************************************
Host - BBW_PxHost - has been created successfully
Host - BBW_PxHost - has been mapped successfully - WIN-8BPNTQKTJ5M
HostInstance - BBW_PxHost - has been installed successfully - WIN-8BPNTQKTJ5M
************************************************************
DONE!
************************************************************
```

10. Open the **BizTalk Administration Console**, point to the **Applications** node and import the `BizTalk Benchmark Wizard.msi` found in the folder `[Installation folder]\Artefacts\BizTalk`.

11. Run the `BizTalk Benchmark Wizard.msi` on all BizTalk servers to add the assemblies to the **Global Assembly Cache** (**GAC**).

12. Go to **Start | All Programs | BizTalk Application Wizard** to start the application.

When the installation of the BBW is successful, you can start it from `C:\Program Files\ Blogical\BizTalk Benchmark Wizard` and follow the steps given next:

1. You will be welcomed first and then you will have to set up some prerequisites such as the BizTalk Management Database:

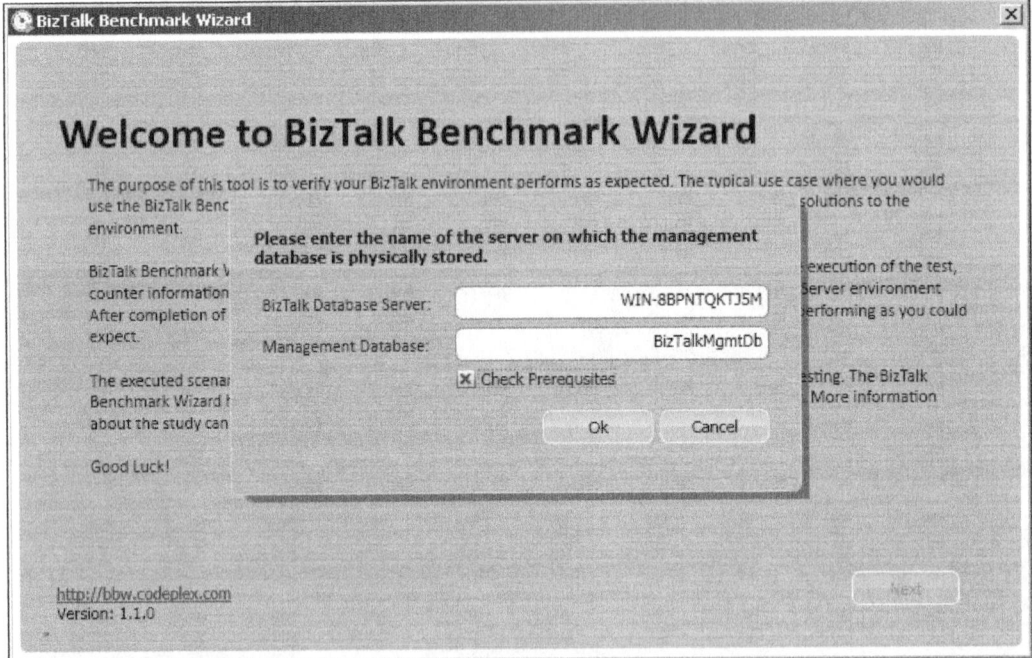

2. The user can opt to collect data for further analysis but this is optional. Collection of datasets enables the creation of a log file that contains all information of a Benchmark run. This log can be analyzed later using, for instance, the PAL tool:

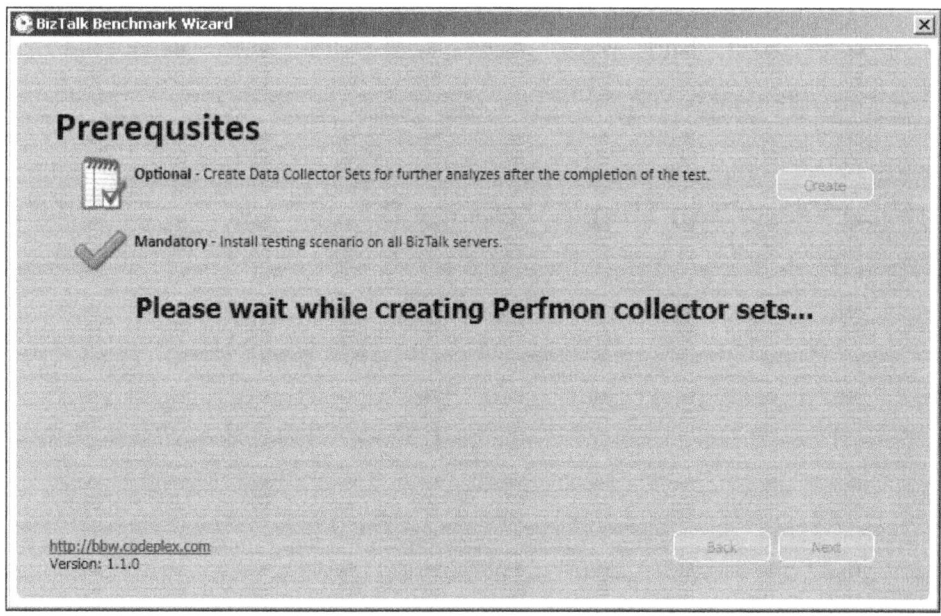

3. Then the user gets to select one of the two scenarios—Messaging or Orchestration. Each scenario has a set of tested environments as follows:

- ❏ Single server (2*Quad CPU, 4GB RAM)

- ❏ 1*BTS (1*Quad CPU. 4GB RAM) + 1*SQL(1*Quad CPU, 8GB RAM)

- ❏ 2*BTS (2*Quad CPU. 8GB RAM) + 2*SQL(2*Quad CPU, 16GB RAM)

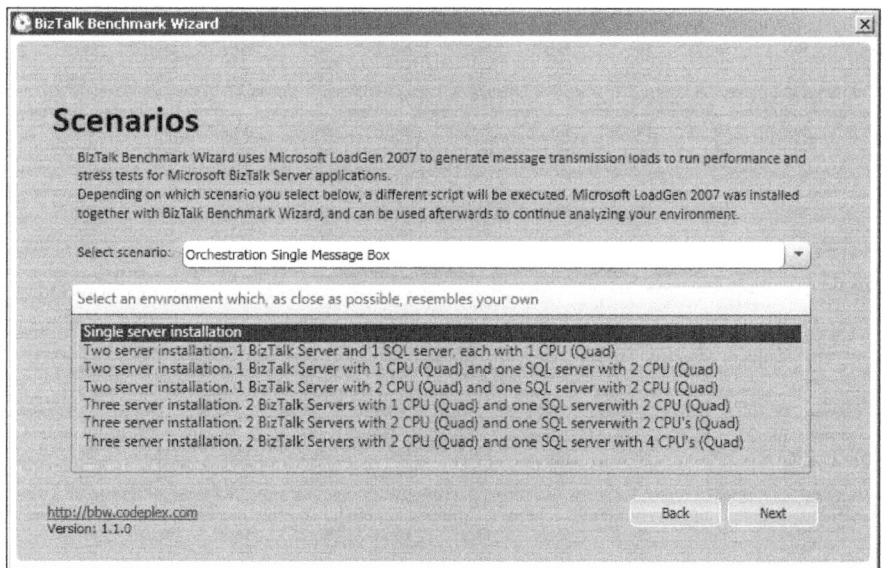

4. The user can select the environment that best resembles his own environment. The next screen will display what will happen given the chosen scenario:

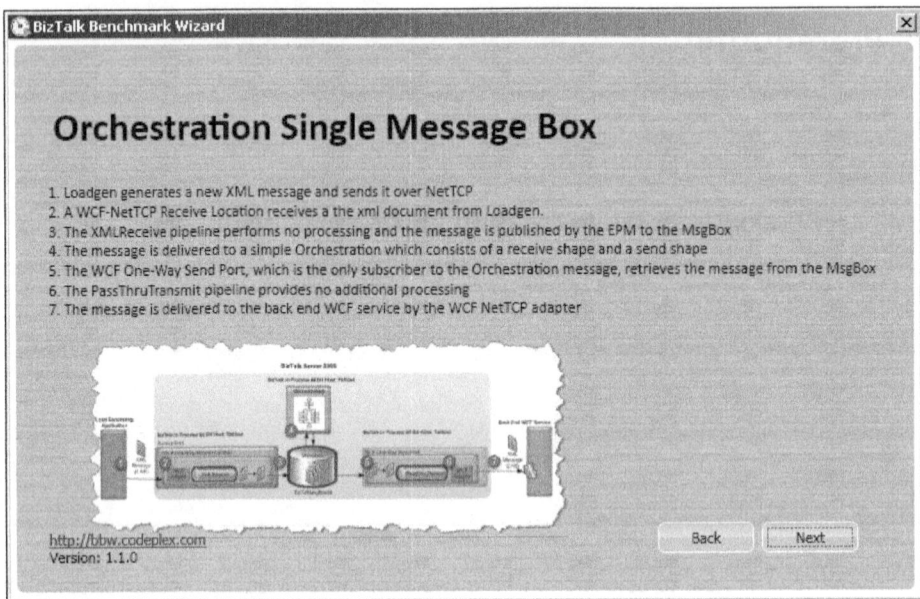

5. As a user, you will have to select where each host instance resides on each machine, if applicable. In case of a single-server installation, all the hosts are on the same machine:

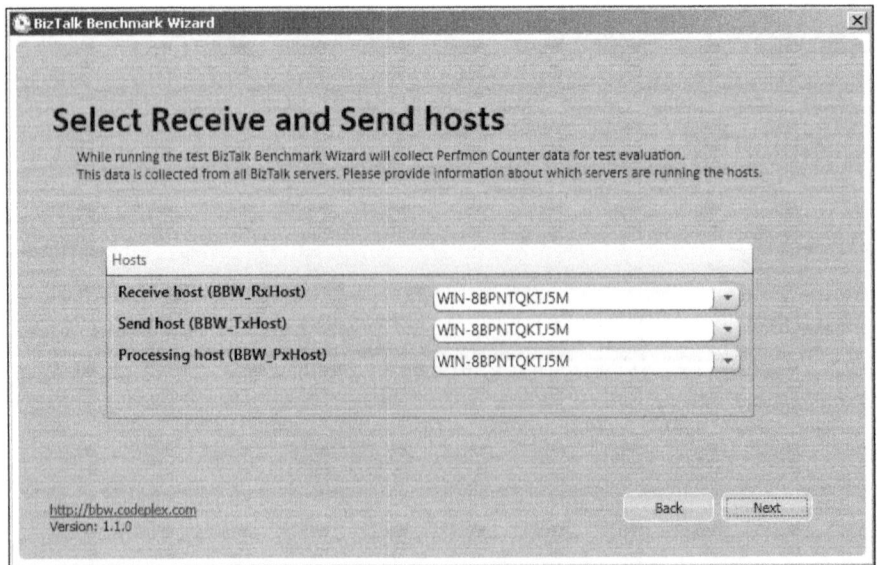

6. One of the following steps is to configure the Indigo Service, a console application hosting service which will be called from the BizTalk Send port. You will have to either host the service on a separate server or go to the folder [Installation folder]\Artefacts\IndigoService and then right-click **IndigoService**. In the BBW, you will have to either follow instructions and/or fill the Server name and click **Test the Indigo Service**. There is also the option of collecting performance counters:

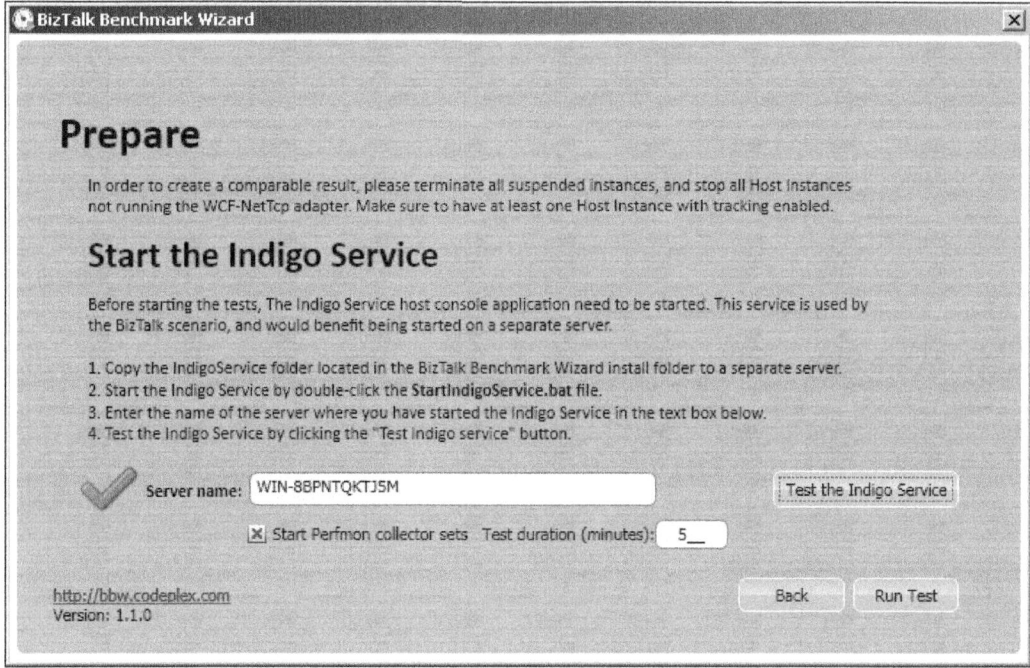

7. As the user clicks **Run Test**, the tool continues to start ports and orchestrations. It will also start the **Perfmon collector** sets if the user has chosen to create those (refer to step 2).

8. As the test proceeds, the user can monitor the counter values through the gauges (**Avg Received msgs/sec** and **Avg Processed msgs/sec**). The default test duration is 30 minutes, with a warm-up of two minutes. In this case, five minutes has been chosen.

9. After warming up, the test will run and you will see the gauges moving certain values.

10. Finally, the user is presented with a result, which is either **Succeeded**, **Acceptable**, or **Failed**. After the test is run, you can save a report:

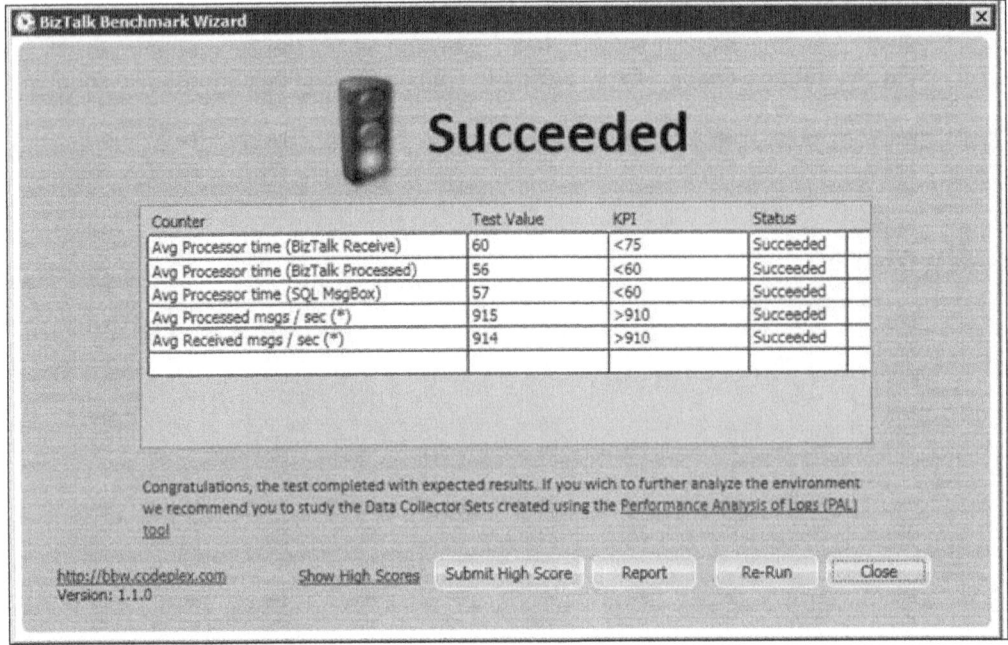

How it works...

By completing the BizTalk Benchmark wizard installation, the following artifacts have been created:

- Three hosts – BBW_RxHost, BBW_PxHost, BBW_TxHost
- Three host instances
- Two adapter handlers for NetTcp
- One BizTalk application
- Two Receive ports
- Two Send hosts
- One Orchestration

Hosts and instances are created through scripts and ports, orchestration is created through installing the msi files. The user can start the wizard and, at the end, run a test based on the selections made. During the test, loadgen will generate the xml messages that will be sent over NetTcp to BizTalk. The messages will be published in the MessageBox database and picked up either by the subscribing send port or orchestration. Finally, the messages will be sent to the backend web service through the WCF-NetTcp adapter.

There's more...

The following section deals with KPIs in detail for certain scenarios.

KPIs

The test run failed as it did not meet the KPIs, at least not all of them. Meeting the KPIs is not easy. The following is the list of KPIs for each scenario. They are based on separate machines for BizTalk and the SQL Server instance, Intel Xeon CPUs with multiple cores, x64 bit platforms and software (refer to the Test Environment table).

Scenario KPIs: Messaging a single-message and multi-message box

KPIs for the scenario of Messaging a single-message and multi-message box are stated in the following table:

Number of BTS	CPU BizTalk Server	Number of SQL Servers	CPU SQL Server	Msg/Sec Received	Msg/Sec Processed
1	1 Quad	1	1 Quad	160	200
1	1 Quad	1	1 Quad	280	350
1	1 Quad	1	2 Quads	390	490
1	1 Quad	1	2 Quads	560	700
2	1 Quad	1	2 Quads	620	770
2	2 Quads	1	2 Quads	730	910
2	2 Quads	1	4 Quads	780	980

Scenario KPIs: Orchestration single-message box

KPIs for the scenario of an orchestration single-message box are stated in the following table:

Number of BTS	CPU BizTalk Server	Number of SQL Servers	CPU SQL Server	Msg/Sec Received	Msg/Sec Processed
1	1 Quad	1	1 Quad	110	140
1	1 Quad	1	1 Quad	170	210
1	1 Quad	1	2 Quads	190	240
1	1 Quad	1	2 Quads	220	270
2	1 Quad	1	2 Quads	230	290
2	2 Quads	1	2 Quads	260	320
2	2 Quads	1	4 Quads	300	370

Test Environment

Each has a Windows 2008 Enterprise x64 Edition as the operating system, with 64 bit CPUs having four cores:

Type	Model	CPU Type	Number of CPU	Logical Disks	Software
Database	DL875	Intel Xeon	8 * 2,4 Ghz	2 x 72gb 10k*	SQL Server 2008 SP1
BTS Host Receive	R805	Intel Xeon	2 * 2,33 Ghz	2 x 72gb 10k SAS	BizTalk Server 2009
BST Host Send	R805	Intel Xeon	2 * 2,33 Ghz	2 x 72gb 10k SAS	BizTalk Server 2009
Load	R805	Intel Xeon	2 * 2,33 Ghz	2 x 72gb 10k SAS	BizTalk Benchmark Wizard
Backend	R805	Intel Xeon	2 * 2,33 Ghz	2 x 72gb 10k SAS	Indigo Service

Following is the configuration of the test environment for Storage: EMC Clarion CX-240 (five solid state drives):

▶ Global tracking enabled

▶ Partitioning of the `TempDb` (SQL Server system database), `BizTalkDTADb` and `BizTalkMsgBoxDb` to as many files as CPUs

▶ Separation of the BizTalk MessageBox database into multiple file groups or files

▶ Enabled the *T1118* flag on the SQL service

▶ Disabled throttling on send and processing hosts

▶ Updated the thread settings (CLR Hosting) on all hosts (there you will find the update install path of `BBW artefacts\registry settings`)

There are a couple of things you can do to improve performance and one is to use the PAL tool before applying changes. Usage of the PAL tool is explained in the next recipe. Actions that can be done, based on analysis are scaling out your environment.

Microsoft case studies

Finally, you can read more on case studies from Microsoft, where tests have been run on different sets of hardware.

- `http://blogs.msdn.com/b/ewanf/archive/2010/01/12/benchmark-your-biztalk-server-part-3.aspx`
- `http://msdn.microsoft.com/en-us/library/ee377068%28BTS.10%29.aspx`

See also

- Refer to the *Automating performance analysis by using the PAL tool* recipe later in this chapter

Automating performance analysis by using the PAL tool

The **Performance Analysis of Logs** (**PAL**) tool is a powerful tool that reads in a performance monitor counter log (any known format) and analyzes it using known thresholds. Basically, it automates the analysis of performance counter logs, for instance, one that is generated by the Benchmark Wizard. At the end, you can generate an HTML or XML-based report that graphically charts important performance counters and throws alerts (in red), when thresholds are exceeded. The thresholds are originally based on thresholds defined by the Microsoft product teams, including the BizTalk Server, and members of Microsoft support.

Before PAL, it was quite hard to analyze logs, which had to be done manually and required quite extensive knowledge of the Windows Architecture. It could also require a lot time to analyze the logs and so investment in money. There are tools that could help in the analysis such as the Microsoft System Center Operation Manager, but might not collect critical data that is necessary or the Microsoft Server 2008 Performance toolkit, which is limited for Windows 2003. There was not really a tool that could analyze log file(s) easy and fast. PAL does just that, it analyzes logs and does not require much time, and is free. This tool has the following benefits:

- Consolidated guidance, central repository of guidance gathered from multiple sources
- Log file data access layer using the Microsoft Log Parser
- Analyzes more data points, breaks down the data into smaller slices, and analyzes them individually
- Dynamically changing thresholds, learning environment asking questions
- Reusable (open source); code is open source
- Extensibility of thresholds; add, edit, or delete thresholds

Getting ready

The PAL tool is available through CodePlex version 2.0.8 (`http://pal.codeplex.com/`) and it requires the Microsoft Log Parser. The latter is a powerful, versatile tool that provides universal query access to text-based data such as log files, XML files, and CSV files, as well as key data sources on the Windows operating system such as the event log, the registry, the filesystem, and the Active Directory Service. Log Parser version 2.2 is available at `http://www.microsoft.com/downloads/en/details.aspx?FamilyID=890cd06b-abf8-4c25-91b2-f8d975cf8c07&displaylang=en`. Other prerequisites are as follows:

- ► Microsoft .NET Framework 3.5 Service pack 1
- ► Microsoft Chart Controls for Microsoft .NET Framework 3.5
- ► PowerShell 2.0

How to do it...

You can start PAL from `<install path>\PAL\PAL v2.0.7\PALWizard`, where the install path is presumably `C:\Program Files`.

You will now go through a Wizard, where the following steps will be performed:

1. Select the log files to analyze.
2. Select the time frame for the analysis.
3. Select the appropriate threshold file.
4. Answer questions.
5. Select the analysis interval.
6. Select the output options.
7. Execute or add to the queue.
8. Select the template.

With the following steps you can perform analysis of a BizTalk Benchmark Wizard log file:

1. With the PAL tool you can select, for instance, the **Counter Log** generated by the BizTalk Benchmark wizard. These files can usually be found at `<install path Benchmark Wizard>\Blogical\BizTalk Benchmark Wizard\COUNTERLOGS\<machine name>\<machine name>_BizTalk Server\<sequence number>\<machine name>` or `\<machine name>_SQL_Server\<sequence number>\<machine name>`:

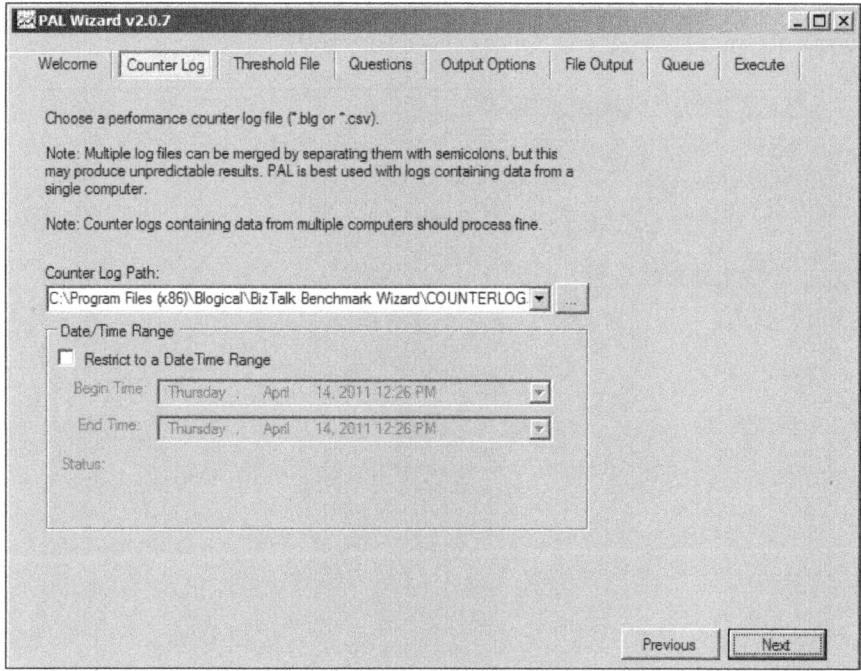

2. Next, you can select the appropriate **Threshold File**. You will select the Microsoft BizTalk Server 2006/2009/2010 file. You are able to edit this file if you wish to do so:

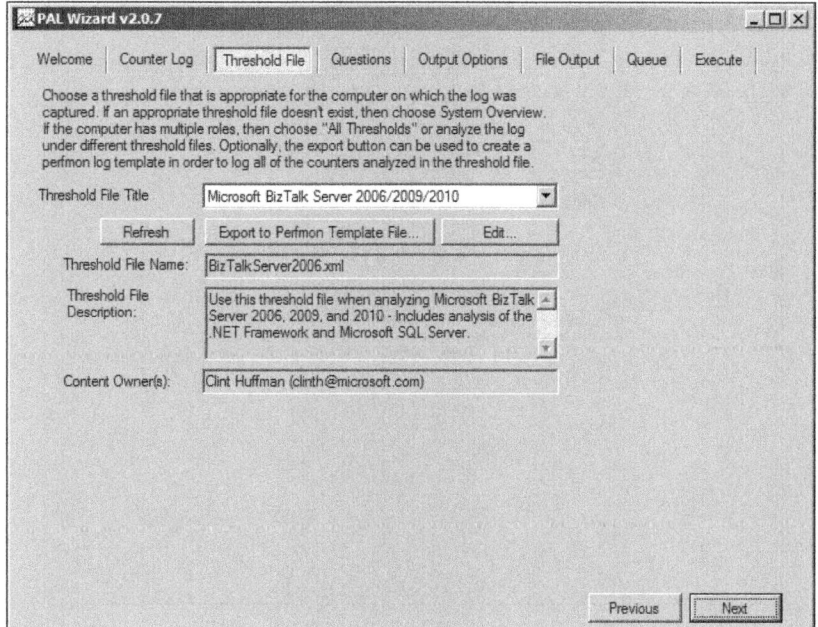

3. Next, you will find the **Questions** tab, where you need to answer questions on your environment regarding the memory, processor, and platform:

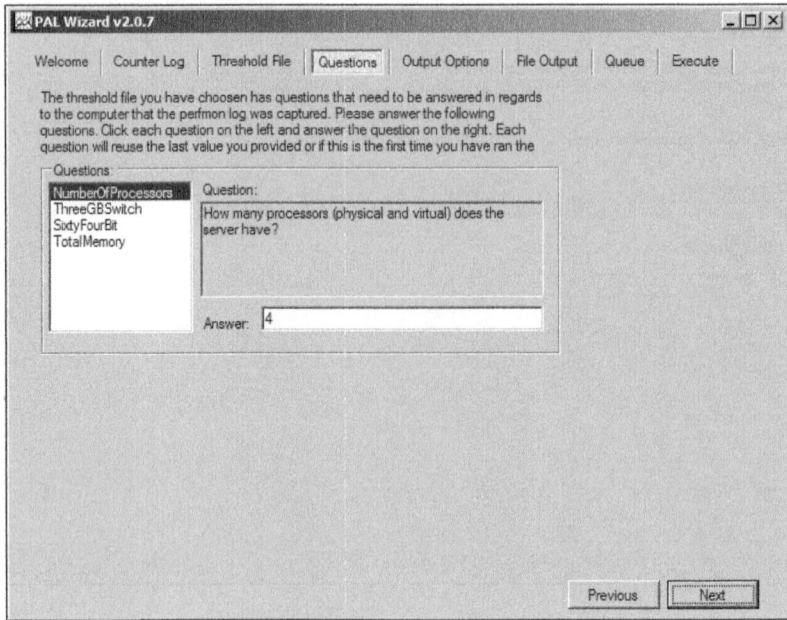

4. In the next tab, you will be able to select the **Output Options**:

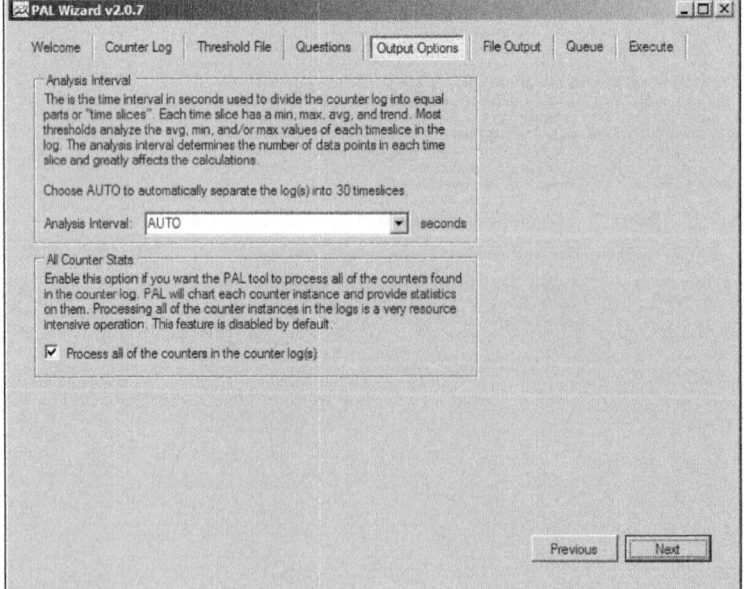

5. After determining the output options, you should select **Output Directory** and which format you want your report in—HTML or XML:

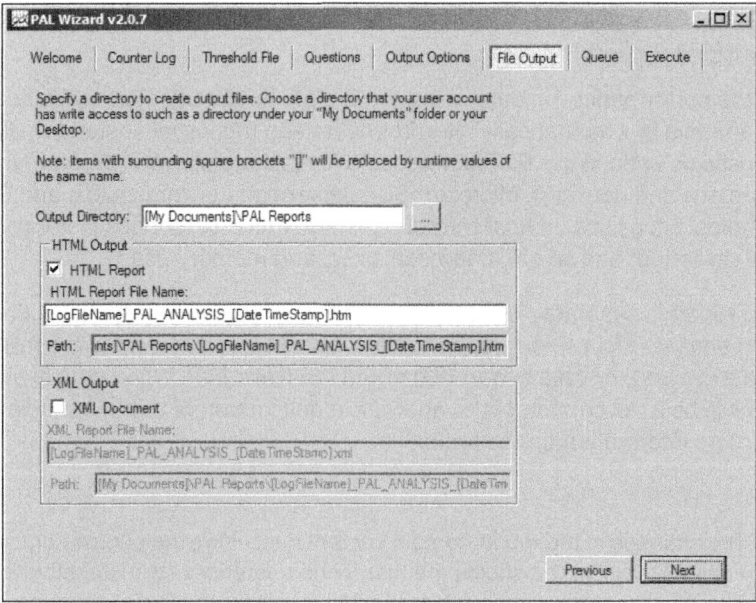

6. Now, you will be able to queue the analysis, if there is any. This can be done by using the **Queue** tab:

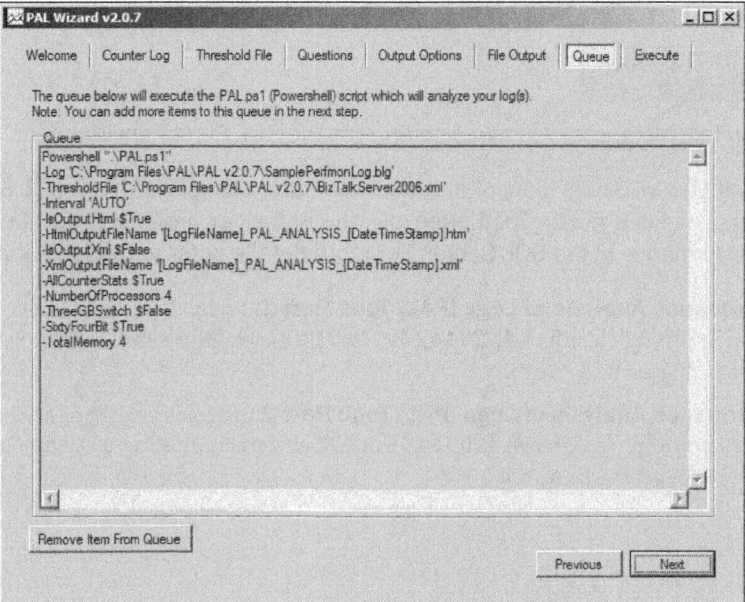

7. Finally, you can execute the analysis. After the analysis, you can open the report and investigate the possible issues.

How it works...

PAL analyzes the performance log data using the BizTalk thresholds. The tool aids in performance analysis by automatically interpreting data in the log file instead of doing it manually. Thresholds used in the BizTalk threshold file include operating system thresholds (CPU, disk, memory, and network), Microsoft SQL Server counter thresholds, and BizTalk counter thresholds. Focus lies on host throttling, adapter latency, service instance statistics (suspended, dehydrated, and so on), database sizes, and memory usage.

The generated report is separated by categories and each category has a collection of analyses. Each analysis focuses on a specific performance counter. An alert is raised when thresholds are exceeded, by yellow (warning) or red (critical) color. When critical alerts are present, there will be a description of the analysis, a description of the thresholds used, and a link for more information on the topic.

The analyses in the report contain content describing the purpose of the analysis, why the thresholds are there, and references for more information. To learn more about interpreting the PAL report for the BizTalk analysis, read the article available at (BizTalk 2006 related, but still applicable to 2010):

`http://msdn.microsoft.com/en-us/library/cc296652.aspx`.

There's more...

Besides the BizTalk instances, you can also analyze the SQL Server environment.

On MSDN blogs, you will find a story of around three parts using PAL for the SQL Server. The PAL tool is useful in analyzing bottlenecks in the BizTalk environment, but you can also analyze the performance in the SQL Server. For more details, refer to the following documents:

▶ **Performance Analysis of Logs (PAL) Tool: Part 1**: `http://blogs.msdn.com/b/temenosonsql/archive/2010/04/30/performance-analysis-of-logs-pal-tool-part-1.aspx`

▶ **Performance Analysis of Logs (PAL) Tool: Part 2**: `http://blogs.msdn.com/b/temenosonsql/archive/2010/05/03/performance-analysis-of-logs-pal-tool-part-2.aspx`

- **Performance Analysis of Logs (PAL) Tool: Part 3**: `http://blogs.msdn.com/b/temenosonsql/archive/2010/05/03/performance-analysis-of-logs-pal-tool-part-3.aspx`

The creator of the PAL tool is Clint Huffman and he has a blog related to his tool at `http://blogs.technet.com/b/clinth/`.

Managing the SSO system

The BizTalk Server and another Microsoft Server product, **Host Integration Server** (**HIS**), both support an extension of the Windows Enterprise Security integration called **Enterprise SSO**. You will notice that Enterprise SSO is one of the BizTalk features during installation. Enterprise SSO in total is provided by a set of processes that run on network servers to provide the following services for heterogeneous systems:

- User account and password mapping and caching
- SSO to multiple Windows domains and host security systems
- Password synchronization to simplify administration

The services mentioned earlier are mandatory for the BizTalk Server, even if you do not require them. The BizTalk Server uses the SSO to help secure information for the receive locations. When the Enterprise SSO service gets started, it retrieves the encryption key called master secret from the Master Secret Server. The **Master Secret Server** is another Enterprise SSO service that has an additional subservice that distributes and maintains the master secret. What the Enterprise SSO service does is that it caches the master secret after it has been retrieved. Every 60 seconds the service synchronizes the master secret with the Master Secret Server.

As you can see, the Master Secret Server plays an important role like MSDTC (refer to the *Configuring MSDTC for multi-server BizTalk platforms* recipe later in this chapter). Regardless of whether you will use the Enterprise SSO service for credential mapping or not, it has to be available in any kind of BizTalk configuration.

Getting ready

With the **Microsoft Management Console** (**MMC**) or command line `ssomanage` utility, you are able to manage the SSO system. With either of these tools, you can update the SSO database, adding, deleting, and managing applications, and administer user mappings. In the MMC, you will find all programs of your operating system. Refer to the following screenshot:

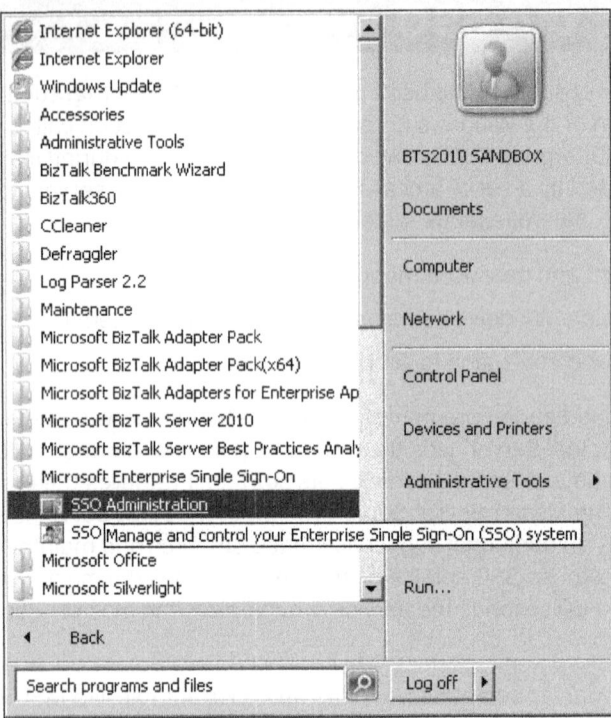

The command line `ssomanage` is available in `C:\Program Files\Common files\Single Sign On`. You will also find the `ssoconfig` command-line tool at the specified location, which is a utility to configure your password synchronization settings.

How to do it...

The following steps describe how to work with the `ssomanage` and `ssoconfig` commands:

1. You can start `ssomanage` from the command line and with the command `ssomanage -?`. You will see all the functions, as shown in the following screenshot:

```
C:\Program Files\Common Files\Enterprise Single Sign-On>ssomanage -?
ssomanage commands -

 Configuration functions -

-server          : set SSO server name (for current user)
-serverall       : set SSO server name (for all users)
-showserver      : show the SSO server name(s)

 Administration functions -

-updatedb        : update SSO database
-enablesso       : enable SSO
-disablesso      : disable SSO
-tickets         : control SSO ticket behavior
-enable          : enable SSO features
-disable         : disable SSO features
-displaydb       : display current SSO database settings

 Application functions -

-listapps        : list existing applications
-displayapp      : display application information
-createapps      : create new applications
-deleteapp       : delete an existing application
-updateapps      : update existing applications
-enableapp       : enable application
-disableapp      : disable application
-purgecache      : purge the credential cache for an application

 Mapping functions -

-listmappings    : list mappings for a user
-createmappings  : create mappings for users
-deletemappings  : delete mappings for users
-enablemapping   : enable a single mapping for a user
-disablemapping  : disable a single mapping for a user
-deletemapping   : delete a single mapping for a user
-setcredentials  : set external credentials for a user
```

2. You can change the global information in the SSO database, such as the Master Secret Server identification, the account names, and so on. This information can be updated by using the `-update` command providing the `update` file containing this information. Refer to the following command line:

    ssomanage -updatedb <update file>, where <update file> is the path and name of the file

3. The `update` file (xml) will have the following format:

    ```
    <sso>
      <globalnfo>
        <ssoAdminAccount>YourDomain\Accountname</ssoAdminAccount>
        <ssoAffiliateAdminAccount> YourDomain
        \Accountname</ssoAffiliatcAdminAccount>
        <secretServer>ServerName</secretServer>
        <auditDeletedApps>1000</auditDeletedApps>
        <auditDeletedMappings>1000</auditDeletedMappings>
        <auditCredentialLookups>1000</auditCredentialLookups>
        <ticketTimeout>2</ticketTimeout>
        <credCacheTimeout>60</credCacheTimeout>
      </globalInfo>
    </sso>
    ```

4. The `ssoconfig` command can be started from the command line and with the command `ssoconfig -?`. You will see all the functions again, as shown in the following screenshot:

```
C:\Program Files\Common Files\Enterprise Single Sign-On>ssoconfig -?
ssoconfig commands -

-setDB                : set SQL Server and SSO database names
-showDB               : show the SQL Server and SSO database names
-createDB             : create SSO database
-upgradeDB            : upgrade SSO database
-generateSecret       : generate new SSO master secret
-backupSecret         : backup current SSO master secret
-restoreSecret        : restore SSO master secret
-auditLevel           : set SSO server audit level
-setSSL               : set SSL encryption
-replayFiles          : set directory for replay files
-syncAge              : set maximum password age (for password sync)
-remoteLookup         : allow remote lookup of credentials
-discover             : discover SSO servers
-status               : display SSO server status
-allowPS              : allow password sync (from PCNS or MIIS)
-reportFilterErrors   : report password filter errors (at runtime)
-scp                  : Service Connection Points (SCP)
```

5. One of the common commands used with `ssoconfig` is the **restoreSecret** for restoring the SSO master secret as a part of the recovery scenario. For restoring the SSO master secret, you should type the following command:

```
ssoconfig -restoreSecret <backup file>
```

The backup file has the name of the master secret file that you backed up during configuration.

See **How to Update the SSO database** document at `http://msdn.microsoft.com/en-us/library/aa559867.aspx`.

How it works...

With the `ssomanage` functions, you can find out, for instance, which SSO server is used, what is the SSO administrator account, and if everything is correctly enabled. `ssomanage` also plays a role during clustering of the Master Secret Server (`http://msdn.microsoft.com/en-us/library/aa561823.aspx`).

With the functions of `ssoconfig`, you can get to know where SSO database is created or upgraded, and also where the SSO master secret is restored in case it has become unavailable.

There's more...

Besides the `ssoconfig` command-line tool, now there is also an MMC Snap-in available and you are able to troubleshoot SSO with command-line tools. Finally, you will find high availability options for a multi-machine BizTalk environment on Microsoft TechNet.

▶ **SSO configuration application MMC Snap-in**: It provides the ability to add and manage applications, add and manage key value pairs, as well as import and export configuration applications so that they can be deployed to different environments. You can download the MMC Snap-in from Microsoft (`http://www.microsoft.com/downloads/en/details.aspx?displaylang=en&FamilyID=94e07de1-1d33-4245-b430-9216979cd587`).

▶ It also provides a client-side class that makes accessing the SSO system to retrieve your key/value pairs easy.

▶ **Troubleshoot Enterprise SSO**: To troubleshoot your SSO environment, it may be useful to walk through certain items described in the troubleshoot enterprise single sign-on table found on MSDN (`http://msdn.microsoft.com/en-us/library/aa953861%28v=bts.70%29.aspx`).

▶ **High availability installation options**: Microsoft TechNet provides high availability options for Enterprise SSO in a multicomputer BizTalk deployment (`http://technet.microsoft.com/en-us/library/aa578263%28BTS.70%29.aspx`).

▶ Through MSDN, you can find information on how to use SSO (`http://msdn.microsoft.com/en-us/library/aa561654.aspx`).

See also

▶ Refer to the *Configuring MSDTC for multi-server BizTalk platforms* recipe later in this chapter

Configuring MSDTC for multi-server BizTalk platforms

In a multiserver environment, the BizTalk Server runtime requires MSDTC. The runtime operations need MSDTC support to ensure that the operations are transactionally consistent. The runtime also depends upon some other components, such as SSO, BizTalk host instances, and any SQL Server instances that are connected to the BizTalk Server. In case MSDTC is not functioning properly, these components will get affected.

MSDTC is a component inside **Component Services**, as shown in the following screenshot:

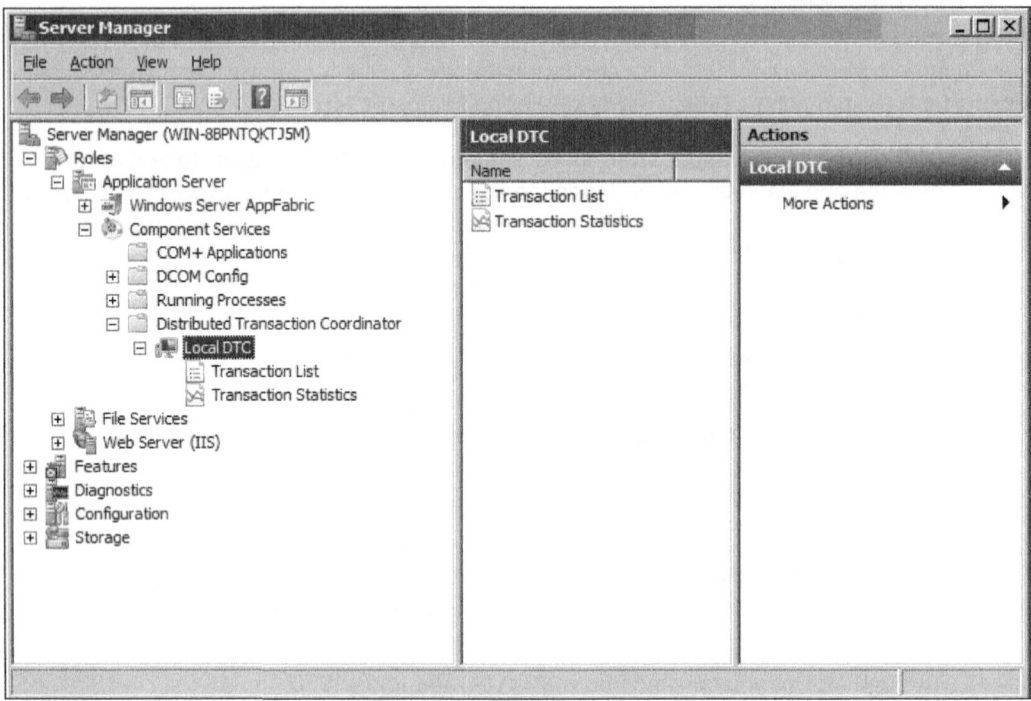

As you can imagine, it is important in a multi-server environment to have MSDTC properly setup and configured. Especially, the security settings need to be set appropiately. This recipe will show how to use DTCPing and DTCTester to aid you in validating and troubleshooting the MSDTC configuration.

Getting ready

To validate the connection between the BizTalk Server and the SQL Server machines, you can use DTCPing and detect it if a firewall is blocking the access. Distributed Transactions (specifically OleTx transactions) use the **Microsoft Remote Procedure Call** (**MSRPC**) protocol to talk to MSDTC on the other machine. You have to make sure that the two machines are able to communicate with each other using the MSRPC protocol. With the DTCPing tool (http://www.microsoft.com/downloads/en/details.aspx?FamilyID=5e325025-4dcd-4658-a549-1d549ac17644&DisplayLang=en) running on both the machines, you can test whether the normal **Remote Procedure Calls** (**RPC**) communication is working or not. After testing, download and unzip the file to a destination folder.

Another tool is the DTCTester (`http://support.microsoft.com/kb/293799`) utility to verify transaction support between two computers, if the SQL Server is installed on one of the computers (multi-server BizTalk environment). The DTCTester utility uses ODBC to verify the transaction support against a SQL Server database.

After you have downloaded the tool, you can run the self-extracting file and place it somewhere on your machine. You will have to create an **Open Database Connectivity** (**ODBC**) data source for your SQL Server through the ODBC utility in the Control Panel. DTCTester is a 32 bit tool, and accesses the ODBC for the 32 bit client. If you have a 64 bit environment, do not use the ODBC client that is in the administration console. To access the 32 bit client, you will have to open up `c:\windows\syswow64\odbcad32.exe.c:\windows\syswow64\odbcad32.exe`.

How to do it...

The following steps describe how to work with DTCPing:

1. Run the DTCPing tool and in the **Remote Server Name** type in the right server name and click **PING**. If everything works fine, you should see the following message being returned by the tool:

   The DTCPing only works with NetBIOS name.

   Refer to the following screenshot:

4. From the second machine you would see that the ping has been received. Refer to the following screenshot:

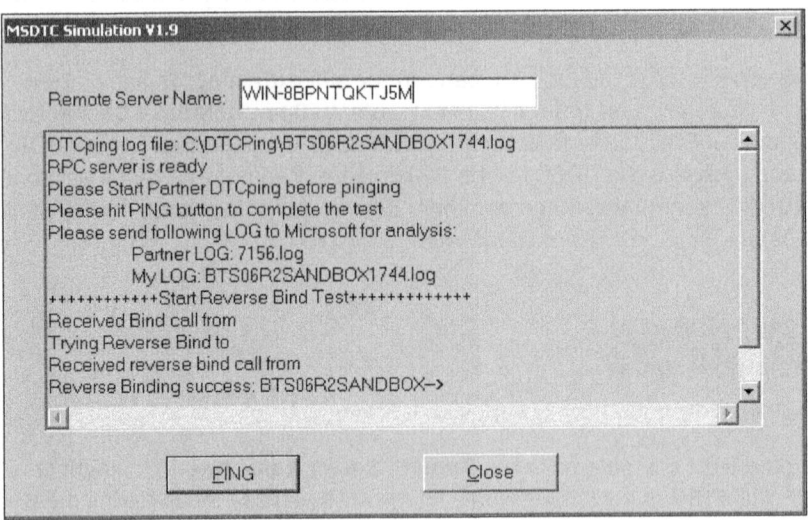

5. From this machine you can ping back to the other machine and the test is complete. Refer to the following screenshot:

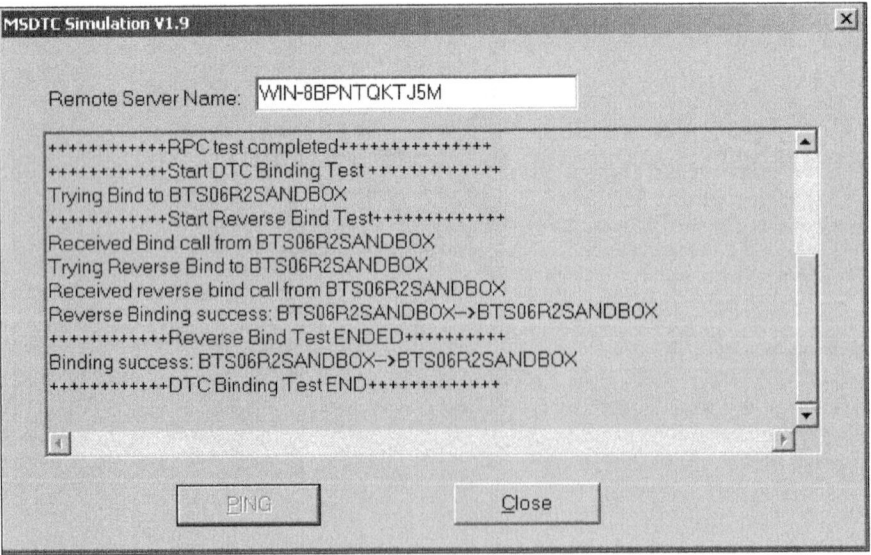

6. DTCTester can be started from the command line, where it has been installed. Execute the following from the command line:

```
dtctester <dsn name><user name><password>
```

7. Replace the values in brackets as appropriate for your environment:

```
D:\BizTalk Cook Book\Chapter 1 - BizTalk Server Environment\Resources\DTCTester>
dtctester VMSQL sa administrator
Executed: dtctester
DSN:  VMSQL
User Name: sa
Password: administrator
tablename= #dtc23687
Creating Temp Table for Testing: #dtc23687
Warning: No Columns in Result Set From Executing: 'create table #dtc23687 (ival
int)'
Initializing DTC
Beginning DTC Transaction
Enlisting Connection in Transaction
Executing SQL Statement in DTC Transaction
Inserting into Temp...insert into #dtc23687 values (1)
Warning: No Columns in Result Set From Executing: 'insert into #dtc23687 values
(1)'
Verifying Insert into Temp...select * from #dtc23687 (should be 1): 1
Press enter to commit transaction.

Commiting DTC Transaction
Releasing DTC Interface Pointers
Successfully Released pTransaction Pointer.
Disconnecting from Database and Cleaning up Handles
```

How it works...

When running DTCPing, it will provide output of any success or error messages obtained when attempting to communicate between servers. A ping from one server will be sent to another server, where an instance of DTCPing is running. Result of the ping is displayed in a running instance of DTCPing and from this instance a ping is sent back to the other server. The result of this ping will also be displayed. A user can verify if there are issues with communication between the two servers.

To be able to verify if an actual transaction in a database can be performed, DTCTester comes into play. When running DTCTester, it establishes a connection to the SQL Server by using a **Data Source Name** (**DSN**). It also provides the username and password that you provide on the command line by using the default network library. Then, a temporary table is created and the connection is enlisted in the transaction. An insert on a temporary table is done and this transaction is committed. The transaction is verified by the execution of a select statement. Finally, the connection is closed.

There is a clear distinction between both tools. DTCPing focuses on connectivity and DTCTester on transaction. An analogy to these tools is that you could see DTCPing as authentication and DTCTester as authorization.

There's more...

There are some resources regarding MSDTC and BizTalk you can benefit from:

- ▶ **Troubleshooting MSDTC issues with the DTCPing tool**: If you encounter errors during testing with the DTCPing tool, then you can report it to the Distributed Services Support Team. It has a blog entry with details on possible errors and how to resolve them (`http://blogs.msdn.com/b/distributedservices/archive/2008/11/12/troubleshooting-msdtc-issues-with-the-dtcping-tool.aspx`).

- ▶ **Troubleshooting MSDTC issues in general**: You will find more information on the Microsoft website on troubleshooting MSDTC at `http://msdn.microsoft.com/en-us/library/aa561924%28v=bts.20%29.aspx`.

- ▶ **BizTalk and MSDTC**: You can get more information at `http://soa-thoughts.blogspot.com/2010/01/biztalk-and-msdtc.html`.

See also

- ▶ Refer to the *Managing the SSO system* recipe earlier in this chapter

2
BizTalk Server Automation: Patterns

In this chapter, we will cover:

- ▸ Implementing the splitter pattern
- ▸ Developing an asynchronous aggregation pattern
- ▸ Creating a FIFO solution
- ▸ Developing a parallel convoy solution
- ▸ Routing using the resequencer messages in an orchestration
- ▸ Implementing a retry pattern in an orchestration
- ▸ Calling a pipeline in an orchestration

Introduction

As a developer, you can solve challenges that you face while implementing a BizTalk solution for a particular requirement by using one of the existing patterns. These patterns are available for BizTalk orchestrations and messaging. This chapter will focus mainly on existing patterns for orchestrations, which you can leverage in your solution or can inspire you to create your own. With the BizTalk Server, you can automate technical processes (machine-to-machine) to support business processes and implement one of the existing patterns, if applicable. These automated processes are supported in BizTalk through orchestration.

An **orchestration** is an executable code that runs a workflow supporting a technical process. An orchestration interacts with outside entities by using the ports. These things together are a powerful infrastructure to perform process automation and support integration with different subsystems.

In an orchestration, you can logically and chronologically design a set of activities (shapes) in order to achieve a certain goal. To be able to interact with other systems and applications outside the boundaries of the orchestration, you can use the Send and Receive ports. With Visual Studio, you can visually model the orchestrations, which are then compiled into .NET assemblies that are deployed in the Global Assembly Cache and registered in the BizTalk Management database. Within the BizTalk runtime, the life cycle of the orchestrations are managed—such as instantiation, execution, termination, and migration—across host instances, as well as scheduled and monitored with external entities.

Orchestrations play an important role when it comes down to implementing messaging integration patterns and automating a technical process. In this chapter, a few patterns will be described with the focus on implementation and how they work. To describe every BizTalk pattern, there is a need to justify a book by itself. So this chapter will limit itself to the most used and common patterns (recipes) for integration (messaging) and automating processes. With each recipe, you will be provided with sufficient background information and links to other resources.

Implementing the splitter pattern

A splitter pattern is used when a batch of messages is received and you need to process them individually. With this pattern you can process such a message by splitting it into small messages. Imagine you have a large message containing multiple orders by different stores and you want to separate each order from each store into a single message, then this pattern can be a fit-for-purpose.

There are different ways to implement this pattern in BizTalk, such as using a pipeline or an orchestration using maps, XSLT, and XPath. As there are multiple ways to implement this pattern, it is good to know what the pros and cons are of each implementation. Envelope debatching or Receive port pipeline debatching is fast, very fast, and suitable for the message only scenarios. The drawback of using this implementation is that when something fails in the pipeline then the entire message fails, so it has less flexibility. This can be resolved enabling the recoverable interchange feature (`http://msdn.microsoft.com/en-us/library/aa578714(v=bts.70).aspx`). Using debatching in an orchestration with map, custom XSLT, or XPath will give you more flexibility. You will have more control over each individual message, and you can do sequential, ordered processing. The drawback of this implementation is that when the number of messages increase the performance will decrease quickly and require a lot of system resources. In this recipe, we will show splitter pattern implementation through messaging and in an orchestration.

Downloading the example code

You can download the example code files for all Packt books you have purchased from your account at http://www.packtpub.com. If you purchased this book elsewhere, you can visit http://www.packtpub.com/support and register to have the files e-mailed directly to you.

Getting ready

Open Visual Studio 2010 and create a solution for the debatching process. For reference you can download the source code (BTS.Cookbook.SplitterPattern) belonging to this chapter.

How to do it...

Suppose you are receiving a message that contains multiple records and in order to process each message individually you want to debatch/split the message by using a pipeline, there are a few steps involved to achieve this, as follows:

1. First, you should create a document schema (see the following screenshot showing document schema) that contains all the elements:

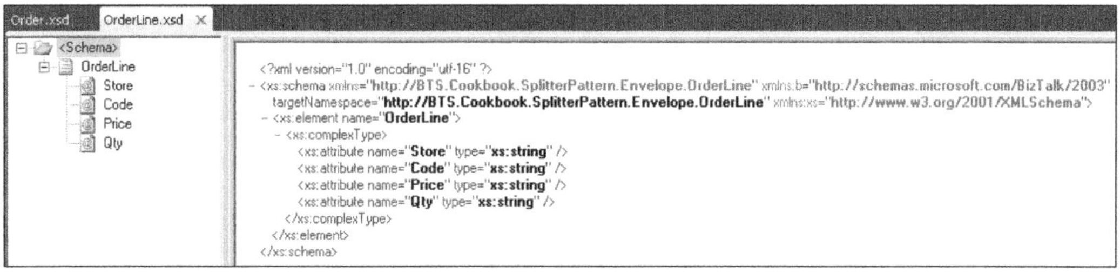

2. Next, you can create an envelope schema (see the following screenshot) that imports the document schema:

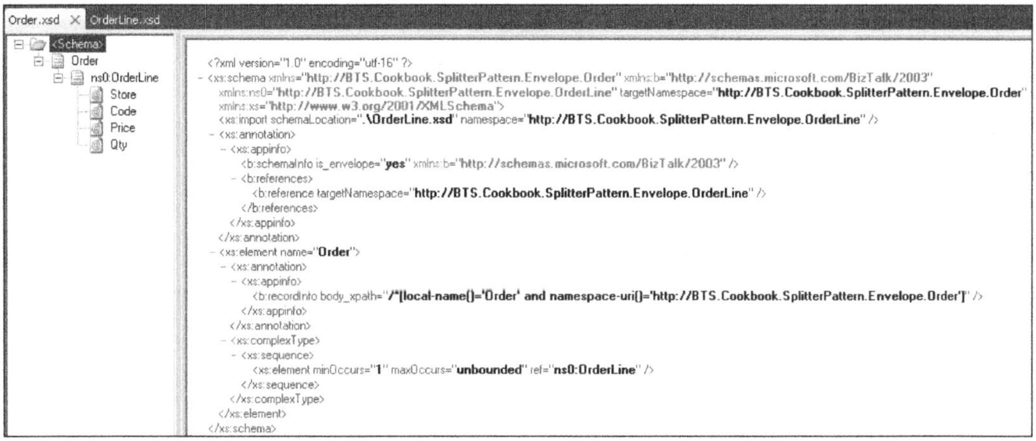

3. For creating a schema, you can right-click on your BizTalk project and click on **Add New Item**. Then select a schema and give it a name. For an envelope schema, you will need to set the **Envelope** property in the schema to **Yes** and import the document schema through **Imports**, as shown in the following screenshot:

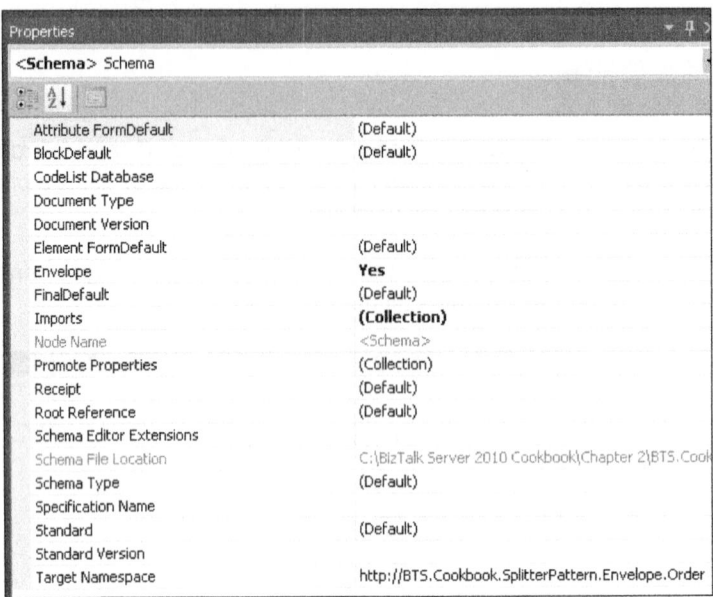

4. In **Properties | Imports**, you can add your document schema through **BizTalk Type Picker**, as shown in the following screenshot:

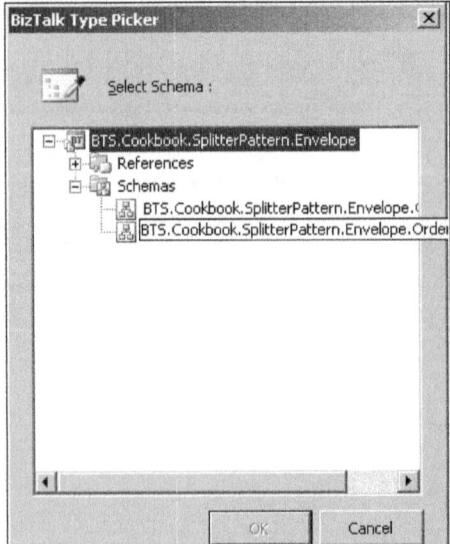

5. In your envelope schema, you can create a child record with a root node name of the document schema and change **Data Structure Type**, as shown in the following screenshot:

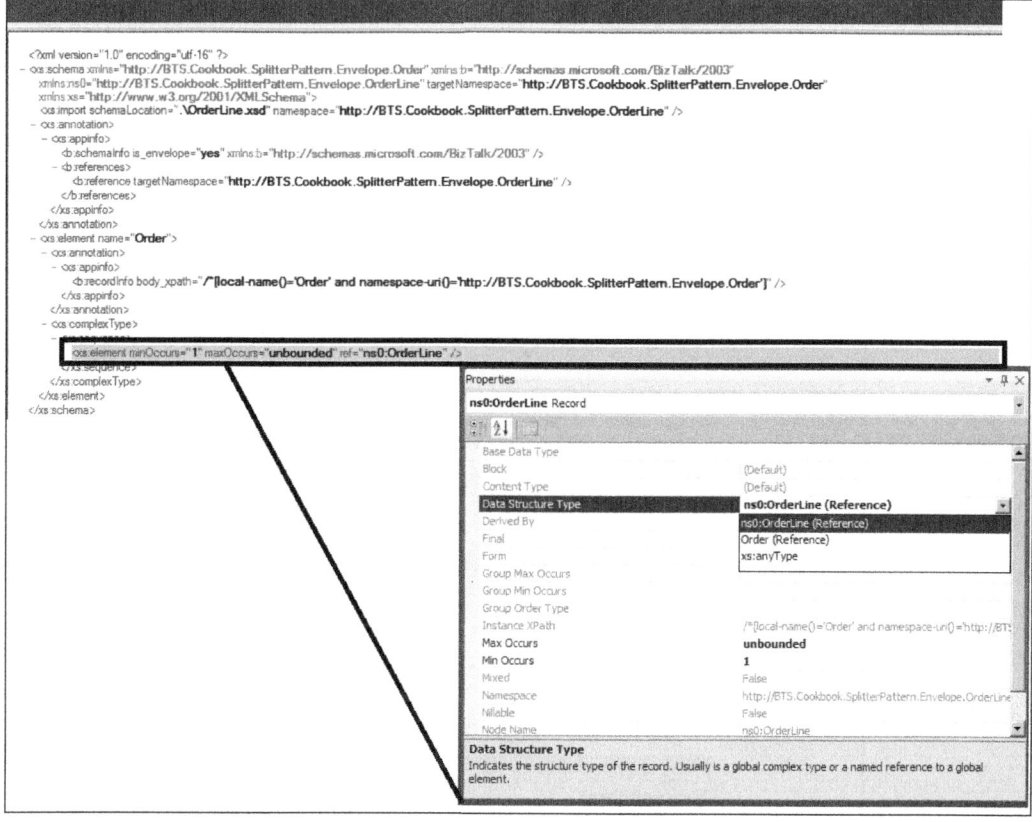

6. Finally, you have to change `body_xpath` to `/*[local-name()='Order' and namespace-uri()='http://BTS.Cookbook.SplitterPattern.Envelope.Order'].`

7. Before you create the pipeline, you can create a message through the `generate` instance that contains multiple records and test it using the `XmlDAsm.exe` tool found In `C:\Program Files\Microsoft BizTalk Server 2010\SDK\Utilities\PipelineTools`. This tool enables you to explore the disassemble behavior. You will have to copy the envelope and document schemas, together with the generated XML file (see the following screenshot):

```
<ns0:Order xmlns:ns0="http://BTS.Cookbook.SplitterPattern.Envelope.Order">
  <ns1:OrderLine Store="A" Code="X123456" Price="22.00" Qty="1" xmlns:ns1="http://BTS.Cookbook.SplitterPattern.Envelope.OrderLine" />
  <ns1:OrderLine Store="B" Code="X123457" Price="43.00" Qty="10" xmlns:ns1="http://BTS.Cookbook.SplitterPattern.Envelope.OrderLine" />
  <ns1:OrderLine Store="C" Code="X123458" Price="63.00" Qty="5" xmlns:ns1="http://BTS.Cookbook.SplitterPattern.Envelope.OrderLine" />
</ns0:Order>
```

8. You can execute `XmlDAsm.exe` with appropriate parameters, as shown in the following screenshot:

```
C:\Program Files (x86)\Microsoft BizTalk Server 2010\SDK\Utilities\PipelineTools
>XmlDasm Order.xml -ds OrderLine.xsd -es Order.xsd
```

9. You will see the preceding screenshot as a message, whether or not debatching of the XML file (message) occurs. If you see multiple messages appearing in the folder, you can check if each message contains a single record. This way you will be sure while creating the pipeline that the debatching process at runtime will succeed.

10. You can create a custom receive pipeline, as shown in the following screenshot. Drag an **XML disassembler** form from the pipeline component in the toolbox to the **Disassemble** stage. Then change the document and envelope schemas accordingly:

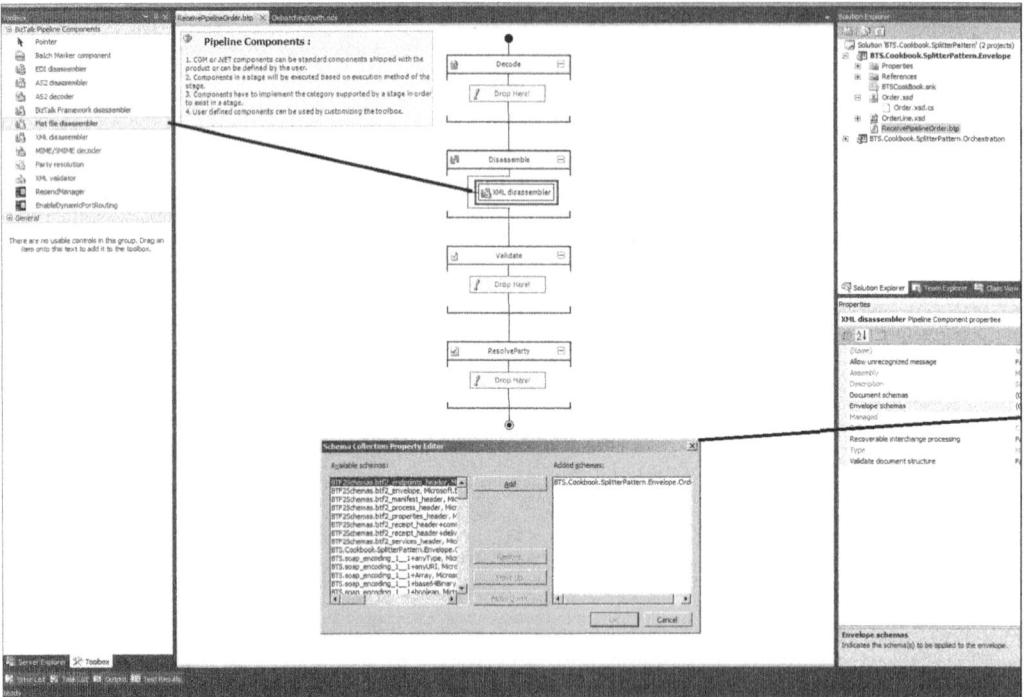

11. After creating your pipeline, you will have to sign your project with a strong name. Give the application a name and deploy it to the BizTalk Server through BizTalk.

12. You will have to create a Receive port with the created custom pipeline and a Send port with filters in the Administration Console to make it able to test the application with the pipeline.

You can also debatch a message inside an orchestration. There are some drawbacks to this approach; you will have to watch out for them. The drawbacks are as follows:

- ▸ Performance as each message performs a send operation resulting in a persistence point
- ▸ If one message fails, the subsequent messages are not sent
- ▸ Complexity with the XPath query

Still, it may be possible that you could choose to do it this way in a situation where you need more control over the debatching process and you are not doing anything transactional.

Instead of using an `xpath` expression in the **envelope** schema, you will have one expression to count the records and one expression to extract each record out of a message. Follow the steps given next:

1. You should create an orchestration with the Receive shape followed by an Expression shape. Then create a message based on an applicable schema and give it a name.

2. Next, you can create a variable called `dRecordCount` and use that in the **Expression** shape to assign the result of the `xpath` expression:

```
dRecordCount = System.Convert.ToDouble(xpath(msgOrder,
"count(/*[local-name()='Order' and namespace-uri()='http://
BTS.Cookbook.SplitterPattern.Orchestration.Order']/*[local-
name()='OrderLine' and namespace-uri()='http://BTS.Cookbook.
SplitterPattern.Orchestration.Order'])"));
```

3. Then, create another variable called **dLoopCount** to hold the loop counter and set its initial value to **1**, as shown in the following screenshot:

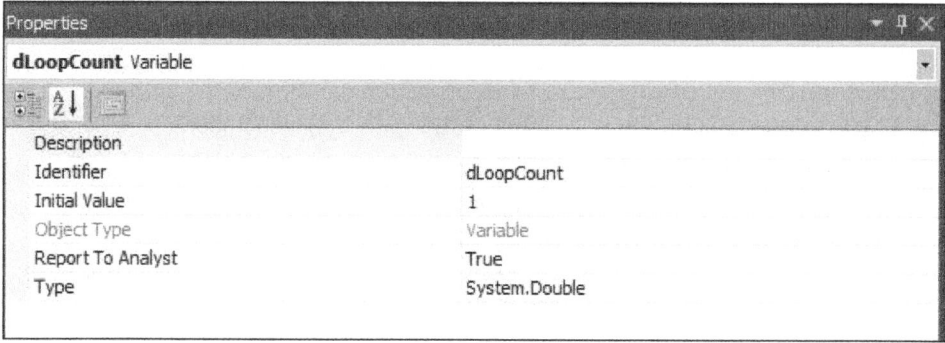

4. Now, you can add a **Loop** shape and set its expression in the form of dLoopCount <= dRecordCount. Inside **Loop** shape, you can place a **Construct** shape for creation of the single message. In the **Construct** shape you can place a **Message Assign** shape. Another variable called sXpath needs to be created for the type string to be able to assign the Xpath query, so that a single message can be extracted from the incoming message:

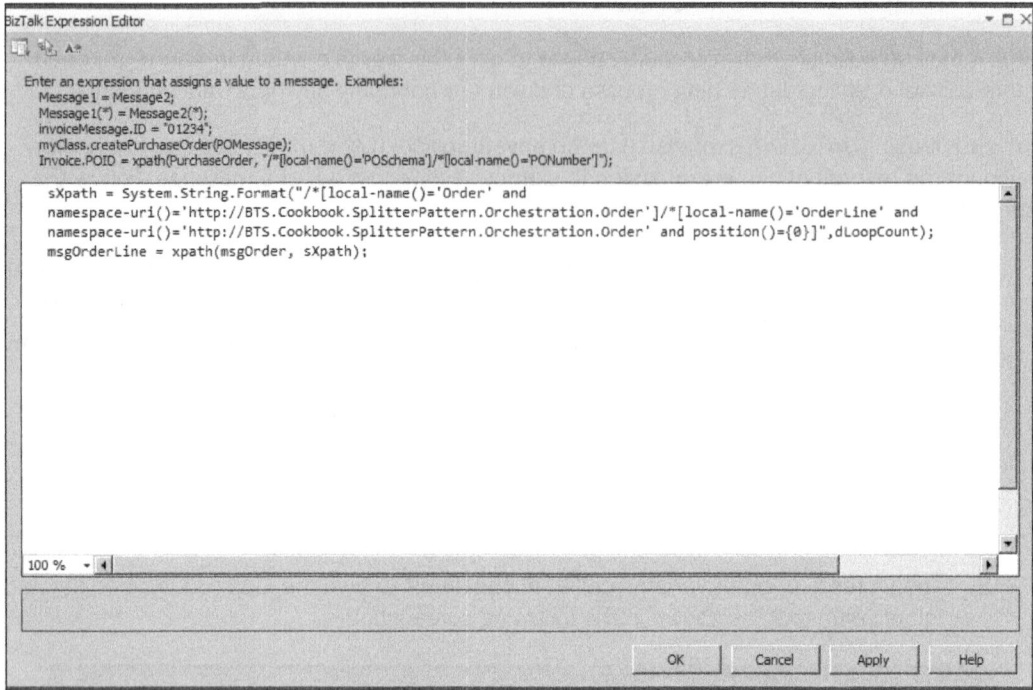

5. Next, you can add a **Send** shape to associate the message to the port and below an **Expression** shape, where the counter (dLoopCount) is increased by 1.

6. Finally, you will add two ports—one to receive a message and one to send the message. The orchestration will appear as shown in the following screenshot:

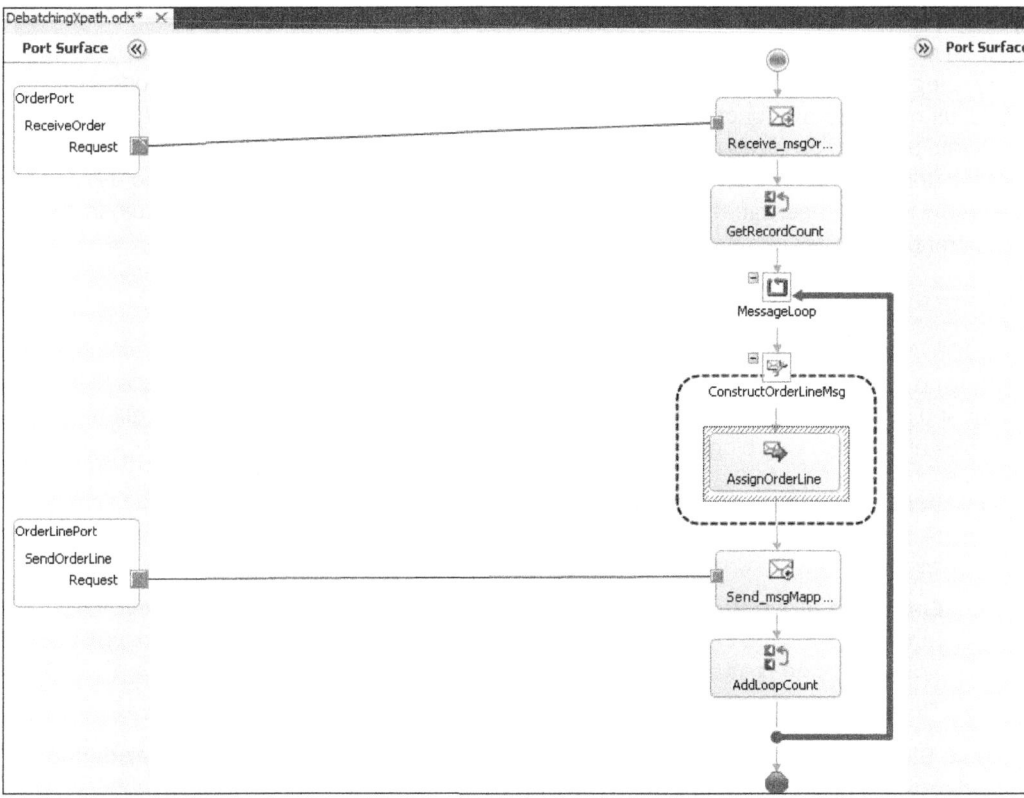

You will find this sample also in the code belonging to this book.

How it works...

First, let us see what happens in envelope debatching. When a message is picked up through, let's say a receive location with a file adapter, the XML disassembler will receive the message. The XML disassembler will retrieve the root node name and target the namespace from the document and construct the message type. It will then query the BizTalk management database (BiztalkMgmt.Db) to retrieve the schema. It will check the schema for any promoted properties and/or distinguished fields and then check if it is an envelope message. If it is an envelope, it will strip out each child node from the body_xpath node (/*[local-name()='Order' and namespace-uri()='http://BTS.Cookbook.SplitterPattern.Envelope. Order']) into the original message and construct a new message for each. It will now repeat the process of determining the message type of each debatched message and retrieving the schema from the BiztalkMgmtDb, promoting any properties, and so on. This is more or less how envelope debatching works. In this recipe, a custom pipeline is used with the XML disassembler in the Disassemble stage, but you can also use an XmlReceive pipeline in the solution instead of a custom pipeline. The XML disassemble component in the XmlReceive pipeline debatches (splits) the envelope message into its separate messages.

Debatching in an orchestration works differently than the published message, which is picked up by an orchestration. The number of records within a message is determined by an XPath query using the `count` function. This function returns the number of nodes in a node set. The result of the `count` function is assigned to a variable. A loop inside an orchestration will iterate as many times as the determined number is assigned to a variable. Within each iteration another XPath query will retrieve a record from the message, which will be assigned to a newly-created message that can be sent to be processed. If you want to debatch in an orchestration, a better alternative can be using a pipeline in an orchestration.

There's more...

Splitting up messages can be useful in many scenarios; you could poll data from the SQL Server and split each record to create a message and send it out. You will find excellent examples at the following blogs:

> **Debatching Inbound Messages from BizTalk WCF SQL Adapter**: `http://seroter.wordpress.com/2010/04/08/debatching-inbound-messages-from-biztalk-wcf-sql-adapter/`

> **Enterprise Integration Pattern Part 4 – Splitter (Debatching multiple records)**: `http://abdulrafaysbiztalk.wordpress.com/2009/11/07/enterprise-integration-pattern-part-4-%E2%80%93-splitter-debatching-multiple-records/`

In 2004, Stephen Thomas wrote an article called **Debatching Options and Performance Considerations in BizTalk 2004** (`http://geekswithblogs.net/sthomas/archive/2004/12/12/17373.aspx`) on debatching options, which provides a good insight of options you have. Envelope and orchestration are the most powerful ones in performance or flexibility.

Saravana Kumar also wrote a good post called **Message Debatching inside Biztalk Orchestration, with TargetNamespace** (`http://blogs.digitaldeposit.net/saravana/post/2006/12/18/Message-Debatching-inside-Biztalk-Orchestration-with-TargetNamespace.aspx`) on debatching later.

See also

> Refer to the *Developing an asynchronous aggregation pattern* and *Calling a pipeline in an orchestration* recipes later in this chapter

Developing an asynchronous aggregation pattern

An asynchronous aggregation pattern continues where the previous splitter pattern ended. By implementing this pattern, you can aggregate results of processed, smaller messages into a large message. Each processed message represents an individual unit of work that has no dependency on other messages. It can be useful when a client sends a batch to be processed and expects a batch response, with results for each message in the batch.

Getting ready

Open Visual Studio 2010 and create a solution for the debatching process. For reference, you can download the source code (BTS.Cookbook.AsyncAggPattern) belonging to this chapter.

How to do it...

First, you will debatch the message using the *Implementing the splitter pattern* recipe. For instance, you can use envelope debatching. There will be orchestration(s) subscribing to the resulting messages, which can be any kind of orchestration(s) processing the messages. Results of processing can be aggregated and it is detailed in the following steps:

1. First, you need to generate a schema based on the stored procedure, as displayed in the following code snippet. The stored procedure will insert each debatched message into the SQL Server table:

```
CREATE PROCEDURE [dbo].[bts_InsertXMLDebatchedMessage]
    @InterchangeID uniqueidentifier,
    @InterchangeSequenceNumber nvarchar(3),
    @LastInterchangeMessage nvarchar(5),
    @source nvarchar(64),
    @destination nvarchar(64),
    @table nvarchar(64),
    @message xml
AS
    -- Set the transaction isolation level to read committed
    SET TRANSACTION ISOLATION LEVEL READ COMMITTED
    SET XACT_ABORT ON
    SET NOCOUNT ON
    -- Declare @parameters and @command variables
    DECLARE @command nvarchar(4000)
    DECLARE @parameters nvarchar(4000)
```

```
DECLARE @bLastInterchangeMessage bit

If (@LastInterchangeMessage = 'true')
  SET @bLastInterchangeMessage = 1
ElSE
  SET @bLastInterchangeMessage = 0
  -- Set @parameters variable
  SET @parameters = N'@InterchangeID uniqueidentifier,
  @InterchangeSequenceNumber int, @LastInterchangeMessage bit,
  @source varchar(50), @destination varchar(50), @message xml'
-- Set @command variable
  SET @command = N'INSERT INTO [' + @table + ']
  ([InterchangeID], [InterchangeSequenceNumber],
  [LastInterchangeMessage], [source], [destination], [message])
  VALUES(@InterchangeID, @InterchangeSequenceNumber,
  @LastInterchangeMessage, @source, @destination, @message)'
-- Execute command
  EXEC sp_executesql @command, @parameters, @InterchangeID,
  @InterchangeSequenceNumber, @LastInterchangeMessage, @source,
  @destination, @message
IF @@ROWCOUNT = 0
BEGIN
  RAISERROR (N'The bts_InsertXMLDebatchedMessage stored
  procedure failed to insert a record.', 16, 1);
END
SET XACT_ABORT OFF
```

2. Second, you need to do a mapping from the original message to the insert message (based on the generated schema). Refer to the following screenshot:

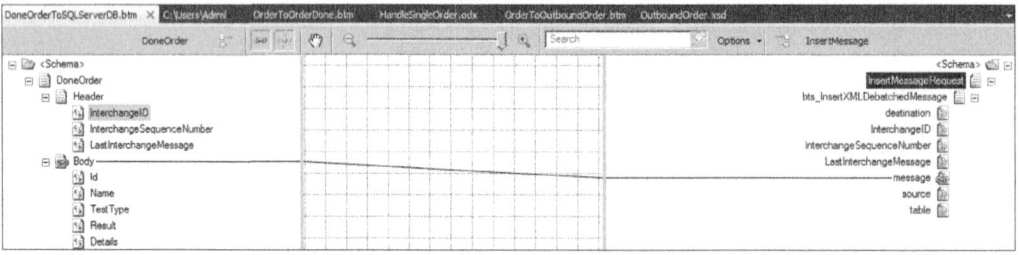

3. After building and deploying your complete solution, you need to configure a Send port responsible for inserting the message in the database. You can see the configuration of the Send port with the SQL Adapter responsible for calling the stored procedure, as shown in the following screenshot:

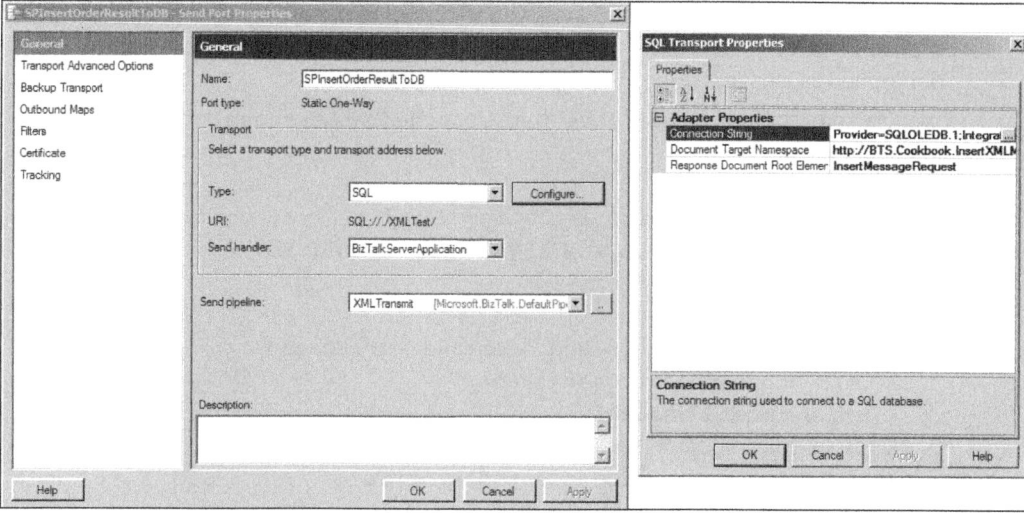

4. With the Send port, you will also configure outbound mapping as mapping needs to take place between the original message and the insert message:

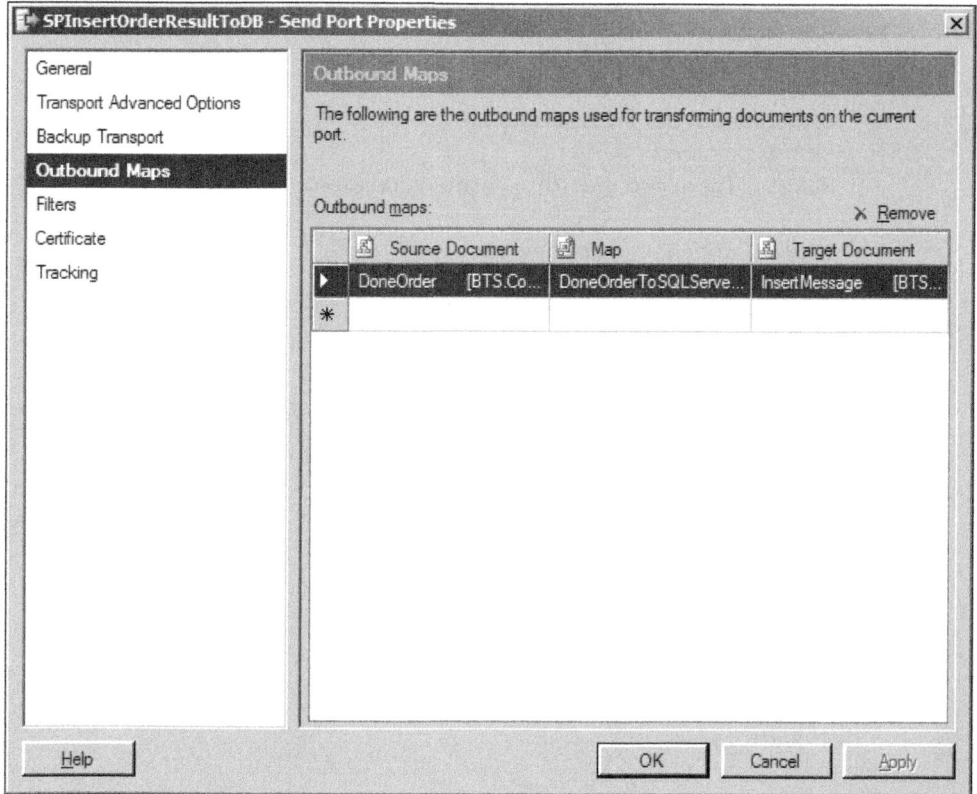

5. To aggregate the complete sequence, you will need to create another stored procedure given in the following code snippet. This procedure will retrieve the debatched messages:

```
CREATE PROCEDURE [dbo].[bts_GetDebatchedXMLMessages]
AS
  BEGIN
  -- Set the transaction isolation level to read committed
  SET TRANSACTION ISOLATION LEVEL READ COMMITTED
  SET XACT_ABORT ON
  SET NOCOUNT ON
  -- Declare @parameters and @command variables
  DECLARE @command nvarchar(4000)
  -- Set @command variable
  SET @command = N'
  DECLARE @InterchangeID uniqueidentifier

  SELECT TOP 1 @InterchangeID=InterchangeIDFROM
  DebatchedStatistics WHERE TotalCnt = ResultCnt And Consumed = 0


  IF (@@ROWCOUNT = 1)
    BEGIN

      UPDATE dbo.DebatchedMessage
      SET [Consumed] = 1
      WHERE [InterchangeID] = @InterchangeID

      UPDATE dbo.DebatchedStatistics
      SET [Consumed] = 1
      WHERE [InterchangeID] = @InterchangeID

      SELECT [Message]
      FROM DebatchedMessage WITH (ROWLOCK READPAST)
      WHERE [InterchangeID] = @InterchangeID AND [Consumed]=1
      ORDER BY interchangeSequenceNumber

      DELETE DebatchedMessage
      WHERE [InterchangeID] = @InterchangeID

    END'
  -- Execute command
  EXEC sp_executesql @command
    SET XACT_ABORT OFF
  END
```

6. Create a Receive port and corresponding receive location. In **Receive port**, select **Type** as **SQL** and configure it accordingly:

  ❑ Connection string to the database: Your database

    ❑ Document Root Element Name: `DoneData`

  ❑ **Document Target Namespace**: **http://BTS.Cookbook.DoneEnvelope**

  ❑ SQL command: `EXEC bts_GetDebatchedXMLMessages`

  ❑ **URI**: **SQL://./XMLTest/**

7. Next, you create a Send port with a descriptive name and configure it with the **File** port and **Filter** set to **Receive port**.

How it works...

The asynchronous aggregation process follows some specific steps:

1. Consider an XML message.

2. It is debatched first into smaller messages.

3. These messages are published to the message box database or to the file folder.

4. An orchestration will subscribe to these messages and process them according to certain business requirements and/or send it to an application that will process the message and return the result.

5. In the sample provided by this book, the orchestration is just a simulation of handling messages. The responses from the orchestration (process) will be aggregated by either an aggregator, which can be an orchestration or a SQL stored procedure.

6. The aggregator will submit the final aggregated result after polling the database and the last interchange flag is set to true.

The following diagram outlines the asynchronous aggregation process implemented in the provided code sample:

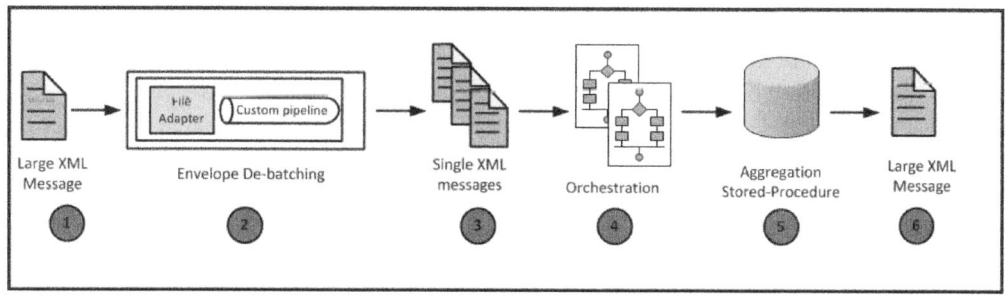

There's more...

Asynchronous aggregation is detailed by the Windows Server AppFabric Customer Advisory Team in the document **BizTalk Patterns part 1 – Asynchronous Aggregation** at `http://blogs.msdn.com/b/appfabriccat/archive/2010/09/29/biztalk-patterns-part-1.aspx`.

The sample provided in this book is derived from the code made by Ji Young Lee (Microsoft South Korea). There is a document **BizTalk Patterns part 2 – Sync Async** at `http://blogs.msdn.com/b/appfabriccat/archive/2010/10/16/biztalk-patterns-part-2-sync-async.aspx`.

Aggregation can also be done through aggregation service orchestration, as shown in the document **Implementation of an Asynchronous Aggregation Pattern** at `http://geekswithblogs.net/synBoogaloo/archive/2005/09/23/54705.aspx`.

See also

▸ Refer to the *Routing using the resequencer messages in an orchestration* recipe later in this chapter

Creating a FIFO solution

Real time ordered delivery can be achieved if you can control the sending of messages. A regular orchestration with a single activation will not do the trick as messages in the `MessageBox` will be picked up by the XLANG engine, which will spin up as many instances of orchestration as there are messages. Messages can be different in size, and different amounts of time will, therefore, likely be required to process them through BizTalk. Therefore, the message order can easily change during the processing of messages. To be able to do it in a **First In First Out** (**FIFO**) manner, the first message needs to be completed before the next message is picked up to be processed. You will basically need one instance of an orchestration to complete all processing of messages. Implementing a FIFO pattern requires you to build a sequential convoy using message correlation and ordered delivery flags in BizTalk.

Convoys are a well known concept in the BizTalk world. Convoys are used when you receive related messages from different sources or systems and in a different order and on a different time interval. Using convoys, you can start the orchestration process and keep receiving the correlated messages either in parallel or sequential form.

Thus, there are two kinds of convoys possible:

▶ **Sequential**: When you need to receive messages in a predefined order then you need to use sequential convoy

▶ **Parallel**: When you can receive the related messages in any order then you need to use parallel convoy, also referred to as concurrency convoy

The FIFO pattern is useful when you need to maintain the message order. Basically, you want to control which message will come out first in BizTalk. In a scenario, where a FIFO-ordered delivery is required, sequential convoys handle the race condition that occurs as BizTalk attempts to process subscriptions for messages received at the same time. A scenario you can think of is financial transactions. Think of a common scenario, where you want to deposit and withdraw money from your bank account. If you do not have enough money in your bank account and you make a deposit of 100 Euros, and then a withdrawal of 50 Euros, it is important that these transactions are committed in the correct order. If the withdrawal transaction would occur first, then you will most likely be informed that you have insufficient funds, even though you have just made a deposit.

Getting ready

Open Visual Studio 2010 and create a solution for the debatching process. For reference, you can download the source code (`BTS.Cookbook.FifoPattern`) belonging to this chapter.

How to do it...

Sequential convoys are implemented by message correlation and ordered delivery flags in the BizTalk Server, as outlined in the following steps:

1. Create a new BizTalk project and add the schema of the message you require in the project you require.

2. Subsequently add a new orchestration to the project and give it a descriptive name.

3. Create a new message in the **Orchestration View** window, and specify the name and type.

4. In the **Orchestration View** window, expand the **Types** node of the tree view so that the **Correlation Types** folder is visible.

5. Right-click on the **Correlation Types** folder, and select **New Correlation Type**, which creates a correlation type and launches the **Correlation Properties** dialog box.

6. In the **Correlation Properties** dialog box, select the properties that the convoy's correlation set will be based on. For example, you can select the **BTS. ReceivePortName** property, which indicates the Receive port through which the message was received.

7. Click on **New Correlation Type**, and give it a descriptive name in the **Properties** window.

8. In the **Orchestration View** window, right-click on the **Correlation Set** folder, select **New Correlation Set**, and specify a name and correlation type.

9. The parallel convoy configuration is shown in the following screenshot:

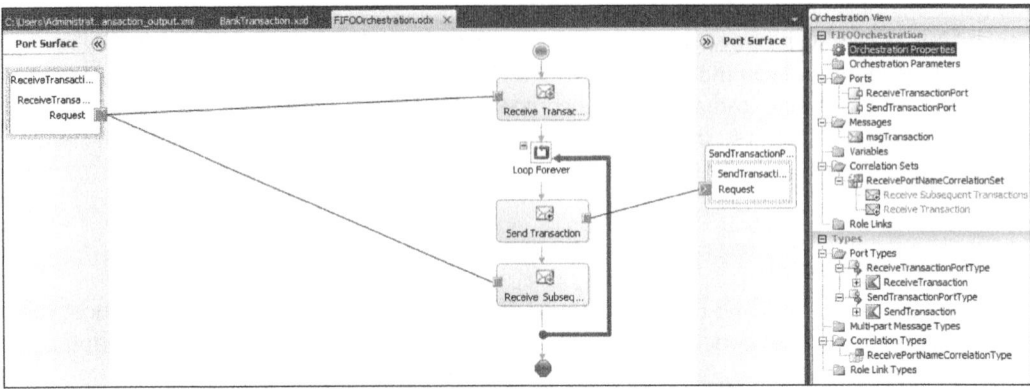

10. From the toolbox, drag the following onto the design surface in top-down order:

   ❑ Drag the **Receive** shape to receive the initial order message. This shape should be configured to use the message created earlier, to activate the orchestration, to initialize with the created correlation set, and to use an orchestration Receive port.

   ❑ Drag the **Loop** shape to allow the orchestration to receive multiple messages This shape should be configured with the expression `true` (allowing the orchestration to run in perpetuity).

   ❑ Drag the **Send** shape within the **Loop** shape. This delivers the message to the destination system. This shape should be configured to use an orchestration Send port.

   ❑ Drag the **Receive** shape within the **Loop** shape. This receives the next message (based on the older messages which were received) in the convoy. This shape should be configured to use the created message, to follow the create correlation set, and to use the same orchestration Receive port as the first Receive shape.

11. Sign the project with a strong name.

12. Subsequently go to the deployment and give it an appropriate application name.

13. Build and deploy the BizTalk project.

14. Create a Receive port and receive location to receive messages from the file system.

15. Create a Send port to deliver messages to the destination system. You could create an MSMQ queue. In the **Transport Advanced Options** section of the **Send Port Properties** dialog box, select the **Ordered delivery** option, as shown in the following screenshot:

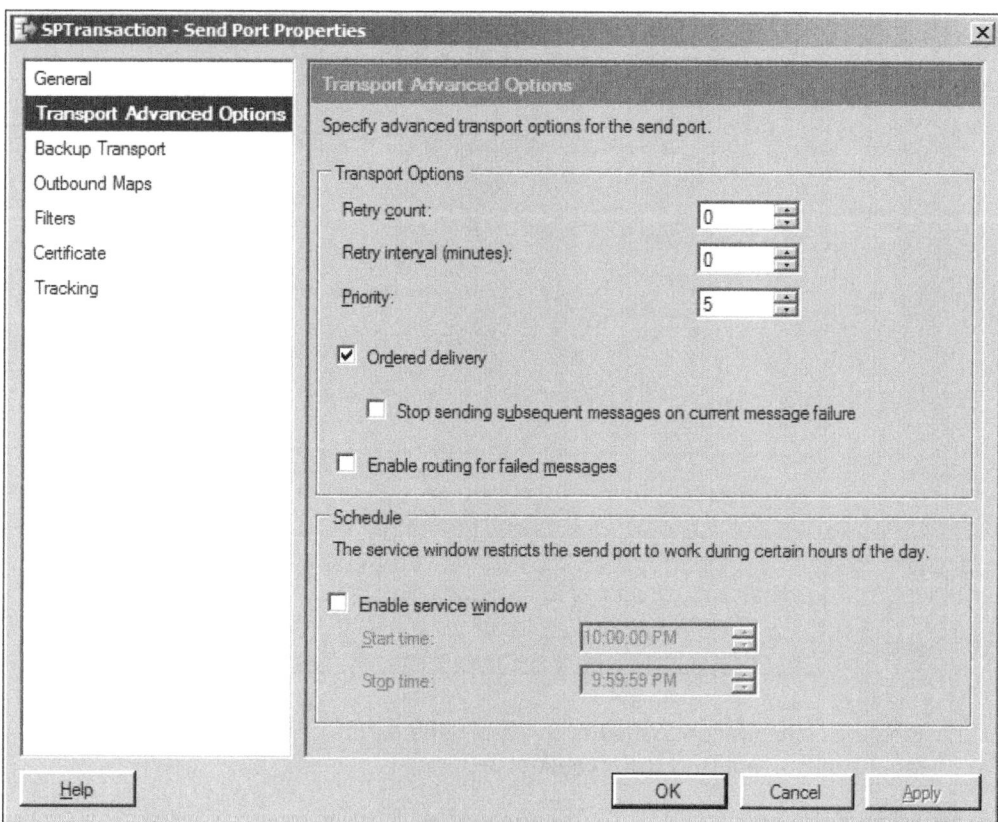

16. For the receive location, you need to select an adapter that implements ordered delivery like WCF-NetMsmq:

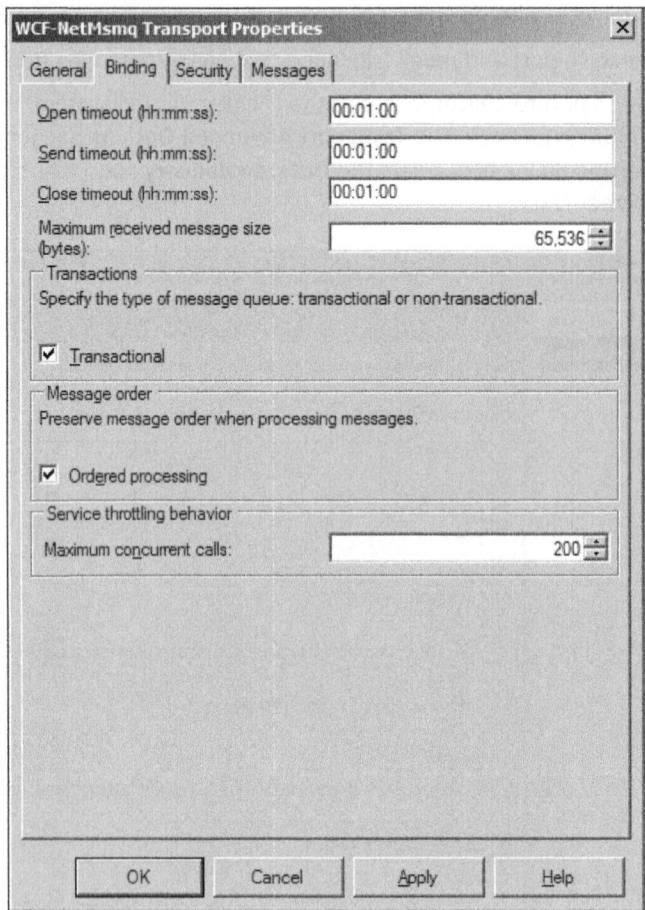

17. Bind the orchestration to the Receive and Send ports, configure the host for the orchestration, and start the orchestration.

How it works...

Sequential convoy implementation can be used to sequentially handle messages within an orchestration. It consists of a correlation set and ordered delivery flags specified on the receive location and Send port to support first-in, first-out flow. The first Receive shape initializes the correlation set, which is based on the Receive port name, by which the order was consumed. This will instruct the BizTalk runtime to associate the correlation type data with the Receive port name by which the message was consumed. It will subsequently associate the correlation type data with the orchestration instance.

All messages with an identical correlation type criteria will be routed to the same instance. With the Ordered Processing flag, the BizTalk runtime will be instructed to maintain the order, determining which message should be delivered to the orchestration instance.

Working with convoys has its pros and cons. One of the disadvantages of using convoys is that the orchestration is always active and thus, wasting resources ("never ending" convoy orchestrations). For processing thousands of messages, this pattern will not be efficient. Another disadvantage is potential risks of zombie messages (`http://geekswithblogs.net/LeonidGaneline/archive/2011/02/05/biztalk-instance-subscription-details.aspx`). Advantages of convoys are sequential handling of messages, as shown in this recipe, or joining multiple single items together to achieve something that an individual item cannot accomplish by itself.

There's more...

This recipe shows implementation of a sequential convoy to support the FIFO pattern. Sequential convoy itself can be fine-tuned to handle sequential processing in a different manner. In this recipe, the orchestration handles each message received from a queue in order (the MSMQ Adapter supports ordered delivery). Basically, the orchestration is a single-thread process (one instance) and is good for maintaining the FIFO process. By not using ordered delivery and having a correlation set based on just a Receive port name, you can have a different correlation set based on the ID in the message and have multiple receive locations. This way more messages can be handled simultaneously and the performance of the process could be increased.

You can find more on sequential convoys through the following resources:

- **Sequential Convoys**: `http://msdn.microsoft.com/en-us/library/aa561843%28v=bts.70%29.aspx`
- **Sequential Convoys in BizTalk**: `http://www.biztalkgurus.com/biztalk_server/biztalk_blogs/b/biztalk/archive/2004/08/23/sequential-convoys-in-biztalk.aspx`
- **BizTalk 2004 Convoy Deep Dive**: `http://msdn.microsoft.com/en-us/library/ms942189%28v=bts.10%29.aspx`

See also

- Refer to the *Developing a parallel convoy solution* recipe later in this chapter

Developing a parallel convoy solution

This recipe will go into implementing a parallel convoy. An example scenario where a parallel convoy can be applicable is when the order can only be shipped if the payment is approved and the stock-level has been verified. Payment comes from a financial system, while stock-level information comes from an inventory system. Both will publish their respective messages for a specific order before the order will get processed further.

Getting ready

Open Visual Studio 2010 to develop the parallel convoy. For reference, you can download the source code (`BTS.Cookbook.ParallelConvoy`) belonging to this chapter.

How to do it...

A parallel convoy can be implemented by performing the following steps:

1. Create a new BizTalk Project and add schemas in the project you require. Schemas in these steps are available in the code sample for this recipe.

2. Create a property schema and rename **property1** to a desired name and set the type as required by the base correlation set.

3. Promote the field element (`Id` in the sample) in both schemas as a promoted property using the property schema necessary to correlate on.

4. Next, add a new orchestration to the project, and give it a descriptive name.

5. Create two new messages in the **Orchestration View** window, and specify the name and type for each of them.

6. In the **Orchestration View** window, expand the **Types** node of the tree view so that the **Correlation Types** folder is visible.

7. Right-click on the **Correlation Types** folder, and select **New Correlation Type**, which creates a correlation type and launches the **Correlation Properties** dialog box.

8. In the **Correlation Properties** dialog box, select the properties that the correlation will be based on, as shown in the following screenshot:

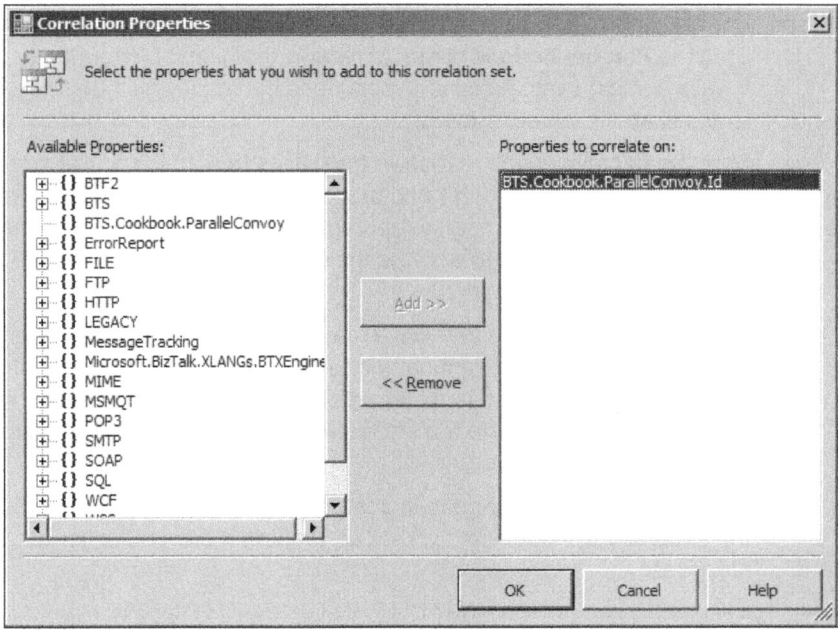

9. Click on the **New Correlation Type**, and give it a descriptive name in the **Properties** window.

10. In the **Orchestration View** window, right-click on the **Correlation Set** folder. Select **New Correlation Set** and specify a name and correlation type.

11. The parallel convoy configuration is shown in the following screenshot:

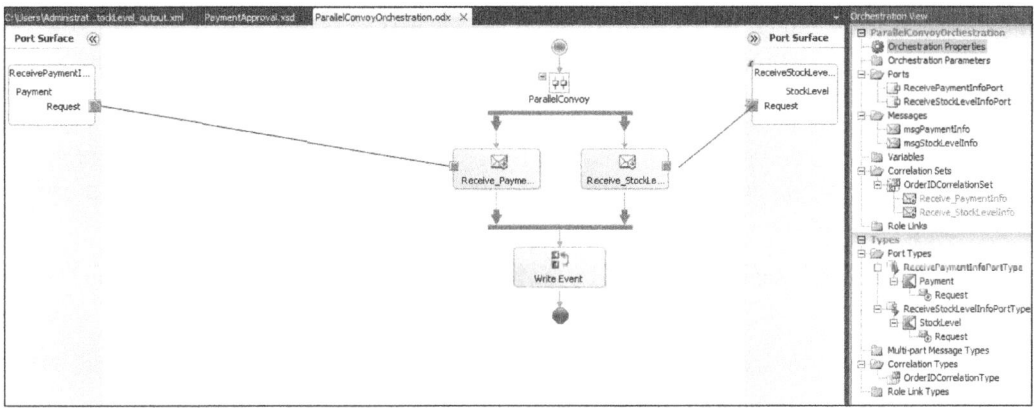

12. From the toolbox, drag the following onto the design surface in top-down order:

- ❑ Drag the **Parallel Actions** shape to receive the response from other systems. If we assume a sample scenario described earlier, it would be from the financial and inventory system.

- ❑ Drag the **Receive** shape to receive messages from the financial system. Place this shape on the left-hand branch of the **Parallel Actions** shape. Configure this shape to use the appropriate message, to initialize the created correlation set, to activate the orchestration, and to use an orchestration Receive port.

- ❑ Drag the **Receive** shape to receive messages from the inventory system. Place this shape on the right-hand branch of the **Parallel Actions** shape. Configure this shape to use the appropriate message, to initialize the correlation set, to activate the orchestration, and to use an orchestration Receive port.

- ❑ Drag the **Expression** shape to indicate further processing of the order. In the **Expression** shape, simply write an event in the event log for diagnostic purposes:

```
System.Diagnostics.EventLog.WriteEntry("Application", "Order
with ID = " + msgPaymentInfo(BTS.Cookbook.ParallelConvoy.
Id));
```

How it works...

A parallel convoy consists of a correlation set and Parallel Actions shape. Each Receive shape in the Parallel Actions shape initializes the correlation set, which is based on the case ID. With a correlation set, BizTalk is instructed to associate the correlation type data with the orchestration instance, so it can route all messages that have identical correlation-type criteria to the same instance. In this case, with a specific ID. Each receive shape has its Activate property set to `true` and its initializing correlation configured to the same correlation set. One of the two Receive shapes will receive the first message and handle the activation of the orchestration instance and initialization of the correlation set. Regardless of the fact that the other Receive shape also has its Activate property set to `true`, it will not activate a new orchestration instance.

Based on the example scenario, messages for two different orders would be handled in the following manner:

1. A payment message from a financial system is received in BizTalk with the ID 12345, orchestration A will be instantiated.

2. A stock level message from an inventory system is received in BizTalk with the ID 6789, orchestration B will be instantiated.

3. Subsequently, the financial system sends a payment message with the ID 6789 to BizTalk and this will be correlated and delivered to orchestration B. This orchestration will continue with the processing.

4. Subsequently the inventory system sends a stock level message with the ID 12345 and this will be correlated and delivered to orchestration A. This orchestration will continue with the processing.

There's more...

The recipe explains a scenario using only a single correlation set, while multiple correlation sets can be used to implement a parallel convoy. Then, the convoy is initialized on multiple branches of a Parallel Actions shape within an orchestration. It does not matter how many correlation sets are used; if multiple Receive shapes initialize a convoy set in a Parallel Actions shape, the same correlation sets must be initialized on all of the Receive shapes.

It is important for a developer to have a good understanding of correlation and correlation sets while building a parallel convoy in BizTalk. You will find more information through the following resources:

▶ **Correlation Sets**: `http://msdn.microsoft.com/en-us/library/aa560163%28v=bts.70%29.aspx`

▶ **BizTalk Server 2004 Convoy Deep Dive**: `http://msdn.microsoft.com/en-us/library/ms942189%28v=bts.10%29.aspx`

See also

▶ Refer to the *Creating a FIFO solution* recipe earlier in this chapter. There you can read more about a sequential convoy being implemented.

Routing using the resequencer messages in an orchestration

The resequencer pattern is one of the **Enterprise Application Integration** (**EAI**) message routing patterns like the previously described splitter pattern. Many EAI patterns can be found through the Enterprise Application Integration site `http://www.eaipatterns.com/`. The resequencer pattern can be used to collect and reorder messages, so that they can be published in a specified order. An orchestration receives a number of messages in a different order and they are reordered within the orchestration. Basically, the orchestration acts as a buffer to store out-of-sequence messages until a complete sequence is obtained. These messages are then sent through a port that preserves the order.

Getting ready

Create a solution in Visual Studio 2010. For reference, you can download the source code (`BTS.Cookbook.ResequencerPattern`) belonging to this chapter.

How to do it...

A resequencer pattern can be implemented as follows:

1. Create a new BizTalk project and add schemas in the project you require. Schemas should include an identifier such as `BatchId` and fields containing the sequence number and the total messages belonging to the sequence.

2. Add the `c#` class library to the project and rename `class1.cs` to a descriptive name.

3. Add the following code to the class, as follows:

```csharp
using System;
using System.Collections.Generic;
using System.Xml;
using System.Xml.Serialization;
using System.Collections;

namespace ResequencerHelperClass
{
  [Serializable]
  public class InMemoryResequencer
  {
    // Sortedlist member
    SortedList sequenceMessages;

    /// <summary>
    /// Constructor
    /// </summary>
    public InMemoryResequencer()
    {
      //Not implemented
    }

    /// <summary>
    /// Method to instantiate Sortedlist object
    /// </summary>
```

```
/// <param name="messageCount">Message Counter as
integer</param>
public InMemoryResequencer(int messageCount)
{
  sequenceMessages = new SortedList(messageCount);
}


/// <summary>
/// Methode to add message to sortedlist
/// </summary>
/// <param name="index">Index as integer</param>
/// <param name="xmlString">xmlString containing
message</param>
public void AddMessageToSortedList(int index, string
xmlString)
{
  sequenceMessages[index] = xmlString;
}

/// <summary>
/// Method to dequeue the messages
/// </summary>
/// <param name="index">Index as integer</param    ///
<returns>Message(xml) as string</returns>
public string DeQueueMessages(int index)
{
  return sequenceMessages[index] as string;
}
  }
}
```

4. Provide the project with a strong name and build.

5. In the BizTalk project, add a reference to the c# class library project.

6. Create a property schema and rename **property1** to a desired name and type required to the base correlation set (BatchId).

7. Promote the field element in the schema as a promoted property using the property schema necessary to correlate on.

8. Through show promotions, create two distinguished fields for sequence number and total messages:

```xml
<?xml version="1.0" encoding="utf-16" ?>
- <xs:schema xmlns:b="http://BTS.Cookbook.ResequencerPattern.Order" xmlns:b="http://schemas.microsoft.com/BizTalk/2003" xmlns:ns0="https://BTS.Cookbook.ResequencerPattern.PropertySchema"
    targetNamespace="http://BTS.Cookbook.ResequencerPattern.Order" xmlns:xs="http://www.w3.org/2001/XMLSchema">
  - <xs:annotation>
    - <xs:appinfo>
      - <b:imports>
          <b:namespace prefix="ns0" uri="https://BTS.Cookbook.ResequencerPattern.PropertySchema" location=".\PropertySchema.xsd" />
        </b:imports>
      </xs:appinfo>
    </xs:annotation>
  - <xs:element name="Order">
    - <xs:annotation>
      - <xs:appinfo>
        - <b:properties>
            <b:property distinguished="true" xpath="/*[local-name()='Order' and namespace-uri()='http://BTS.Cookbook.ResequencerPattern.Order']/*[local-name()='SequenceNumber' and namespace-uri()
              ='']" />
            <b:property distinguished="true" xpath="/*[local-name()='Order' and namespace-uri()='http://BTS.Cookbook.ResequencerPattern.Order']/*[local-name()='TotalMessages' and namespace-uri()='']" />
            <b:property name="ns0:BatchId" xpath="/*[local-name()='Order' and namespace-uri()='http://BTS.Cookbook.ResequencerPattern.Order']/*[local-name()='BatchID' and namespace-uri()='']" />
          </b:properties>
        </xs:appinfo>
      </xs:annotation>
    - <xs:complexType>
      - <xs:sequence>
          <xs:element name="SequenceNumber" type="xs:int" />
          <xs:element name="TotalMessages" type="xs:int" />
          <xs:element name="BatchID" type="xs:int" />
        - <xs:element name="Data">
          - <xs:complexType>
            - <xs:sequence>
                <xs:element name="Details" type="xs:string" />
              </xs:sequence>
            </xs:complexType>
          </xs:element>
        </xs:sequence>
      </xs:complexType>
    </xs:element>
  </xs:schema>
```

9. Next, add a new orchestration to the project, and give it a descriptive name.

10. Create a new message in the **Orchestration View** window, and specify the name and type.

11. In the **Orchestration View** window, expand the **Types** node of the tree view so that the **Correlation Types** folder is visible.

12. Right-click on the **Correlation Types** folder, and select **New Correlation Type**, which creates a correlation type and launches the **Correlation Properties** dialog box.

13. In the **Correlation Properties** dialog box, select the properties that the correlation will be based on.

14. In the **Orchestration View** window, create the following variables:

Variable name	Type	Initializing value
messageCounter	System.Int32	1
messageReturnCounter	System.Int32	1
messageString	System.String	N.A.
resequencerHelper	YourHelperClass.ClassName	N.A.
totalMessages	System.Int32	N.A.
xmlDocument	System.Xml.XmlDocument	N.A.

15. From the toolbox, drag the following onto the design surface in top-down order:

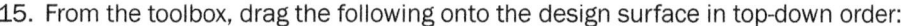

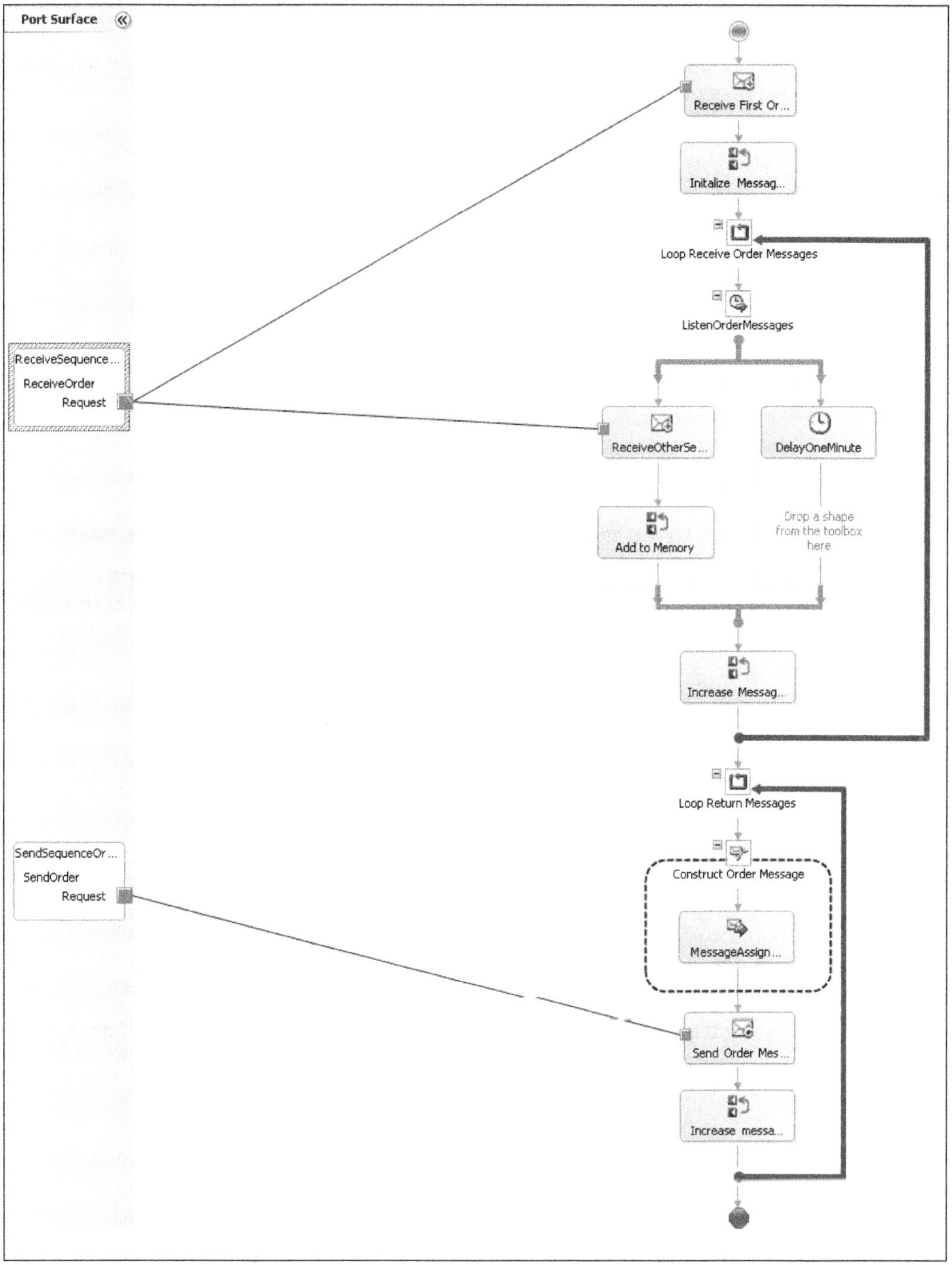

❑ Drag the **Receive** shape and give it a descriptive name. Configure this shape to use the appropriate message, to initialize the created correlation set, to activate the orchestration, and to use an orchestration Receive port.

❑ Drag the **Expression** shape under the **Receive** shape and fill in the following expression (this is based on the sample provided with this book):

```
//Assign total messages counter
totalMessages = orderMsg.TotalMessages;


xmlDocument = orderMsg;
messageString = xmlDocument.OuterXml;
resequencerHelper = new ResequencerHelperClass.InMemoryReseq
uencer(messageCounter);
resequencerHelper.AddMessageToSortedList(orderMsg.
SequenceNumber,messageString);
```

❑ Drag the **Loop** shape below the **Expression** shape and configure it with the following expression:

```
messageCounter <= totalMessages
```

❑ Drag the **Listen** shape in the **Loop** shape and give it a descriptive name.

❑ Drag the **Receive** shape to the left branch of the **Listen** shape and configure this shape to use the appropriate message, to follow the created correlation set, and to use the same orchestration Receive port as the first Receive shape.

❑ Drag the **Expression** shape below the **Receive** shape and fill in the following expression (this is based on the sample provided with this book):

```
xmlDocument = orderMsg;
messageString = xmlDocument.OuterXml;
resequencerHelper.AddMessageToSortedList(orderMsg.
SequenceNumber,messageString);
```

❑ In the right branch, drag the **Delay** shape and give it a descriptive name. Fill in the following expression:

```
new System.TimeSpan(0,0,60)
```

❑ Below the **Listen** shape, drag an Expression shape and fill in the following:

```
messageCounter = messageCounter + 1;
```

- ❑ Drag a new **Loop** shape below the first Loop shape and configure with the following expression:

  ```
  messageReturnCounter <= totalMessages
  ```

- ❑ Drag the **Construct** shape in the **Loop** shape and give it a descriptive name.

- ❑ In the **Construct** shape, drag the **Message Assign** shape and fill in the following expression:

  ```
  messageString =  resequencerHelper.DeQueueMessages(messageRe
  turnCounter);
  xmlDocument.LoadXml(messageString);
  orderMsg = xmlDocument;
  ```

- ❑ Drag the **Send** shape below the **Message Assign** shape and use an orchestration Send port.

- ❑ Drag the **Expression** shape below the **Send** shape and fill the following in the expression:

  ```
  messageReturnCounter = messageReturnCounter + 1;.
  ```

16. Sign the BizTalk project with a strong name and build.

How it works...

If there is a resequencer mechanism working, then there is a correlation set too. This correlation set is for incoming messages on an ID shared by all messages. In this recipe, ID is BatchId. The correlation set is based upon this ID. The correlation is initialized by the first Receive shape and the orchestration is instantiated by the first message that arrives. This message is saved in the memory through a call to the helper class in a SortedList of type string. When the method AddMessageToSortedList is called, the message is passed as a string with a sequence number (int). Basically, the message and sequence number are saved as a key/value pair.

The sequence of messages coming in is determined by the sequence number within the message. Each message belonging to a chain of messages sharing the same BatchId has a certain sequence number. After the first message, all subsequent messages are received in a running orchestration instance based on the correlation. The loop terminates as soon as all the messages are received.

In the next loop, a number of calls are made to the helper class to retrieve each message from the SortedList based upon the index. The index starts at 1 and is provided to the method call to retrieve messages from the SortedList. Next, the message is sent and the index is raised. The loop terminates as soon as all the messages are retrieved and sent.

When implementing this pattern, it is important to consider what caching option to choose. Messages come with a need to be stored temporarily, sorted, and finally sent in a sequence. Messages can be stored in memory as depicted in this recipe later on, but it is not a good option if the message size is large. A better approach in such a scenario would be using a file or database. Storing it as a file results in more I/O and a decrease in performance. A database, on the other hand, will give a better performance, but brings some more complexity with configuration of the SQL or Oracle ports.

There's more...

Resequencing, debatching, and aggregation are patterns that are described in this chapter and are also applicable with the ESB Toolkit using `ESB.Extensions`. There are other situations, where the resequencer pattern can be useful. There are some resources you can look into regarding the resequencer pattern:

  ▸ **Debatching, aggregation and resequencing using the BizTalk ESB Toolkit 2.0 and ESB.Extensions**: `http://bveldhoen.wordpress.com/2010/09/05/debatching-aggregation-and-resequencing-using-the-biztalk-esb-toolkit-2-0-and-esb-extensions/`

  ▸ **Implementing the Resequencer Pattern with BizTalk 2009 and Frends**: `http://geekswithblogs.net/michaelstephenson/archive/2009/01/01/128295.aspx`

  ▸ **In-Memory BizTalk Resequencer Pattern**: `http://seroter.wordpress.com/2008/10/09/in-memory-biztalk-resequencer-pattern/`

  ▸ **Enterprise Integration Patterns Part-3 – Resequencer**: `http://abdulrafaysbiztalk.wordpress.com/2009/10/20/enterpriseintegrationpattern_resequencer/`

See also

  ▸ Refer to the *Implementing the splitter pattern* and *Developing an asynchronous aggregation pattern* recipes earlier in this chapter

Implementing a retry pattern in an orchestration

A challenging situation with a BizTalk orchestration can be when communication with the external system fails and we have no idea what to do next. You can, for instance, in a Send port, configure a number of tries before an error message is generated by BizTalk. In case there is no properly planned action, the message and orchestration both are suspended in the BizTalk Administration Console and cannot be resumed in a fashionable manner. Once the communication is restored, resuming messages may work, but messages sent from an external system will not connect with the corresponding orchestration. Resuming the orchestration could fail if it is waiting for a specific message type. What you could do in this situation is to implement a retry pattern. This pattern basically has some logic programmed into an orchestration that will suspend it so it can be resumed properly by an administrator.

Getting ready

Open Visual Studio 2010 to develop the parallel retry pattern. For reference you can download the source code (`BTS.Cookbook.RetryPattern`) belonging to this chapter.

How to do it...

A retry pattern can be implemented by performing the following steps:

1. Create a new BizTalk project and add schemas in the project you require.

2. Create the necessary messages in the **Orchestration View** window, and specify the name and type of each.

3. Create a variable in the orchestration named `nRetryCounter` of type `int32`. The retry counter setting can be set, that is hardcoded, yet obtaining the value from the configuration files or databases, such as `BTSNTSvc.exe.config`, BRE, or SSO. However, a database is a better option than using a file (`http://geekswithblogs.net/michaelstephenson/archive/2008/05/25/122381.aspx`).

4. From the toolbox, drag the following onto the design surface in top-down order:

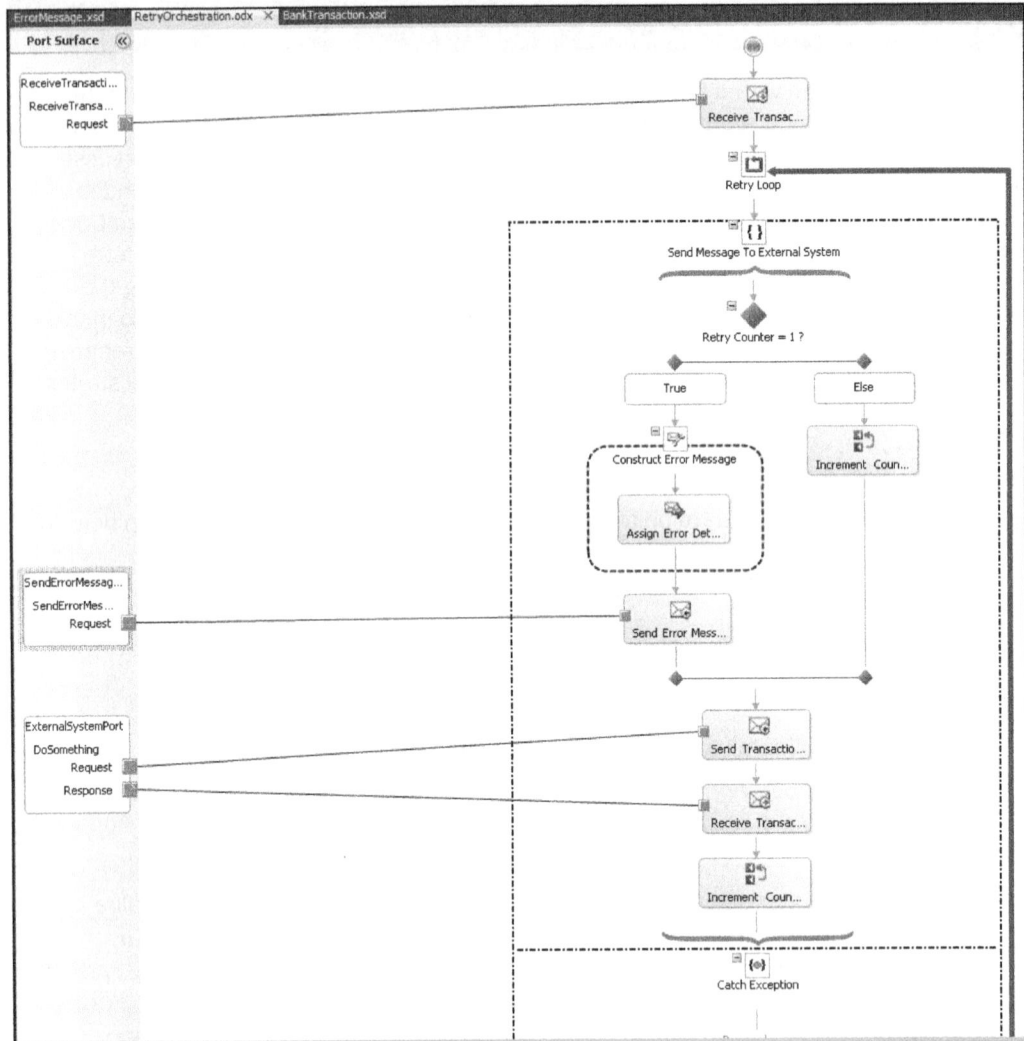

❑ Drag the **Receive** shape and give it a descriptive name. Configure this shape to use the appropriate message, to activate the orchestration, and to use an orchestration Receive port.

❑ Next, drag the **Loop** shape below the **Receive** shape and configure it using the following expression:

```
nRetryCounter < 5
```

❑ Again in this sample it is set as hardcoded, yet obtaining the value from the configuration files or databases such as `BTSNTSvc.exe.config`, BRE, or SSO. However, a database is a better option than using files.

❑ Drag the **Scope** shape in the **Loop** shape and give it a descriptive name.

❑ Right-click on the **Scope** shape and add a new exception handler. Configure the exception handler by entering a descriptive name for the exception object name and choose **Exception Object Type System.Exception**.

❑ Drag the **Decide** shape in the **Scope** shape and give it a descriptive name. In the left branch, add the following expression:

```
nRetryCounter == 5
```

❑ Again in this sample it is set as hardcoded, yet obtaining the value from the configuration files or databases such as `BTSNTSvc.exe.config`, BRE, or SSO. However, a database is a better option than using files.

❑ In the left branch add the **Construct Message** shape and give it a descriptive name. Select the message to construct (that is, Error message).

❑ Drag the **Message Assign** shape in the **Construct Message** shape and assign error information to the message as follows:

```
msgError = new System.Xml.XmlDocument();
msgError.Message = "Error occured in external system";
msgError.Code = "100";
msgError.Source = "External System";
msgError.InnerException = "";
```

❑ Drag the **Send** shape below the **Message Construct** shape and use an orchestration Send port.

❑ Below the **Send** shape add a **Suspend Orchestration** shape and place the following expression:

```
"Error occured in process";
```

❑ In the right branch, add an **Expression** shape and place the following expression:

```
nRetryCounter = nRetryCounter + 1;
```

❑ Below the **Scope** shape, drag the **Receive** and **Send** shapes to send the message to the external system or service. This depends on your situation:

❑ Below the **Send** shape, add an **Expression** shape and place the following expression:

```
nRetryCounter = nRetryCounter + 1;
```

5. Sign the BizTalk project with a strong name and build.

6. In the BizTalk Administration Console, set the retry count in the Advanced Transport Options of the Send Adapter, if applicable, to 0. Only then the fault will be thrown and the execution will come in the exception handler block. Otherwise, the port will try to resend the message three times by default after the specified interval.

How it works...

If a retry mechanism is working in the orchestration then a Scope shape is embedded within a Loop shape. The Loop shape checks the `nRetryCounter` variable that has a default value of 0. The Loop shape determines if its value is less than 5. The Decide shape checks if `nRetryCounter` is equal to 5. When the orchestration is instantiated for the first time, the check will resolve in false, `nRetryCounter` is set to 1, and call to external system is made (or any other calls to any system, service, and so on). If a response message is returned that is, not erroneous, then `nRetryCount` is raised to two and another retry will occur until `nRetryCount` reaches five, then it will exit the loop. However, if an error occurs, that is no message is returned or a fault message and exception is thrown, then the exception handler will kick in.

The scope has an exception handler that catches all errors from the two-way Send port calling the external system as it is using System.Exception and does not include any logic. After the exception handler executes, the Loop shape continues with the process. During the next evaluation of `nRetryCounter` at the Decide shape, its value is still five and the `true` branch is executed. Therefore, the orchestration is suspended and an error message is created and sent.

If an error occurs, then the message will be suspended. With "Failed Message Routing" on Send ports, you can route them to another Send port with a Filter if `ErrorType.ErrorMessage` shows `FailedMessage` and handle the error as needed.

There are some points to consider while implementing this pattern. While sending the messages if the message fails to get transported, then the message to be sent will go into a Suspended (Resumable) state. If the administrator resumes both the orchestration service instance and the send service instance (that is, the original suspended message), you will send the same message twice. To work around this problem, you can use delivery notifications and a Nack Handler to automatically clean-up the send service instances.

There's more...

The retry pattern is one of the patterns you can implement in an orchestration to support process automation. You can leverage this pattern or combine multiple patterns (some provided with this book) to design your business process. You will find more design patterns like aggregation, scatter-gather, and content-based routing on MSDN in the document **Implementing Design Patterns in Orchestrations** at http://msdn.microsoft.com/en-us/library/aa561967%28v=bts.70%29.aspx.

▸ Refer to the *Calling a pipeline in an orchestration* recipe later in this chapter

Calling a pipeline in an orchestration

BizTalk 2006 introduced the feature of calling a pipeline from within an orchestration. As a developer, you are now able to use pipeline-processing stages within an orchestration, such as validating a document. Calling a pipeline can make your orchestration more efficient by minimizing the interactions between the orchestration and the `MessageBox` database. Through programmatic interface inside pipelines, you can call, receive, and send pipelines directly from an orchestration.

Getting ready

Open Visual Studio 2010 and create a solution. For reference, you can download the source code belonging to this chapter.

How to do it...

As an example, a message is de-batched through calling a pipeline in an orchestration. To call a pipeline in an orchestration, you can perform the following steps:

1. Create a new BizTalk project and add schemas in the project you require. Schemas in these steps are available in the code sample for this recipe. There is one `envelope` schema and one `single record` schema.

2. In project references, add a reference to `Microsoft.XLANGs.Pipeline` assembly found in `C:\Program Files\BizTalk Server 2010`.

3. Create a new pipeline through **Add New Item**, select the **Receive** pipeline and give it a descriptive name.

4. Next, add a new orchestration to the project, and give it a descriptive name. Configure the orchestration by setting the transaction type to **Atomic**.

5. Create two new messages in the **Orchestration View** window, and specify the name and type of each. In this case, one for the full message of type `System.Xml.XmlDocument` and one for the single message of type `singleOrderLine`.

6. Drag an **XML disassembler** pipeline component from the toolbox into the **Disassemble** stage.

7. In the **Orchestration View** window, create a new variable with type `Microsoft.XLANGs.Pipeline.ReceivePipelineOutputMessages`.

8. From the toolbox, drag the following onto the design surface in top-down order, as shown in the following screenshot:

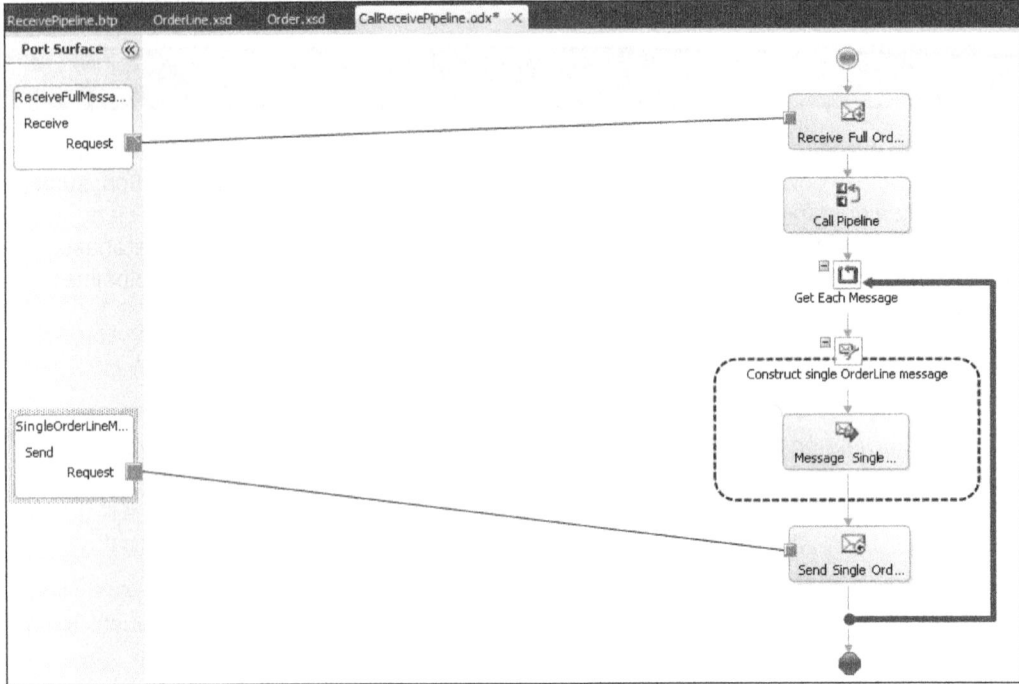

- Drag the **Receive** shape and configure this shape to use the appropriate message, to activate the orchestration, and to use an orchestration Receive port.

- Drag the **Expression** shape and give it a descriptive name. Within the **Expression** shape, place the following code:

```
receivePipeline = Microsoft.XLANGs.Pipeline.
XLANGPipelineManager
```

- Execute `ReceivePipeline` (type of (`BTS.Cookbook.CallPipeline. Orchestration.pipelinename`), `fullOrderMessage`).

- Drag the **Loop** shape and give it a descriptive name. Configure the **Loop** shape within the **Expression** shape by adding the following expression:

```
receivePipeline.MoveNext()
```

- Drag the **Construct** shape and select the message to be constructed.

❑ Drag the **Message Assign** shape and place the following statements:

```
singleOrderLineMessage = new System.Xml.XmlDocument();
receivePipeline.GetCurrent(singleOrderLineMessage);
```

❑ Drag the **Send** shape and give it a descriptive name and use an orchestration Send port.

9. Sign the project with a strong name.

10. Subsequently, go to the deployment and give it an appropriate application name.

11. Build and deploy the solution.

12. Bind the orchestration to the Receive and Send ports, configure the host for the orchestration, and start the orchestration.

How it works...

The message is received by BizTalk and routed to the subscribing orchestration. Within the orchestration, the pipeline is executed with the Expression shape. To be able to call pipelines, a reference must be set to the `Microsoft.XLANGs.Pipeline` assembly. This assembly contains the `Microsoft.XLANGs.Pipeline.XLANGPipelineManager` class that has two methods that can be called:

▶ `ExecuteReceivePipeline(System.Type, Microsoft.XLANGs.BaseTypes.XLANGMessage)`

▶ `ExecuteSendPipeline(System.Type, Microsoft.XLANGs.Pipeline.SendPipelineInputMessages, Microsoft.XLANGs.BaseTypes.XLANGMessage)`

> The BizTalk Server .NET Class reference provides information on `Microsoft.XLANGs.Pipeline` assembly: `http://technet.microsoft.com/en-us/library/microsoft.xlangs.pipeline%28BTS.70%29.aspx`.

Depending on what kind of pipeline you have created, you have to call one of these methods. When calling `ExecuteReceivePipeline`, you will need a variable with the type `Microsoft.XLANGs.Pipeline.ReceivePipelineOutputMessages` to reference the object.

For `ExecuteSendPipeline`, you need a variable with the type `Microsoft.XLANGs.Pipeline.SendPipelineInputMessages`. `ReceivePipelineOutputMessages` class has a method `MoveNext()` implemented, so you are able to iterate from message to message. In the provided sample, you could process each message returned by the pipeline based on this method.

Calling a pipeline in an orchestration has some limitations, for instance, providing per instance configuration is not possible (on the receive pipeline), it must run in an atomic scope and does not support recoverable interchanges. Yet the benefit of using this pattern is that calling a pipeline can make your orchestration more efficient by minimizing the interactions between the orchestration and the `MessageBox` database. It supports receiving multiple messages returned from the pipeline and can use enumeration to process each message.

There's more...

Stephen W. Thomas wrote about calling a pipeline in an orchestration, when the feature was introduced back in 2005 for the upcoming BizTalk 2006 version. The recipe described is derived from his samples:

 ▶ **How To Call A Receive Pipeline In an Orchestration**: `http://www.biztalkgurus.com/biztalk_server/biztalk_blogs/b/biztalk/archive/2005/06/16/how-to-call-a-receive-pipeline-in-an-orchestration.aspx`

 ▶ **Calling Send and Receive Pipelines from the orchestration expression shapes**: `http://www.codeproject.com/Articles/36884/Calling-Send-and-Receive-Pipelines-from-the-orches`

MSDN provides information on calling pipelines in an orchestration. It states that:

"BizTalk Server has the ability to synchronously call a pipeline from within an orchestration. This enables orchestrations to leverage the message processing encapsulated within a pipeline (either send or receive) against a body of data without having to send that data through the messaging infrastructure."

`http://msdn.microsoft.com/en-us/library/aa562035%28v=bts.70%29.aspx`

See also

 ▶ Refer to the *Implementing the splitter pattern* recipe explained earlier in this chapter

3
BizTalk Server Instrumentation, Error Handling, and Deployment

In this chapter, we will cover:

- ▶ Tracing BizTalk applications using DebugView
- ▶ Monitoring BizTalk solution behavior with Log4Net
- ▶ Applying event logging in BizTalk solutions
- ▶ Enabling Failed Message Routing in BizTalk
- ▶ Implementing error handling in an Orchestration
- ▶ Exploring BizTalk's out of the box deployment
- ▶ Using the Deployment Framework for BizTalk

Introduction

This chapter will contain recipes on how to instrument your BizTalk solution for monitoring and tracing purposes, how to implement error handling, and deploying your BizTalk solutions. These recipes are around important BizTalk application aspects—monitoring behavior of BizTalk applications, how to control errors, and how to deploy them. Using instrumentation in your BizTalk solution you have the ability to monitor behavior or to diagnose errors and to write trace information. In general, when an error occurs for instance, in an orchestration, a pipeline, or map, it will be logged in the event log, which can be viewed with the event viewer. Information provided can be enough for you to diagnose or understand the error as most of the time the stack trace is provided, too. But it may not be enough to find the root cause of the error. Instrumentation can aid in tracking an error and diagnosis, enabling you to find the root cause more efficiently. As a BizTalk developer, you can code instructions that write information to an event log, a log file, or a database. There are also tools available such as DebugView, which enables you to view, at runtime, what is happening inside your BizTalk application.

Diagnosis can be one purpose of using instrumentation; another can be that you want to log or trace what is happening in a BizTalk application. You can simply use `System.Diagnostics.Trace` or `System.Diagnostics.Eventlog` namespaces to write either an event log of DebugView. During development you can use this option; but if you need more flexibility, Log4net is a better option. With Log4net you are able to write information to other sources such as a file, databases (for example, Oracle, MS Access, SQL Server, and so on), and send e-mails. Log4net can impact performance, which is not desirable in production environments. An alternative to Log4net is to use the BizTalk CAT Instrumentation Framework that leverages the **Event Logging for Windows** (**ETW**) infrastructure. This infrastructure provides the ability to start and stop event tracing sessions, monitor their status, configure a variety of logging settings such as buffer size, flush interval, stop conditions, and more.

Another aspect of BizTalk applications is error handling. Exceptions can easily happen at the backend server you integrate with or within services you consume in your BizTalk application. You can implement error handling in BizTalk on messaging level and in orchestration. On the messaging level, you can use failed message routing and handle the failed message through a custom process or notification mechanism that you have in place. Within orchestrations, you can use the scope shape that enables you to add exception handlers. Through failed message routing and usage of scopes in orchestration you can make your BizTalk application more robust.

Besides error handling and instrumentation, you as a developer will also be involved in deployment of your BizTalk application. There are a number of options when it comes to deployment of BizTalk applications. BizTalk's out of the box deployment offers functionality to build and deploy your application from Visual Studio to the BizTalk Runtime. From the BizTalk Administration Console, you are able to export the application as an MSI (Windows Installer Component) file. You can use the MSI file to deploy your application in another environment. The MSI file can also be created by using the command line tool, `BTSTask.exe`. Besides creating an MSI file, this tool can also aid in automating the build and deployment through scripting. Another option for deployment is to use the Deployment Framework for BizTalk offered through CodePlex. This framework extends the ability and flexibility for deploying BizTalk applications.

Tracing BizTalk applications using DebugView

With Log4Net and ETW, you are able to do event logging and see what happens in your BizTalk solution. Another option is to use DebugView to trace what is happening. **DebugView** is an application that lets you monitor the debug output on your local system, or any computer on the network that you can reach via TCP/IP. Its current version, at the time of writing this book, is 4.76, which supports 32 and 64 bits. The tool displays both kernel-mode and Win32 debug output, so you don't need a debugger to catch the debug output of your BizTalk applications, for example, when instrumenting it with Log4Net.

Getting ready

Download DebugView from Windows Sysinternals site (`http://technet.microsoft.com/en-us/sysinternals/bb896647`) and then unpack the ZIP file on your machine. For reference, you can download the source code (`BTS.Cookbook.DebugView`) belonging to this chapter.

How to do it...

Within your orchestration, expression shapes can be added that contain `System.Diagniostics.Trace.Write` or `System.Diagnostics.Debug.Write` statements. You can download the DebugView example belonging to this book. The following screenshot is of the splitter pattern solution that debatches messages in an orchestration (see the *Implementing the Splitter Pattern* recipe in *Chapter 2, BizTalk Server Automation: Patterns*):

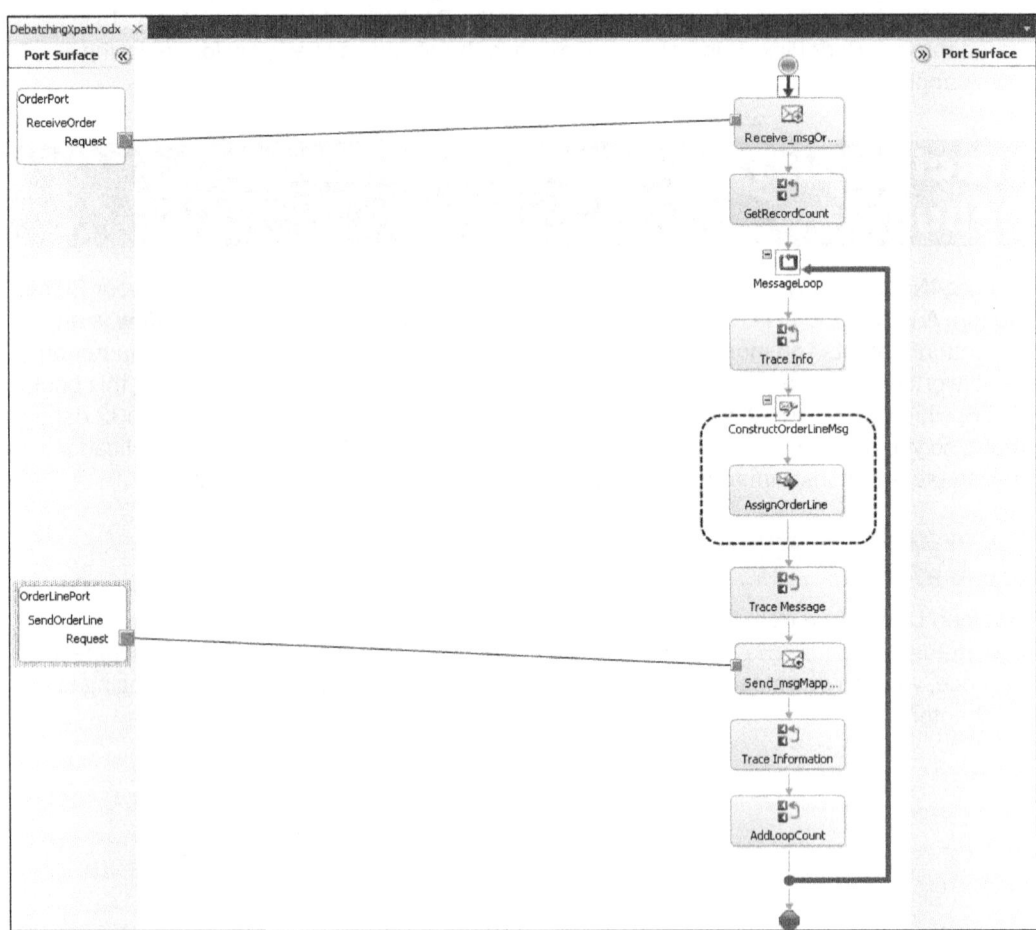

There are a couple of expression shapes in the orchestration that contain statements for the trace output.

The first expression statement has the following trace statement:

```
//Tracing DebugView
System.Diagnostics.Trace.Write(System.String.Format("Number of records
is : {0}", dRecordCount.ToString()));
```

The second expression statement, Trace Info, has the following statement:

```
//Tracing DebugView
System.Diagnostics.Trace.Write(System.String.Format("Record number :
{0}", dLoopCount.ToString()));
```

The Trace Message expression shape has the following statement:

```
//Assign message to xmldoc variable
xmlDoc = msgOrderLine;
//Tracing DebugView
System.Diagnostics.Trace.Write(xmlDoc.InnerXml);
```

The final expression shape named Trace Info, again, has the following statement:

```
//Trace DebugView
System.Diagnostics.Trace.Write("OrderLine Message Sent");
```

All these statements show that you can place certain information in the `Write` method. You can start DebugView from the location where you unpack the ZIP file:

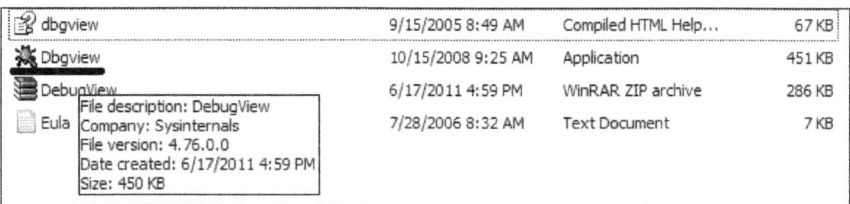

In DebugView, you have to enable **Capture Global Win32** under the **Capture** menu item. You can now drop a message for the BizTalk debatch solution. As soon as BizTalk picks up the message, you will see the trace output in the DebugView window:

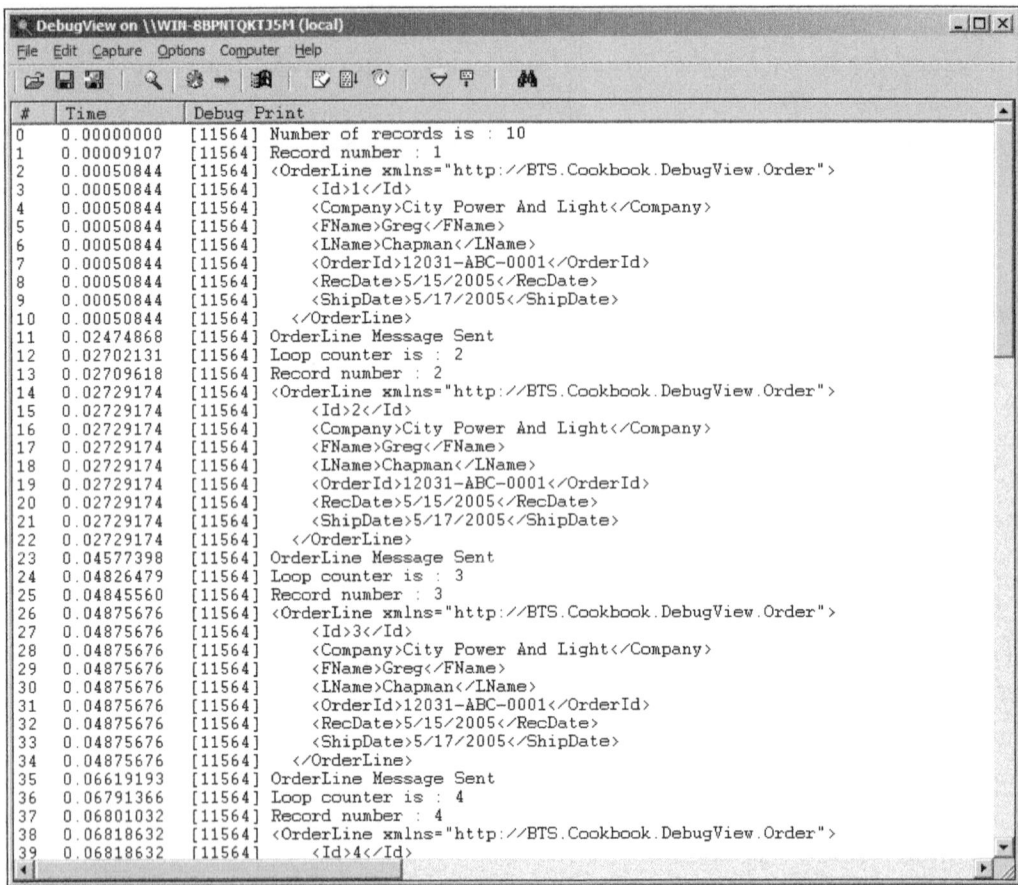

How it works...

When you execute the DebugView program file (`dbgview.exe`) it will immediately start capturing the debug output. The `Write` method of `System.Diagnostics.Trace` will write the value to the trace listeners. So tracing events are written to what is called the `OutputDebugString` via the `DefaultTraceListener` trace listener. What this listener does is that it writes the output to `OutputDebugString` (which DebugView can monitor), and a managed debugger (if one is attached).

There's more...

With DebugView, you have an option to trace what is happening in your orchestration as shown with the example. Possible drawback is that you will have to remove the expression shapes when bringing your solution to production, or that you have not incorporated the ability to turn tracing off. However, you can turn it off using debug statements only as these are not compiled into a release build. Richard Seroter has two blog posts on conditional tracing, where you as a developer can configure the trace to be on or off. Besides that, there is more information on how to extend tracing within the BizTalk solution. You can find these blog posts at the following URLs:

- ▸ http://seroter.wordpress.com/2007/01/22/biztalk-application-tracing-part-i/

- ▸ http://seroter.wordpress.com/2007/01/22/biztalk-application-tracing-part-ii/

The following post explains why having tracing in a production environment is not an option as it impacts performance:

- ▸ http://blogs.msdn.com/b/darrenj/archive/2007/04/03/watch-out-debugview-outputdebugstring-performance.aspx

See also

Refer to the following recipes on logging and tracing in this chapter:

- ▸ *Applying event logging in BizTalk solutions*
- ▸ *Monitoring BizTalk solution behavior with Log4Net*

Monitoring BizTalk solution behavior with Log4Net

Log4Net is a port of the log4j framework to the .NET runtime and part of the Apache Logging Services project. This project is intended to provide cross-language logging services for the purposes of application debugging and auditing. It is a tool that helps the programmer to output log statements to a variety of output targets. It can enable to track orchestration events, without using the orchestration debugger and can be viewed as a substitute for it. Orchestration debugger has its limitations as it is used in conjunction with breakpoint and only gives visibility in intermediate values of variables and messages.

Getting ready

You can use the Log4Net code accompanied with this book, that has been ported to the .NET 4 Framework. Log4Net source code that is available at `http://logging.apache.org/log4net/download.html` is still at version .NET 2.0. To be able to use Log4Net inside BizTalk, Scott Colestock created a project called **log4net.Ext.Serializable_For1.2.10**. This has also been ported to .NET 4.0 and compiled at the ported Log4Net. The .NET 4.0 version of log4net.Ext.Serializable_For1.2.10 is also accompanied with this book.

Open Visual Studio and open the sample from the `<installation path>:\Program Files (x86)\Microsoft BizTalk Server 2010\SDK\Samples\Orchestrations\CallOrchestration` solution. For reference you can download the source code (`BTS.Cookbook.Log4Net`) belonging to this chapter.

How to do it...

There are some steps involved to be able to use Log4Net to monitor in this solution:

1. First you need to reference your BizTalk project to both `log4net` and `log4net.Ext.Serializable`.

2. Create a variable called `logger` in the orchestration viewer of the type, `log4net.Ext.Serializable.SlogManager`.

3. After the **Receive** shape in your orchestration (the soonest possible option) you place an Expression shape that contains statements to initialize Log4Net:

   ```
   logger = log4net.Ext.Serializable.SLogManager.GetLogger(@"BTS.
   Cookbook.Log4Net",log4net.helpers.CallersTypeName.Name);
   logger.RegistryConfigurator();
   logger.Debug("New PO request arrived...");
   ```

4. Subsequently, another **Expression** shape is added with the following statements:

   ```
   logger.Debug("Call Orchestration find shipping price");
   logger.Debug(System.String.Format("PO Number is {0}",
   IncomingPOMessage(BTS.Cookbook.Log4Net.PO_Num)));
   logger.Debug(System.String.Format("Weight is {0}",
   IncomingPOMessage(BTS.Cookbook.Log4Net.Weight)));
   logger.Debug(System.String.Format("Shipment Price is {0}",
   IncomingPOMessage(BTS.Cookbook.Log4Net.shipmentPrice)));
   ```

5. In the Find orchestration that is called from the ReceivePO orchestration two expression shapes are added to each branch with the following statements:

```
logger.Debug(System.String.Format("Less Than Min, Shipment Price
is {0}", POMessageParameter(BTS.Cookbook.Log4Net.shipmentPrice)));
```

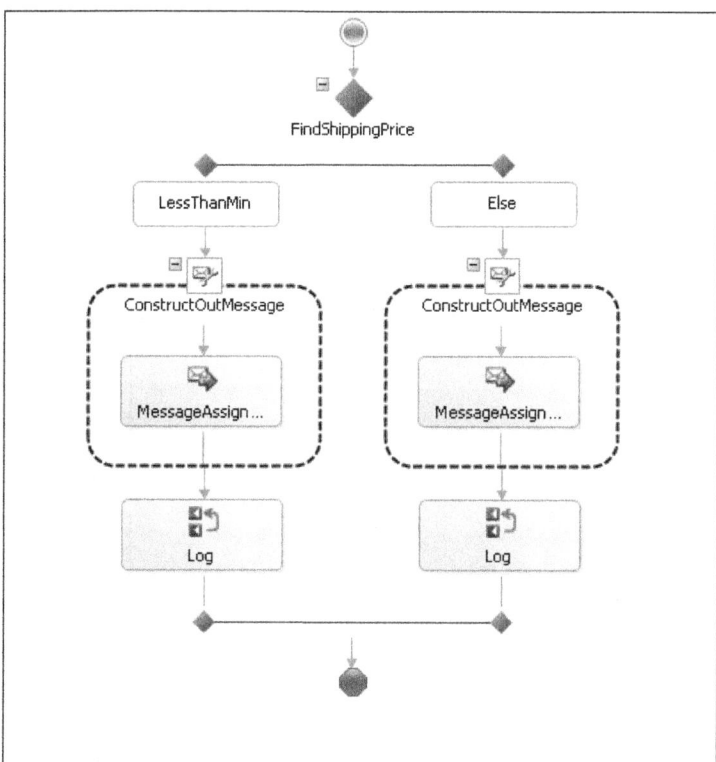

6. After the **CallOrchestration** shape another **Expression** shape is placed with the statement:

```
logger.Debug("Send PO");
```

The ReceivePO orchestration is shown in the following screenshot:

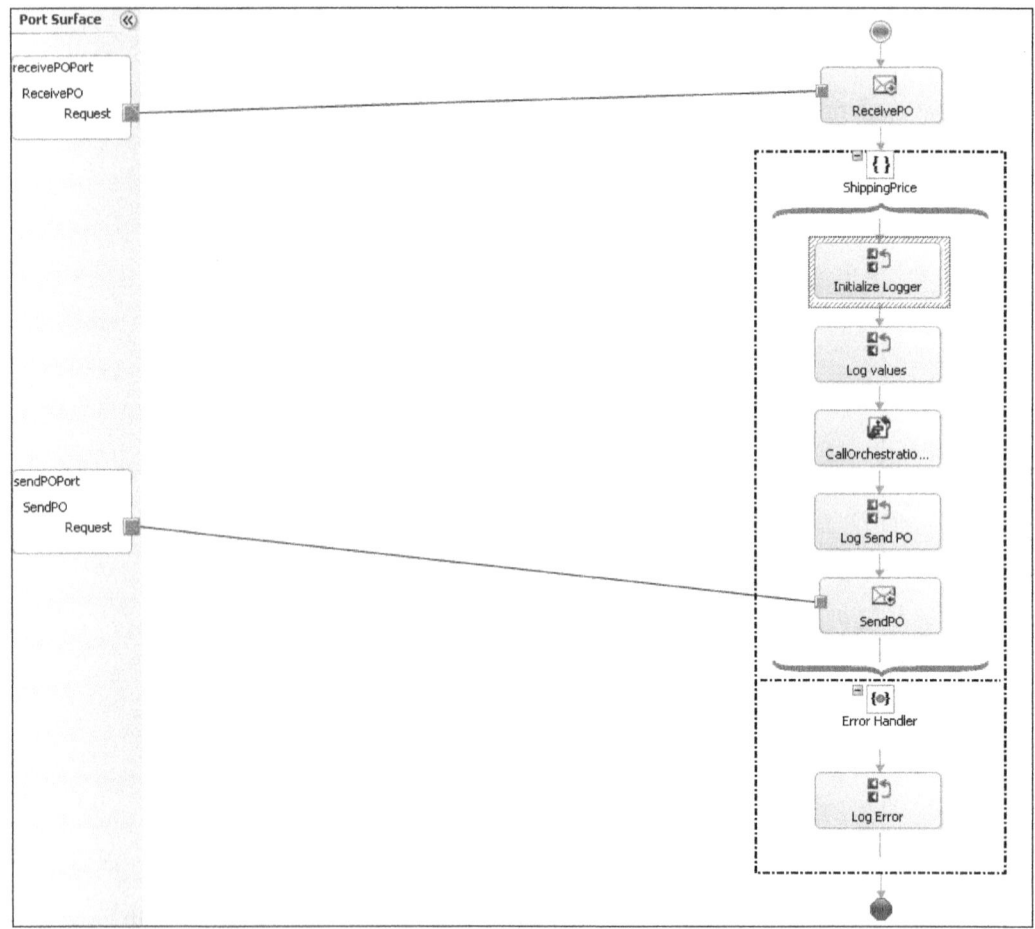

Generally, for any orchestration the first step is mandatory and others are optional and depend on how you want to monitor/debug your solution. Next step is to configure how you want to log the information choosing an appender.

7. Create a Log4Net file by opening a notepad and pasting the following, which is an example of file appender:

```xml
<?xml version="1.0" encoding="utf-8" ?>
<log4net>
<appender name="FileAppender" type="log4net.Appender.FileAppender,
log4net,Version=1.2.10.0,Culture=Neutral,PublicKeyToken=ef9ea2b5a7
ffdc67">
    <file value="C:\\BizTalk Server 2010 Cookbook\\Chapter 3\\BTS.
Cookbook.Log4Net\\BTS.Cookbook.Log4Net\\Log\\BTSCookbook.txt" />
    <appendToFile value="true" />
    <lockingModel type="log4net.Appender.FileAppender+MinimalLock"
/>
    <layout type="log4net.Layout.PatternLayout">
        <conversionPattern value="%date [%thread] %-5level %logger
[%property{NDC}] - %message%newline" />
    </layout>
</appender>
        <root>
            <level value="ALL"/>
            <appender-ref ref="FileAppender"/>
        </root>
</log4net>
```

8. Save the file solution name as `BTS.Cookbook.Log4Net.log4net`.

9. Open the registry and create a key at location `HKLM\SOFTWARE\` for 32 bit machines and `HKLM\SOFTWARE\Wow6432Node` called `BTS.Cookbook.Log4Net`.

10. In the key, create a string value named `log4netConfig` with the location of the `.log4net` file. For instance, (based on sample) `C:\BizTalk Server 2010 Cookbook\Chapter 3\BTS.Cookbook.Log4Net\BTS.Cookbook.Log4Net.log4net`.

How it works...

Using Log4Net instrumenting orchestrations, as in the given sample, you can log it to file (text), event log, database, and so on based on the chosen appender. In sample events it will be logged to a text file, which takes place as soon as the logger is initialized. Log4Net consists of three main components, logger, appenders, and layouts. These components work together to help you to log messages (logger) according to the message type and level, and to control at runtime how these messages are formatted (layout) and where they are reported (appenders). The logger (emit trace output) in BizTalk is instantiated and associated with the Log4Net file that has information on where to report events and in what format. With `GetLogger` and `RegistryConfigurator` the name and location of the Log4Net file are determined. Logger now knows where, and in which format, it can write event's that occur. For each event that you want to log, the logger can be used. In our preceding example, a file appender is used and when this log is opened you can see the logged events:

There's more...

Scott Colestock was one of the first BizTalk pros that documented the use of Log4Net. This document named **Diagnostic Tracing with BizTalk 2004** can be found at the following URL:

`http://www.traceofthought.net/PermaLink,guid,62b858b4-d8ba-4fc4-92aa-35a4ff1ba00a.aspx`

More examples of appenders can be found at the Log4Net website at:

`http://logging.apache.org/log4net/release/config-examples.html`

See also

▸ The *Tracing BizTalk applications using DebugView* and *Monitoring BizTalk solution behavior with Log4Net* recipes.

Applying event logging in BizTalk solutions

Logging and tracing in BizTalk can be achieved by using Log4Net or DebugView in combination with `System.Diagnostics.Trace` or `System.Diagnostics.Debug`. Previous recipes have shown these options. Both can be used, but do not deliver the desired level of agility and performance according to research conducted by the Application Server Group ISV Partner Advisory Team (`http://blogs.msdn.com/b/asgisv/archive/2010/05/11/best-practices-for-instrumenting-high-performance-biztalk-solutions.aspx`). Their findings were as follows:

- ▶ High CPU utilization while using DebugView when monitoring BizTalk applications

- ▶ High impact on application performance when running DebugView during stress testing

- ▶ Burden on the administrator to restart BizTalk host instance when any changes in the tracing configuration such as enabling, disabling or changing the trace level were required

Log4Net and DebugView are not good options to use in production environment when performance is the key factor. Both are more valuable on a developer machine. A better option, the team thought, was to leverage the Event Logging for Windows (ETW) infrastructure that enables you to take advantage of the general purpose, high-speed tracing facility provided by the OS kernel. To use ETW, you do have to use a framework and it is more complex compared to DebugView and Log4Net.

The Microsoft's BizTalk **Customer Advisory Team** (**CAT**) built a framework on top of the ETW infrastructure. They also built the BizTalk CAT Instrumentation Framework Controller, which is an easy-to-use GUI for the BizTalk CAT Instrumentation Framework. This controller enables you to start and stop a trace and adjust filter options, and can easily enable real-time tracing for Microsoft SysInternals DebugView (or other debuggers), to a log file or to both at the same time.

Getting ready

Download the BizTalk Solution Instrumentation Framework v1.4 found on MSDN (`http://archive.msdn.microsoft.com/appfabriccat/Release/ProjectReleases.aspx?ReleaseId=4355`) and the BizTalk CAT Instrumentation Framework Controller on codeplex (http://btscatifcontroller.codeplex.com/).

For reference, you can download the source code for CAT (`BTS.Cookbook.CAT`) belonging to this chapter.

How to do it...

There are some steps involved to be able to use the Controller to be able to monitor, for instance, an orchestration. First you need to port the Framework to .NET 4 by performing the following steps:

1. Unpack the BizTalk Solution Instrumentation Framework V1.4 to a folder.

2. Open the solution with Visual Studio 2010 and convert.

3. Right-click on the **Microsoft.BizTalk.CAT.BestPractices.Framework** project and select **Properties**.

4. Click on the **Build** tab and change the **Target framework** to **.NET Framework 4**.

5. Sign the project with a strong name.

6. Build the project.

7. Use the `gacutil` command to place the assembly in the GAC:

```
Administrator: Visual Studio Command Prompt (2010)
AT.BestPractices.Samples.Framework\bin\Release>gacutil /i Microsoft.BizTalk.CAT.
BestPractices.Framework.dll
Microsoft (R) .NET Global Assembly Cache Utility.  Version 4.0.30319.1
Copyright (c) Microsoft Corporation.  All rights reserved.

Assembly successfully added to the cache

C:\Resources\BizTalk Solution Instrumentation Framework V1.4\Microsoft.BizTalk.C
AT.BestPractices.Samples.Framework\bin\Release>_
```

The `Microsoft.BizTalk.CAT.BestPractices.Framework.dll` assembly is necessary for your BizTalk project as a reference. As an example, we will use the splitter pattern solution that debatches messages in an orchestration (see the Implementing the Splitter Pattern recipe). For enabling tracing in any orchestration by using `Microsoft.BizTalk.CAT.BestPractices.Framework`, you will have to follow these steps:

1. Create a variable in the Orchestration View window and give it a descriptive name and select the **Type** as **System.Guid**.

2. Within orchestration, drag an **Expression** shape at the start of the orchestration after the Receive shape and add the following statement:

```
<your variable name> = Microsoft.BizTalk.CAT.BestPractices.
Framework.Instrumentation.TraceManager.WorkflowComponent.
TraceIn();
```

3. Add a few more Expression shapes to monitor your orchestration. With examples belonging to this book, you see that before and after the Expression shape (Record Count), and in the Message Loop, Expression shapes are placed with statements like:

```
Microsoft.BizTalk.CAT.BestPractices.Framework.Instrumentation.
TraceManager.WorkflowComponent.TraceInfo(System.String.
Format("Record count is : {0}",dRecordCount.ToString()));
```

4. At end of the orchestration an **Expression** Shape is placed with the following statement:

```
Microsoft.BizTalk.CAT.BestPractices.Framework.Instrumentation.
TraceManager.WorkflowComponent.TraceOut(<your variable name>);
```

5. After you have placed the **Expression** shapes within your orchestration you can build and deploy your solution.

The Controller can be installed by executing the MSI and following the steps in the wizard. You can start the Controller from the Windows menu and you will be presented with a UI, as shown in the following screenshot:

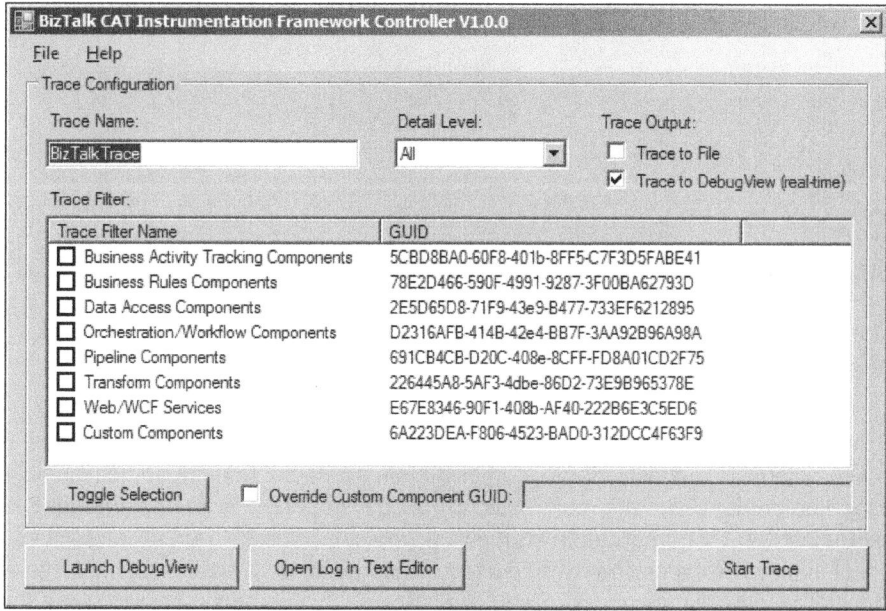

You need to perform the following steps to view the trace output in DebugView:

1. Check **Orchestration/Workflow** as the **Trace Filter** option.

2. In the **File** option, select the location of your DebugView tool or the location of where the text file needs to be placed.

3. Click on **Start Trace**.

4. Click on **Launch DebugView**.

5. Drop the file to initiate the orchestration.

In the **DebugView** window, you will see the output of the trace, as shown in the following screenshot:

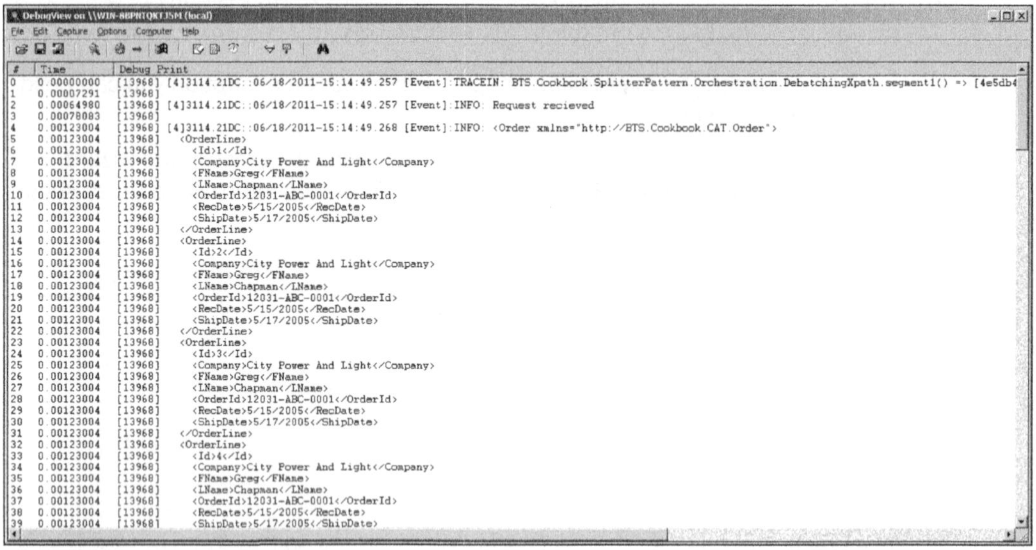

How it works...

As with other options such as Log4Net and DebugView/`System.Diagnostics.Trace` (Debug), instrumenting orchestration is the key to help you in diagnosing and troubleshooting behavioral problems in orchestrations or other BizTalk artefacts. Usually, some issues are not foreseen beforehand and are manifested during development. With implementing tracing using the BizTalk CAT Instrumentation Framework, you can leverage tracing capabilities with a high level of agility. The framework can be used within maps, business rules, business activity, and so on. With orchestration example, you see that an entry point is recorded using TraceIn immediately at the first available opportunity; for example, after the first Receive shape. Then the internal state of orchestrations is traced; for example, messages, result of the XPath queries, and so on. Finally, the exit point from an orchestration is recorded using TraceOut at the very last step in the orchestration.

There's more...

The article by the advisory team at `http://blogs.msdn.com/b/asgisv/archive/2010/05/11/best-practices-for-instrumenting-high-performance-biztalk-solutions.aspx` lists more possibilities to leverage the BizTalk CAT Instrumentation Framework by tracing events in the following:

▶ Custom Pipeline Components

▶ BizTalk Maps

- ▸ Business Rules
- ▸ Custom Components

More background information on ETW can be found in MSDN magazine for April 2007 at `http://msdn.microsoft.com/en-us/magazine/cc163437.aspx` and introduction of the ETW article at `http://blogs.msdn.com/b/matt_pietrek/archive/2004/09/16/230700.aspx`.

Finally, in the BizTalk Hotrod issue 2010, Q2 you can find an article by Valery Minonov called **Instrumentation Best Practices for High Performance BizTalk Solutions** at `http://biztalkhotrod.com/Documents/Issue10_Q2_2010.pdf`.

See also

- ▸ The *Tracing BizTalk applicationss using DebugView* and *Monitoring BizTalk solution behavior with Log4Net* recipes for more details on other options for monitoring behavior in BizTalk solutions.

Enabling Failed Message Routing in BizTalk

The BizTalk product team introduced the Failed Message Routing feature in version 2006. Before that there was not an out of the box ability to resume messages that could not be routed or failing for another reason. Failed messages were placed into the Message Box and suspended, and no BizTalk application could subscribe to these messages for either troubleshooting or repair actions. For BizTalk 2006 and subsequent versions, failed message routing allows you to enable routing for failed messages. It means a developer can create an orchestration process or message Send ports that subscribe to any exceptions that occur at messaging level. These exceptions at this level can occur in adapter processing, pipeline processing, mapping, or message routing and will result in an error message if routing for failed messages is enabled. Through simple configuration you can act on failures happening on BizTalk boundaries.

Getting ready

There is an example of Failed Message Routing found in the BizTalk SDK at `<InstallationDrive>: \Program Files\Microsoft BizTalk Server 2010\SDK\Samples\Messaging\ErrorHandling\ErrorHandler`.

How to do it...

To enable Failed Message Routing and to have an orchestration process to handle them or having a send port route them to, for instance a folder, you can follow these steps:

1. First step in having Failed Message Routing enabled in your BizTalk application(s) is to check the **Enable routing for failed messages** checkbox on the Receive port on which you wish to have this ability:

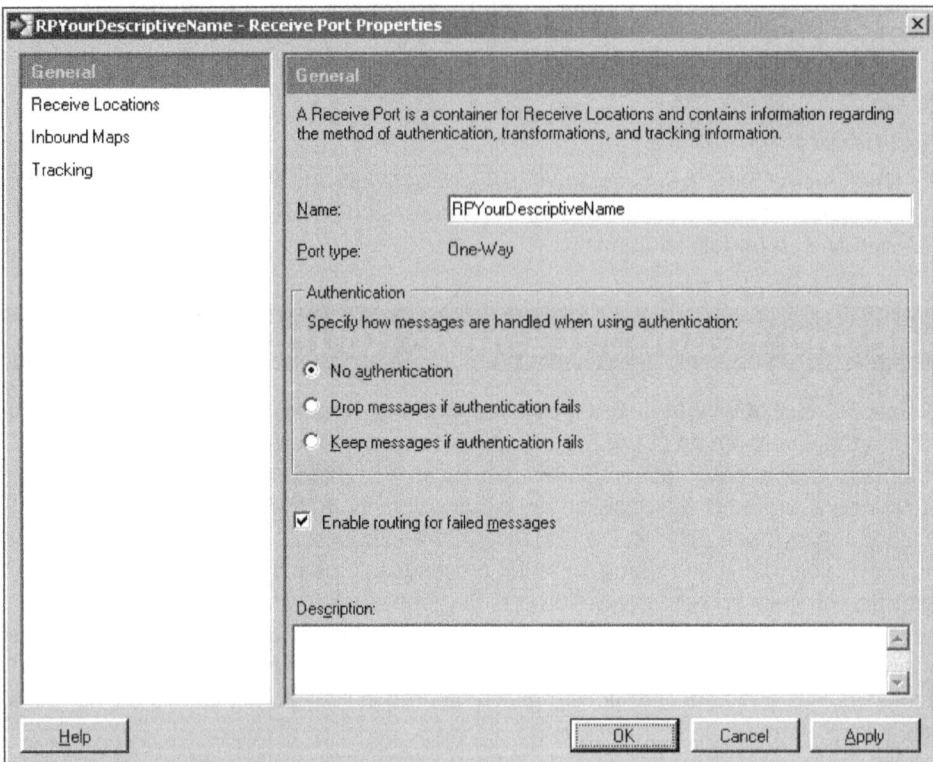

2. Subsequent step is to enable Failed Message Routing on the Send port, if applicable for your solution:

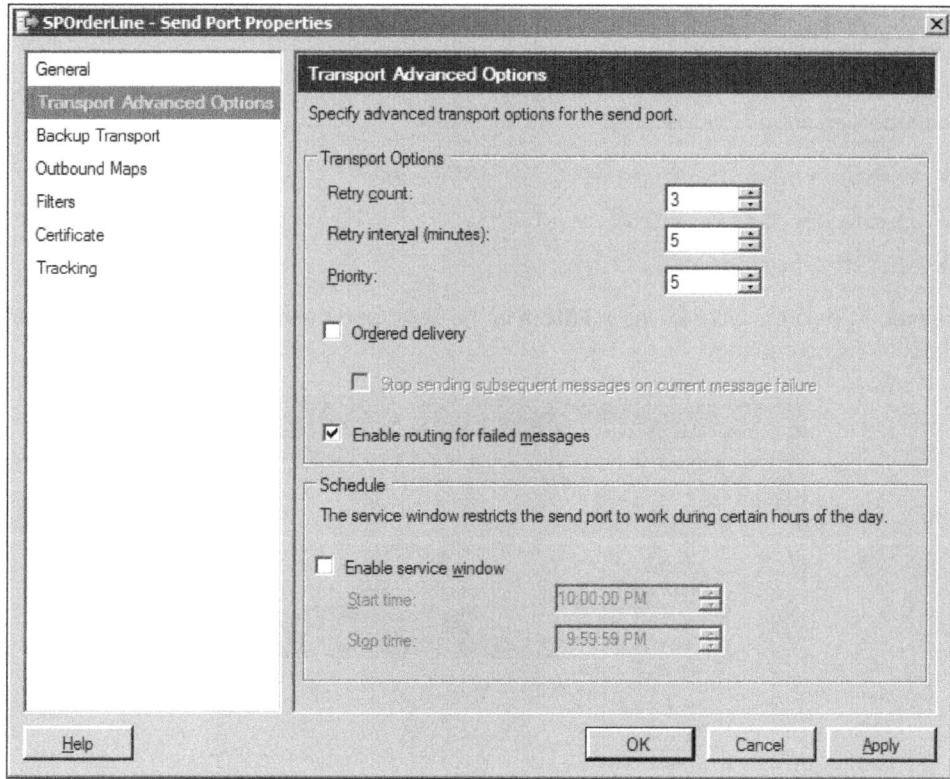

3. Create a Send port that subscribes to the failed message. Give it a descriptive name and set, for instance, the following filter expression:

```
ErrorReport.MessageType = YourMessageType
```

4. If you want an orchestration to pick up failed messages and process them, you can do the following:

   ❑ Create a message in the **Orchestration View** window, and specify the name and type as **System.Xml.XmlDocument**.

   ❑ Drag a **Receive** shape and give it a descriptive name. Configure this shape to activate the orchestration, give an appropriate message with a filter expression such as `ErrorReport.MessageType == YourMessageType`, and to use an orchestration Receive port.

5. Drag subsequent shapes to process the message. This depends on how you want to process the message. For instance, send a message to an administrator or log to a custom database.

How it works...

When you enable routing for failed messages, a set of properties will be promoted. Some of these properties are as follows:

- ▸ `ErrorReport.FailureCode`
- ▸ `ErrorReport.FailureCategory`
- ▸ `ErrorReport.MessageType`

These properties are available under **Filters** in the Send ports and orchestrations, as shown in the following screenshot:

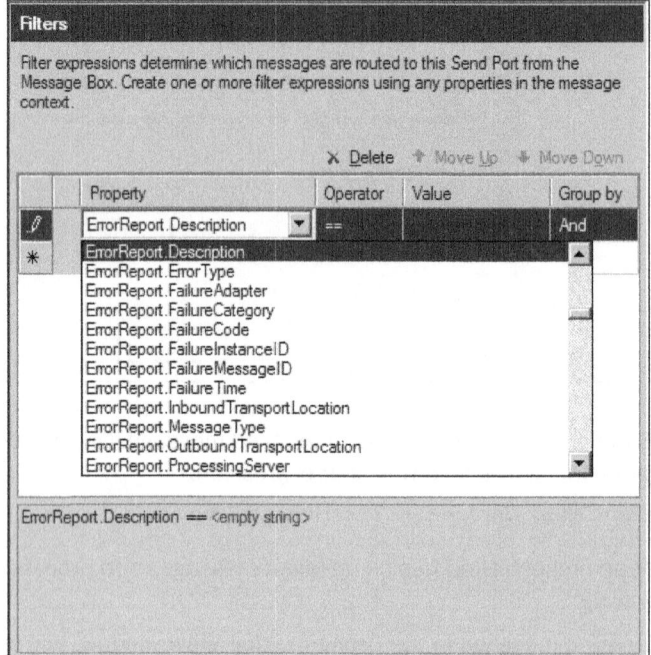

With filters, you basically create a subscription on a certain error message. You can, as a developer, define an error-handling mechanism specifically for a single integration point, an application, or an entire BizTalk environment. The mechanism can be a simple notification by an e-mail, or an orchestration as in the sample belonging to this recipe.

There's more...

When dealing with failed messages there are some considerations on retrying them. These considerations are discussed in the **Considerations When Retrying Failed Messages in BizTalk or the ESB Toolkit** document found at the following URL:

```
http://seroter.wordpress.com/2010/01/18/considerations-when-retrying-
failed-messages-in-biztalk-or-the-esb-toolkit/
```

See also the **Using Failed Message Routing** document at the following URL:

```
http://msdn.microsoft.com/en-us/library/aa578516%28v=bts.70%29.aspx
```

See also

> ▸ The *Implementing Error Handling in an Orchestration* recipe will show how to handle an error in an orchestration process.

Implementing error handling in an orchestration

With developing an orchestration, you will have to bear in mind that errors can occur. Within an orchestration, you can implement error handling through usage of the Scope shape. The Scope shape allows you to use transactions and for exception handlers similar to try/catch block in .NET. The exception handlers allow you to specify different kinds of exceptions. You can resolve errors within the orchestration like with the try/catch mechanism. There are situations when errors can occur in an orchestration when messages cannot be sent or transformation goes wrong. With the exception handler shape, you act upon the error and write some custom code for logging purposes such as writing to the Microsoft Event Log and sending an alert to an administrator.

Getting ready

Open visual studio and create a solution. For reference, you can download the source code for error handling (BTS.Cookbook.Orchestration.ErrorHandling) belonging to this recipe.

How to do it...

Error handling by using a scope can be implemented by following these steps:

1. Create a new BizTalk project and add schema(s) of message(s) you require in the project.
2. Subsequently, add a new orchestration to the project and give it a descriptive name.

3. Create a new message in the **Orchestration View** window, and specify the name and type.

4. Following steps involve the process you want to implement (these steps are just an example:

5. Drag a **Receive** shape to the orchestration canvas to receive the initial order message. Configure this shape to use the message created earlier and activate the orchestration. Also, configure this shape to use an orchestration Receive port.

6. Drag a **Scope** shape from the toolbox onto the orchestration design surface, set the **Transaction Type** property to **None** and give a name to the Scope shape.

7. Right-click on the name of the new **Scope** shape, and select **New Exception Handler** from the Context menu:

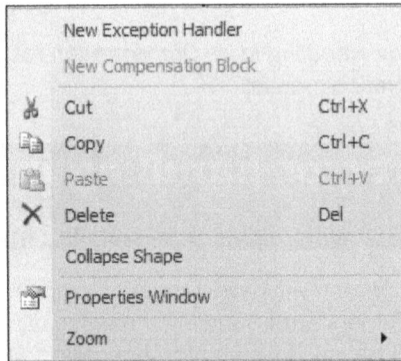

8. Right-click on the name of the exception handler created in the previous step, and select **Properties Window** from the Context menu.

9. Set the **Exception Object Type** property to **General Exception** or a .NET exception that you require and the **Name** property to a descriptive name. If you choose to use a .NET exception type, you need to set the **Exception Object Name** property.

10. Within the Exception Handler, you can drag an **Expression** shape and have, for instance, the following statement:

```
System.Diagnostics.EventLog.WriteEntry("Application", "An
Exception occurred")
```

11. You can see the result of having a scope and error handling block in the following screenshot (this orchestration belongs to the example belonging to this book):

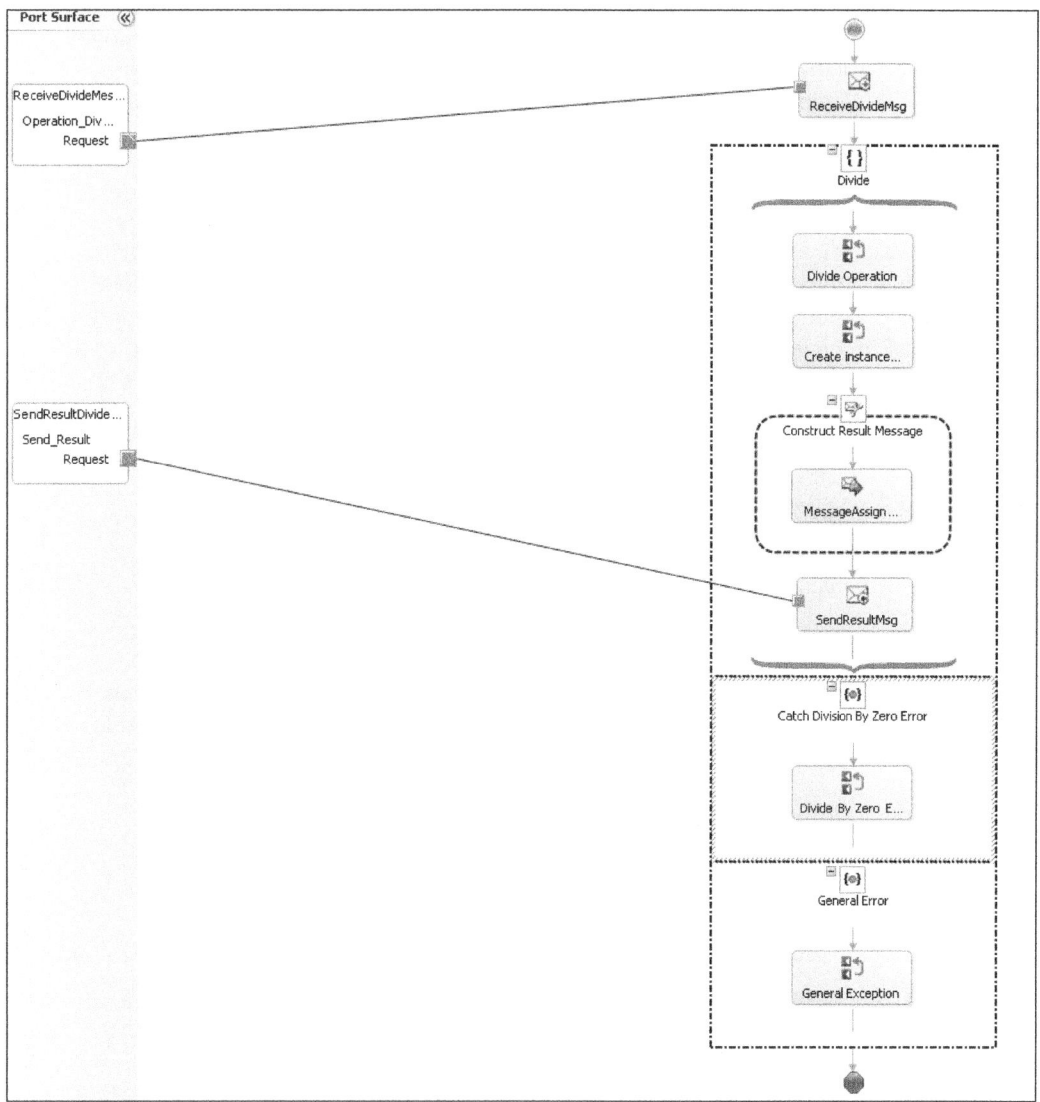

How it works...

With the Scope shape, you are able to catch an error that occurs with the scope boundaries in an orchestration. If BizTalk encounters an exception processing the orchestration logic within scope, it will invoke the Expression shape. The Expression shape writes an error message to the Windows application log. As a developer, you can choose to define a stricter error-resolution procedure. With the Error Handler block, you can invoke an exception-handling framework or invoke another orchestration to trigger a process for resolving the error.

Exception handling in orchestration works like .NET—an exception, once thrown, it will continue outward through error handlers added to the scope. Scope can have multiple exception handlers added to them with different exception types, but only of the general exception type. If the latter is not present, and there is no explicit exception handler for a thrown exception, the BizTalk orchestration engine handles the exception and writes an event to the operating system's event log.

There's more...

At the following MSDN URL, you can find an example of error handling, but it has a dependency with Microsoft Office InfoPath:

```
http://msdn.microsoft.com/en-us/library/aa578190%28v=bts.70%29.aspx
```

On the Code Project site, you will find a guide on handling exceptions in BizTalk, which basically sketches a few scenarios with error handling in an orchestration. You are able to find it on the Code Project site at the following URL and it is provided with code:

```
http://www.codeproject.com/KB/biztalk/ExceptionDemo.aspx
```

At the following MSDN URLs, you can see more information and examples of handling exceptions:

- ▶ `http://msdn.microsoft.com/en-us/library/aa561229(BTS.70).aspx`
- ▶ `http://msdn.microsoft.com/en-us/library/aa578190(v=bts.70).aspx`
- ▶ `http://msdn.microsoft.com/en-us/library/aa578012(v=bts.70).aspx`

On the MSDN Code Gallery, you can find error handling samples You can find the **BizTalk: Sample: Error Handling** document at the following URL:

```
http://code.msdn.microsoft.com/BizTalk-Sample-Error-69c099be
```

For error handling in web services, see the blog post on Best practices for handling web service exceptions in the BizTalk Server at the following URL:

```
http://blog.codit.eu/post/2012/01/13/Best-Practices-for-consuming-
Web-Services-from-within-BizTalk-Server.aspx
```

See also

▸ A good sample of error handling when a message cannot be sent can be found in the *Implementing a retry pattern in an orchestration* recipe in *Chapter 2, BizTalk Server Automation: Patterns*.

Exploring BizTalk's out of the box deployment

A developer builds a BizTalk solution and deploys it to his own BizTalk environment and tests it. As soon as he determines that his BizTalk application is finished enough, he can export it from the BizTalk Administration Console. An MSI and binding file (XML) are extracted and can be viewed as a complete "backup" of the application. The MSI and binding files can be separate or binding files are included within the MSI. Both can be used to install an application in another BizTalk environment. The administrator does not have to rely on Visual Studio to deploy straight from the code as the ability to create an MSI is offered through the BizTalk Management Console.

The drawback with MSI is that it represents a certain version, and when outdated an extraction of the right version is required. Deployments to different stages (test, acceptance, and production) are manual tasks and require some discipline by administrators. Besides that, versioning is important to keep a track of different versions of the application. Discipline by administrators is key when building and maintaining the MSIs.

An administrator can also use `BTSTask.exe` found at `<install path>:\Program Files (x86)\Microsoft BizTalk Server 2010`. `BTSTask.exe` is a command line utility that can be used for performing many application deployment tasks from the command line, such as:

▸ Exporting an application and its artifacts to a `.msi` file by using the `ExportApp` command

▸ Exporting binding information to a `.xml` file by using the `ExportBindings` command

- ▸ Importing an application from a `.msi` file by using the `ImportApp` command
- ▸ Importing binding information from a `.xml` file by using the `ImportBindings` command

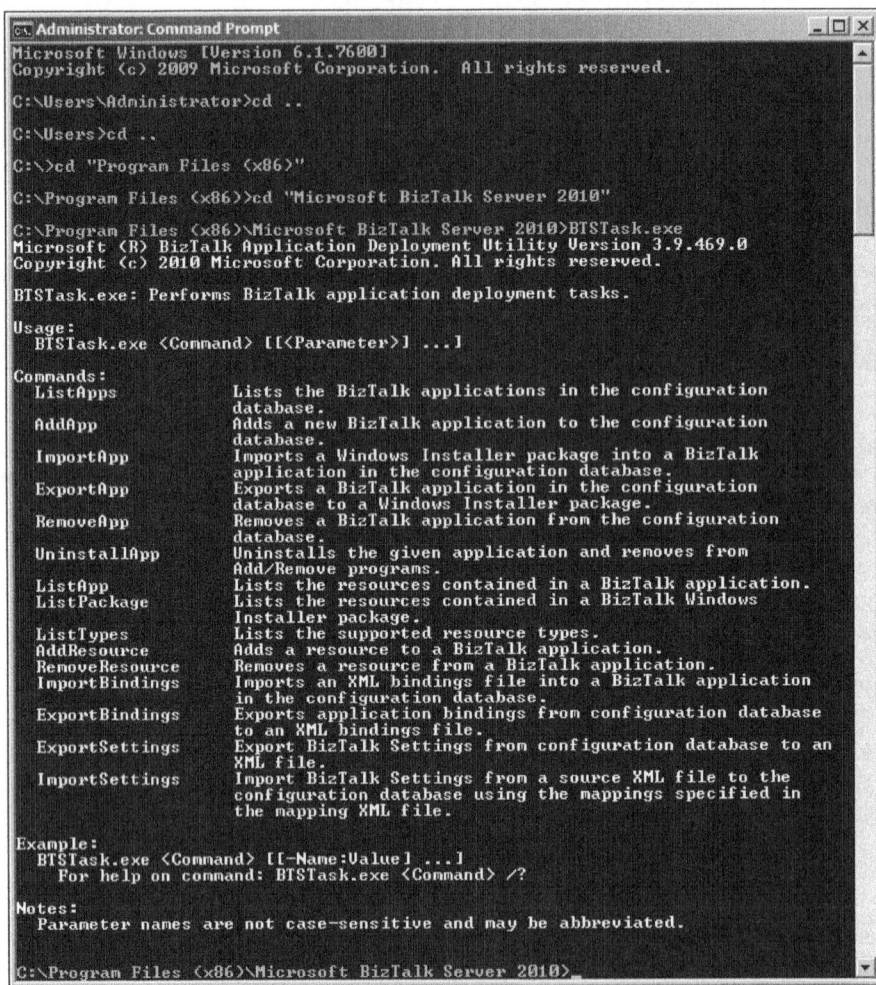

You will find the BTSTask Command-Line Reference document on MSDN at the following URL:

`http://msdn.microsoft.com/en-us/library/aa559686%28v=bts.70%29.aspx`

How to do it...

There are two ways of out-of-box deployment offered by BizTalk and one via the BizTalk Administration Console. The following steps are involved:

1. Open the BizTalk Server Administration Console and navigate to your BizTalk application.

2. Right-click on your solution and select **Export | MSI file**, as shown in the following screenshot:

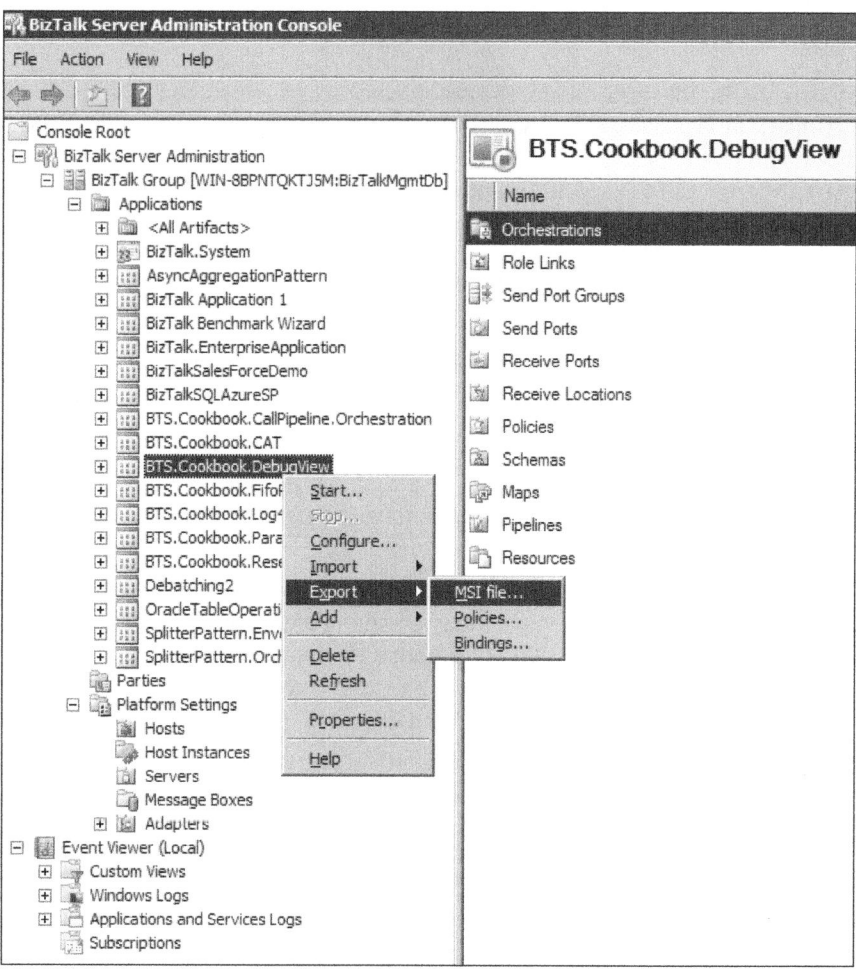

3. A wizard will start and you can walk through several steps:

4. Welcome screen; click on Next

5. Resources to export

6. Specify IIS hosts

7. Dependencies

8. Destination (version!)

9. Progress

10. Summary

11. Export bindings

When installing the BizTalk application, the resources (DLL) are installed in three different places—BizTalk Database, filesystem, and GAC—an essential step is, before doing the solution export, you should go to resources and for each resource you should use the reserved variable, `%BTAD_InstallDir%`. This will prevent the DLLs from spreading in the filesystem.

The `BTAD_InstallDir` variable contains the installation path of the BizTalk application, in other words, it is the name of the folder that the user selects when he/she runs your MSI file (the default value is `%ProgramFiles%Generated by BizTalk<application name>`).

When including binding files (Resources to export step) to the MSI you need to consider the following:

▶ Host instance names in target environments (test, acceptance, and production), if these are different then you need to take that into account when creating the binding files for these environments. For more information on customizing binding files, go to `http://msdn.microsoft.com/en-us/library/aa559898.aspx`.

▶ Multiple binding files can be included, and if targeted to the same environment all of them are applied during installation, so see to it each binding file is targeted to a different environment. For more information on applying multiple BizTalk bindings to the same environment, go to `http://seroter.wordpress.com/2009/05/04/applying-multiple-biztalk-bindings-to-the-same-environment/`.

▶ Passwords should not be stored in the binding file. When exporting a binding file BizTalk removes the passwords.

Another way of deployment is using `BTSTask.exe` to export the BizTalk application using the `ExportApp` command. This command enables you to export a BizTalk application to an `.msi` file. The following steps are involved:

1. Open the command prompt and navigate to the folder where `BTSTask.exe` resides.

2. Enter the following command:

```
ExportApp /ApplicationName:MyApplication /Package:C:\<destination
folder>\MyApplication.msi
```

3. Execute the command and you will get the output, as shown in the following screenshot:

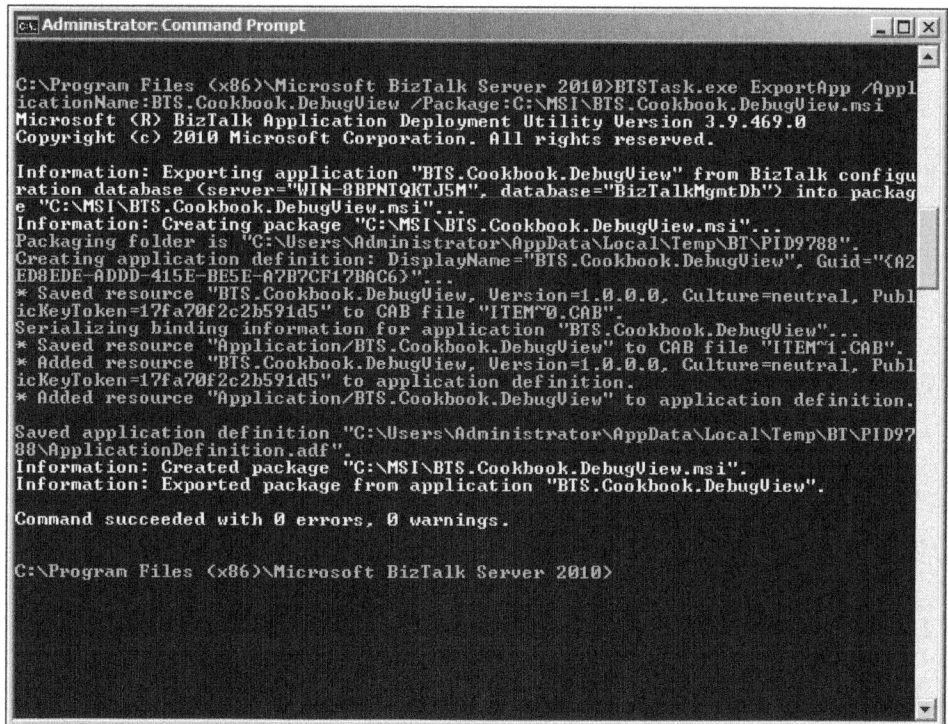

With a batch file, you can allow MS-DOS and Microsoft Windows users to create a list of commands to run in sequence once the batch file has been executed. This offers the opportunity to automate the deployment using a few commands to `btstask.exe` that will perform a number of tasks. You can, for instance, create an MSI and include multiple bindings for different environments (UAT and production). You will have to perform the following steps listed, for example:

1. Create a directory called `build`.

2. Create a directory called `bindings`.

3. Deploy your application into BizTalk using Visual Studio.

4. Once you have successfully deployed the application go to the BizTalk Administration Console.

5. Navigate to your application and extract the bindings file by right-clicking on the application and selecting **Export bindings**.

6. Save the file under <path> <your solution name> build folder with the name, `Production_<solution name>.BindingInfo.xml`.

   For our sample, you will find `C:\BizTalk Server 2010 Cookbook\Chapter 3\BTS.Cookbook.CAT\ BTS.Cookbook.CAT \build\ Production_BTS. Cookbook.CAT.BindingInfo.xml`.

7. Change binding setting for production environment, if necessary.

8. Copy the binding file in the bindings folder and copy it to the build folder and rename it to 9. `UAT_<solution name>.BindingInfo`.

   For our sample, you will find `C:\BizTalk Server 2010 Cookbook\Chapter 3\BTS.Cookbook.CAT\ BTS.Cookbook.CAT \build\ Production_BTS. Cookbook.CAT.BindingInfo.xml`.

9. Change the binding setting for UAT environment, if necessary.

10. In the solution folder, run the following command:

```
btstask listapp -ApplicationName:" <your solution name> "
-ResourceSpec: <your solution name> ResourceSpec.xml
```

   For example, following command can be run:

```
btstask listapp -ApplicationName:" BTS.Cookbook.CAT "
-ResourceSpec: BTS.Cookbook.CAT .ResourceSpec.xml
```

11. With the following `MSIBuild.bat` file, you can create an MSI with binding files included for production and UAT environments:

```
btstask addresource /ApplicationName:" <your solution name> " /
Type:System.BizTalk:BizTalkBinding  /Property:TargetEnvironment=
"Production"  /Source:"bindings\Production_<your solution name>.
BindingInfo.xml" /Overwrite

btstask addresource /ApplicationName:" <your solution name> " /
Type:System.BizTalk:BizTalkBinding  /Property:TargetEnvironment="
UAT"  /Source:"build\UAT_<your solution name>.BindingInfo.xml" /
Overwrite

btstask exportapp /ApplicationName:" <your solution name> " /
Package: <your solution name>.msi
/ResourceSpec:Build/<your solution name>.ResourceSpec.xml
```

How it works...

Using the BizTalk Administration Console or command-line window, results in the creation of MSI. As default all application artifacts are incorporated in the MSI, but as a developer you can select a subset. With MSI, you can easily migrate your solution to other BizTalk environments. When creating an MSI, there are some considerations to be taken into account:

- **Configuration settings**: When exporting your application as a configuration, settings in the `BTSNTSvc.exe.config` file are not exported. If artifacts in a BizTalk solution rely on a custom configuration value existing in this file, a developer must use another mechanism (manual or otherwise) to add that same configuration value to the target environment.

- **Security credentials**: Depending on the solution, an MSI package may contain sensitive information such as passwords and should be appropriately secured. You can move or have passwords in port bindings, because they are removed from all bindings when you export directly from an application. If you require persisting passwords in a binding file, you must create a binding file with the passwords in it and then add the binding file to the application as a file resource.

- **Security authorization**: During the export process all permission settings on files and folders are removed. For web directory resources, the security settings in place, at the time of export, are written to the MSI package.

With a batch file you can automate deployment by executing a sequence of commands. Creation of MSI, and including different binding files and/or other resources, can be performed in one action.

There's more...

On MSDN, you will find more resources on deployment of a BizTalk application:

Find the **Deploying BizTalk Applications** document at
`http://msdn.microsoft.com/en-us/library/aa561812.aspx`

Find the **Deploying and Managing BizTalk Applications** document at
`http://msdn.microsoft.com/en-us/library/aa578693.aspx`

You can also use PowerShell as post-processing script for advanced deployment functionalities, such as modifying the BizTalk config file, creating receive locations, creating an Event Log Application sink, and adding an SSO application store configuration. For an example refer to the **Using PowerShell in BizTalk Post-Processing Scripts** document at the following URL:

`http://geekswithblogs.net/EltonStoneman/archive/2009/06/08/using-powershell-in-biztalk-post-processing-scripts.aspx`

See also

- For more details on out of the box deployment of BizTalk applications, refer to the *Using the Deployment Framework for BizTalk* recipe.

Using the Deployment framework for BizTalk

The **BizTalk Deployment Framework** (**BTDF**) supports deployments for BizTalk applications that go far beyond BizTalk's out of the box deployment functionality described in the *Exploring BizTalk out of the box deployment* recipe. It has a number of tools that can improve developers' and administrators' productivity, such as binding file management. The framework version 5.0 supports BizTalk Server 2010 and has a couple of advantages for the developers, as well as for the administrators:

▶ Ability to eliminate all manual steps in BizTalk deployments

▶ Maintains all environment-specific configurations and runtime settings in an Excel spreadsheet

▶ Single binding file can be applied for all deployment (Development, Test, Acceptance and Production) environments

▶ Re-use of scripts to deploy applications to different servers

▶ Low cost as the framework is free of charge

Though this framework has the advantages mentioned above, it comes with a price, creating a non-compatible BizTalk MSI (the framework creates WiX based MSI's). Furthermore, it brings more complexity with moving parts and investment in learning the framework and its deployment approach.

Getting ready

Download the BizTalk Deployment Framework from CodePlex `http://biztalkdeployment.codeplex.com/` and install it on your machine. As an example, the solution from the *Applying event logging in BizTalk solutions* recipe is used called `BTS.Cookbook.CAT`.

How to do it...

To be able to leverage features that the deployment framework offers and to get started you can do the following:

1. Open the BizTalk solution in Visual Studio.

2. Add a new project from BizTalk projects, you will notice that, after installing the framework, there is a new template called **Deployment Framework** for the BizTalk Project; give it a name of the solution ending with `.Deployment` such as `BTS.Cookbook.CAT.Deployment`.

3. The Project Options window will pop up, as shown in the following screenshot:

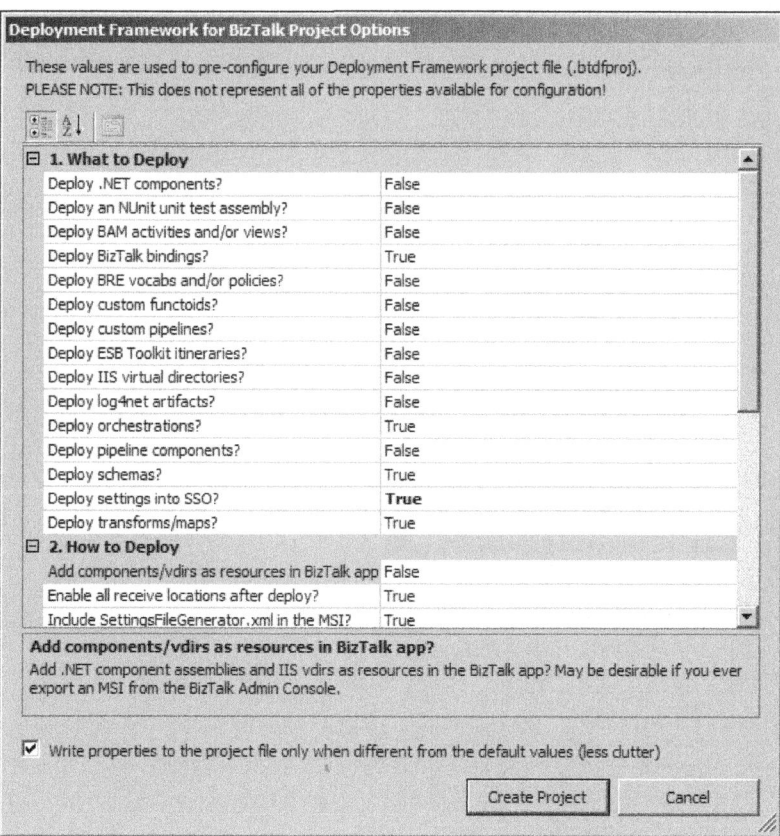

4. Select appropiate values and click on the **Create Project** button.

5. A project will be created and you will see a dialog box, as shown in the following screenshot:

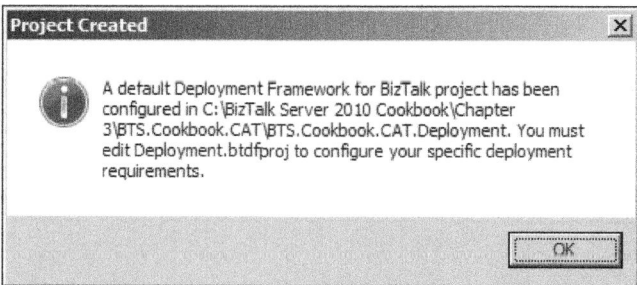

6. Click on **OK** and then you will find the project file, `btdfproj`. You can change the setting to match your environment:

```xml
Deployment.btdfproj ×
<?xml version="1.0" encoding="utf-8"?>
<!--
  Deployment Framework for BizTalk 5.0
  Copyright (C) 2008-2010 Thomas F. Abraham and Scott Colestock
-->
<Project xmlns="http://schemas.microsoft.com/developer/msbuild/2003" DefaultTargets="Deploy">
  <PropertyGroup>
    <Configuration Condition="'$(Configuration)' == ''">Debug</Configuration>
    <Platform Condition="'$(Platform)' == ''">x86</Platform>
    <SchemaVersion>1.0</SchemaVersion>
    <ProjectName>BTS.Cookbook.CAT</ProjectName>
    <ProjectVersion>1.0</ProjectVersion>
    <IncludeSSO>True</IncludeSSO>
    <UsingMasterBindings>True</UsingMasterBindings>
  </PropertyGroup>
  <PropertyGroup>
    <!-- Properties related to building an MSI for server deployments -->
    <!-- BizTalk App Version Upgrade -->
    <!-- For each new product release to be deployed to your BizTalk servers: -->
    <!--     1) Increment ProductVersion -->
    <!--     2) Generate a new GUID and update ProductId with the new GUID -->
    <!--   This allows the new MSI to automatically uninstall (not undeploy!) the old MSI and install the new one. -->
    <ProductVersion>1.0.0</ProductVersion>
    <ProductId>d8aed154-6a67-4a76-8930-09f10faf4fb8</ProductId>
    <!-- BizTalk App Version Upgrade -->
    <ProductName>BTS.Cookbook.CAT for BizTalk</ProductName>
    <Manufacturer>Deployment Framework User</Manufacturer>
    <PackageDescription>BTS.Cookbook.CAT</PackageDescription>
    <PackageComments>BTS.Cookbook.CAT</PackageComments>
    <!-- NEVER change the ProductUpgradeCode. -->
    <ProductUpgradeCode>d8f124db-ebf5-4608-a932-2f9d5391d501</ProductUpgradeCode>
  </PropertyGroup>
  <PropertyGroup Condition="'$(Configuration)' == 'Debug'">
    <DeploymentFrameworkTargetsPath>$(MSBuildExtensionsPath)\DeploymentFrameworkForBizTalk\5.0\</DeploymentFrameworkTargetsPath>
    <OutputPath>bin\Debug\</OutputPath>
    <DeployPDBsToGac>false</DeployPDBsToGac>
  </PropertyGroup>
  <PropertyGroup Condition="'$(Configuration)' == 'Release'">
    <DeploymentFrameworkTargetsPath>$(MSBuildExtensionsPath)\DeploymentFrameworkForBizTalk\5.0\</DeploymentFrameworkTargetsPath>
    <OutputPath>bin\Release\</OutputPath>
    <DeployPDBsToGac>false</DeployPDBsToGac>
  </PropertyGroup>
  <PropertyGroup Condition="'$(Configuration)' == 'Server'">
    <DeploymentFrameworkTargetsPath>Framework\</DeploymentFrameworkTargetsPath>
    <!-- Get our PDBs into the GAC so we get file/line number information in stack traces. -->
    <DeployPDBsToGac>true</DeployPDBsToGac>
  </PropertyGroup>
  <ItemGroup>
    <PropsFromEnvSettings Include="SsoAppUserGroup;SsoAppAdminGroup" />
  </ItemGroup>
  <ItemGroup>
    <Schemas Include="YourSchemas.dll">
      <LocationPath>..\$(ProjectName)\bin\$(Configuration)</LocationPath>
    </Schemas>
  </ItemGroup>
  <Import Project="$(DeploymentFrameworkTargetsPath)BizTalkDeploymentFramework.targets" />
  <!--
    The Deployment Framework automatically packages most files into the server install MSI.
    However, if there are special folders that you need to include in the MSI, you can
    copy them to the folder $(RedistDir) in the CustomRedist target.
    To include individual files, add an ItemGroup with AdditionalFiles elements.
  -->
  <Target Name="CustomRedist">
  </Target>
</Project>
```

7. Rename the deployment. `btdfproj` to
   `<your solutionname>.Deployment.btdfproj`. For example, `BTS.Cookbook.CAT.Deployment.btdfproj`.

8. Next steps involve the following environmental settings:

9. Open the `SettingsFileGenerator` file.

10. An excel sheet, as shown in the following screenshot, will appear where you can fill in
    the details for different BizTalk environments such as test and production:

11. You can add settings for the application version, Receive Host, Send Host, Processing
    Host, Tracking Host, Default Host, and so on.

12. Save this file.

13. Next, you will create a master binding file, as instructed in the following steps:

14. Deploy your application into BizTalk using Visual Studio.

15. Once you have successfully deployed the application, go to the BizTalk
    Administration Console.

16. Navigate to your application and extract the bindings file, by right-clicking on the
    application and choosing **Export Bindings**.

17. Save the file to `<path> <your solution name>.<deployment folder with name> <your solution name>.PortBindingsMaster.xml`. For example, in
    our sample you will give a name such as `C:\BizTalk Server 2010 Cookbook\Chapter 3\BTS.Cookbook.CAT\BTS.Cookbook.CAT.Deployment\PortBindingsMaster.xml`.

18. Finally, go to **Tools** in the menu and select **Deployment Framework for BizTalk | Build Server Deploy MSI**, as shown in the following screenshot:

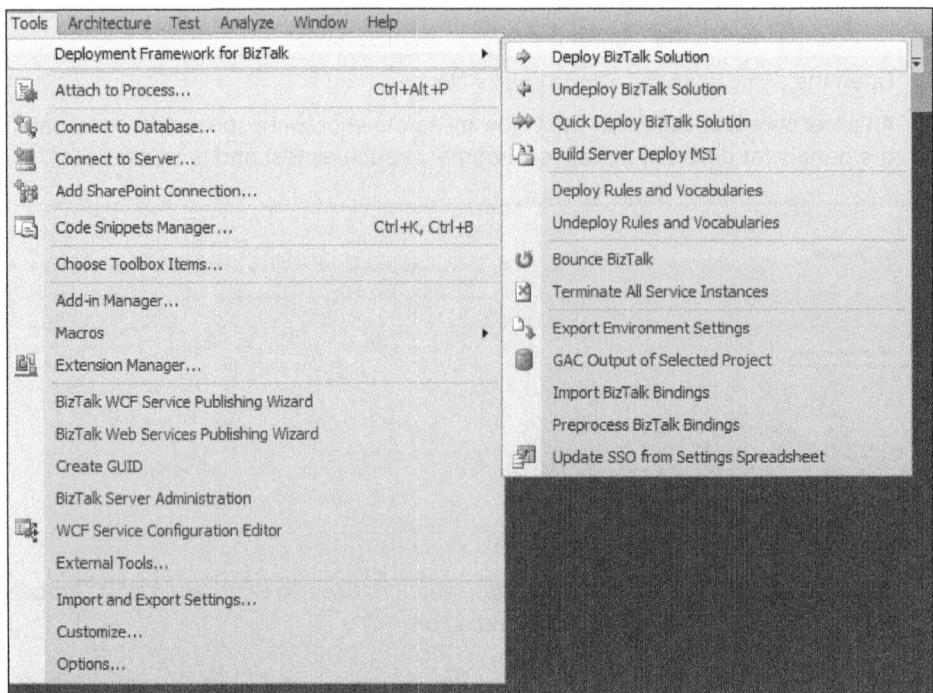

How it works...

Deployment framework for BizTalk has a lot of features that you, as a developer, can leverage. The most important feature is building a deployment project file (`.btdfproj`), which is created when adding a new deployment framework for the BizTalk Project. First, when you add this project template, a folder is created based on the name you give, with a `.Deployment` extension. Next, based on the options chosen in the **Deployment Framework for BizTalk Project** options, a `.btdfproj` file is created with `BuildDebugMsi.bat`, `BuildReleaseMsi.bat`, `InstallWizard.xml`, `license.txt` and `UnInstallWizard.xml` files and a folder named `EnvironmentSettings` containing a `SettingsFileGenerator.xml` file. The latter can be used to set different environmental settings for UAT or production environments.

By exporting a binding file, a developer can create a `PortBindingsMaster` file containing the configuration of the BizTalk application. With BizTalk deployment, there is always the question on how to manage your binding files; hence, these files are hardly readable and it is easy to make mistakes.

Deployment framework for BizTalk contains a `SettingsFileGenerator.xml`, where you can specify values to be shown up in the bindings. When the deployment is started, the settings are parsed and merged with the `PortbindingsMaster` file to a file called `PortBindings.xml`. This file is used to import bindings to the just deployed application. If you don't need to parse anything, you can instruct the framework to use the `PortbindingsMaster` file instead of the `PortBindings` file, by setting the `<UsingMasterBindings>` element to `true`.

There's more...

It will be hard to find information on the deployment framework other than blogs by its creators Scott Colestock and Thomas F.Abraham at the following URLs:

- `http://traceofthought.com/`
- `http://www.tfabraham.com/blog/`

See also

- The *Exploring BizTalk out of the box deployment* recipe shows the deployment option BizTalk itself offers.

4
Securing your Message Exchange

In this chapter, we will cover:

- ▶ Importing certificates
- ▶ Using MIME/SMIME pipeline components
- ▶ Signing and verifying a message
- ▶ Encrypting and decrypting a message
- ▶ Configuring BizTalk and SSL (Transport)

Introduction

Microsoft BizTalk Server 2010 can make use of **Public Key Infrastructure** (**PKI**) digital certificates (`http://msdn.microsoft.com/en-us/library/windows/desktop/aa381975.aspx`) for purposes of document encryption and decryption, document signing and verification (non-repudiation), and party resolution.

With this infrastructure, BizTalk provides security at its boundaries when messages are received over some communication channels or sent to a party or channel. In general, BizTalk provides message-level security for:

- Inbound messages:
    - Receiving trusted data
    - Authenticating message sender party

- Outbound messages:
    - Sending out trusted data

- Trust between processes

Within the BizTalk runtime architecture, receive and send handlers are involved in message-level security. The receive handler is responsible for receiving messages from channels containing one or more receive locations. Such a receive location is a combination of a receive adapter and a pipeline. The receive pipeline contains four stages:

- Decode
- Disassemble
- Validate
- Resolve party

The first and last stages (decode and resolve party) in the receive pipelines deal with message security. These stages can decrypt a message and verify its digital signature with the help of certificates. A send handler has a different role and it fetches messages from the `MessageBox` through subscriptions, and pushes these messages to a channel. A send handler is a combination of a send adapter and a pipeline. The send pipeline contains three stages:

- Preassemble
- Assemble
- Encode

The last stage (encode) can be configured to encrypt or digitally sign messages.

Receive and send handlers, together with orchestrations, run under what is called a host, which is a logical entity (container). It represents BizTalk runtime services, which facilitates the operation of these components. A host can be mapped to a BizTalk physical machine in the BizTalk Server Group. This mapping is named **host instance** and runs under a certain Windows account. This account acts as a principle identity (Service account) of the running host instance and plays a role in message-level security by providing access to its certificate store.

In this chapter, recipes will be introduced to aid you in securing the message exchange between the BizTalk Server and the external party with which it communicates. In your BizTalk solution, you may face security requirements dictating the encryption of messages from and to external parties. These requirements could stem from:

- Sensitive data such as financial or healthcare
- Privacy regulations

If encryption is not a requirement, you will have to sign your messages or verify the messages from partners. By signing and verifying messages, you ensure that the data in messages has not been tampered with.

Importing certificates

The BizTalk Server depends mainly on security provided by certificates and uses them for encryption and digital signatures. By using certificates for encryption and digital signatures, The BizTalk Server can:

- Send and receive data that can be trusted
- Make sure that the data it processes is secure
- Make sure that the authorized parties receive its messages
- Make sure that it receives messages from the authorized parties

The underlying methodology of digital certificates is called **PKI**. Here, a user has a key pair consisting of a public and a private key. Any encryption performed with a private key can be decrypted with the corresponding public key, and vice versa. As the terms imply, the private key remains under the sole control of the user and the public key is made publicly available. For the public to know who is the owner of a certain public key, data that identifies the owner is added to that key. The combination of that data and the public key is referred to as a **digital certificate**.

Digital certificates are stored in certificate stores. A certificate store often has numerous certificates, possibly issued by a number of different certification authorities. There are two locations (stores) that BizTalk uses:

- Other People certificate store
- Personal certificate store

Through the **Other People** certificate store, BizTalk retrieves the public key certificates needed to encrypt outgoing messages and to verify the digital signatures on incoming messages. All users can read and use the certificates in this store. The following screenshot shows the **Other People** certificate store that the BizTalk Server uses for public key certificates:

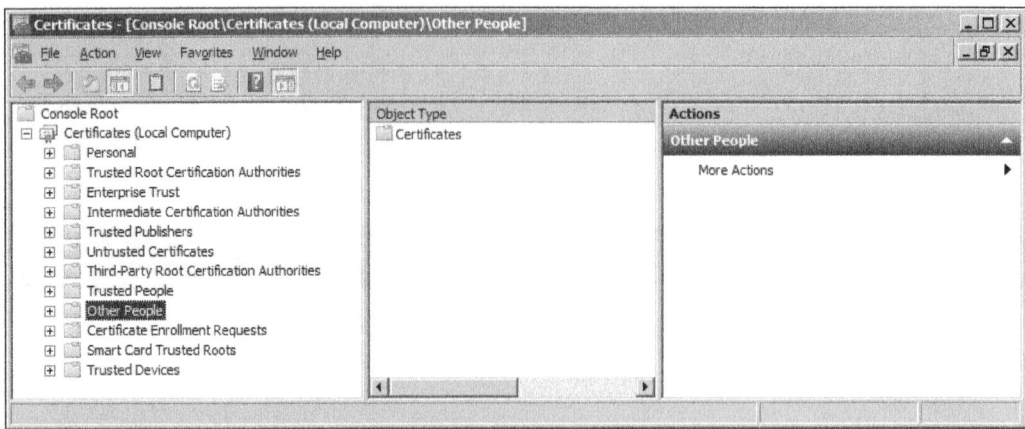

BizTalk uses the **Personal** certificate store to create an association to a private key needed to decrypt incoming messages and sign outbound messages. The personal certificate store of the host instance is used to access the private key associated with that service account. Every Windows account enabled to log on interactively on a computer has a **Personal** certificate store that only that account can access.

When a running host instance needs to decrypt incoming or sign outbound messages, it requires a private key. The certificate that corresponds to that private key must be stored in the **Personal** certificate store for the service account that runs that host instance. The following screenshot shows the **Personal** certificate store that the BizTalk Server uses for certificates that have an associated private key:

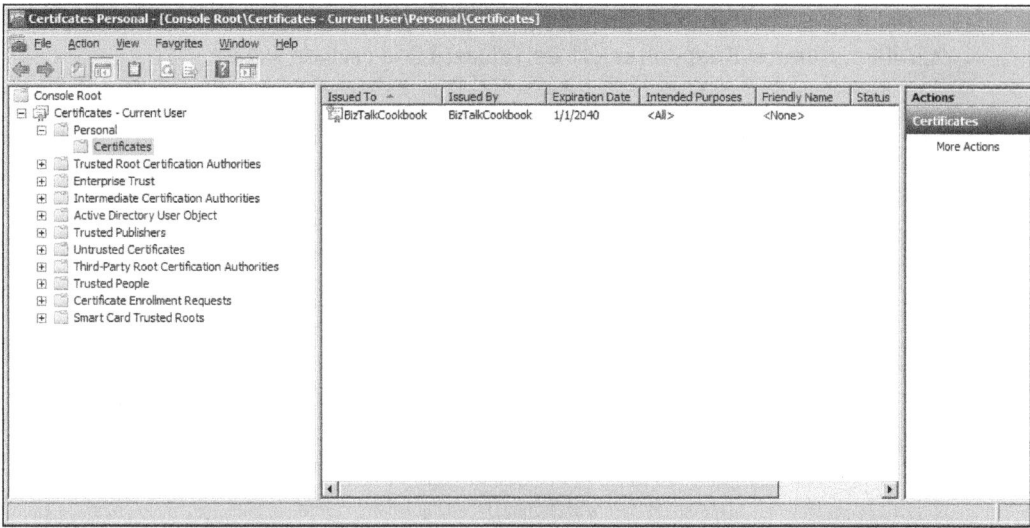

Getting ready

For this recipe, you will need a certificate from an external party or you will have to create one. You can create certificates by using the `Makecert.exe` command-line tool. This tool is part of the SDK belonging to your specific Windows OS (that is, for BizTalk 2010 this would be Windows 7, Windows 2008, or 2008 R2). This SDK can be downloaded as:

- ISO: `http://www.microsoft.com/download/en/details.aspx?displaylang=en&id=18950`

- Web setup: `http://www.microsoft.com/download/en/details.aspx?displaylang=en&id=3138`

How to do it...

To import certificates, you can use **Microsoft Management Console** (**MMC**) or the command-line tool `CertWizard`.

Through the MMC, you have to perform the following steps:

1. Type `mmc` at the command line.
2. The console will appear and you can select **File**.

3. Navigate to **Add/Remove Snap-ins**.

4. In **Add or Remove Snap-ins** select **Certificates** and click on **Add**:

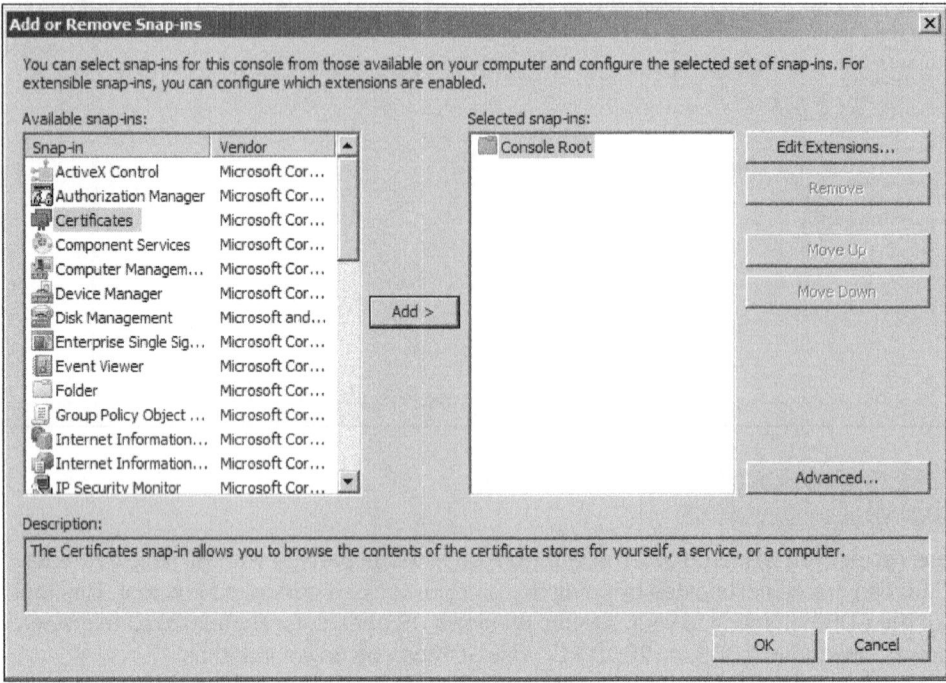

5. A **Certificates Snap-ins** dialog screen will appear with three options detailing how snap-ins should manage the certificates:

   ❑ **My user account**

   ❑ **Service account**

   ❑ **Computer account**

6. Select one of the options and click on **Finish** (note that I normally select **Computer account**).

7. You can repeat steps 4 to 6 if you need to manage more than one certificate store. In the **Select Computer** window, select the option **Local Computer** (the computer this console is running on) and click on **Finish**.

8. Once you have the desired snap-ins, click on **OK**:

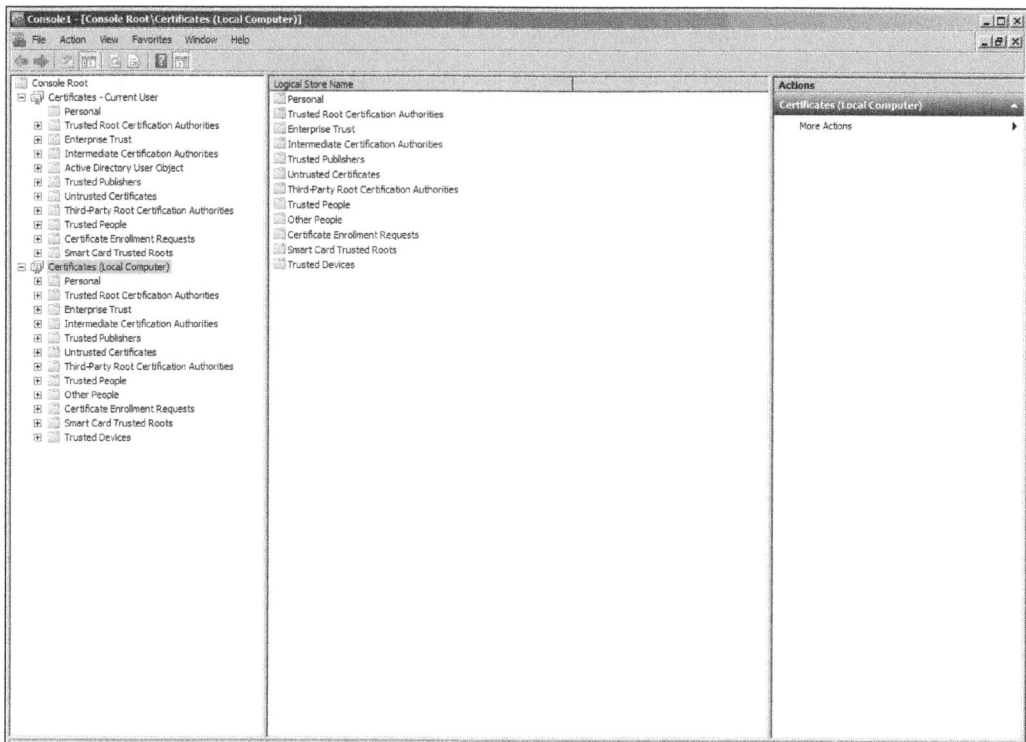

9. You are now able to import certificates in the key store you require by right-clicking a store and selecting **All Tasks | Import**.

10. You will be guided by the **Certificate Import Wizard**.

11. When the wizard fires up, you can see the welcome screen indicating that you can now copy a certificate or revocation list to a certificate store. Click on **Next**.

12. Specify the file to import using the **Browse...** button and navigate to the location of the file. Click on **Next**.

13. In the **Certificate Store** screen, you have to indicate where the certificates need to be placed:

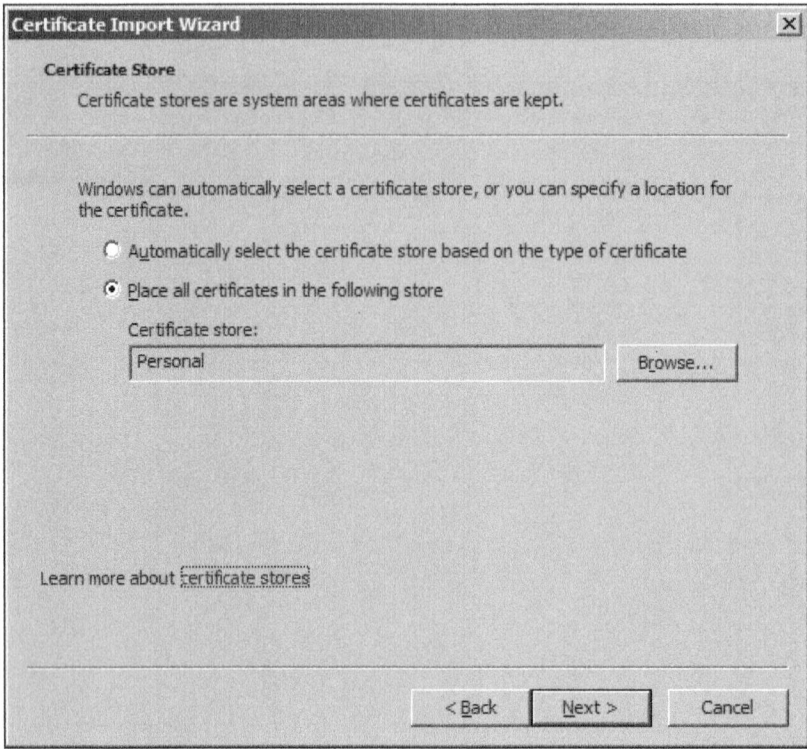

14. You can either let the wizard automatically select the store based on the type of the certificate or manually place it in a store. In that case, the certificate store where you have started the wizard is selected (that is, **Personal**). You can use the **Browse...** button to select another store. Click on **Next**.

15. You will see a summary of where the certificate will be placed. Click on **Finish**.

With the `CertWizard` command-line utility, you can import a certificate from a `.pfx` or `.cer` file into a private or public store for use with the Microsoft BizTalk Server. A `.pfx` file contains both, a private key and certificate while `.cer` file holds the certificate only. This utility first has to be built in Visual Studio before you can use it. The source code for `CertWizard` can be found in the `C:\Program Files\Microsoft BizTalk Server 2010\SDK\Utilities\ Certificate Wizard` folder. In a 64-bit version of the operating system and BizTalk Server 2010, it will be in the `C:\Program Files (x86)\Microsoft BizTalk Server 2010\ SDK\Utilities\Certificate Wizard` folder.

To use the `CertWizard` utility, open the solution in Visual Studio 2010 and build it. Now, perform the following steps to import a certificate:

1. Open a command prompt and navigate to the folder where `CertWizard` resides (that is, `C:\Program Files\Microsoft BizTalk Server 2010\SDK\Utilities\Certificate Wizard\bin\Debug`).

2. The syntax for importing a private key is as follows:

   ```
   CertWizard /Privatekey <filename>.pfx [/Filepassword
   <filepassword>] [/Useridentity <useridentity>] [/
   Password <password>] [/Thumbprint <thumbprint>] [/Usage
   sign|decrypt|both|none] [/Exportable true|false]
   ```

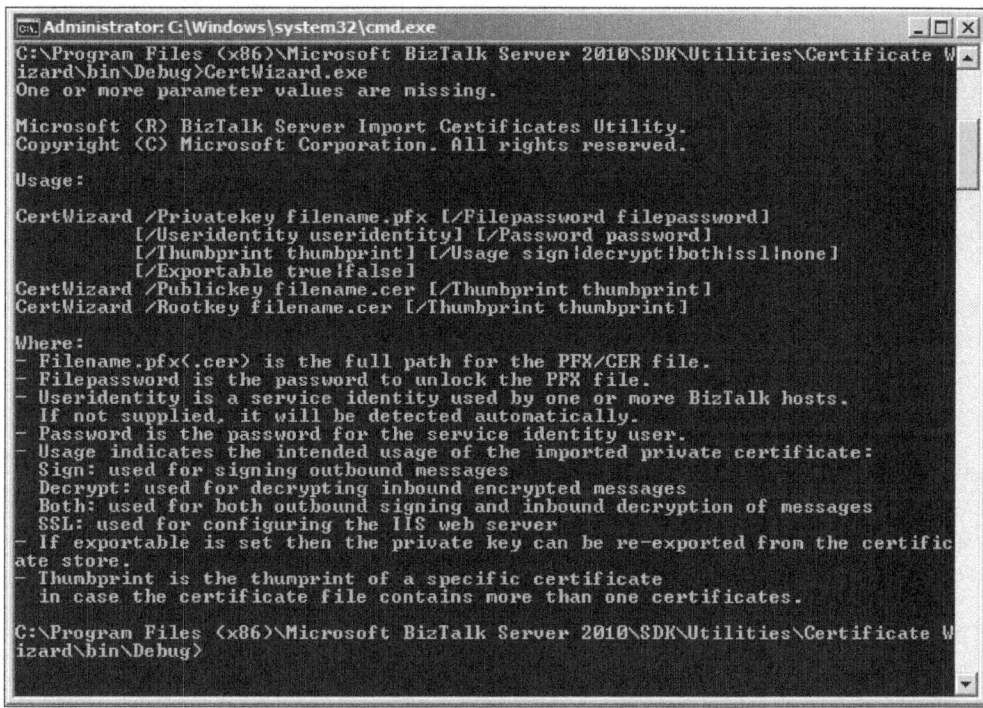

3. You can also use `CertWizard` to import a root key (such as the one provided with this book) by using the following command:

```
CertWizard /Rootkey filename.cer
```

 A **root key** is either an unsigned public key certificate or a self-signed certificate that identifies the Root **Certificate Authority** (**CA**).

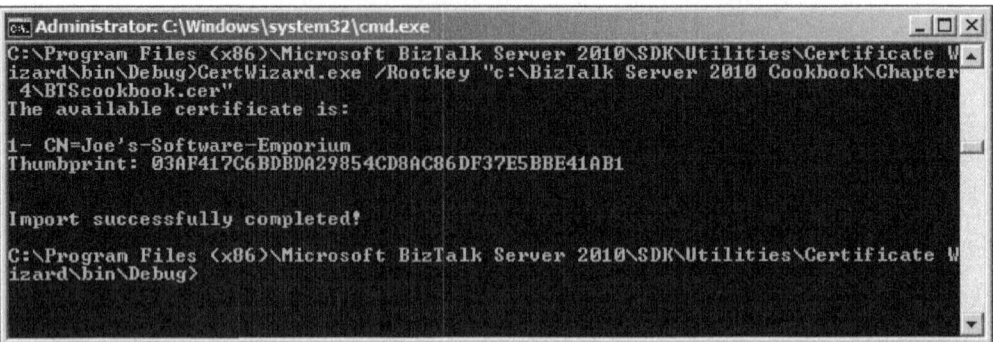

How it works...

Importing certificates can be done through the MMC snap-in or the command-line tool. Using the MMC, a user can easily manage certificates. Through the **All Tasks** menu item, the user is able to import certificates with the guidance of a wizard, which guides him/ her through several steps to ultimately have the certificate imported in the desired store. This can also be achieved using the `CertWizard` command-line tool. With certificates in the appropriate stores, BizTalk has the capability to sign and encrypt messages to facilitate message-level security.

There's more...

The previous recipe describes how to import certificates. In general, you need a good understanding on how to manage digital certificates used with the BizTalk Server 2010. Installation of certificates is one thing, but you also need to know in which folder to install the certificates.

For a checklist of steps to install the certificates, you can see the document **Checklist: Installing and Configuring Certificates** at `http://msdn.microsoft.com/en-us/library/gg634541%28v=BTS.70%29.aspx`.

Besides the checklist, you can review the following resources on MSDN:

- **Best Practices for Managing Certificates**: `http://msdn.microsoft.com/en-us/library/gg634535%28v=BTS.70%29.aspx`

- **Known Issues with Certificates in BizTalk Server**: `http://msdn.microsoft.com/en-us/library/gg634590%28v=BTS.70%29.aspx`

- **Installing and Configuring Digital Certificates**: `http://msdn.microsoft.com/en-us/library/gg634475%28v=BTS.70%29.aspx`

The BizTalk Server uses two types of certificate stores; the Other People certificate store for public key certificates and the Personal certificate store of each host instance service account for certificates with associated private keys:

- **Certificate Stores that BizTalk Server Uses**: `http://msdn.microsoft.com/en-us/library/aa559322%28v=BTS.70%29.aspx`

- **Display Certificate Stores**: `http://technet.microsoft.com/en-us/library/cc725751.aspx`

Finally, PowerShell is a good tool to see where the certificates are installed. Using the MMC, you can see all the certificates installed in the machine, but we cannot search by thumbprint. See Sandro Pereira's post **BizTalk**, **Certificates and PowerShell** at `http://sandroaspbiztalkblog.wordpress.com/2010/10/11/biztalk-certificates-and-powershell/`.

See also

- Refer to the *Signing and verifying a message* and *Encrypting and decrypting a message* recipes later in this chapter. There you can find out how to configure the BizTalk Server to use the certificate for MIME/SMIME

Using MIME/SMIME pipeline components

Out of the box, BizTalk provides several pipeline components to be used when creating a pipeline. These components are available inside the Visual Studio Toolbox. Two of these components are called the **Multipurpose Internet Mail Extensions/Secure Multipurpose Internet Mail Extensions (MIME/SMIME) Decoder pipeline component** and **Encoder pipeline component**.

The first component can be used for decoding and decrypting (MIME/SMIME) encoded messages and verifying digital signatures of signed messages. The second is used to encode and encrypt outgoing messages and sign these messages. These pipeline components can be inserted in either the encoding or the decoding stage of a pipeline and aid in encoding or decoding a message:

▶ The encoding pipeline component is used on outgoing messages. It enables you to encode, encrypt, and sign these messages. This is useful when you want to initiate a secured document interchange between the BizTalk Server and external partners. You can also use this component to send multi-part messages with the BizTalk Server.

▶ The decoding pipeline component enables you to decode and decrypt SMIME encoded messages and to verify digital signatures of signed messages. This component is useful when the secured document interchange starts at an external partner and terminates at your BizTalk Server. This component can also be used for receiving messages with attachments.

Getting ready

You can download the BizTalk project for this recipe from the website accompanying this book.

How to do it...

To use components in a pipeline, you need to create a new BizTalk project and follow the steps according to the pipeline.

Receive pipeline

To create a receive pipeline, perform the following steps:

1. Add a new receive pipeline by right-clicking on the project. Select **Add New Item** and **Receive Pipeline** from the **Add New Item** dialog. Give a descriptive name to the pipeline.

2. Drag the **MIME/SMIME decoder** pipeline component into the **Decode** stage of your receive pipeline.

3. Select and right-click on the component, and select **Properties**.

4. Now you are able to change four properties:

   ❑ **Allow non-MIME message**
   ❑ **Body type content type**
   ❑ **Body part index**
   ❑ **Check revocation list**

Send pipeline

To create a send pipeline, perform the following steps:

1. Add a new send pipeline by right-clicking on the project. Select **Add New Item** and **Receive Pipeline** from the **Add New Item** dialog. Give the pipeline a descriptive name.

2. Drag the **MIME/SMIME encoder** pipeline component into the **Encode** stage of your send pipeline.

3. Select and right-click on the component, and select **Properties**.

4. Now you are able to change five properties:

   ❑ **Check revocation list**

   ❑ **Content transfer encoding**

   ❑ **Enable encryption**

   ❑ **Send body part as attachment**

   ❑ **Signature type**

How it works...

A receive pipeline consists of four stages; decode, disassemble, validate, and party resolution. The decode stage is where the MIME/SMIME Decoder pipeline component can play a role in the pre-processing of a message such as verifying message signatures to ensure integrity, or decoding the MIME/SMIME messages. Up to 255 components can be placed in this stage. If, for example, a message is encrypted and then digitally signed, this stage would have two subsequent components, one for each task. The BizTalk Server uses these out of the box components by default. It can process messages and attachments (if any) in either MIME or SMIME format and can also verify signatures and decrypt MIME/SMIME messages. The component is able to convert messages of both types into an XML format.

A send pipeline consists of three stages; pre-assemble, assemble, and encode. The encode stage is where the MIME/SMIME Encoder pipeline component can play a role in the post-processing of a message so that the external system can process it properly. As the message is converted to the external format, any additional processing required on the message can be executed. Possible processing in this stage includes MIME/SMIME encoding, custom encryption of the message, digitally signing it to maintain its integrity, or any other processing that can be required to encode the message. Like the Decode stage in the receive pipeline, this stage can contain up to 255 components. The BizTalk server uses these out of the box components by default to digitally sign or encrypt messages.

There's more...

You will find more information on MIME/SMIME pipeline components on MSDN:

▶ **How to Configure the MIME/SMIME Encoder Pipeline Components**:
  `http://msdn.microsoft.com/en-us/library/aa561432(v=bts.70).aspx`

▶ **How to Configure the MIME/SMIME Decoder Pipeline Components**:
  `http://msdn.microsoft.com/en-us/library/aa578427(v=bts.70).aspx`

There are some differences between configuring these components inside Visual Studio (at the time of development) and configuring them inside the BizTalk Administration Console, the values are different. You can find more in the document **BizTalk Pipeline Configuration – Configure the properties for the MIME/SMIME Encoder pipeline component** at `http://sandroaspbiztalkblog.wordpress.com/2009/12/18/biztalk-pipeline-configuration-configure-the-properties-for-the-mimesmime-encoder-pipeline-component/`.

See also

▶ Refer to the *Signing and verifying a message* and *Encrypting and decrypting a message* recipes later in this chapter

Signing and verifying a message

To prevent tampering with a message, it can be signed with a certificate to guarantee it is authentic. The BizTalk Server uses a private key to sign outgoing messages. The signing of messages can be achieved by using the standard encoding component (MIME/SMIME) in the send pipeline. The encoding component then needs to be configured to sign all outgoing messages. The signing key and certificate that are used to sign the outgoing message are retrieved from the personal certificate store for the host service account where the pipeline is running.

The following table describes the keys and certificates that need to be installed to sign and verify messages:

Certificate purpose	Certificate type	Certificate store
Signing	Own private key with associated certificate	Personal store for each service account of a host instance that has a send pipeline with a MIME/SMIME Encoder pipeline component configured to sign messages (Add Signing Cert To Message property set to true).

Certificate purpose	Certificate type	Certificate store
Verifying signature	Partner's public key, found in the Partner's certificate	Other People store on each computer that has a host instance that uses a receive pipeline with a MIME/SMIME Decoder pipeline component.

The BizTalk Server supports only one personal certificate for each BizTalk group. A BizTalk group can represent an entire enterprise, a department, a hub, or another business unit. The personal certificate that is used by the BizTalk group is specified by setting the thumbprint of the personal certificate in the BizTalk group properties. To conclude, a BizTalk group is limited by using one certificate to be used for signing a message. You must make sure that the signing certificate is available in the certificate store of the service account of the hosts, where the send pipelines are running:

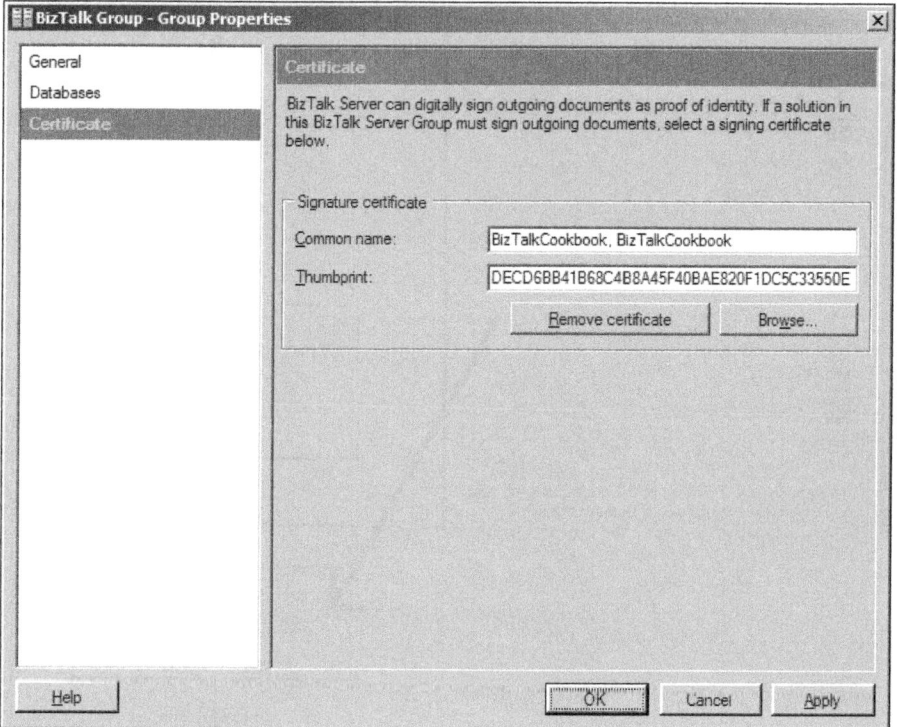

Getting ready

Request a digital signature certificate with a private-public key pair from the CA for the BizTalk Server to use. Send the certificate with the public key to the communication partner(s) that need to verify the digital signature on your messages. You can also use `Makecert.exe` command-line tool to create the certificate.

How to do it...

The following steps need to be performed to be able to send a digitally signed message:

1. In the BizTalk Server, log on with the Service account for the host instance running the handler that will send messages to the partner(s). Install the private key certificate that the BizTalk Server will use to sign messages in the personal store for the Service account.

2. Create a new BizTalk project and add a new send pipeline by right-clicking on the project. Select **Add New Item** and **Send Pipeline** from the **Add New Item** dialog. Give a descriptive name to the pipeline.

3. Drag the **MIME/SMIME encoder** component from the **BizTalk Pipeline Components** section of the **Toolbox** to the **Encode** stage of the send pipeline:

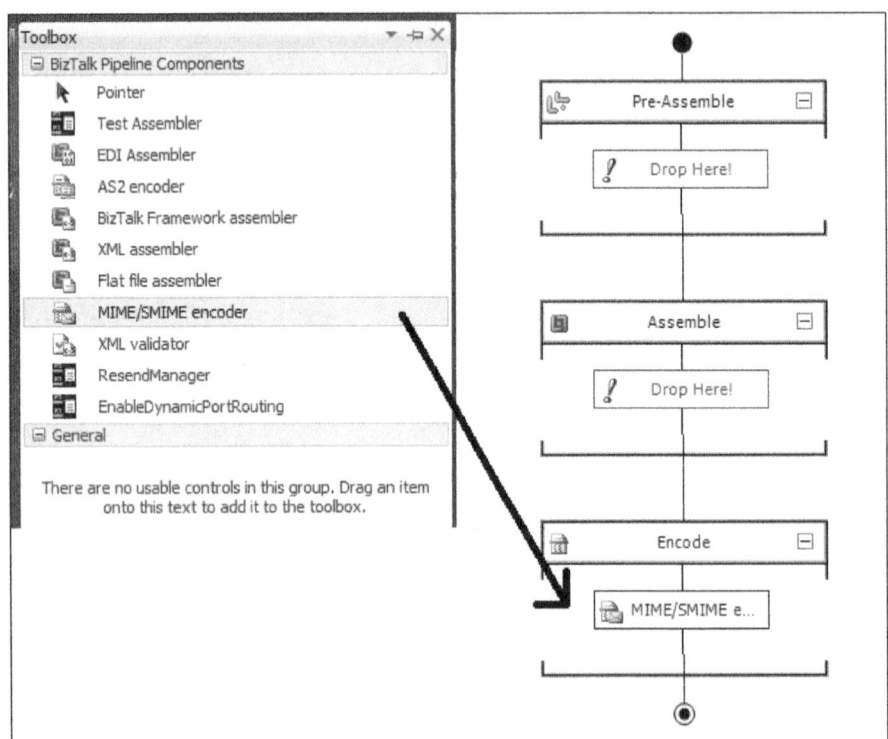

4. Select and right-click on the component, and select **Properties**. Change the value of the **Signature type** to **Clear Sign**. This will ensure that the certificate is appended to the message:

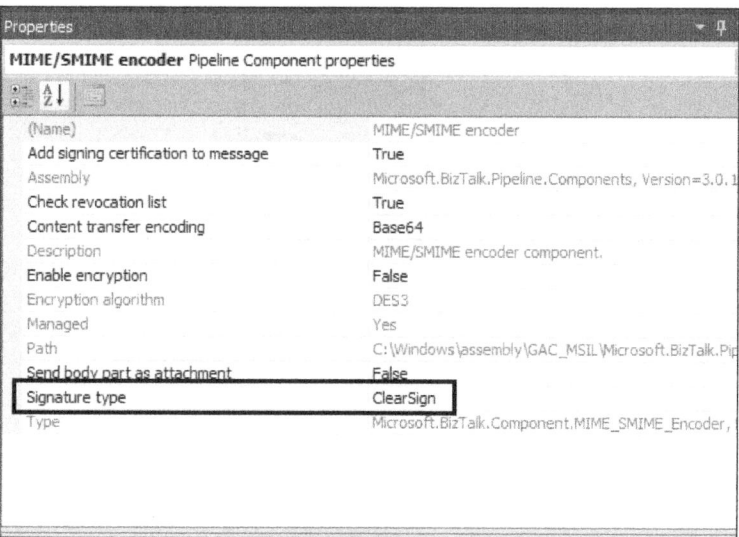

5. Sign the project with a strong name.

6. Subsequently, go to the deployment and give an appropriate name to the application.

7. Build and deploy the BizTalk project.

8. Create a Send port to deliver the message to the recipient, using any transport adapter desired. The sample code provided by this book uses the File adapter.

The following steps need to be performed to be able to verify a digitally signed message:

1. Install the public key certificate of your communication partner(s) in the **Other People** store. This certificate is used to verify the digital signature of the messages of your partner(s).

2. Create a new BizTalk project and add a new receive pipeline by right-clicking on the project. Select **Add New Item** and **Receive Pipeline** from the **Add New Item** dialog. Give the pipeline a descriptive name.

3. Drag the **MIME/SMIME decoder** component from the BizTalk Pipeline Components section of the toolbox to the **Decode** stage of the send pipeline:

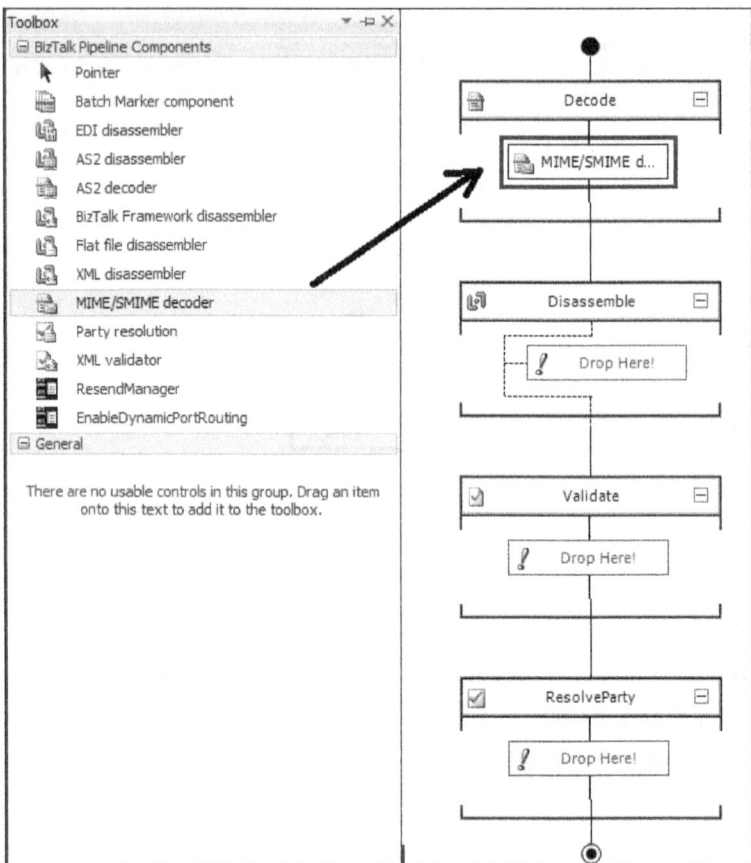

4. Leave the properties as they are (default).

5. Subsequently, go to deployment and give the application an appropriate name.

6. Build and deploy the BizTalk project.

7. Create a Receive port and a receive location to accept the signed message from the sender, using an appropriate transport adapter. Give a descriptive name to the port and the receive location.

8. Open the **BizTalk Administration Console**, and navigate to **Platform Settings**. Select **Host Instances**. Right-click on the **BizTalk host** that will receive the signed message and select **Properties**.

9. Specify the certificate that BizTalk will use to validate incoming messages. Paste the thumbprint of that certificate into the thumbprint field in the **Certificates** section of the **Host Properties** dialog box.

How it works...

Signing messages in BizTalk occurs inside the encode stage of a send pipeline. The MIME/SMIME Encoder pipeline component within the pipeline signs the message by using the BizTalk Server private key that is stored in the Personal store of the Service account of a host instance configured for the send handler. To enable signing using the MIME/SMIME encoder the **Signature type** property of the **MIME/SMIME encoder** component must be set to either **Clear Sign** or **Blob Sign**. Both types append the signature to the message, where only **Blob Sign** can be used in combination with encryption. See the following diagram for the flow of a message from the MessageBox database being signed and sent to an external party:

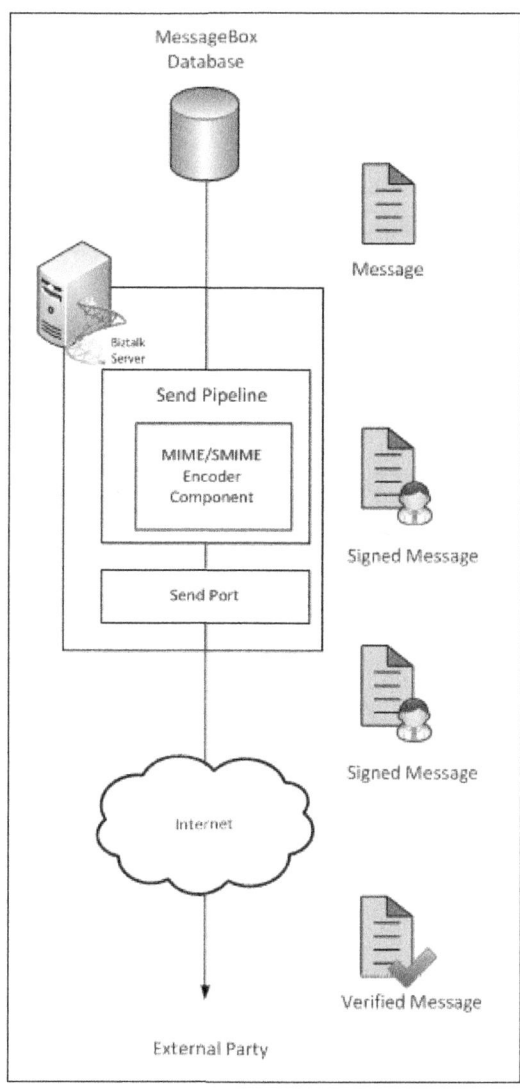

Verifying messages in BizTalk occurs inside the decode stage of a receive pipeline. The MIME/SMIME Decoder pipeline component within the pipeline verifies the signature by using the partner's public key that is stored in the **Other People** store on the machine that has a host instance configured for the receive handler. See the following diagram for the flow of a message from an external party sending a signed message to the publishing of the verified message in the MessageBox database:

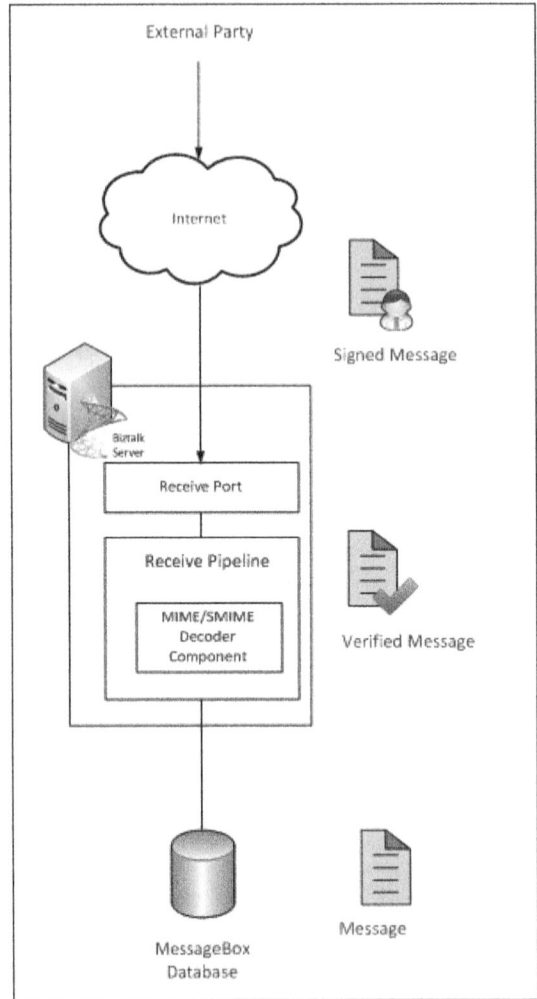

There's more...

The BizTalk Server supports signing outbound messages and signature verification for inbound MIME/SMIME messages. The BizTalk Server uses S/MIME versions 2 and 3 to sign outbound messages and to validate the signature of inbound messages. You can find more in the document **Certificates that BizTalk Server Uses for Signed Messages** at `http://msdn.microsoft.com/en-us/library/aa547244%28v=BTS.70%29.aspx`.

More information on how to configure BizTalk Server pipelines, receive locations, ports, and the BizTalk Server environment to receive and send signed messages can be found in the document **Sending and Receiving Signed Messages** at `http://msdn.microsoft.com/en-us/library/aa559190(v=bts.70).aspx`.

The `MakeCert.exe` command-line tool generates X.509 certificates for testing purposes only. It creates public and private key pairs for digital signatures and stores them in a certificate file. This tool also associates the key pair with a specified publisher's name and creates an X.509 certificate that binds a user-specified name to the public part of the key. For more information, see the document **Makecert.exe (Certificate Creation Tool)** at `http://msdn.microsoft.com/en-us/library/bfsktky3(v=VS.100).aspx`.

Based on the security policies in your company, you may want to consider the questions provided through MSDN in the document **Planning Message Security** at `http://msdn.microsoft.com/en-us/library/aa578453(v=BTS.70).aspx`.

See also

▶ Refer to the *Using MIME/SMIME pipeline components* recipe earlier in this chapter

Encrypting and decrypting a message

In certain communication scenarios between two parties, you may need an encryption mechanism for outbound messages, as well as a decryption mechanism for the inbound messages. Information in messages can be of a sensitive nature or bound to privacy law. This can be data such as social security numbers, bank account numbers, addresses, phone numbers, and so on. The BizTalk Server offers encryption capabilities using certificates. These certificates contain cryptographic key pairs consisting of a public and a private key. The owner of a certificate, for instance BizTalk, can share the public key with communication partner(s). These partners use that public key to encrypt their messages. As the message can only be decrypted with the corresponding private key, the partner(s) are certain that the message can only be decrypted by the owner of the certificate. This means that the private key has to be kept secure and should be protected by the owner.

BizTalk can send secure, encrypted messages to partners by using the public key certificate of each of them. A host can have many public keys for sending encrypted messages, but it can only use one certificate for decrypting messages. The following table describes the keys and certificates that need to be installed for encrypting and decrypting messages:

Certificate purpose	Certificate type	Certificate store
Decryption	Own private key	The Personal store for each Service account of a host instance that has a receive pipeline with a MIME/SMIME Decoder pipeline component.
Encryption	Partner's public key	The Other People store on each computer that has a host instance, which has a send pipeline with a MIME/SMIME Encoder pipeline component configured to encrypt messages.

Every certificate contains a unique identifier called a **thumbprint**, which BizTalk uses to identify the correct certificate. The thumbprint is calculated by applying a hashing algorithm to the certificate. Thumbprints are used while configuring a host or a Send port.

Getting ready

For this recipe, you will need the public key certificate from the party that will receive the encrypted message or create your own certificate.

How to do it...

To be able to send encrypted messages, you will need to install the certificate in the **Local Computer\Other People** store. Then the following steps have to be performed:

1. Create a new BizTalk project and add a new send pipeline by right-clicking on the project. Select **Add New Item** and **Send Pipeline** from the **Add New Item** dialog. Give the pipeline a descriptive name.

2. Drag the **MIME/SMIME encoder** component from the **BizTalk Pipeline Components** section of the **Toolbox** to the **Encode** stage of the send pipeline (refer to the *Signing and verifying a message* recipe earlier in this chapter).

3. Select and right-click on the component, and select **Properties**. Change the value of the **Enable encryption** property from **False** to **True**. Choose the **Encryption algorithm** you desire (the options are, from **strong to weak, DES3, DES**, or **RC2**):

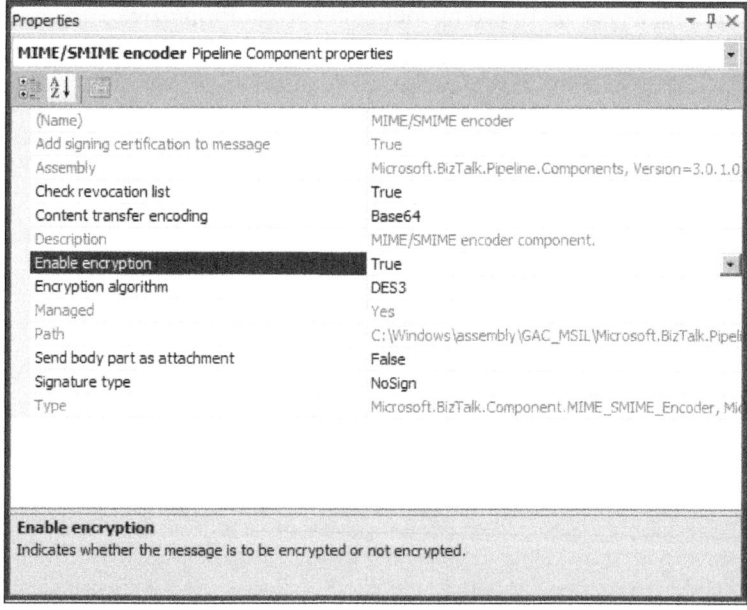

4. Sign the project with a strong name.

5. Subsequently, go to the deployment and give an appropriate name to the application.

6. Build and deploy the BizTalk project.

7. Create a Send port to deliver the message to the recipient, using any transport adapter desired. The sample code provided with this book uses the File adapter.

8. Create a Send port and give it a descriptive name. Select an appropriate Adapter and choose the send pipeline you deployed.

9. In the Send port, choose **Certificate** and select the **Public-key Certificate** of the message receiver for the **Certificate Name** property.

To be able to receive encrypted messages, you will need to obtain a certificate from the CA containing a private key, or create one using the MakeCert.exe command-line tool. Then, the following steps have to be performed:

1. Create a new BizTalk project and add a new receive pipeline by right-clicking on the project. Select **Add New Item** and **Receive Pipeline** from the **Add New Item** dialog. Give the pipeline a descriptive name.

2. Drag the **MIME/SMIME decoder** component from the **BizTalk Pipeline Components** section of the **Toolbox** to the **Decode** stage of the receive pipeline (refer to the *Signing and verifying a message* recipe earlier in this chapter).

3. Select and right-click on the component, and select **Properties**:

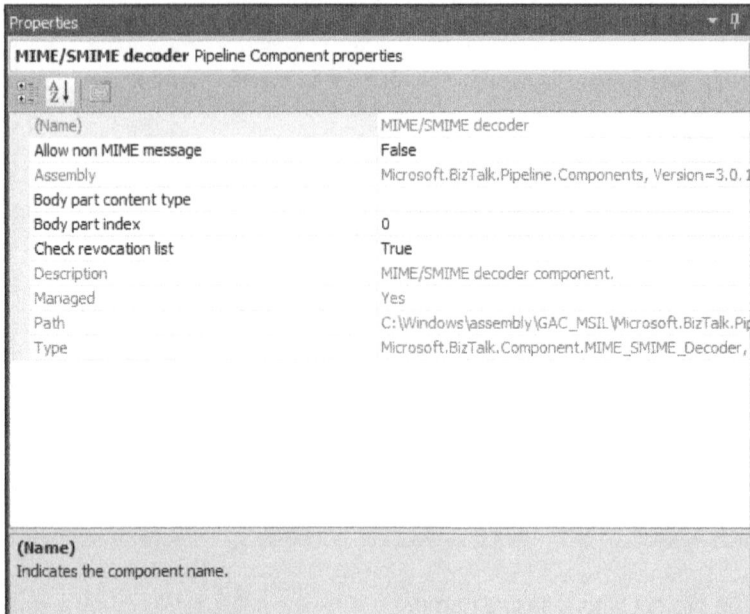

4. Sign the project with a strong name.

5. Subsequently, go to the deployment and give an appropriate name to the application.

6. Build and deploy the BizTalk project.

7. Create a Receive port and a receive location to accept the encrypted message from the sender, using an appropriate transport adapter. Give a descriptive name to the port and the receive location.

8. Open the **BizTalk Administration Console**, and navigate to **Platform Settings**. Select **Host Instances**. Right-click on the **BizTalk host** that will receive the encrypted message and select **Properties**.

9. Specify the certificate that BizTalk will use to decrypt the messages. Paste the thumbprint of this certificate into the thumbprint field in the **Certificates** section of the **Host Properties** dialog box.

How it works...

Encryption of messages in BizTalk occurs inside the **Encode** stage of a send pipeline. The MIME/SMIME Encoder pipeline component within the pipeline encrypts the message by using the public key of the communication partner(s). This key is stored in the **Other People** store on the machine of the host instance configured for the send handler. To enable encryption using the MIME/SMIME encoder, the **Enable encryption** property must be set to **True**.

Furthermore, the **Encryption algorithm** can be set to **DES**, **3DES**, or **RC2**. See the following diagram for the flow of a message from the **MessageBox** database being encrypted and sent to an external party:

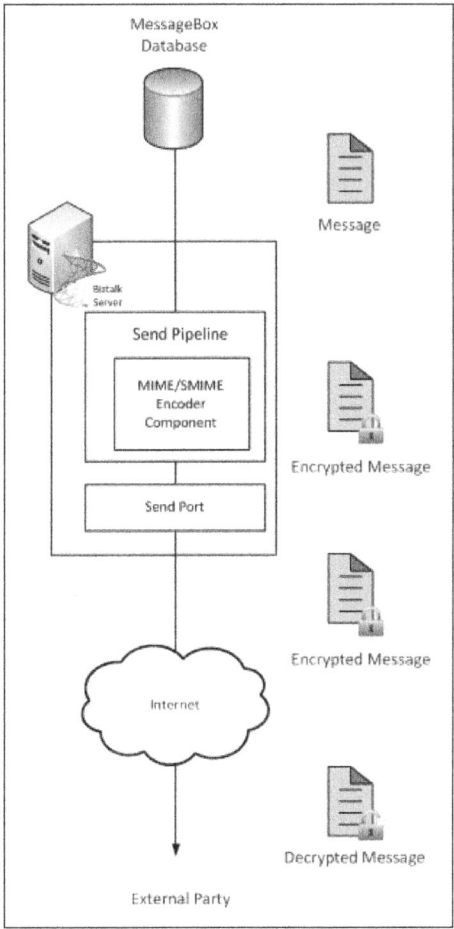

Decryption of messages in BizTalk occurs inside the decode stage of a receive pipeline. The MIME/SMIME Decoder pipeline component within the pipeline decrypts the message by using the BizTalk Server private key that is stored in the personal store of the service account of a host instance configured for the receive handler.

See the following diagram for the flow of a message from an external party sending an encrypted message for publishing the decrypted message in the `MessageBox` database:

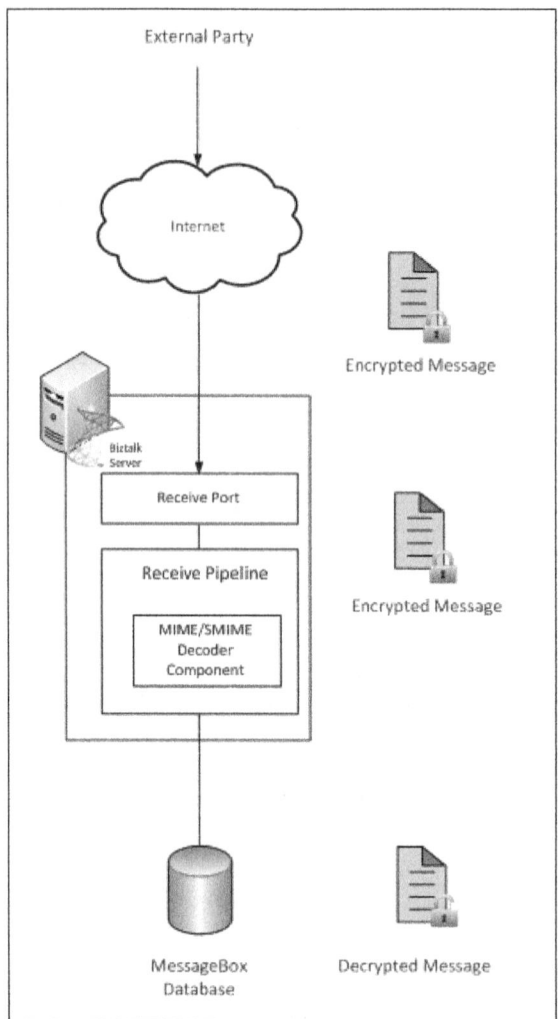

There's more...

The BizTalk Server supports encryption of outbound messages and decryption of inbound messages based on **Secure Multipurpose Internet Mail Extensions (S/MIME)**. The BizTalk Server uses S/MIME version 3 for encryption of outbound messages, and S/MIME versions 2 and 3 for decryption of inbound messages. You can find more in the document **Certificates that BizTalk Server Uses for Encrypted Messages** at http://msdn.microsoft.com/en-us/library/aa559843%28v=BTS.70%29.aspx.

The code project website contains a BizTalk project with guidance on securing messages with encryption in the document **Secure Messaging Solution** at `http://www.codeproject.com/KB/biztalk/SecureMessaging.aspx`.

There is another good sample from Richard Seroter you can use as guidance for encryption and decryption of messages. It can be found in the blog post called **Building a Complete Certificate Scenario With BizTalk Server 2006** at `http://seroter.wordpress.com/2007/03/05/building-a-complete-certificate-scenario-with-biztalk-server-2006/`.

Alternatives for encryption can be BizCrypto for BizTalk. It offers adapters and pipeline components that integrate into the BizTalk Server. You can find more in the document **Biztalk adapters and pipelines for secure data storage and transfer** at `http://www.eldos.com/bizcrypto/biztalk.php`.

See also

▸   Refer to the *Importing certificates* recipe earlier in this chapter

Configuring BizTalk and SSL (Transport)

Secure transport can be provided by HTTPS, which is a combination of the **Hypertext Transfer Protocol** (**HTTP**) with **Secure Sockets Layer** (**SSL**)/**Transport Level Security** (**TLS**) protocol to provide encrypted communication and secure identification of a network web server. SSL provides secure connections by allowing two applications connecting over a network connection to authenticate the identity and by encrypting the data exchanged between the applications. Authentication allows a server and optionally a client to verify the identity of the application on the other end of a network connection. Encryption makes data transmitted over the network intelligible only to the intended recipient. Where message level security focuses on data in the message itself, transport-level security focuses on protecting the data while it is in transit from the sender to the recipient. With BizTalk, transport-level security can be accomplished with HTTP, FTP, WCF-BasicHttp adapters, and WCF-WSHttp adapters.

Secure communication between the BizTalk Server and an external party can be configured using one-way or two-way SSL authentication. With a one-way SSL, the server is required to present a certificate to the external party, but the external party is not required to present a certificate to the server. To successfully negotiate an SSL connection, the external party must authenticate the server, but the server will accept any external party into the connection. A one-way SSL is common on the Internet where users want to create secure connections before they share personal data. With a two-way SSL, the client also presents a certificate to the server. A server can be configured with a requirement for the clients to submit valid and trusted certificates before completing the SSL connection.

Getting ready

Depending on the type of communication, one-way or two-way SSL, you will need a certificate for yourself to get identified by another party and a certificate to authenticate the other party.

How to do it...

To have transport-level security through SSL, you need to configure the appropriate send adapter when sending a message securely to an external party. After you have deployed your BizTalk solution, you will configure Send ports that require transport security. Some steps to establish a one way SSL with BizTalk HTTP, WCF-BasicHttp, and WCF-WSHttp are discussed in the following sections.

For the HTTP Adapter you use the following configuration:

1. Create a Send Port and give it an appropriate name.
2. Select **Type HTTP** and click on **Configure**.
3. Select the **Authentication** tab.
4. Select the **Authentication type** according to your requirements.
5. Paste the **thumbprint** of the client certificate. Refer to the following screenshot:

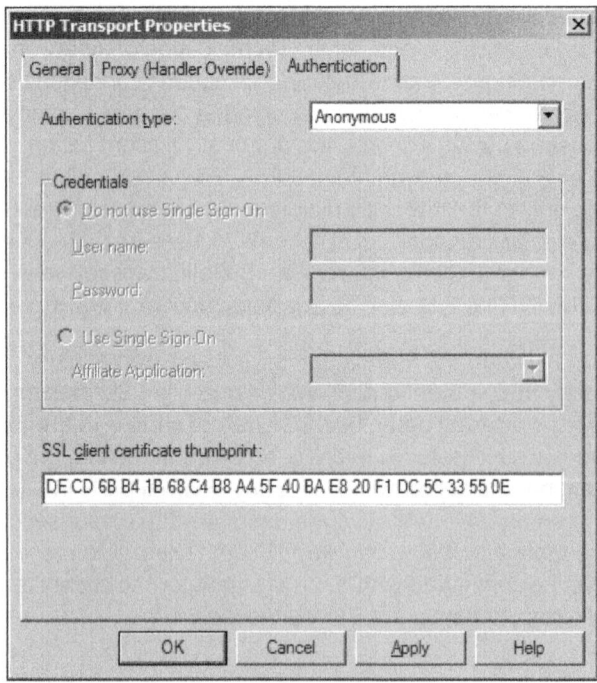

The WCF-BasicHttp adapter can be configured as follows:

1. Create a Send port and give it an appropriate name.
2. Select **Type WCF-BasicHttp** or **WCF-WSHttp** and click on **Configure**.
3. Select the **Security** Tab.
4. In **Security mode** choose **Transport**.
5. In **Transport client credential type** choose **Certificate**.
6. In **Client certificate**, click on **Browse...** and select the appropriate certificate. Refer to the following screenshot:

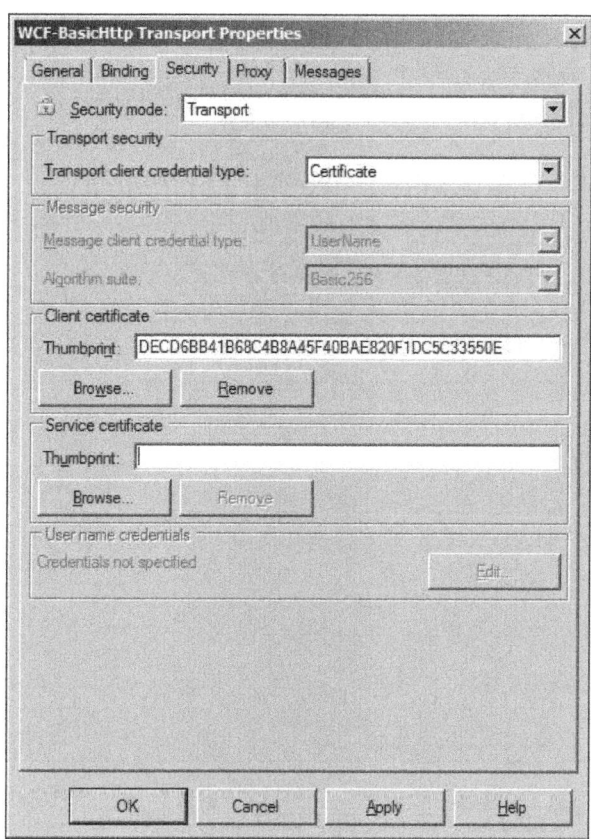

For the WCF-WSHttp adapter you can use the following configuration:

1. Create a Send port and give it an appropriate name.
2. Select **Type WCF-BasicHttp** or **WCF-WSHttp** and click on **Configure**.
3. Select the **Security** tab.

4. In **Security mode**, choose **TransportWithMessageCredential**.

5. In **Message security** choose **Certificate**.

6. Choose the appropriate **Algorithm suite**.

7. In **Client certificate**, click on **Browse...** and select the appropriate certificate. Refer to the following screenshot:

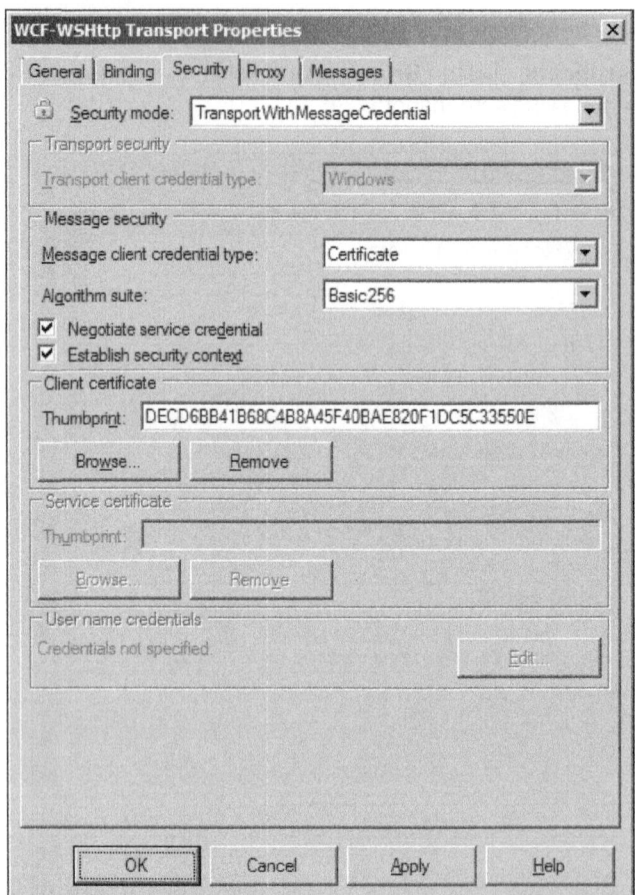

How it works...

SSL uses public key encryption technology for authentication. With public key encryption, a public key and a private key are generated for a server. These keys are related in such a way that data encrypted with the public key can only be decrypted using the corresponding private key and vice versa. The private key is carefully protected so that only the owner can decrypt messages that were encrypted using the public key.

The public key is embedded in a digital certificate with additional information describing the owner of the public key, such as the name, street address, and e-mail address. A private key and digital certificate provide the identity for the server. To make itself identified by an external party, BizTalk uses a certificate from the Personal Certificate store of the user under which the BizTalk Windows Service is running. The thumbprint of this certificate is used to configure the adapter.

The data embedded in a digital certificate is verified by a certificate authority (also referred to as a trusted certificate authority) and digitally signed with the certificate authority's digital certificate. Well-known certificate authorities include VeriSign and Entrust.net. Their digital certificates are trusted by the Windows OS by default. A trusted certificate authority establishes trust for a server.

An application participating in an SSL connection is authenticated when the other party evaluates and accepts their digital certificate. Web browsers, servers, and other SSL-enabled applications generally accept, as genuine, any digital certificate that is signed by a trusted certificate authority and is otherwise valid. For example, a digital certificate can be invalidated because it has expired or the digital certificate of the certificate authority used to sign it expired. A server certificate can be invalidated if the hostname in the digital certificate of the server does not match the hostname specified by the client.

There's more...

Find more about security recommendations for a BizTalk Server deployment in the document **Security Recommendations for a BizTalk Server Deployment** at `http://msdn.microsoft.com/en-us/library/aa546779(v=bts.70).aspx`.

In BizTalk 2010, the FTP Adapter has been enhanced and supports SSL. You can find more in the document **Enhancements to the FTP Adapter in BizTalk Server 2010** at `http://msdn.microsoft.com/en-us/library/ff629768%28v=bts.70%29.aspx`.

In general, you can review the overall security of BizTalk through MSDN articles. You can find more about it in the document **Securing Your Deployment of BizTalk Server 2010** at `http://technet.microsoft.com/en-us/library/aa577802(BTS.70).aspx`.

Richard Seroter has written a series of articles on BizTalk and WCF and one of them focuses on security patterns. That document is **BizTalk and WCF: Part II, Security Patterns** (`http://seroter.wordpress.com/biztalk-and-wcf-part-ii-security-patterns/`).

As alternatives, BizCrypto provides adapters to FTP and FTP-over-SSL client functions to your BizTalk orchestrations. You can find more about it in the document **FTP and FTPS Adapters for BizTalk** at `http://www.eldos.com/bizcrypto/biztalk-ftps-adapter.php`.

See also

▸ Refer to the *Importing certificates* recipe earlier in this chapter

5
WCF Services with BizTalk

In this chapter, we will cover:

- ► Creating a canonical schema
- ► Exposing schemas as a WCF Service
- ► Consuming WCF services in a BizTalk orchestration
- ► Consuming WCF services in a BizTalk messaging only solution
- ► Exposing orchestrations with BizTalk
- ► Exposing systems with the BizTalk Server Adapter Pack 2010

Introduction

The first thing that will come up if you talk about **Service Oriented Architecture (SOA)** is services. Services are building blocks of SOA and gain more momentum on the Web, which is an excellent platform for services. It is not just the Web, also within enterprise more and more services are being created to satisfy business needs and opening systems/applications to enable them to exchange information with each other.

BizTalk has evolved over the years and has capabilities on board to simplify exposing systems or processes and consuming services. The BizTalk WCF Services Publishing Wizard is offered by BizTalk out of the box. It offers two options—Publish orchestrations or schemas as WCF services, enabling a developer to expose schemas or orchestrations as services to be consumed by the outside world or other systems. The ability to expose existing IT investments to a broader set of consumers was one of the concepts in the SOA reference model which Microsoft set up a few years earlier. The reference model, as depicted in the following diagram, is based on three concepts expose, compose, and consume:

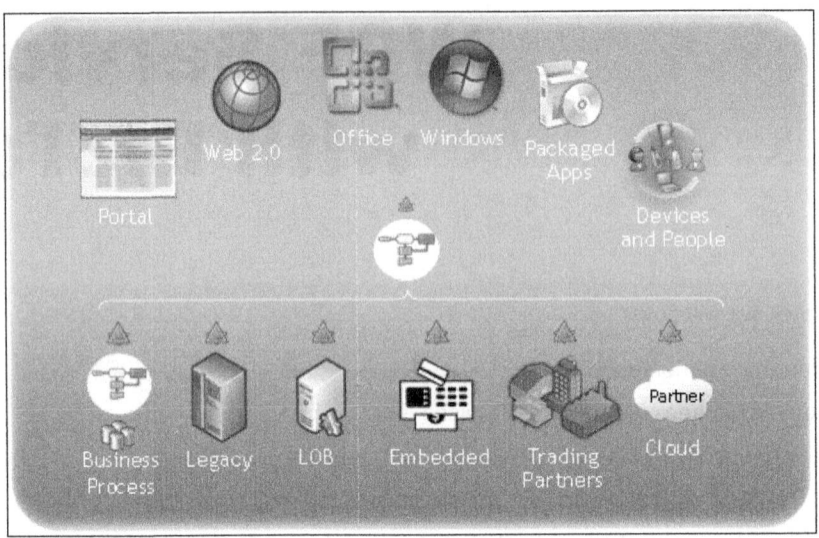

Compose focuses on combining services into applications or cross-functional business processes. Orchestration provides capability to compose services into larger constructs, such as business processes. It also enables consuming services, increase in productivity for the business, and enhancing insight in the business performance. Consumers of services can be a portal, a windows application, devices, and so on.

In composing a process, a BizTalk orchestration can consume one or more services with the Consume WCF Service Wizard which is also delivered out of the box. With this ability, BizTalk can provide services that support business processes. Yet, BizTalk focuses on exposing systems through its adapters such as the BizTalk adapter pack, host integration adapters (part of Host Integration Server included in the BizTalk package), and adapters delivered with accelerators.

In this chapter, focus lies on exposing BizTalk artefacts that is, schemas and orchestration as WCF services, consuming services, and exposing systems leveraging the BizTalk adapter pack. Another artefact that plays an important role is a schema. To achieve loose coupling between systems in BizTalk, a canonical schema can be developed.

Creating a canonical schema

A canonical schema is a design pattern, which is applied within a service-oriented paradigm, and within the BizTalk Server context to establish loose coupling between systems. Through performing transformation of messages from one system to a canonical schema and from a canonical schema to a message of another system, systems have no direct relationship with each other. A canonical schema can also be viewed as an internal schema in BizTalk and aid you in structuring your solution through the best practice of creating separate projects for maps, orchestrations, internal and external schemas.

Another advantage of using a canonical schema is that it reduces the number of transformations you need. If you need to map a few types of inbound messages coming from different parties to a few outbound messages, you can create a map to your canonical schema for each inbound schema and then a map from your canonical schema to each outbound schema. For example, if you have three types of incoming messages that need to be mapped to three types of outgoing messages, you will need to build and maintain only six maps instead of nine.

As you can see in the following diagram, without a canonical schema, you can map each incoming message to one outgoing message resulting in nine maps. When applying the pattern of a canonical schema, you will only need six maps, as you will reuse maps:

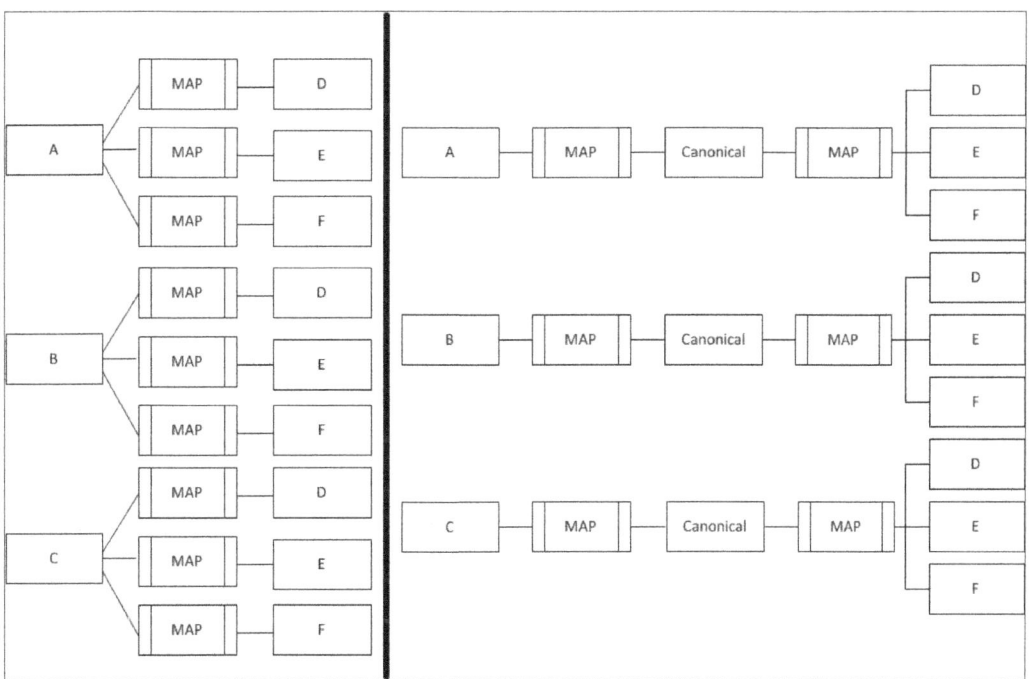

A canonical schema in BizTalk can be a combination of multiple schemas into one master schema. This schema should not be exposed to the outside world, as this would complicate the change and induce tighter coupling. A canonical schema represents a data model and the one created in this recipe is a generic schema built from scratch.

A canonical schema can also be application driven, where a single back-office application such as an ERP (SAP, Oracle E-Business Suite) system is used to generate all outgoing messages and process all incoming messages. The format in a canonical schema will match the format used in, for instance, a SAP system such as SAP IDOC. Another type of canonical structure is B2B driven and its format, which is used, is from partners such as EDIFACT. With this type, you can have very large and complex structures.

It is important that common business entities are known in an organization and the developer can craft these entities into a canonical schema and leverage reuse. These entities can exist in one leading system in an enterprise, such as SAP. You can derive your canonical schema of these entities. Another option is to create a complete canonical schema from scratch, based on the defined entities within the enterprise. This recipe will show how to create a canonical schema manually. The recipe simply shows how to build a canonical schema and the entities such as Employee, Contract, and Department which are fictive.

Getting ready

Before you start, you will need a general data model or business entity that will represent the canonical schema that is, an internal schema. For reference, you can download the source code belonging to this chapter.

How to do it...

The following steps illustrate the process of creating a canonical schema which can be found with the code accompanying this book:

1. Open Visual Studio 2010.
2. Create a new BizTalk project and give it a descriptive name.
3. Right-click on the project and choose **Add | New Item...**.
4. In the **New Item** dialog screen, choose **Schema** and name it **Employee**.
5. Rename the root element to **Employee**.

6. Create the following elements (all type `xs:string`):

   - ❑ **FirstName**
   - ❑ **LastName**
   - ❑ **FullName**
   - ❑ **EmployeeNumber**
   - ❑ **SocialSecurityNumber**
   - ❑ **Contract**
   - ❑ **Department**

7. Right-click on the project and choose **Add | New Item...**.

8. In the **New Item** dialog screen, choose **Schema** and name it **Contract**.

9. Rename the root element to **Contract**.

10. Create the following elements:

    - ❑ **Type** (`xs:string`)
    - ❑ **Function** (`xs:string`)
    - ❑ **Salary** (`xs:int`)
    - ❑ **Benefits** (`xs:int`)
    - ❑ **Pension** (`xs:int`)

11. Right-click on the project and choose **Add | New Item...**.

12. In the **New Item** dialog screen, choose **Schema** and name it **Department**.

13. Rename the root element to **Department**.

14. Create the following elements (all type `xs:string`):

    - ❑ **Name**
    - ❑ **Head**

15. Right-click on the project and choose **Add | New Item...**.

16. In the **New Item** dialog screen, choose **Schema** and name it **Canonical**.

17. Add three child records naming them **Record1**, **Record2**, and **Record3**.

18. Go to the **Properties** of **Schema** node and click on ellipsis of Imports.

19. An **Imports** dialog will pop up. Click on the **Add** button.

20. The **BizTalk Type Picker** dialog will appear with a list of the schemas you have created:

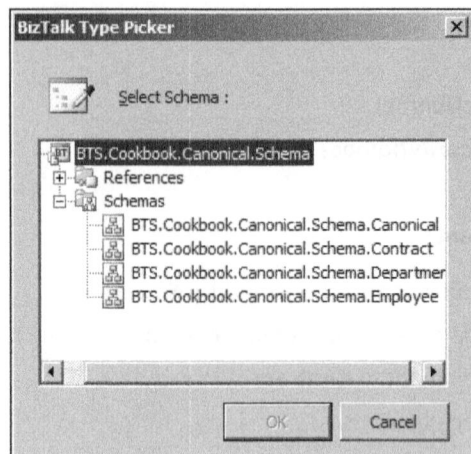

21. Select the **Employee** schema and click on **OK**.

22. Repeat steps 20 to 22 for the **Contract** and **Department** schemas.

23. Click on the **abl** button to edit the prefix for each imported schema into **emp** for **Employee**, **con** for **Contract** and **dep** for **Department**.

24. Finally, click on **OK**.

25. Select **Record1** and in **Data Structure Type** choose **emp:Employee** (reference).

26. Select **Record1** and in **Data Structure Type** choose **con:Contract** (reference).

27. Select **Record1** and in **Data Structure Type** choose **dep:Department** (reference).

28. The schema will now look similar to the following screenshot:

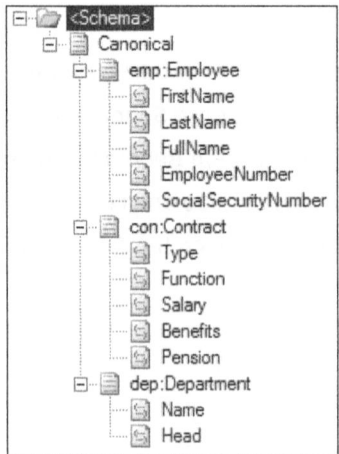

How it works...

Creating a canonical schema from scratch will mean that you have assembled a canonical schema from different generic schemas. Schemas can be created manually through Visual Studio or can be generated from existing messages. Creating a canonical schema of an entity and implementing it into your solution will help you to anticipate on changes in the future.

By using a canonical schema as an internal schema, you can introduce loose coupling and have less overheads in maintaining mappings. For instance, if you would use external schemas, your schema will be more susceptible to changes to that schema. However, with a canonical schema, you may only have to update the transformation and continue to publish the canonical messages to the `MessageBox` without further changes to any subscribing orchestrations. This really shows it is worth using canonical schemas when you have multiple subscribers to a single published message, as you have a single change to make. Canonical schemas are also very useful for versioning multiple releases of external schemas. Different versions can map to the same internal/canonical schema.

In simple messaging scenarios, using a canonical schema can result in too much overhead and you will be adding more complexity to the solution than necessary. You will be fine just using source and destination schemas for mapping.

There's more...

A general description of this pattern can be read on Wikipedia in the article **Canonical schema pattern** at `http://en.wikipedia.org/wiki/Canonical_Schema_pattern`.

There is a whitepaper called **Using canonical formats with BizTalk Server** (`http://www.motion10.com/us/library/`) that can be obtained through motion10. This article describes the best practices of using canonical formats in BizTalk.

See also

▸ Refer to the *Exposing schemas as a WCF service* recipe discussed later in this chapter, where you can see mapping between external schema, that is exposed as a web service, and an internal schema.

Exposing schemas as a WCF Service

A process can be exposed in two different ways as a service. You can either expose an orchestration as a web service or you can create web services based on the schema file. In case of an orchestration, you will be converting an HTTP SOAP request to a BizTalk message. Then you can perform all your processing based on the message within BizTalk and then return a SOAP response. With exposing schemas as a WCF Service, you can first focus on designing a schema and then you can craft your service before hosting it in BizTalk, where it resides as an endpoint. The endpoint can serve as an entry point for the process to kick-off, or aggregate some data. With this concept of exposing schemas as a service, you can push the boundaries of BizTalk and enhance connectivity with the outside world.

Getting ready

You may want to expose schemas as services for consumers. In this recipe, a sample schema is used that you can find with the code belonging to this book.

How to do it...

To have schemas exposed as a web service, you have to create your schema first:

1. Open Visual Studio 2010.
2. Create a new BizTalk project and give it a descriptive name.
3. Right-click on the project and choose **Add | New Item...**.
4. In the **New Item** dialog screen, choose **Schema** and name it **EmployeeContractService**.
5. Rename the root element to **Request**.
6. Add the record and name it **Response**.
7. Select the **EmployeeRequest** record. Add a child element and name it **SocialSecurityNumber** (type `xs:string`).
8. Add another child element and name it **FullName** (type `xs:string`).
9. Select the **EmployeeResponse** record and add the following child elements:
    - **Type** (`xs:string`)
    - **Function** (`xs:string`)
    - **Salary** (`xs:int`)
    - **Benefits** (`xs:int`)
    - **Pension** (`xs:int`)
10. Sign the project with a strong name. Provide the project with a strong name key and build it. Subsequently, go to the deployment and give it an appropriate application name.

Now, you have your schema ready and you can create a BizTalk application through the management console:

1. Open **BizTalk Management Console**.

2. Navigate to **Applications** and right-click on it. Then, select **New | Application**.

3. Give a name to the application.

The following steps involve using **BizTalk WCF Service Publishing Wizard**:

1. Navigate to **BizTalk Server Menu** on your system.

2. Choose **BizTalk WCF Service Publishing Wizard**.

3. A dialog will appear, welcoming you, click on **Next**.

4. A **WCF Service Type** dialog appears and you can choose **Transport Type** (**WCF-BasicHttp**, **WCF-WSHttp**, or **WCF-CustomIsolated**). Choose **WCF-BasicHttp**.

5. Check the option **Enable on-premise metadata exchange**.

6. Check the option **Create BizTalk receive location in the following application**.

7. Choose the BizTalk application you just created.

8. The next dialog will show options for creating the service, choose **Publish schemas as WCF service** and click on **Next**:

 We can perform these steps directly from Visual Studio, no need to go to the BizTalk Management Console.

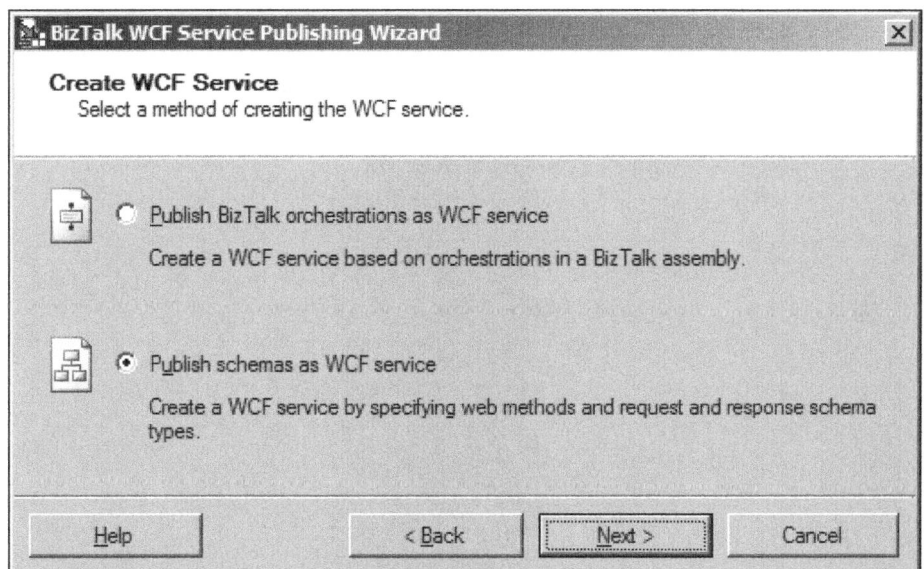

9. You can now describe your service by giving it a name and naming the operation:

    a. Right-click on **Service1** and rename it appropriately.

    b. Right-click on **Operation1** and rename it appropriately.

    c. Right-click on **Request** and select **Schema Type**. A dialog will appear and you will need to browse to the .dll file containing the schema you made. You will see the schema and the corresponding message types.

    d. Choose **Request Type** and click on **OK**.

    e. Right-click on **Response** and select the schema type. A dialog will appear, as shown in the following screenshot:

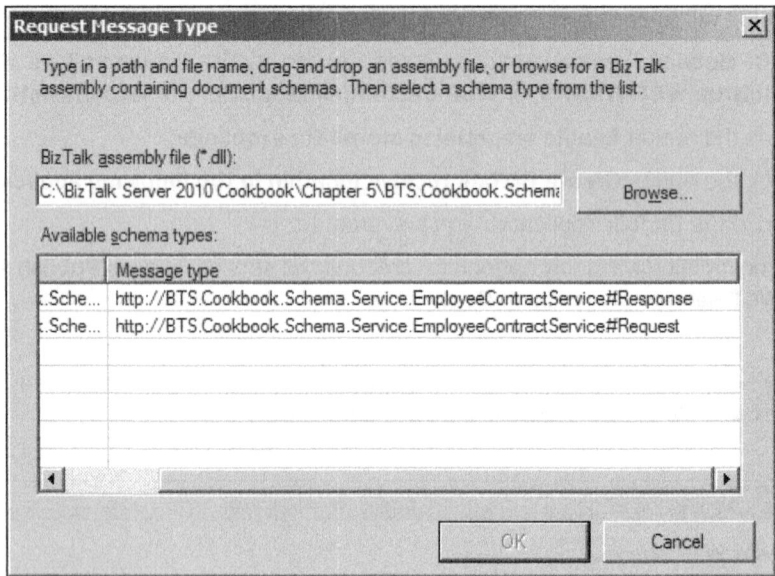

    f. Choose **Response Type** and click on **OK**.

10. The WCF Service would look similar to the following screenshot:

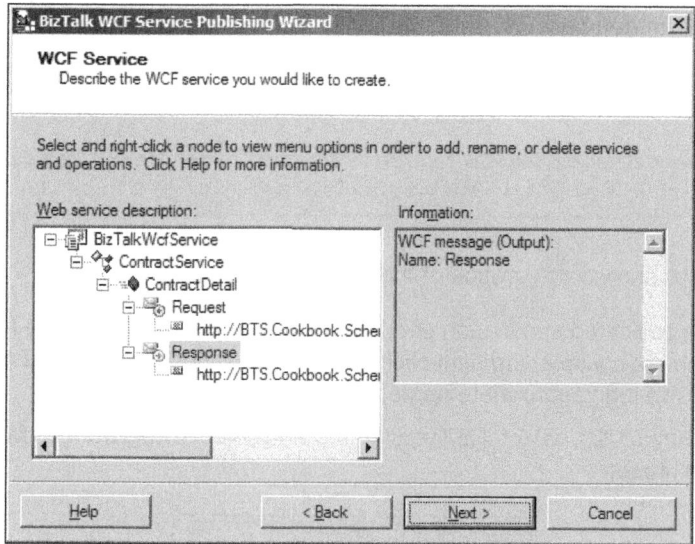

11. Click on **Next** and a new dialog will appear giving you an opportunity to give a name to the service for the target namespace. You can leave it as it is and click on **Next**.

12. In the next dialog, you need to determine the location (`http://host[:port]/path`) of your service and check **Allow anonymous access to WCF Service** if you require. Click on **Next**.

13. The final dialog will show a summary of options you selected. You can click on **Create Now**.

14. Now, the wizard will create the service, receive locations in the application, and host the service on IIS.

15. When the wizard is done, it will display whether the creation was succesful or not and give you access to see the location of the service. You can click on **Finish**.

16. You can now go to **BizTalk Administration Console** and navigate to the application and select **Receive Location**. You will see a **Receive Location** with the **URI** you chose. Right-click on the location and enable it.

Finally, to make the service accessible, you need to ensure that the application pool in IIS is set up properly. The DefaultAppPool, for instance, does not have sufficient rights to access the BizTalk Management database:

> Server Error in '/BTS.Schema.Service' Application.
>
> *Cannot open database "BizTalkMgmtDb" requested by the login. The login failed. Login failed for user 'IIS APPPOOL\DefaultAppPool'.*

The following steps show configuration of the service on IIS:

1. Create a dedicated application pool for the service on IIS 7. Go to the IIS 7 management console and right-click on application pools, select **Add Application Pool...**. Give it an appropriate name.

2. With BizTalk 2010, select .NET version 4.0 and select **Integrated** as **Managed pipeline mode**:

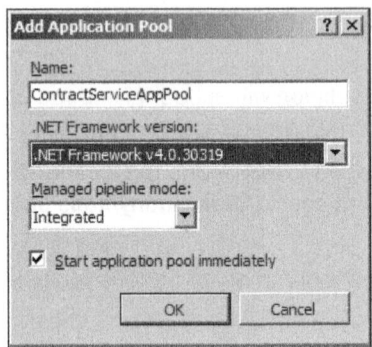

3. Click on **OK**.

4. Right-click on the newly-created application pool and select **Application Pool Defaults**.

5. In the **Process Model** section, select **Identity** and click on the ellipsis (**...**).

6. You can now set the custom account, that has the appropiate right to the BizTalk management database, by choosing **Set Custom Account**.

7. A new dialog will pop up, as shown in the following screenshot:

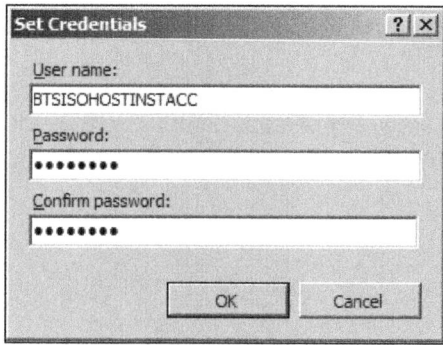

8. Set the **User name** and **Password**, as shown in the previous screenshot, and click on **OK**.

9. You can now go to your service by selecting it in the IIS Management Console and then choose **Advanced Settings** in the action pane.

10. Select **Application Pool** and click on the ellipsis (**...**).

11. A **Select Application Pool** dialog will pop up and you can select the newly-created **Application Pool**.

12. Click on **OK** and then again click on **OK**.

13. You can now open a browser and go to your service that is, `http://localhost/path/servicename.svc`, as shown in the following screenshot:

BizTalkServiceInstance Service

You have created a service.

To test this service, you will need to create a client and use it to call the service. You can do this using the svcutil.exe tool from the command line with the following syntax:

```
svcutil.exe http://win-8bpntqktj5m/BTS.Schema.Service/ContractService.svc?wsdl
```

This will generate a configuration file and a code file that contains the client class. Add the two files to your client application and use the generated client class to call the Service. For example:

C#

```
class Test
{
    static void Main()
    {
        ContractServiceClient client = new ContractServiceClient();

        // Use the 'client' variable to call operations on the service.

        // Always close the client.
        client.Close();
    }
}
```

Visual Basic

```
Class Test
    Shared Sub Main()
        Dim client As ContractServiceClient = New ContractServiceClient()
        ' Use the 'client' variable to call operations on the service.

        ' Always close the client.
        client.Close()
    End Sub
End Class
```

How it works...

A schema can be exposed by using in the BizTalk WCF Service Publishing Wizard, where a developer is guided through a number of steps before it creates the WCF Service that will be hosted on IIS. These steps involve choosing the desired binding:

- WCF-BasicHttp
- WCF-WSHttp
- WCF-CustomIsolated

By using first binding, WCF-BasicHttp, you can do cross-computer communication with legacy ASMX-based web services and clients that conform to the WS-I Basic Profile 1.1, using either the HTTP or HTTPS transport with text encoding. However, you will not be able to take advantage of the features that are supported by WS-protocols, which is where second binding, WCF-WSHttp comes into the picture. The last binding, WCF-CustomIsolated, enables you to use the WCF extensibility components in the BizTalk Server with an isolated host.

Besides binding, you can describe the service by giving it a name and you can name the operation or operations. You can add more operations to the service if you wish to do so. In the wizard, you can also determine the location of the service (`http://host[:port]/path`) and determine security (that is, allow anonymous or not). Other security details of the service are set in IIS while configuring the application pool.

The wizard generates the following files in the root folder (that is, `C:\inetpub\wwwroot\servicename\`) of the created web application:

- **WCF Service**: It contains metadata of the service. It is a `.svc` file.
- **Web Config**: It is the ASP.NET configuration file that contains information for the ASP.NET Web application behaviors, the published WCF service behaviors, the metadata endpoint, and the BizTalk-specific settings.
- **In AppData directory**:
  - **BizTalk schema** (`xsd` **file**): It defines the structure of the XML instance messages, which are used in the WCF receive location.
  - `SchemaIndex` (`xml` **file**): It is a file that indicates the XML schema files used in the WCF receive location.
  - `Serialization` (`xsd` **file**): It is a schema exported by `DataContractSerializer` for the types, elements, and attributes from the namespace (`http://schemas.microsoft.com/2003/10/Serialization/`).
  - `ServiceDescription` (`xml` **file**): It is a file that describes the published WCF Service contracts including the message types.

▶ **In Temp directory**:

❑ `BindingInfo` **(**`xml` **file)**: It is a binding file that can be imported by the development command-line tool or wizard to configure the receive locations. The published WCF Services do not use this file in the Temp folder at runtime.

❑ `WcfServiceDescription` **(**`xml` **file)**: It is a file that summarizes the settings that you used with the BizTalk WCF Service Publishing Wizard to create this web application. The published WCF services do not use this file and the Temp folder at runtime.

You now have an endpoint (interface) at the receive location of the BizTalk application. The contract is defined by a schema and the binding is configured by running the wizard. Implementation of the service itself is for processing the message separated from the interface.

Basically, now you have a service based on a schema. An orchestration can, for instance, subscribe to the message, perform the processing, and return a message that will be returned to the caller of the service. Another option is to have a solicit response to the Send port which communicates with a database, ERP system (such as SAP, Oracle E-Business Suite) or any other web service.

There's more...

This recipe demonstrated how to publish schemas as a WCF Service and how you can use the BizTalk WCF Service Publishing Wizard for it. The use of the wizard is also explained on MSDN:

▶ **How to Use the BizTalk WCF Service Publishing Wizard to Publish Schemas as WCF Services**: `http://msdn.microsoft.com/en-us/library/bb246047(v=bts.70).aspx`

▶ **BizTalk WCF Service Publishing Wizard**: `http://msdn.microsoft.com/en-us/library/bb226547(=bts.70).aspx`

For deciding which binding to choose while publishing your schema(s) as services, you have to consider your requirements and decide what fits them best. You can read about the bindings on MSDN:

▶ **WCF-BasicHttp Adapter**: `http://msdn.microsoft.com/en-us/library/bb246098(v=BTS.70).aspx`

▶ **WCF-WSHttp Adapter**: `http://msdn.microsoft.com/en-us/library/bb226477(v=BTS.70).aspx`

▶ **WCF-CustomIsolated Adapter**: `http://msdn.microsoft.com/en-us/library/bb245951(v=BTS.70).aspx`

See also

▶ Refer to the *Exposing orchestrations with BizTalk* recipe discussed later in this chapter. The BizTalk WCF Service Publishing Wizard plays an important role in this recipe.

Consuming WCF Services in a BizTalk orchestration

With BizTalk 2010, you can use the Consume WCF Service Wizard, which comes out of the box and enables you to consume web services from BizTalk. These days there might be many web services in your enterprise, which you may need to consume in your process or web services outside your enterprise. To call a web service, you will need a **Web Services Description Language** (**WSDL**) file of the service. This file provides a machine-readable description of how the service can be called, what parameters it expects, and what data structures it returns. With the Consume WCF Service Wizard, this file can be imported and BizTalk will turn it into a schema that can be read in the same way as a standard XSD, with each web method defining its own schema.

Getting ready

You will need to have the WSDL file or the URI (location) of the WSDL you want to consume. The code accompanied with this book contains a service that you can set up and host on IIS. This service will be used in detailing this recipe. For reference, you can download the source code belonging to this chapter.

How to do it...

The following steps will show how to consume a web service in BizTalk:

1. Open Visual Studio 2010.
2. Create a new BizTalk project and give it a descriptive name.
3. Right-click on the project and choose **Add | Add Generated Items...**.
4. Select **Consume WCF Service** and click on **Add**.
5. You will see the wizard pop up with a welcome message, "**This wizard guides you through the process of consuming a WCF service.**" Then click on **Next**.
6. The next screen will show two options about how to consume metadata of the service. You can choose the first option, which more closely resembles the **Add Web Reference** option—which is an option to choose if the service is running on host. Click on **Next**.

7. In the metadata endpoint step of the wizard, you can enter the **URL** (**MetaData Address**) of the service with the extension **?WSDL**, as shown in the following screenshot, and click on **Get**:

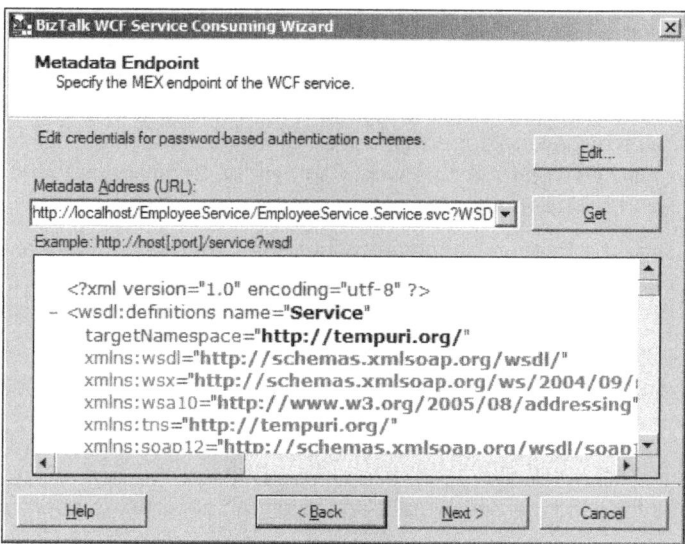

8. The next window will show the summary of the operation. You can click on **Import**.

9. When the import operation has been performed, a final screen will show the result of the import stating that is completed. Click on **Finish**.

10. You can use the generated orchestration (.odx) to consume the service, or create a new orchestration, or rename it if you do wish to redo work.

11. From the toolbox, drag the following onto the design surface in top-down order; the configuration is shown in the following screenshot:

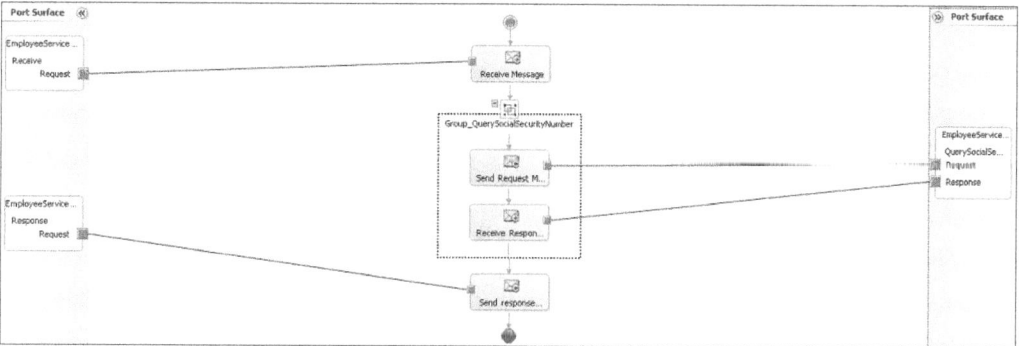

▸ Drag the **Receive** shape to receive the initial message. Configure this shape to use this message, activate the orchestration, and to use an orchestration Receive port. The initial message is of the same message type as the request message type for service.

▸ Drag the **Group** shape below the Receive shape and give it a descriptive name.

▸ Drag the **Send** shape in the **Group** shape and give it a descriptive name. Configure this shape to use the initial message to send. It is possible that you may have to perform a transform of the initial message to request the message type for the service. Connect the Send shape to the generated Send port of the service.

▸ Drag the **Receive** shape below the **Send** shape and give it a descriptive name. Configure this shape to use the response message type of the service. Connect the Receive shape which generates the Receive port of the service.

▸ Below the **Group** shape, place a Send shape and give it a descriptive name. Configure this shape to use the response message type of the service and use an orchestration Send port.

12. Sign the project with a strong name.

13. Subsequently, go to the deployment and give it an appropriate application name.

14. Build and deploy the BizTalk project.

15. Create a Receive port and a receive location to receive messages from the filesystem.

16. Import the binding file created by the Consume Wizard, which will generate an appropriate Send port for calling the service.

17. Create a Send port for sending a response message to the file.

How it works...

The BizTalk WCF Service Consuming Wizard guides the developer, to be able to consume a WCF Service in an orchestration. With this wizard, a wrapper around the WCF proxy is created, which can be invoked in a BizTalk orchestration. When running the wizard, the user enters information in a couple of pre-defined steps, such as selecting an existing **metadata exchange** (**MEX**) endpoint. When the wizard completes, the schemas and types necessary to consume the WCF Services are added to the BizTalk project. Basically, a series of files are added to the BizTalk project. These files include:

▸ `<servicename>_tempuri_org.xsd`: It contains all the operation contracts.

▸ `<servicename>_ Service_schemas_microsoft_com_2003_10_ Serialization.xsd`: It contains all the base XSD types.

▸ `<servicename>.odx`: It holds the multi-part message types and port types for calling the WCF service.

- `<servicename>.BindingInfo.xml`: It is a binding file for the Send port which uses the identified transport.
- `<servicename>_Custom.BindingInfo.xml`: It is another binding file for the WCF-custom adapter, which surfaces many more WCF properties that you may want to use.

These generated files greatly reduce complexity of consuming a WCF Service in BizTalk. The created orchestration can be renamed or a new one is created using message types and ports, which prevent you from redoing your work when the service you consume is changed. This wizard will have to run again resulting in regeneration of all the files.

The `BizTalkServiceInstance.BindingInfo.xml` and `BizTalkServiceInstance_Custom.BindingInfo.xml` can be imported into the BizTalk application generating the Send port for transport. While importing the generated binding file, the `WCF.Action` property, for instance, will be populated in the action mapping format. These files greatly aid the developer in configuring ports for communication with the WCF Service and save a lot of time.

There's more...

This recipe illustrates how to consume a service through a request response operation (two-way). This is the most common message exchange pattern. You can also implement one-way (fire and forget) request and handle exceptions. Through the blog post **BizTalk and WCF: Part I, Operation Patterns** (`http://seroter.wordpress.com/biztalk-and-wcf-part-i-operation-patterns/`) by Richard Seroter, you can see how that is done.

MSDN provides numerous walkthroughs and you can also find one on consuming a WCF service using the WCF-BasicHttp Adapter in the document called **Walkthrough: Consuming WCF Services with the WCF-BasicHttp Adapter** at `http://msdn.microsoft.com/en-us/library/bb246019(v=bts.70).aspx`.

On MSDN you will also found more background information on how to use the BizTalk WCF Service Consuming Wizard in the document called **How to Use the BizTalk WCF Service Consuming Wizard to Consume a WCF Service** at `http://msdn.microsoft.com/en-us/library/bb226552(v=bts.70).aspx`.

See also

- Another way to consume WCF Services is through a messaging solution, where you do not use an orchestration. For this, you can refer to the *Consuming WCF Services in a BizTalk messaging only solution* recipe discussed later in this chapter.

Consuming WCF Services in a BizTalk messaging only solution

In the previous recipe, *Consuming WCF Services in a BizTalk orchestration*, you can read how to consume a WCF Service in an orchestration. Of course there are situations, where you do not need the overhead of orchestration that processes a message in a series of steps. If the processing of a message can be done with the core BizTalk messaging components (Receive ports, Send ports, pipelines, maps, and subscriptions), a messaging-only solution is sufficient. Generally, when complexity and latency need to be kept at a minimum, you need to focus on pure messaging and keep orchestration out of the equation. Orchestration induces an overhead with round trips to the `MessageBox` database as it is stateful and complex with a series of shapes in a flow.

Getting ready

You will need to have the WSDL file or URI (location) of the service you want to consume. The code accompanied with this book contains a service that you can set up and host on IIS. This service will be used in detailing this recipe. For reference, you can download the source code belonging to this chapter.

How to do it...

The first step is to consume a web service according to the following steps:

1. Open Visual Studio 2010.
2. Create a new solution and give it a descriptive name.
3. Create a new BizTalk project and give it a descriptive name.
4. Right-click on the project and choose **Add | Add Generated Items...**.
5. Select **Consume WCF Service** and click on **Add**.
6. You will see a pop up of this wizard with a welcome message – **This wizard guides you through the process of consuming a WCF Service**. Click on **Next**.
7. The next screen will show two options about how to consume metadata of the service. You can choose the first option, which more closely resembles the **Add Web Reference** option—which is an option to choose if the service is running on host. Click on **Next**.
8. In the metadata endpoint step of this wizard, you can enter the URL (metadata address) of the service with the extension **?WSDL** (refer to the *Consuming WCF Services in a BizTalk orchestration* recipe) and click on **Get**.

9. The generated orchestration can be deleted as it will not be used in this solution.

10. Then click on **Add | New Item...**. Then select **Schema**.

11. Give the schema an appropriate namespace.

12. Rename the root node to **Request**. Add another record to the schema and name it **Response**. Now, you have a multi-rooted schema.

13. Add elements to both nodes, as shown in the following screenshot:

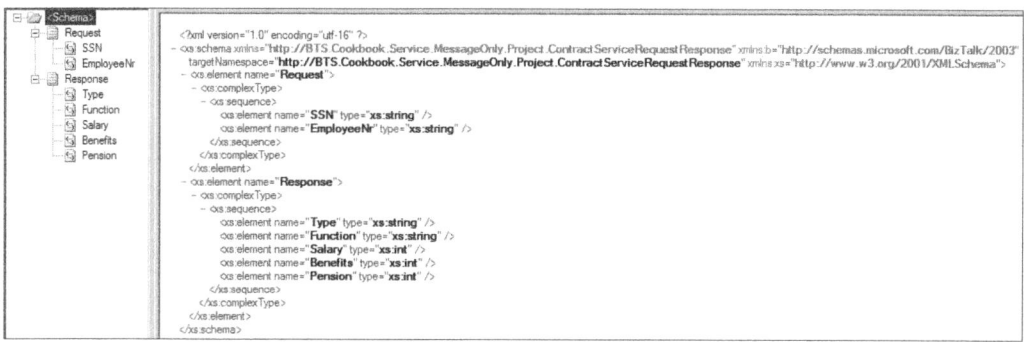

14. Sign the project with a strong name.

15. Subsequently, go to the deployment and give it an appropriate application name.

16. Build this project.

17. Add the project to your solution. This project will contain the maps.

18. Add reference to the project with the schemas.

19. Right-click on the project and choose **Add | New Item...**. Then, select **Map** and give it a descriptive name.

20. **BizTalk Mapper** will appear and you can click on **Open Source Schema**.

21. **BizTalk Type Picker** will appear and you can navigate to the schema you created. Select **Request**.

22. Click on **Open Destination Schema** and **BizTalk Type Picker** will appear again. Select the schema generated by the wizard named ContractService_tempuri_org. Select the correct node (that is, request message).

23. Connect the elements from each schema with each other, as shown in the following screenshot:

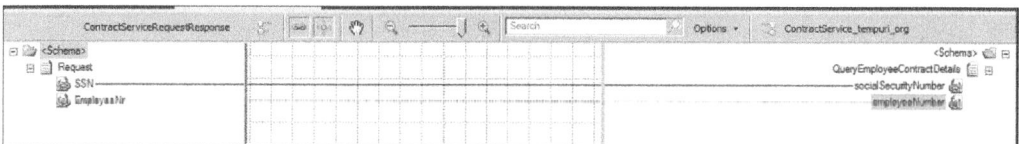

24. Right-click on the project and choose **Add | New Item....** Select **Map** and give it a descriptive name.

25. **BizTalk Mapper** will appear and you can click on **Open Source Schema**.

26. **BizTalk Type Picker** will appear and you can navigate to the schema you created. Select **Response**.

27. Click on **Open Destination Schema** and **BizTalk Type Picker** will appear again. Select the schema generated by the wizard named **ContractService_tempuri_org**. Select the correct node (that is, response message).

28. Connect elements from each schema with each other, as shown in the following screenshot:

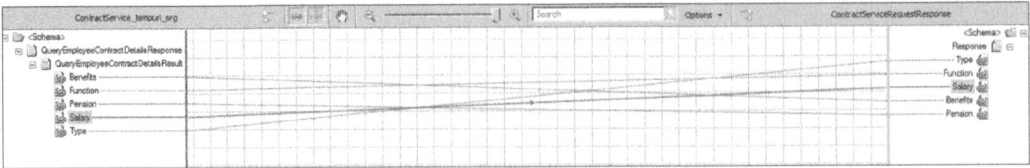

29. Sign the project with a strong name.

30. Subsequently, go to the deployment and give it an appropriate application name.

31. Build this project.

32. Deploy this project. The project with maps and referenced schema project will be deployed.

33. Open **BizTalk Administration Console** and navigate to the application.

34. Right-click on the application, select **Import | Bindings....**

35. A dialog will open and you can navigate to the generated Custom.BindingInfo file and click on **Open**. A Send port will be generated.

36. Click on the generated Send port. Select **Outbound Maps**. In **Outbound Maps**, select the custom-created schema. The map and the target document will be filled in automatically.

37. Subsequently, select **Inbound Maps**. In **Inbound Maps**, select the generated schema, **ContractService_tempuri_org**. The map and the target document will be filled in automatically.

38. Select filters. Choose property **BTS.MessageType** and type in the value `http://BTS.Cookbook.Service.MessageOnly.Project.ContractServiceReques tResponse#Request` (custom-created schema target namespace #rootelement request).

39. Create a Send port and give it an appropriate name.

40. In the newly created Send port, select the filters and choose the property **BTS.MessageType**. Type in the value `http://BTS.Cookbook.Service. MessageOnly.Project.ContractServiceRequestResponse#Response` (custom-created schema target namespace #rootelement response).

41. Configure this Send port to use the File Adapter and send a message to the folder `out`.

42. Create a Receive port with the corresponding receive location. Give appropriate names to both of them. Configure the location to use the File Adapter and pick up the files from folder `in`.

43. Right-click on the application and click on **Start**.

How it works...

The WCF Service can be consumed without using an orchestration. The BizTalk WCF Service Consuming Wizard results in schemas and types necessary to consume the WCF service. The generated orchestration is of no use and can be deleted. The service is called through the Send port and it can call itself by getting initialized through the inbound message, which is routed to the Send port and mapped to the corresponding request message of the service. The response message is subsequently mapped back to the expected response message.

The service is called indirectly through BizTalk by the application or system that wants to consume the service. The system/application does not have any knowledge on where the service resides or how to call it. In this recipe, a request message can be offered to the receive location (folder) and that message is routed to the Send port that has a subscription on the message type. The message is transformed to request the message format for the service. The service is called and the response is received. The response is transformed back to the expected format by another Send port that has a subscription on the message type. This message is sent to another folder.

In the following diagram, you can see the message flow and transformations taking place at the send side. You can opt for the receive side and/or in combination with transforming to and from the canonical schema to enhance loose coupling:

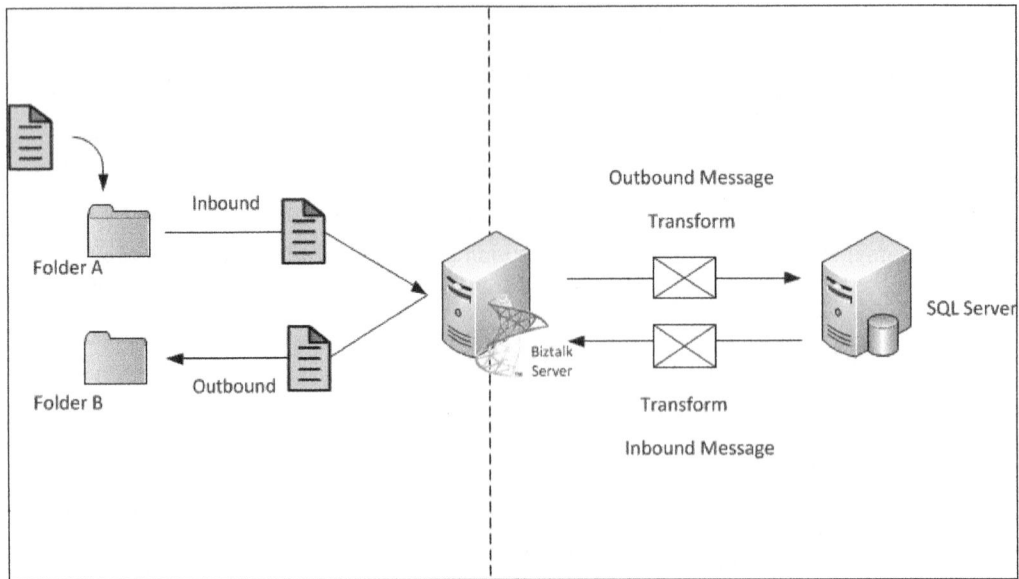

This approach can be beneficial in low-latency scenarios. Yet in hosting services Windows Server AppFabric can be a better alternative. The BizTalk MessageBox can be a bottleneck when it comes to low-latency. However, BizTalk offers a great number of an adapters, which offers more interoperability than Windows Server AppFabric. A BizTalk Messaging-only solution offers better performance, but less control. As discussed in the previous recipe *Consuming WCF Services in a BizTalk orchestration*, you can have more control through usage of orchestration. However, an orchestration means more roundtrips to `MessageBox`, which impacts on the performance more than the message-only solution.

There's more...

The concept of consuming the WCF Services without an orchestration is also detailed in *SOA Patterns with BizTalk Server 2009, Richard Seroter, Packt Publishing*. You can find it at `http://www.packtpub.com/soa-patterns-with-biztalk-server-2009/book`. It shows how to implement SOA concepts in BizTalk solutions.

See also

▶ This recipe showed how to use WCF Services in a messaging-only solution calling a backend system. Another option to get data from a back system is described in the *Exposing systems with the BizTalk Server Adapter Pack 2010* recipe discussed later in this chapter.

Exposing orchestrations with BizTalk

A BizTalk orchestration can be called as a service from an outside application. By exposing it as a service, you are able to call it from the application, as you would normally do with other web services. Exposed orchestrations supporting a generic process can be reused within your enterprise. By exposing orchestrations, you can take advantage of core BizTalk capabilities, such as error handling, document tracking, and integration into downstream BizTalk via the publish/subscribe architecture. From a service-oriented standpoint, you can extend outside your BizTalk environment and support creation of composite applications.

Getting ready

You will need to have an orchestration to expose. The project containing the orchestration must be built before running the BizTalk WCF Service Publishing Wizard. The orchestration must have at least one Receive port whose type modifier is public. The code accompanied with this book contains an orchestration that you can build and use in this recipe.

How to do it...

Using BizTalk, an orchestration can be exposed as a service via the BizTalk WCF Service Publishing Wizard, an out of the box tool which comes with BizTalk. With this tool, you can expose an orchestration as a service. Perform the following steps:

The first step is to create a BizTalk application through the management console:

1. Open the BizTalk Management Console.
2. Navigate to **Applications** and right-click on it. Then, select **New | Application**.
3. Give a name to the application.

The following steps involve using the BizTalk WCF Service Publishing Wizard:

1. Navigate to **BizTalk Server Menu** on your system.
2. Choose **BizTalk WCF Service Publishing Wizard**.

3. You can also choose to open the wizard through Visual Studio:

   a. Open the project in Visual Studio containing the orchestration you want to expose.

   b. In the menu, navigate to **Tools** and choose **BizTalk WCF Service Publishing Wizard**.

4. A dialog will appear, welcoming you. Click on **Next**.

5. The **WCF Service Type** dialog appears and you can choose **Transport Type** (**WCF-BasicHttp**, **WCF-WSHttp**, or **WCF-CustomIsolated**). Choose **WCF-WsHttp**.

6. Check the option **Enable on-premise metadata exchange**.

7. Check the option **Create BizTalk receive locations in the following application**.

8. Choose the BizTalk application you just created.

9. The next dialog will show options for creating the service, choose **Publish BizTalk orchestration as WCF service** and click on **Next**:

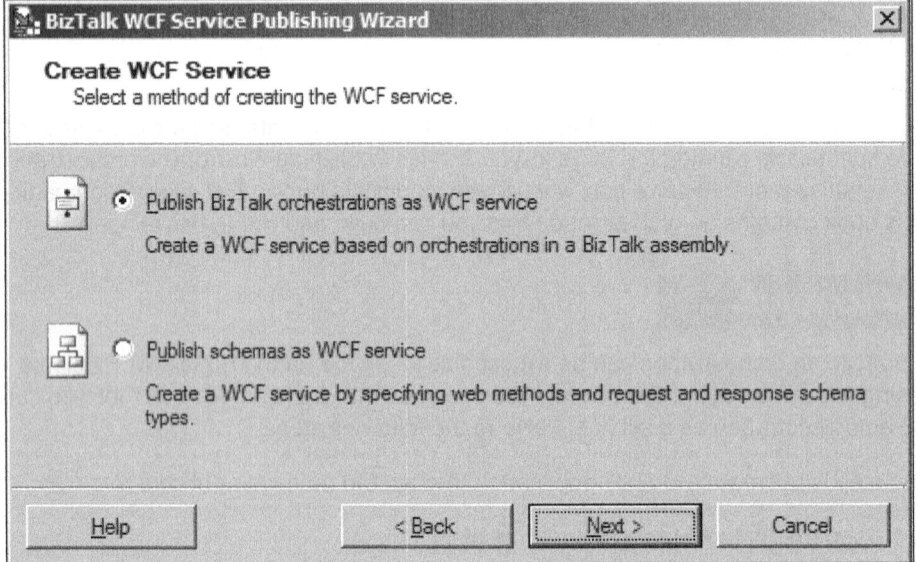

10. On the next dialog of BizTalk, in the BizTalk assembly file (`*.dll`) textbox, type the name of the BizTalk assembly file, or click on **Browse**, to browse to the assembly containing the orchestration(s) to publish, and then click on **Next**.

11. Now, you will see a dialog with orchestrations and ports, which enable you to choose the orchestration to expose (it depends if there are multiple orchestrations in the assembly file). Choose the orchestration and click on **Next**.

12. The next dialog will appear giving you an opportunity to give a name to the service for the target namespace. You can leave it as it is and click on **Next**.

13. In the subsequent dialog, you need to determine the location (`http://host[:port]/path`) of your service and check **Allow anonymous access to WCF Service**, if you require so. Click on **Next**.

14. The final dialog will show a summary of the options you selected. You can click on **Create Now**.

15. When the wizard finishes the operation, it will display whether the creation was succesful or not and give you access to see the location of the service. Then, you can click on **Finish**.

Finally, to make the service accessible, you need to ensure that the application pool in IIS is set up properly. The DefaultAppPool, for instance, does not have sufficient rights to access the BizTalk Management database. The *Exposing schemas as a WCF Service* recipe discussed earlier in this chapter, details more about how to configure the service on IIS 7.

The orchestration which is being exposed, including schema(s), needs to be deployed to the BizTalk runtime. The following steps describe how to configure the application:

1. In the **BizTalk Administration Console**, navigate to the application.

2. Right-click on the application and select **Configure**.

3. Select the orchestration and assign a host to it.

4. Assign the Receive port to the Inbound logical port (this port is generated by the wizard).

5. Next, go to the receive location and right-click on **Select properties**.

6. Click on **Configure** and go through the tabs and fill in appropriate values (that is, **Security**).

7. For testing purposes, you can set security to none first, to be able to test the orchestration quickly.

To be able to consume the orchestration from .NET applications, you need to reference the service.

How it works...

The BizTalk WCF Service Publishing Wizard is used to expose an orchestration as a service. While launching the BizTalk WCF Service Publishing Wizard, the orchestration is interrogated and the Receive port is created with the appropriate binding. Working of the wizard is the same as the WCF Service while exposing the schema. You need to choose a binding:

► WCF-BasicHttp

► WCF-WSHttp

► WCF-CustomIsolated

Then, you need to describe the service by giving it a name and naming the operation or operations. You can add more operations to the service if you wish to do so. In the wizard, you can also determine the location of the service (`http://host[:port]/path`) and determine security (that is, allow anonymous or not). Other security details of the service are set in IIS, while configuring the application pool. This wizard generates a number of files, which are also described in the *Exposing schemas as a WCF Service* recipe, discussed earlier in this chapter.

Now, you have an endpoint (interface) at the receive location of the BizTalk application. The contract is defined by the schema and the binding is configured by running the wizard. Implementation of the service itself is for processing the message that is separated from the interface. Processing is done in orchestration. The developer can create an application which references the service endpoint and sends requests which are published in `MessageBox` and picked up by the orchestration to process.

There's more...

With the BizTalk WCF Service Publishing Wizard, you can publish orchestrations as WCF Services. It is detailed on MSDN in the document **How to Use the BizTalk WCF Service Publishing Wizard to Publish Orchestrations as WCF Services** at `http://msdn.microsoft.com/en-us/library/bb226564(v=BTS.70).aspx`.

There are advantages and disadvantages when it comes to exposing schemas and/or orchestrations as services. Those are listed in the post **Orchestration VS Schemas as a Web Service (BizTalk Web Services Publishing Model)** at `http://lostechies.blogspot.com/2011/03/orchestration-vs-schemas-as-web-service.html`.

See also

▶ The BizTalk WCF Service Publishing Wizard can also be used to expose schemas as WCF services. For this, you can refer to the *Exposing schemas as a WCF Service* recipe, discussed earlier in this chapter.

Exposing systems with the BizTalk Server Adapter Pack 2010

As the BizTalk Server evolved, the number of adapters grew and the Enterprise Adapters became first class citizens of the BizTalk adapter's collection. Out of the box, BizTalk offers a lot of adapters that support numerous databases, protocols, and applications. The BizTalk Server Adapter Pack 2010 extends the number of adapters to provide more integration capabilities. It provides connectivity to SAP, Oracle E-Business Suite, Siebel, and Databases such as SQL and Oracle databases. It is a collection of key **Line of Business** (**LOB**) application adapters that enable any Windows application to integrate with LOB applications using the **Windows Communication Foundation** (**WCF**) programming model.

The BizTalk Server Adapter Pack 2010 gets installed easily through the wizard that guides you through the installation process. As a developer, you can install the WCF-based adapters supported by the latest versions of LOB systems, while you can also install the Microsoft BizTalk Adapters for enterprise applications (non-WCF LOB Adapters), which support older versions of LOB systems. During installation, a few components such as the Add Adapter Service Reference Plug-in and the Consume Adapter Service are installed. The second one is very useful when you want to expose operations in LOB within the enterprise.

Getting ready

For this recipe, the BizTalk Server Adapter Pack 2010 needs to be installed. Installation is pretty straightforward and is guided by the wizard. With the code of this book, the SQL script for creating the database and table is provided.

How to do it...

The following steps will show how to generate schemas to be connected to an external system (for simplicity, the external system is the SQL Server):

1. Open Visual Studio 2010.
2. Create a new BizTalk project and give it a descriptive name.
3. Right-click on the project and choose **Add | Add Generated Items...**.
4. Select **Consume Adapter Service** and click on **Add**.

5. A new dialog screen will appear, as shown in the following screenshot:

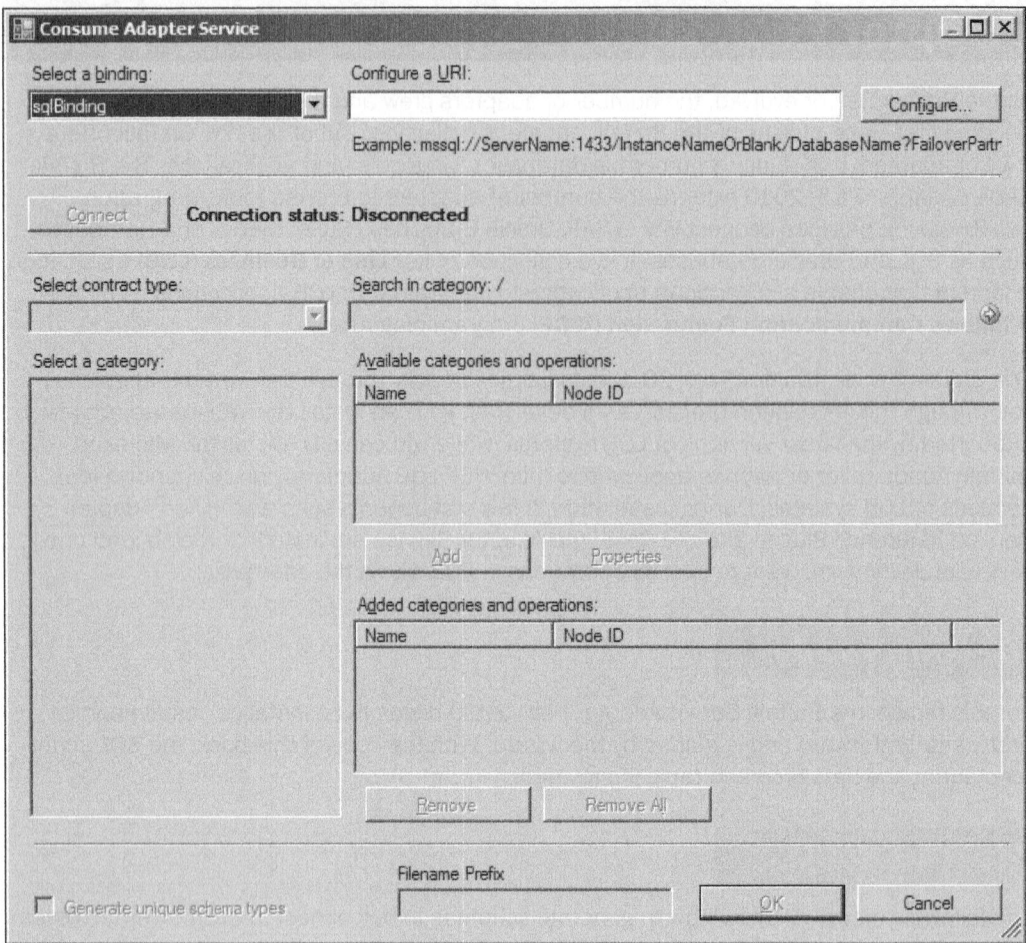

6. In **Select a binding**, choose **sqlBinding**.

7. Click on **Configure** and in the first tab, **Security,** you can choose the appropriate **Client credential type**. Leave it as **None**.

8. In the next tab, **URI Properties**, fill in the properties for **Initial Catalog** and **Server**.

9. In the last tab, **Binding Properties**, you can configure the properties for the binding. Leave properties as it is.

10. Click on **OK**. The **Connect** button is now enabled and you can click on it.

11. If the connection succeeds, you will see that the **Select a category** box is filled with categories. Select the category you want. In this recipe, we have chosen **Tables** and selected the **Products** table:

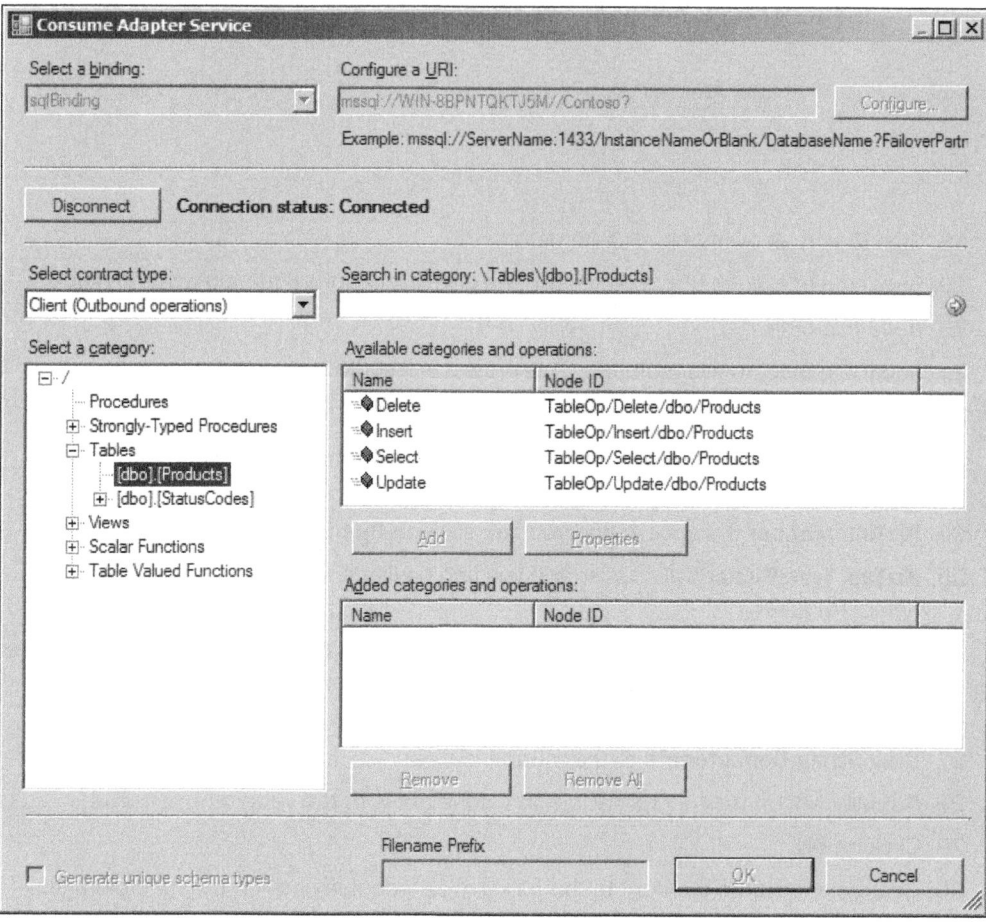

12. In **Available categories and operations**, choose **Select** and click on **Add**.

13. Click on **OK**. Schemas and binding files will be created.

14. Click on **Add | New Item...** and then select **Schema**.

15. Give the schema an appropriate namespace.

16. Rename the root node to **Request**. Add another record to the schema and name it as **Response**. Now, you have a multi-rooted schema.

17. Add elements to both nodes, as shown in the following screenshot:

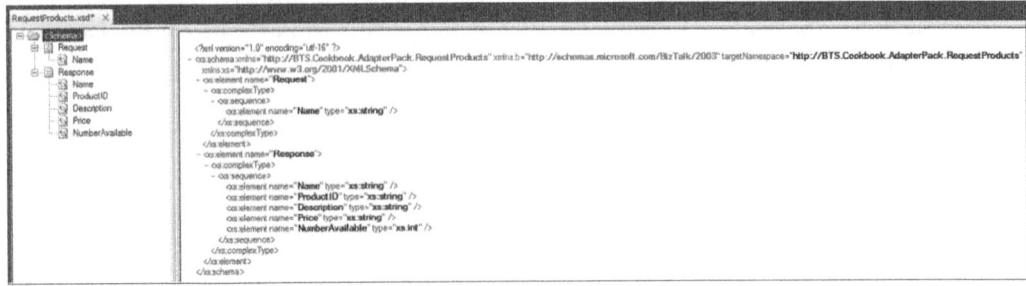

18. Sign the project with a strong name.

19. Subsequently, go to the deployment and give it an appropriate application name.

20. Build this project.

21. Add the project to your solution. This project will contain the maps.

22. Add a reference to the project with the schemas.

23. Right-click on the project and choose **Add | New Item...**. Select **Map** and give it a descriptive name.

24. **BizTalk Mapper** will appear and you can click on **Open Source Schema**.

25. **BizTalk Type Picker** will appear and you can navigate to the schema you created. Select **Request**.

26. Click on **Open Destination Schema** and **BizTalk Type Picker** will appear again. Select the schema generated by the wizard named **TableOperation.dbo.Products.xsd**. Select the correct node (that is, **Select**).

27. Drag **String Concatenate** to the mapper canvas.

28. Double-click on the functoid and add a constant with the value `where name = '`.

29. Click on **OK**.

30. Connect the **Name** element to the functoid and double-click on the functoid again.

31. Add a constant with the value `'`.

32. Connect the functoid with the name value of the destination schema. The schema should look similar to the following screenshot:

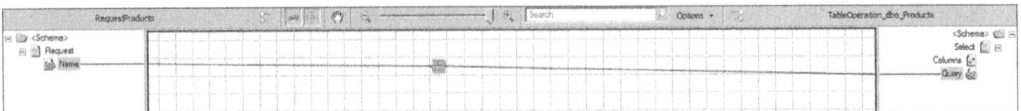

33. Right-click on the project and choose **Add | New Item...**. Select **Map** and give it a descriptive name.

34. **BizTalk Mapper** will appear and you can click on **Open Source Schema**.

35. **BizTalk Type Picker** will appear and you can navigate to the schema you created. Select **Response**.

36. Click on **Open Destination Schema** and **BizTalk Type Picker** will appear again. Select the schema generated by the wizard named **TableOperation.dbo.Products.xsd**. Select the correct node (that is, **SelectResponse**).

37. Connect elements from each schema with the respective elements, as shown in the following screenshot:

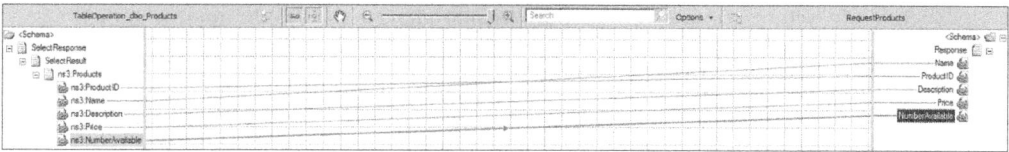

38. Sign the project with a strong name.

39. Subsequently, go to the deployment and give it an appropriate application name.

40. Build this project.

41. Deploy this project. The project with maps and referenced schema will be deployed.

42. Open **BizTalk Administration Console** and navigate to the application.

43. Right-click on the application. Select **Import | Bindings...**.

44. Select the generated binding file (`WcfSendPort_SqlAdapterBinding_Custom.bindinginfo`) in the project directory.

45. Click on **Open**. A Send port will be created.

46. Click on the generated Send port. Select **Outbound Maps**. In **Outbound Maps**, select the custom-created schema. The map and target documents will be filled in automatically.

47. Subsequently, select **Inbound Maps**. In **Inbound Maps**, select the generated schema **BTS.Cookbook.AdapterPack.TableOperation_dbo_Products**. The map and target documents will be filled in automatically.

48. Select filters. Choose property BTS.MessageType and type in the value **http://BTS. Cookbook.AdapterPack.RequestProducts#Request** (custom-created schema target namespace `#rootelement` request)

49. Create a Send port and give it an appropriate name.

50. In the newly created Send port, select filters and choose the property **BTS. MessageType**. Type in the value **http://BTS.Cookbook.AdapterPack. RequestProducts#Response** (custom-created schema target namespace `#rootelement` response)

51. Configure this Send port to use the File Adapter and send the message to the folder `out`.

52. Create a Receive port with the corresponding receive location. Give appropriate names to both of them. Configure the location to use the File Adapter and pick up the files from the folder `in`.

53. Right-click on the application and click on **Start**.

How it works...

The Consume Adapter Service Wizard is a metadata generation tool, included in the WCF LOB Adapter SDK to use with BizTalk projects. It enables you to configure security, line-of-business connection strings and adapter-binding properties. The second step is to select one or more operations based on the contract type, which is either outbound or inbound. Finally, the developer can generate XML schemas and WCF-Custom Receive port binding files, when it concerns an inbound contract type or WCF-Custom Send port binding file for outbound contract type. The binding file contains information to configure (during deployment) a Send and/or Receive port with WCF-Custom transport.

The SQL table operation (Select) is called indirectly through BizTalk by the application or the system that wants to request some information from the table. In this recipe, it is simulated by dropping a request in the folder, let us say Folder A. Then, BizTalk picks up the request and routes it to the subscribing Send port that communicates with the SQL Server. It is transformed to a format for the SQL Server.

The table operation (Select) will be performed in the SQL Server. The response (result of select operation) is transformed back to the expected format by another Send port that has a subscription on the message type. This message is sent to another folder (Folder B), as shown in the following diagram:

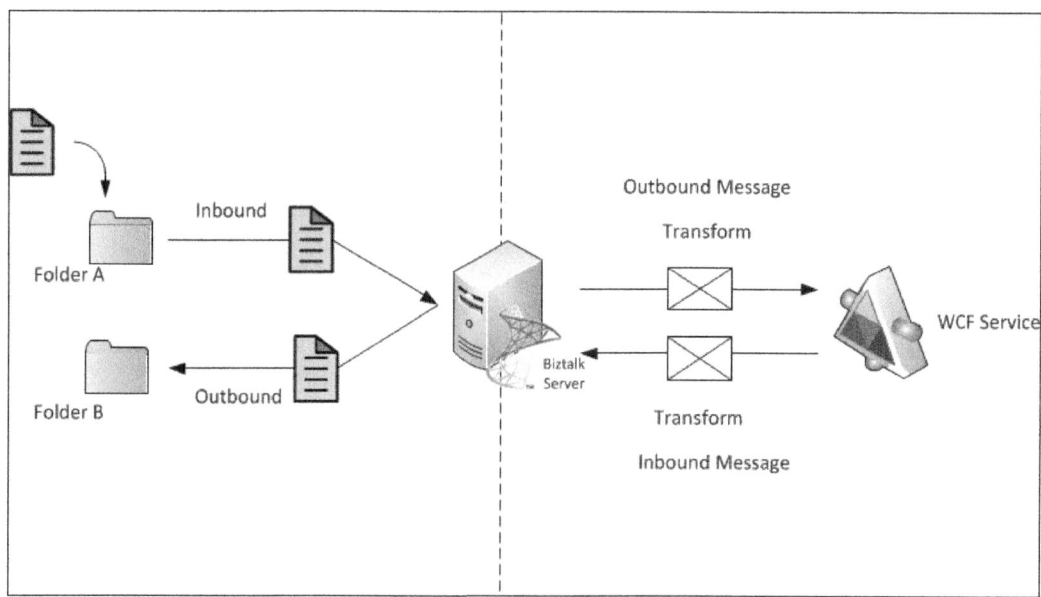

As you can see, files (request message) are being picked up and routed to the SQL Server. However, you can use a WCF Service in front of BizTalk based on the schema, as shown in the *Exposing schemas as a WCF Service* recipe. This would create a message-only scenario, where you call a service that requests data which is being obtained by the SQL Server, or any other system which is supported through the BizTalk Adapter Pack such as the Oracle database, SAP, Siebel, or Oracle E-Business Suite. This recipe shows the concept of exposing data or operations from LOB systems or databases to the enterprise. In the next chapter, you will see how this boundary can be extended outside the enterprise.

There's more...

Microsoft has released the Adapter Pack to simplify interoperability with other systems and the interactive poster **BizTalk Adapter Pack 2.0 Interactive Poster** (http://www.microsoft.com/download/en/details.aspx?displaylang=en&id=20320) to a good overview (it is Adapter Pack 2.0, but it still applies for Adapter Pack 2010).

Another good resource that details interoperability with systems such as SAP, Dynamics CRM/AX, SalesForce, and SharePoint is the *Microsoft BizTalk 2010: Line of Business Systems Integration, Kent Weare, Richard Seroter, Sergei Moukhnitski,* and *Thiago Almeida, Packt Publishing*. This book can be found at http://www.packtpub.com/microsoft-biztalk-2010-line-of-business-systems-integration/book.

Installation of the BizTalk Server Adapter Pack 2010 is pretty straightforward and the necessary steps to be performed for the installation are detailed in the post **Installing the BizTalk Adapter Pack 2010 on x64** at http://soa-thoughts.blogspot.com/2010/11/installing-biztalk-adapter-pack-2010-on.html.

You can also read the document **BizTalk Adapter Pack 2010 Documentation** at http://www.microsoft.com/download/en/details.aspx?displaylang=en&id=1325.

See also

▶ If you just want to call a web service in the messaging-only way, refer to the *Consuming WCF Services in a BizTalk messaging only solution* recipe, discussed earlier in this chapter.

▶ To expose data and operations outside the enterprise, refer to the *Exposing on-premises data in the cloud* recipe in *Chapter 6, BizTalk AppFabric Connect*.

6
BizTalk AppFabric Connect

In this chapter, we will cover:

- ▶ Installing AppFabric Connect and AppFabric Connect for Services
- ▶ Using the BizTalk Mapper in Workflow Services
- ▶ Exposing on-premise data in the cloud
- ▶ Exposing BizTalk applications in the cloud using AppFabric Connect for Services
- ▶ Performing table operations in SQL Azure

Introduction

The BizTalk Server 2010 offers a new feature called **AppFabric Connect**, which allows developers to use the BizTalk Mapper and Adapter Pack capabilities in their solutions, without depending on the BizTalk runtime itself. The developer can use the BizTalk Mapper with the same UI as in BizTalk projects to utilize the XML-based data transformation capabilities and connect to the backend **Line of Business** (**LOB**) systems, such as SAP, Oracle database, Oracle E-Business Suite, Seibel, and the SQL Server without writing custom code for the LOB connectivity. Within a project, the developer uses **Windows Workflow Foundation** (**WF**) activities to programmatically access the BizTalk Server's LOB connectivity and data transformation capabilities. The project can be deployed, hosted, and managed in Windows Server AppFabric/**Internet Information Services** (**IIS**).

In this chapter, you will find a recipe of the application that uses Mapper and LOB connectivity and is hosted on IIS. You can create these kind of applications if you have a scenario, where low-latency LOB integration and other BizTalk built-in features such as scalability, reliability, and so on are not necessary.

Another related feature of AppFabric Connect is the BizTalk Server 2010 AppFabric Connect for Services feature, which allows you to extend the reach of your LOB Services and BizTalk application into Windows Azure AppFabric. The LOB Service or BizTalk application runs on-premise, but can be accessed securely and easily through Windows Azure. The capabilities of the Windows Azure AppFabric Service Bus and Access Control are utilized to publish and secure access to an endpoint definition of your service, the actual calls to the real service are passed to the service which is running on-premise. A developer uses a wizard to provision the service endpoint in the Service Bus. Internal processes or data can be made accessible to users outside your organization as services are accessible in the cloud but you stay in control using your on-premises infrastructure. This chapter contains a recipe which shows how to extend the BizTalk application to the cloud and a recipe on how to expose on-premise data to the cloud.

Both features require the BizTalk Server Adapter Pack 2010 that offers capabilities of getting connected with the backend LOB systems, but it also offers the possibility of getting connected with the cloud SQL database and SQL Azure. SQL Azure is not considered as a backend system. However, you can integrate with it using the WCF-SQL Adapter. There is one recipe in this chapter showing you how to perform table operations in the SQL Azure database.

The BizTalk Server 2010 has evolved a great deal with capabilities on board to get connected with the cloud, which enriches the connectivity of the platform. It does require some effort to have this in place. The first recipe will show you how to install AppFabric Connect and AppFabric Connect for Services, to enable you to use these features.

Installing AppFabric Connect and AppFabric Connect for Services

The BizTalk Server 2010 offers the AppFabric Connect feature to enable developers to use BizTalk Mapper in Workflow projects and the capabilities of the BizTalk LOB adapters (that is, the BizTalk Server Adapter Pack). Besides that, there is also the AppFabric Connect for Services feature that brings connectivity with the cloud and extends the reach of BizTalk to the cloud, which opens up the possibility of hybrid integration solutions with on-premise systems and the cloud. AppFabric Connect for Services is not offered out of the box, but can be obtained through the BizTalk Server 2010 Feature Pack.

To use the AppFabric Connect feature of BizTalk, it needs to be installed and configured on the BizTalk developer machine and runtime environment that is, test, acceptance, and/or production. The operating system required for this feature is Windows 2008 (R2), Vista, or Windows 7. The last two are client operating systems and are not best suited for a BizTalk environment or this feature. Any production environment will have BizTalk installed on a server OS facilitating scalability, availability, and so on. Having a server OS for every environment, it is easy to keep the OS in synchronization throughout the BizTalk solution life-cycle. Any service pack/hotfix can also be kept in synchronization and it introduces less complexity if things turn out to be different the between development and test, for instance. To conclude, it is recommend to have a virtual machine with a server operating system on top of a client OS for development.

Installation of the AppFabric Connect feature depends on installation of the BizTalk Server itself and for a development environment also on Visual Studio 2010. The BizTalk Server 2010, BizTalk Server Adapter Pack 2010, and Windows Azure AppFabric SDK 1.0 or higher are required for installing AppFabric Connect for Services.

Getting ready

Windows Azure is required while making use of the BizTalk AppFabric Connect for Services feature, a new feature available in the BizTalk Server 2010. AppFabric Connect for Services enables you to use BizTalk's capabilities from Windows Azure AppFabric that is, the Service Bus. To be able to do so, you need a Windows Azure account through one of their offerings. Windows Azure has the following offerings:

- ▸ Pay-as-you-go
- ▸ Subscription
- ▸ Member

Through one of these offerings, you have to create an account using Windows LiveID.

Finally, you will need the DVD/ISO BizTalk Server Enterprise, Standard, or Developer Edition according to the version installed in your environment.

How to do it...

To install AppFabric Connect and AppFabric Connect for Services, you will have to perform some steps.

AppFabric Connect

To install AppFabric Connect, you will have to setup the application found in the BizTalk Server folder of the DVD/ISO BizTalk Server Enterprise, Standard, or Developer Edition. Then, select **Install Microsoft AppFabric Connect**, as shown in the following screenshot:

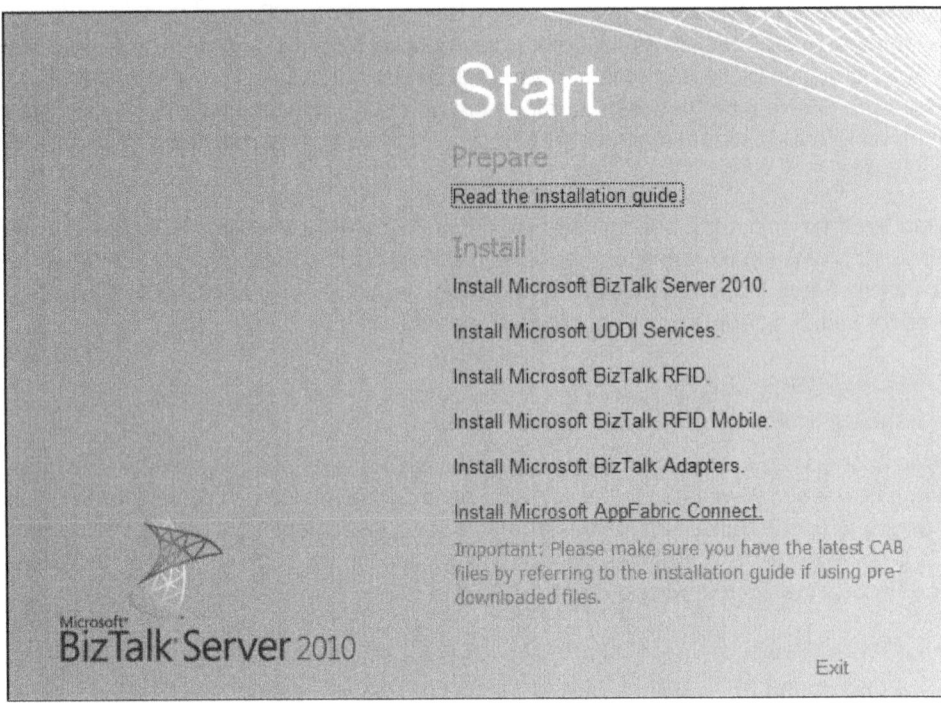

You have to perform the following steps to have the AppFabric Connect feature installed:

1. The first step dictates you to install the BizTalk Server. Most likely that has been already done. Here, it is important to note that, for a development environment the Developer Tools and SDK components of BizTalk are required.

2. The second step is to install the Microsoft WCF LOB Adapter SDK. Click on **Install Microsoft WCF LOB Adapter SDK** and the wizard will pop up, which guides you through the installation. Here, it is important to note that on a development environment, you need **Runtime**, **Tools**, **BizTalk Server Addin**, and **Samples**. If you want just the mapper, then **Runtime** is enough. In non-development environments (UAT, Production), you can install only the **Runtime** option:

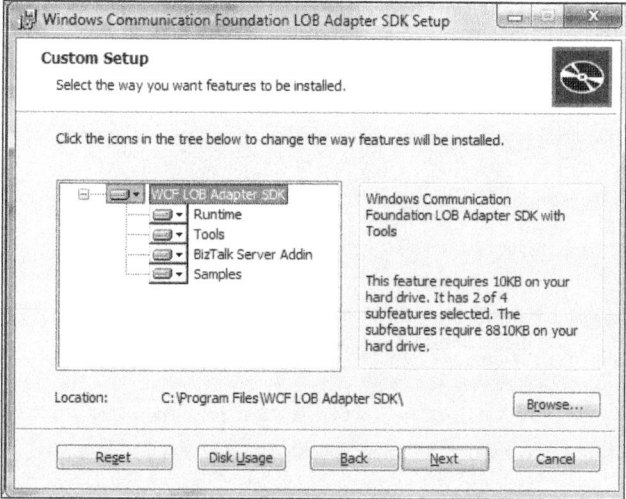

3. The third step is to install **Microsoft BizTalk Adapter Pack**. Click **Install Microsoft BizTalk Adapter Pack** and a wizard will popup that guides you through the installation. You can choose which adapters you want based on your requirements (through custom installation):

   ❑ Microsoft BizTalk Adapter for the Oracle Database

   ❑ Microsoft BizTalk Adapter for the Microsoft SQL Server

   ❑ Microsoft BizTalk Adapter for the Oracle E-Business Suite

   ❑ Microsoft BizTalk Adapter for the mySAP Business Suite

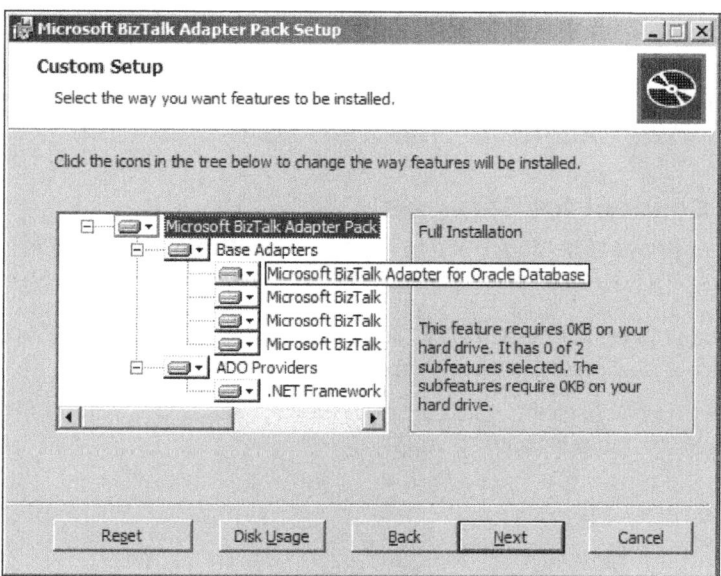

4. When running on 64 bit, you need to install **Microsoft BizTalk Adapter Pack (x64)**.

5. When all components have been installed succesfully for AppFabric Connect, you will see the following screenshot:

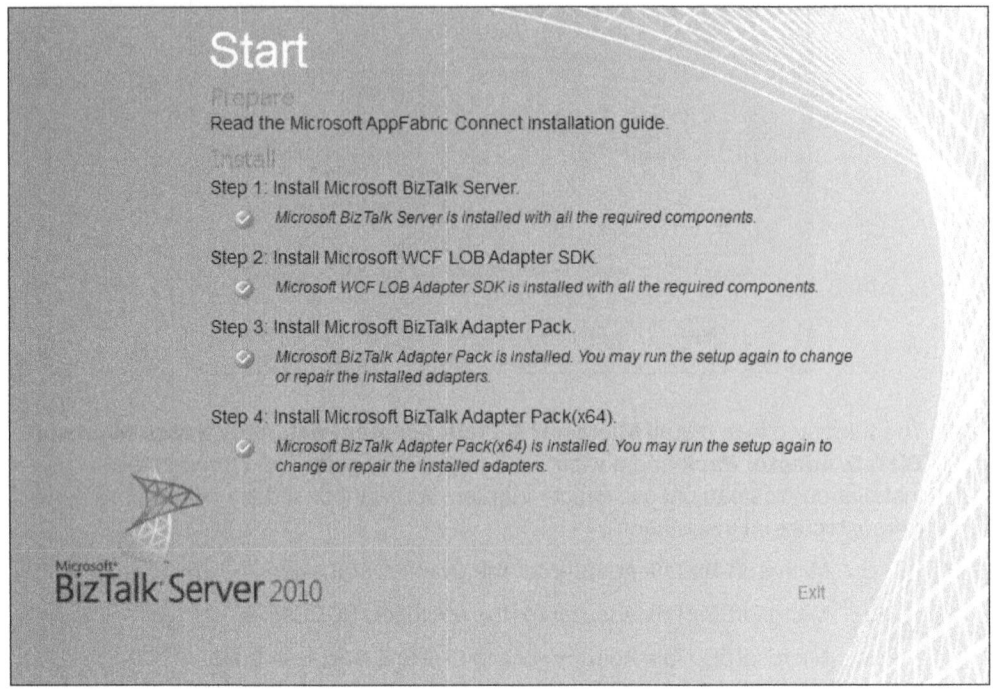

6. Finally, you need to install the **LOB Client library** files required for the LOB adapters to connect to the LOB applications. This depends on which adapters have been selected in step 3. The client libraries you need to install, can be found in the **Adapter Pack Installation** guide at `http://www.microsoft.com/download/en/details.aspx?displaylang=en&id=1325`.

AppFabric Connect for Services

The following steps have to be performed to install the **AppFabric Connect for Services** feature:

1. Download the BizTalk Server 2010 Feature Pack from `http://www.microsoft.com/download/en/details.aspx?id=19638`.

2. Run the `BiztalkServer2010_FeaturePack.exe` and a wizard will pop-up which will guide you through the installation.

How it works...

Installation of the AppFabric Connect feature enables the developer to start a new .NET 4 WCF Workflow Service project or add a new workflow to an existing project. The developer can find the mapper activity in his workflow's toolbox. He/she should also be able to use **Add Adapter Service Reference** from your workflow project to get the LOB activities.

Installation of AppFabric Connect for Services enables you to use one of the following BizTalk wizards:

▶ **BizTalk WCF Service Publishing Wizard**: To publish BizTalk orchestrations or schemas as WCF Services with endpoints in the Windows Azure AppFabric Service Bus

▶ **BizTalk WCF Adapter Service Development Wizard**: To expose on-premise LOB systems by publishing BizTalk WCF LOB Adapters as WCF Services with endpoints in the AppFabric Service Bus

There's more...

Before you create a Windows Azure account, it is very important to choose the right offer by concerning the cost of the tool. You can choose the right offer through the Windows Azure Website (`http://www.microsoft.com/windowsazure/offers/`):

Pick an Offer Type page that also shows the Microsoft tools which help you to calculate Pricing and TCO.

Microsoft has launched a document called **BizTalk Server 2010 AppFabric Connect Feature Frequently Asked Questions** (`http://social.technet.microsoft.com/wiki/contents/articles/biztalk-server-2010-appfabric-connect-feature-frequently-asked-questions-faq.aspx#I_installed_BizTalk_Server_2010_after_installing_the_WCF_LOB_Adapter_SDK_2010,_How_do_I_enable_this_feature_now`) with answers to frequently asked questions when using Visual Studio 2010 to develop WF applications that utilize functionality provided by the BizTalk Server 2010 AppFabric Connect feature.

See also

▶ Refer to the *Using the BizTalk Mapper in Workflow Services*, *Exposing on-premise data in the cloud*, and *Exposing BizTalk applications in the cloud using AppFbric Connect for Service* recipes discussed later in this chapter

Using the BizTalk Mapper in Workflow Services

As a BizTalk developer, you may not easily switch to the .NET development to create a Workflow Service. An orchestration can be built for many integration scenarios within an enterprise. Yet, an orchestration might not always be the right fit. For a low-latency scenario, for instance, where you do not need out of the box BizTalk capabilities such as reliability, the Workflow Service can be the option especially, if you expect a high load and you anticipate that I/O contention is going to impact performance.

However, with the AppFabric Connect feature, you can leverage some of the BizTalk capabilities such as the BizTalk Mapper inside your workflow and besides the Mapper, a developer can even make use of the LOB capabilities using the BizTalk Adapter Pack without installing BizTalk Server Runtime. This enables you to improve latency over a pure BizTalk Server solution, while still utilizing the BizTalk Server's functionality. In this recipe, a Workflow Service will be created which leverages the BizTalk Server Mapper and the LOB Adapter functionality.

Getting ready

To create Workflow Services, you need to have Visual Studio 2010 installed with the BizTalk Developer and Tools feature and the AppFabric Connect feature. For reference, you can download the source code belonging to this chapter. You also need to download the Adventure Works sample database from Codeplex (`http://msftdbprodsamples.codeplex.com/`). Install the AdventureWorksLT2008R2 database on your machine. The AdventureWorks database serves as a source to retrieve the `CustomerAddress` data. Another database script is accompanied with this book.

How to do it...

To create a Workflow Service, you need to perform the following steps:

1. Open Visual Studio.
2. Create a **New Project** dialog box, select **Workflow** and click on the middle pane to select **WCF Workflow Service Application**. Give it a descriptive name and click on **OK**.
3. Select the **Sequential Service** which is displayed in the designer pane and delete it, as it will be replaced with a new **Sequence** shape. Rename the service with an appropriate name for example, **CustomerOperationalDS**.
4. Drag-and-drop the **Sequence** shape from the toolbox to the center of **ExtractDataTransformLoad.xamlx**.

5. Drag-and-drop the **Receive** shape from the toolbox onto the **Sequence** shape, which is displayed in the designer pane. The **Receive** shape is available on the **Messaging** tab of the toolbox.

6. Right-click on the **Receive** shape and select **Properties** from the context menu.

7. In **Properties** for the **Receive** shape, set **OperationName** to **ExtractCustomerAddress** and the **ServiceContractName** property to **IinitializeSvc**. Verify that the **CanCreateInstance** checkbox is selected and that the **SerializerOption** is set to **DataContractSerializer**:

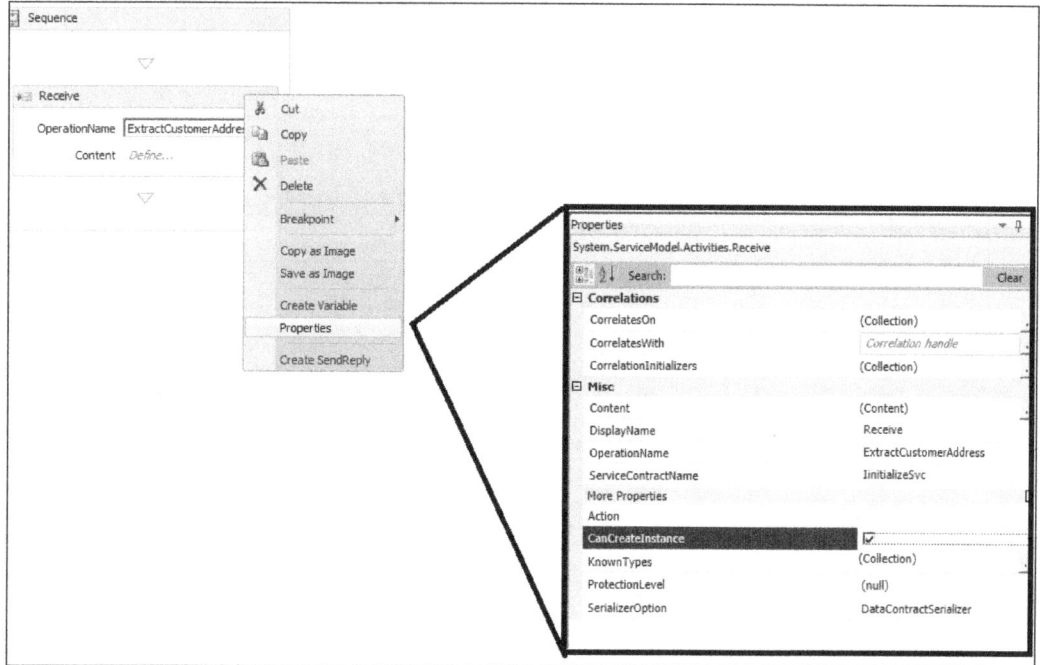

8. Click to select the project in **Solution Explorer**, right-click to display the context menu and click to select **Add Adapter Service Reference** to display the **Add Adapter Service Reference** dialog box. Enter the following values to populate the **Add Adapter Service Reference** dialog box and click on **OK**:

    a. Choose **sqlBinding** in **Select a binding**.

    b. In **Configure a URI**, enter **mssql://localhost//AdventureWorksLT2008R2**.

    c. Click on the **Connect** button to establish a connection to the AdventureWorksLT2008R2 database.

    d. Under **Select contract type**, verify that **Client (Outbound operations)** is selected.

e. In **Select a category** section, click to expand **Views** and select the **[dbo].[SalesLT.vCustomerAddress]** view

f. In the **Available categories and operations** section, select the **Select** operation and then click on the **Add** button

9. Verify that the **Add Adapter Service Reference** dialog box is populated, as shown in the following screenshot, and click on the **OK** button:

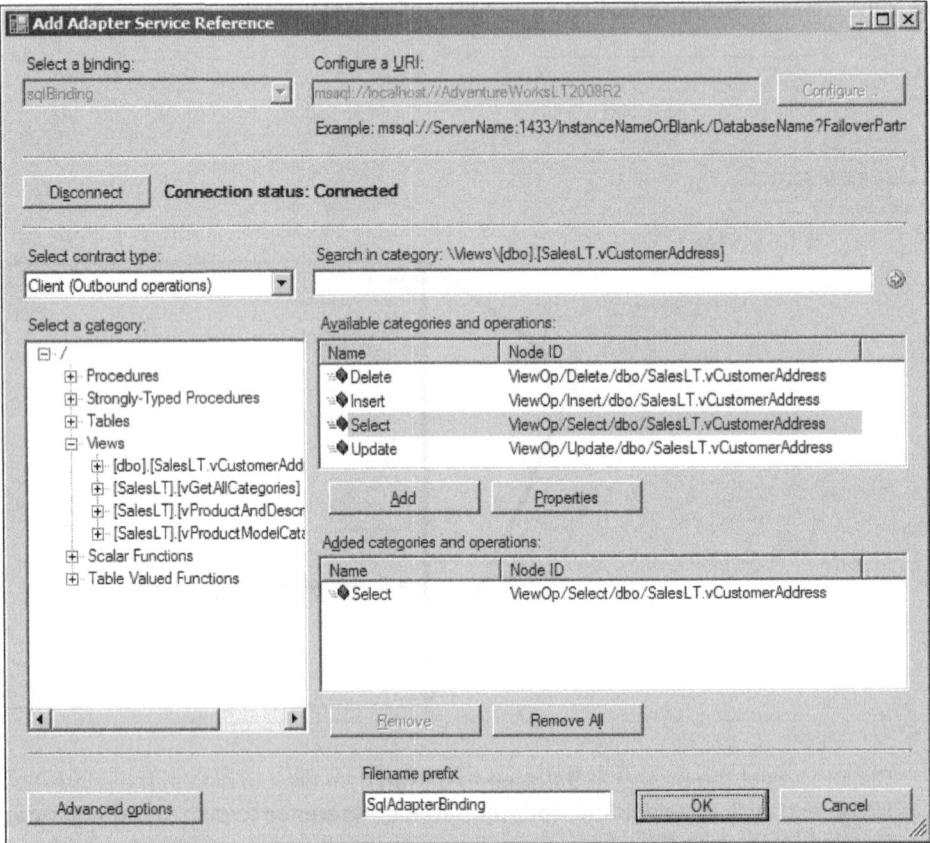

10. In **Solution Explorer**, right-click on the project and select **Build** from the context menu. After building this project with the new adapter service references, the Visual Studio 2010 toolbox should expose one additional tab called **mssql_ViewOp_dbo_SalesLTvCustomerAddress** and this tab will expose **SelectActivity**.

11. Click to select the project in **Solution Explorer**, right-click to display the context menu and click to select **Add Adapter Service Reference** to display the **Add Adapter Service Reference** dialog box. Enter the following values to populate the **Add Adapter Service Reference** dialog box and click on **OK**:

    1. Choose **sqlBinding** in **Select a binding**.

    2. In **Configure a URI**, enter **mssql://localhost//CustomerOperationalDS**.

    3. Click on the **Connect** button to establish a connection to the **CustomerOperationalDS** database.

    4. Under **Select contract type**, verify that **Client (Outbound operations)** is selected.

    5. In the **Select a category** section, click to expand **Tables** and select the **[dbo].[CustomerAddress]** table.

6. In the **Available categories and operations** section, select **Insert** operation and then click on the **Add** button.

12. Verify that the **Add Adapter Service Reference** dialog box is populated, as shown in the following screenshot and click on the **OK** button:

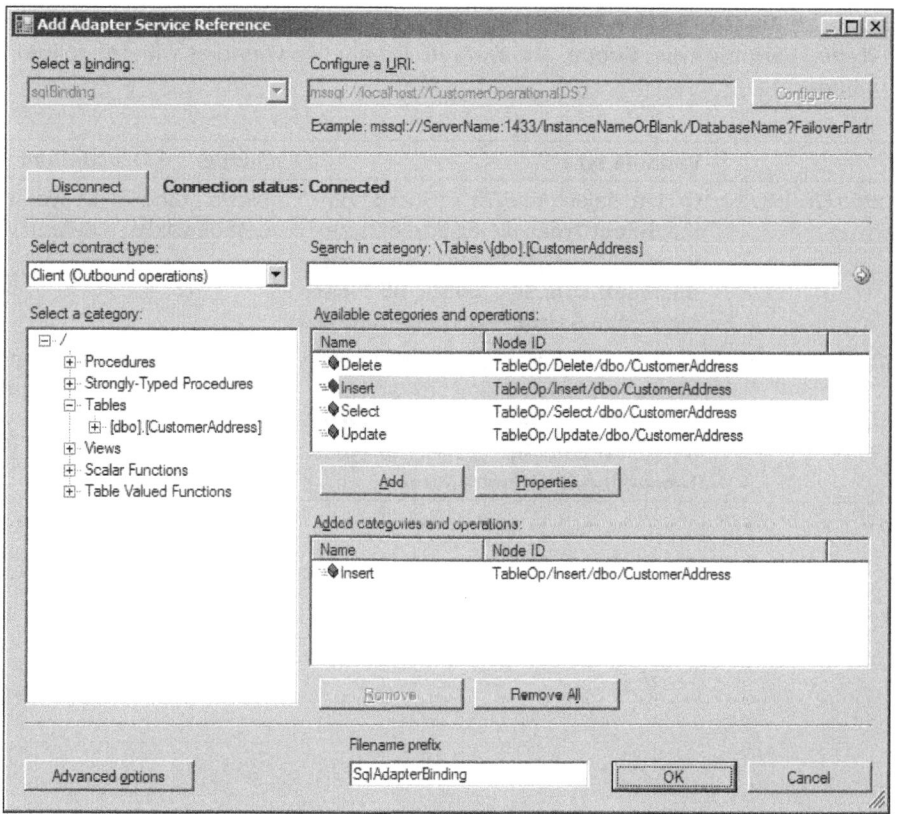

13. In **Solution Explorer**, right-click the project and select **Build** from the context menu. After building this project with the new adapter service references, the Visual Studio 2010 toolbox should expose another additional tab called **mssql_TableOp_dbo_CustomerAddress** and this tab will expose **InsertActivity**:

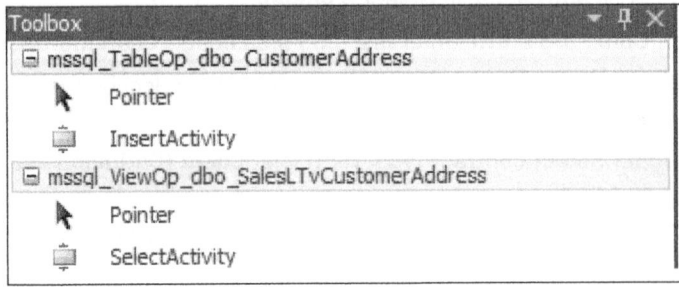

14. Click-and-drag **SelectActivity** and **InsertActivity** from the toolbox onto the **Sequence** shape that is displayed on the designer pane.

15. Click on **Variables** in the bottom-right corner of **Designer** to invoke the **Create Variable** option in **Designer**.

16. Click on **Create Variable** to display a row in the **Designer** that accepts inputs for **Name**, **Variable type**, **Scope**, and **Default**. Create two variables with the following values:

Name	Variable type	Scope	Default
dataLocal	Click to select Array of <T> and from the **Select Types** dialog box, browse to select the **Type Name** of **schemas. microsoft.com.Sql._2008._05.Types. Views.dbo.SalesLTvCustomerAddress**	Leave at the default value	Leave at the default value
dataOperational	Click to select Array of <T> and from the **Select Types** dialog box, browse to select the **Type Name** of **schemas. microsoft.com.Sql._2008._05.Types. Tables.dbo.CustomerAddress**	Leave at the default value	Leave at the default value

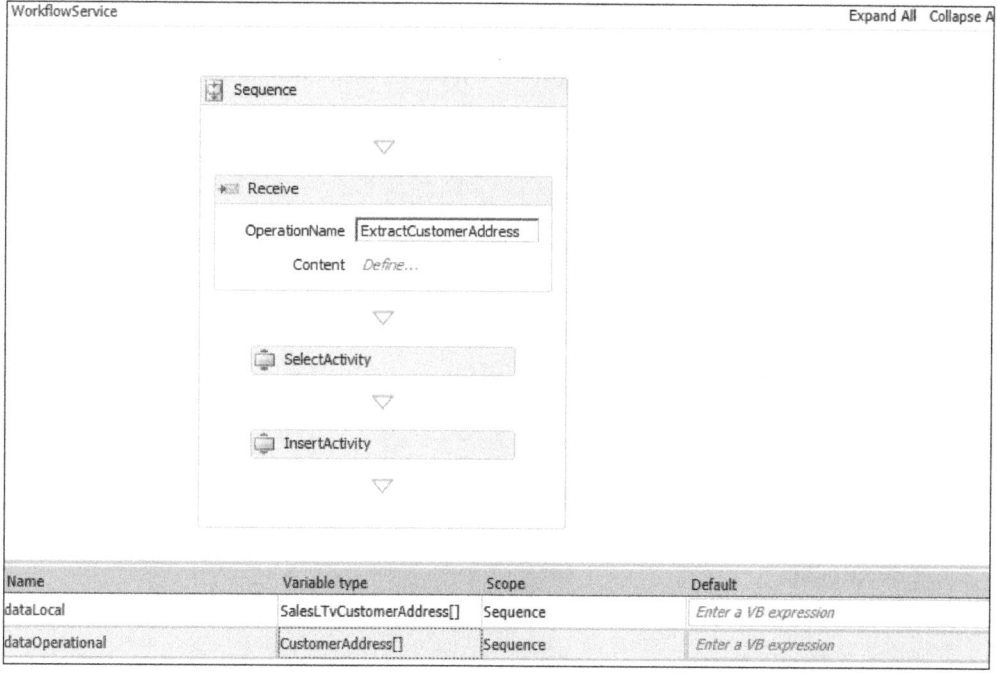

17. Right-click to select the **SelectActivity** item in the Visual Studio Designer and select **Properties** from the context menu. Enter the following values for the **SelectActivity** item properties:

Columns	DisplayName	EndPointConfigurationName	Query	SelectResult
"*"	Leave as default	Leave as default	Leave as default	dataLocal

18. Right-click to select the **InsertActivity** item in the Visual Studio Designer and select **Properties** from the context menu. Leave all values at their default except for **Rows**. Set the value for the **Rows** property to **dataOperational**.

19. Locate the **Mapper** item in the BizTalk category of the toolbox, click to select it and drag it between **SelectActivity** and **InsertActivity**.

20. When you release the left mouse button to drop it onto the **Designer** surface, the **Select Types** dialog box will be displayed. Specify an **InputDataContractType** of **schemas.microsoft.com.Sql._2008._05.Types.Views.dbo. SalesLTvCustomerAddress[]** and specify an **OutputDataContractType** of **schemas.microsoft.com.Sql._2008._05.Types.Tables.dbo.CustomerAddress[]**, then click on **OK**.

21. Click on the **Edit** option that is displayed for the **Mapper** item to display the **Select a Map** dialog box.

22. Verify that the **Create a new Map** radio button is selected, enter a name of **MapToOperational**, verify that **Launch the Map** is checked and click on **OK** to launch the BizTalk Mapper. A new map surface should be displayed that contains the input and output schemas:

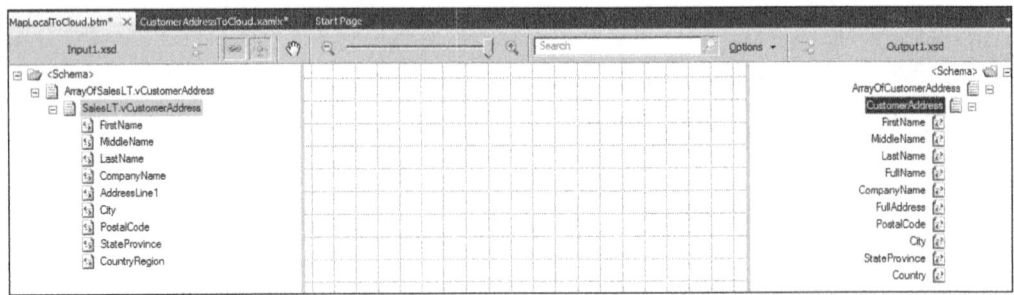

23. Drag-and-drop two **String Concatenate** functoids onto the surface of the Map.

24. Drag-and-drop the following nodes from the schema on the left onto the first **String Concatenate** functoid:

   ❑ **FirstName**

   ❑ **MiddleName**

   ❑ **LastName**

25. Drag-and-drop the output of the **String Concatenate** functoid to the **FullName** node of the right schema.

26. Drag-and-drop the following nodes from the schema on the left, onto the second **String Concatenate** functoid:

   ❑ **AddressLine1**

   ❑ **PostalCode**

   ❑ **City**

27. Drag-and-drop the output of the second **String Concatenate** functoid to the **FullAddress** node of the right schema:

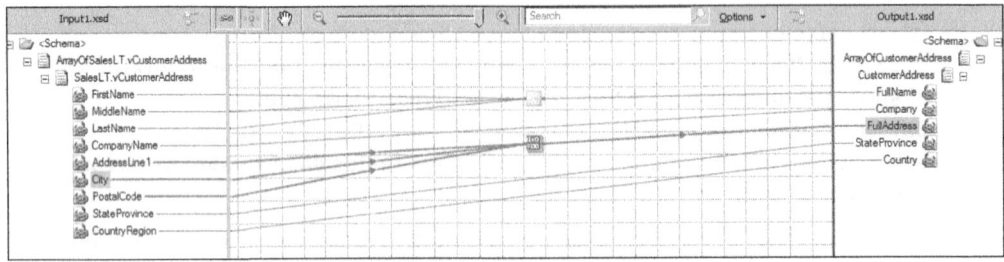

28. Double-click on **ExtractDataTransformLoad.xamlx** in **Solution Explorer** to display the **Designer** surface, right-click on the **Mapper** item and select **Properties** from the context menu to display the Visual Studio properties for the Mapper item.

29. Enter an input value of **dataLocal** in the Visual Studio properties for the Mapper item.

30. Enter an output value of **dataOperational** in the Visual Studio properties for the Mapper item.

31. Click on the Visual Studio 2010 **File** menu and select **Save All** to save the solution and project.

32. In **Solution Explorer**, right-click on the project and click on **Build**.

33. In **Solution Explorer**, right-click on the project and select **Properties** from the context menu to display the properties page for the project.

34. On the **Web** tab of the project properties page, select **Use Local IIS Web server**.

35. In **Solution Explorer**, right-click on the project and select **Publish** from the context menu to display the **Publish Web** dialog box.

36. Enter the following values into the **Publish Web** dialog box (assuming that IIS 7.0 is running locally) and then click on the **Publish** button:

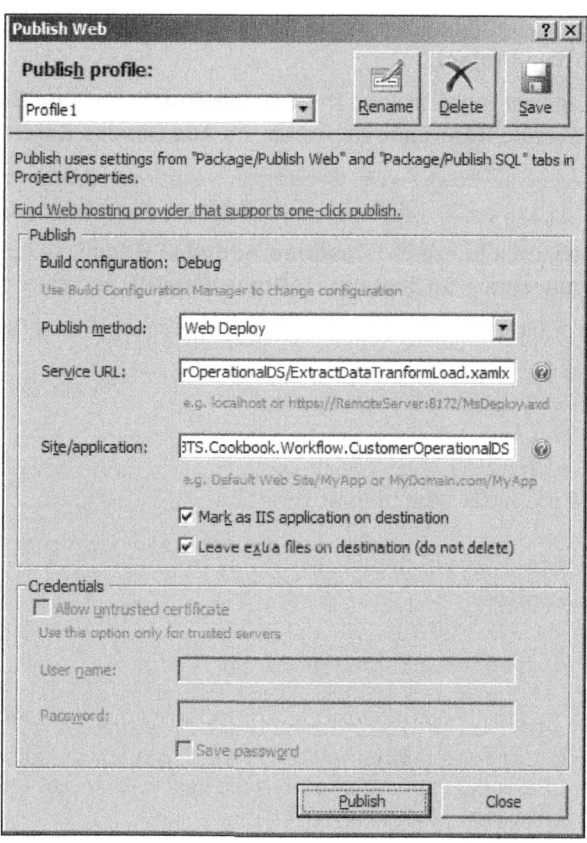

37. Open a browser and navigate to `http://localhost/BTS.Cookbook.CustomerAddress.Workflow/ ExtractDataTranformLoad.xamlx` to verify that the service has been created.

38. Click on the link `http://localhost/BTS.Cookbook.CustomerAddress.Workflow/ ExtractDataTranformLoad.xamlx ?wsdl` to verify that the WSDL is displayed correctly.

39. Since this WCF application will use the WCF SQL Adapter to connect to the AdventureWorksLT2008R2 database, either configure **DefaultAppPool Identity** with an account that has permissions to read from and write to the AdventureWorksLT2008R2 database, or else configure the application in IIS to run in a different Application Pool that is using an identity with an account that has permissions to read from and write to the AdventureWorksLT2008R2 database.

40. Select the solution in **Solution Explorer**, then click on the **File** menu, click on **Add**, and then click on **New Project** to display the **Add New Project** dialog box.

41. In the **Add New Project** dialog box, under **Installed Templates**, click to expand **Visual C#**, select **Windows**, and select **Console Application**.

42. Type **ConsoleTestOperationalDS** for the name of the project and click on **OK**.

43. In **Solution Explorer**, right-click on the **ConsoleTestOperationalDS** project and click on **Set as StartUp Project**.

44. In **Solution Explorer**, right-click on the **ConsoleTestOperationalDS** project again and click on **Add Service Reference** to display the **Add Service Reference** dialog box.

45. Enter `http://localhost/BTS.Cookbook.CustomerAddress.Workflow/ CustomerAddressToCloud.xamlx` into **Address** and click on **Go**.

46. Under **Services**, click to expand **CustomerAddressToCloud**, select **IinitializeSvc** and then name **Namespace SRCustomerToOperationalDS** and click on **OK**.

47. Replace the code that currently exists in `Program.cs` with the following code:

```csharp
using System;
using System.Collections.Generic;
using System.Linq;
using System.Text;
  namespace ConsoleTestOperationalDS
  {
    using SRCustomerToOperationalDS;
    class Program
    {
      static void Main(string[] args)
      {
        Console.WriteLine("Invoking WCF Service to select rows
        from CustomerAddressView local database and insert
        result set into CustomerAddress table in the
        Operational DataStore");
```

```
            IinitializeSvcClient client = new
            IinitializeSvcClient();
            client.ExtractCustomerAddress();
            Console.WriteLine("Done");
            Console.WriteLine("Please press <Enter> to close
            program.");
            Console.ReadLine();
        }
    }
}
```

48. Press *F5* to execute the console application.

49. Open Microsoft SQL Server Management Studio to verify that the rows have been added to the **CustomerAddress** table in the **CustomerOperationalDS** database.

How it works...

Without using the BizTalk runtime, you can use the LOB capabilities offered through the BizTalk Adapter Pack and the BizTalk Mapper. LOB SDK, a dependency of the BizTalk Adapter Pack, offers an Add Adapter Service Reference Visual Studio Plugin, which is a metadata proxy generation tool. This tool is used to generate data contract types which are used in mapping. One data contract is generated from the source view and another from the destination table.

Contracts are based on selected operations and reflected in Visual Studio as activities. The activities can be viewed as visual representations of the logic that will be used to select records from the `SalesLT.vCustomerAddress` view. After performing a BizTalk mapping operation on the selected records, insert the result set into the `CustomersAddress` table in the `CustomerOperationalDS` database. For the select operation activity, you defined a query and variables for both selected data as input into a BizTalk map, as well as the data that is output from the BizTalk map. Mapping data is done through the BizTalk Mapper that is available as an activity from the Workflow toolbox. Mapping experience is the same as when using a mapper in a BizTalk project.

By defining in-project web properties using a local IIS and publishing it, the Workflow Service is deployed locally in IIS. The service needs to run under an account that has sufficient permissions to access the databases and read/write the view/table. You can test the workflow through an application that references the service and call it.

There's more...

You will find a similar sample of a Workflow Service in the wiki article **BizTalk + WF/WCF, Better Together** (http://social.technet.microsoft.com/wiki/contents/ articles/903.aspx) that has served as a template for this recipe.

Another wiki article **Introducing BizTalk Server 2010 AppFabric Connect** (http://social. technet.microsoft.com/wiki/contents/articles/work-with-biztalk- appfabric-connect.aspx) will explain more about the high level AppFabric Connect feature.

There are not many samples or blog posts on the BizTalk AppFabric Connect feature with Workflow Services. Still, there are some that are worth looking into:

> ▸ **Using the BizTalk Adapter Pack and AppFabric Connect in a Workflow Service**: http://seroter.wordpress.com/2011/04/03/using-the-biztalk- adapter-pack-and-appfabric-connect-in-a-workflow-service/

> ▸ **Code Uploaded for WCF/WF and AppFabric Connect Demonstration**: http:// seroter.wordpress.com/2011/04/13/code-uploaded-for-wcfwf-and- appfabric-connect-demonstration/

See also

> ▸ Refer to the *Installing AppFabric Connect and AppFabric Connect for Services* recipe discussed earlier in this chapter

Exposing on-premise data in the cloud

BizTalk AppFabric Connect for services is a feature you can install on top of the BizTalk Server 2010 and/or its Adapter Pack. This feature brings together the capabilities of the BizTalk Server and Windows Azure AppFabric enabling enterprises to extend the reach of their on-premise LOB systems and BizTalk applications to the cloud. Developers can use the BizTalk WCF Service Publishing Wizard and the BizTalk WCF Adapter Service Development Wizard to one of the following:

> ▸ Publish BizTalk orchestrations or schemas as WCF Services with endpoints in the Windows Azure AppFabric Service Bus

> ▸ Expose on-premise LOB systems by publishing BizTalk WCF LOB Adapters as WCF Services with endpoints in the AppFabric Service Bus

With the BizTalk WCF Adapter Service Development Wizard, you can expose on-premise data from, for instance, an Oracle database in the cloud. For instance, you can have a WCF-Service with the endpoint in the cloud, which can be accessed by the application outside your enterprise querying for data in an on-premise Oracle database. This recipe will focus on exposing on-premise data in the SQL Server to the cloud.

Getting ready

To expose on-premise data (LOB data) to the cloud, you need to have the AppFabric Connect feature. You must also have Windows Azure AppFabric SDK version 1.0 (September update or later) and the BizTalk Server 2010 Feature Pack installed. Also, refer to the *Installing AppFabric Connect and AppFabric Connect for Services* recipe discussed earlier in this chapter. Before you can try and use this recipe, you must have registered a service namespace with the Windows Azure AppFabric Service Bus. Go to the Windows Azure AppFabric portal (http://www.microsoft.com/windowsazure/appfabric/) to register a service namespace with the Service Bus.

For reference, you can download the source code belonging to this chapter. You also need to download the Adventure Works sample database from Codeplex (http://msftdbprodsamples.codeplex.com/). Install the AdventureWorksLT2008R2 database on your machine. The AdventureWorks database serves as the source to retrieve the CustomerAddress data.

How to do it...

To expose on-premise data in the cloud, you will have to perform the following steps:

1. Open Visual Studio 2010 and start a new project.

2. In the **New Project** dialog box, from the list of installed templates, click on **Visual C#**. In the right pane, select **WCF Adapter Service**. For the project name, enter an appropriate name (for example, **CustomerAddress_Service**) and then click on **OK**. The **WCF Adapter Service Development Wizard** is launched.

3. In the **Welcome** page, select the checkbox **Create WCF Adapter Service** for the SharePoint client if the service will be consumed by a SharePoint client. If the service will be consumed by any other client, make sure the checkbox is cleared (that is, for this recipe, clear the checkbox).

4. In the **Choose Operations** page, select the operation that you want to expose as a service on the cloud:

    1. From the **Select a binding** drop-down list, select **sqlBinding**.

    2. In the **Configure a URI** textbox, enter the URI to connect to the SQL Server database, AdventureWorksLT2008R2, which contains the CustomerAddress view. A typical URI to connect to the SQL Server is mssql://<server_name>/<sql_server_instance>/<my_database>?.

    3. Click on **Connect**.

    4. From the **Select contract type** dialog box, select **Client (Outbound operations)**.

- From the **Select a category** box, expand the **Views** node, and click on **[dbo]. [SalesLT.vCustomerAddress]**.

- From the **Available categories and operations** box, click on **Select**, and then click on **Add**. The selected operation is now listed in **Added categories and operations box**. The following screenshot shows the selected options and operations:

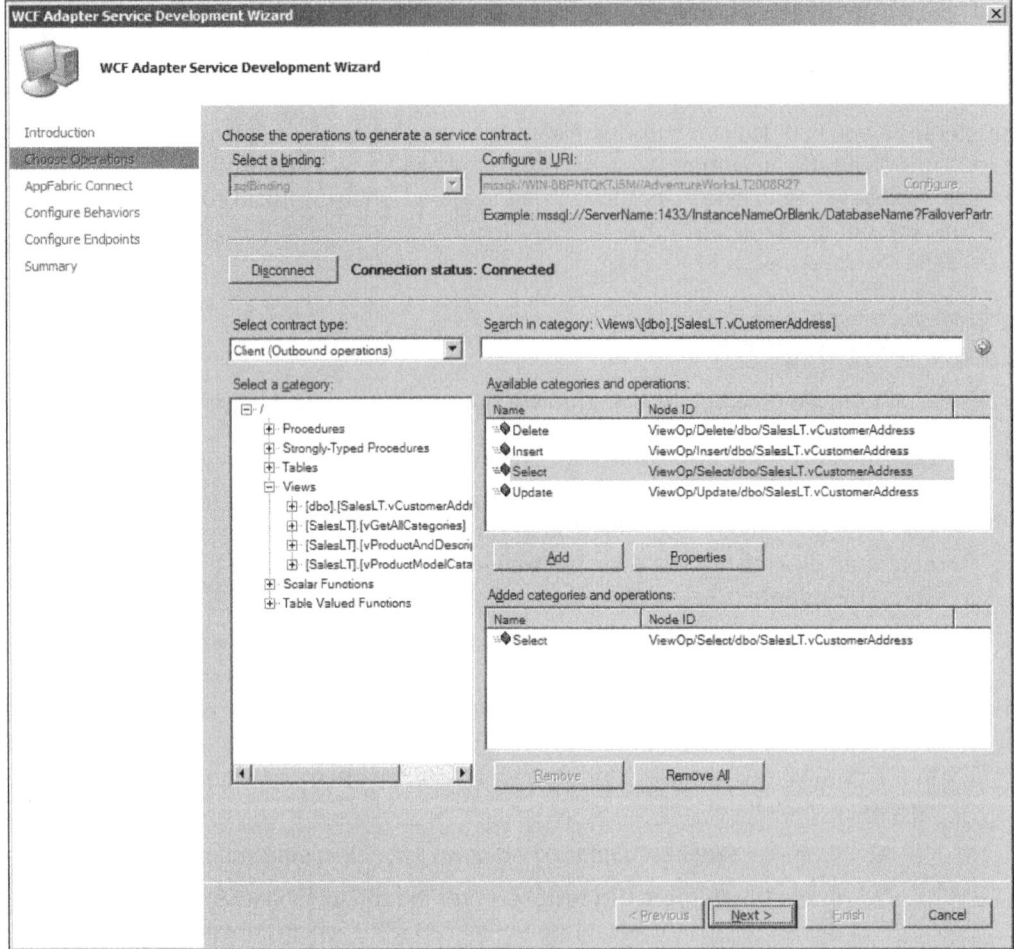

- Click on **Next**.

5. In the **AppFabric Connect** page, select the **Extend the reach of the service on the cloud** checkbox. In the **Service Namespace** text box, enter the service namespace that you have registered with the Service Bus. Click on **Next**.

6. In the **Configure Behaviors** page, configure the service behavior (for both on-premises and cloud-based services) and the endpoint behavior (for only endpoints on the Service Bus). In the **Service Behavior Configuration** section specify the values, as shown in the following screenshot:

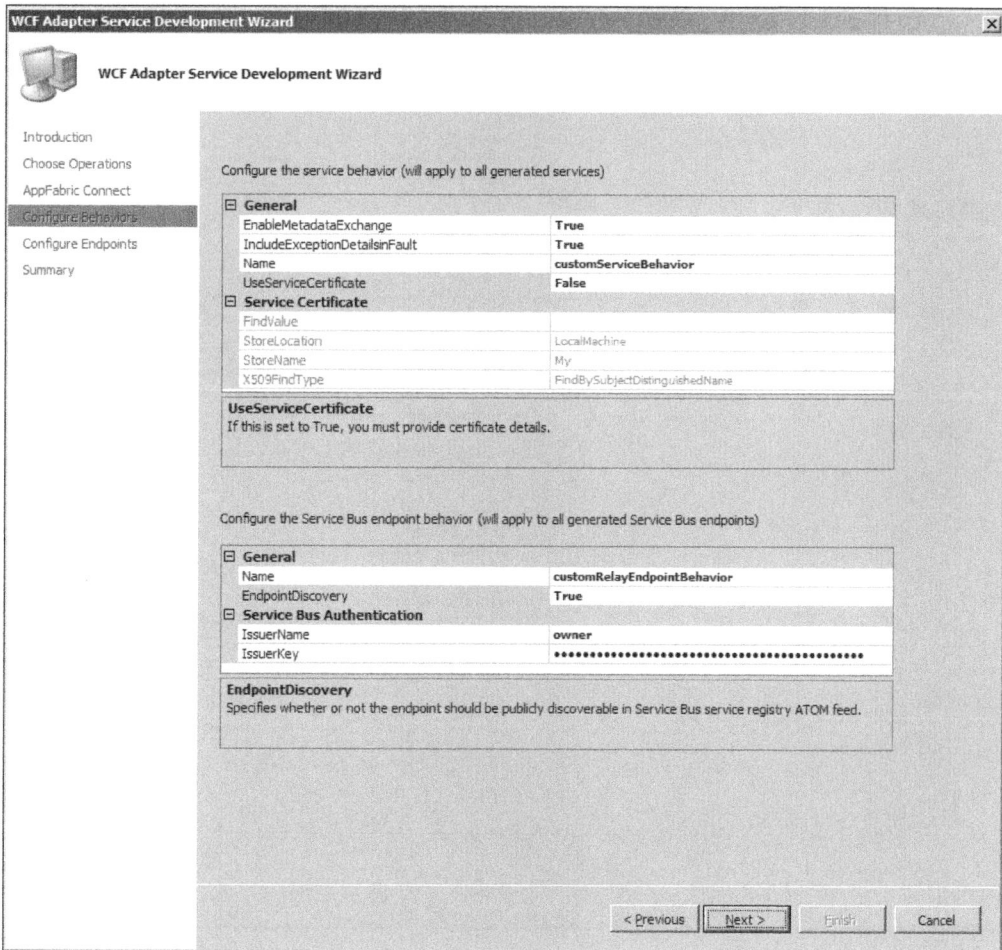

7. Click on **Next**.

8. In the **Configure Endpoints** page, specify properties for both on-premises and the Service Bus endpoint configuration. See the following screenshot for the values to specify:

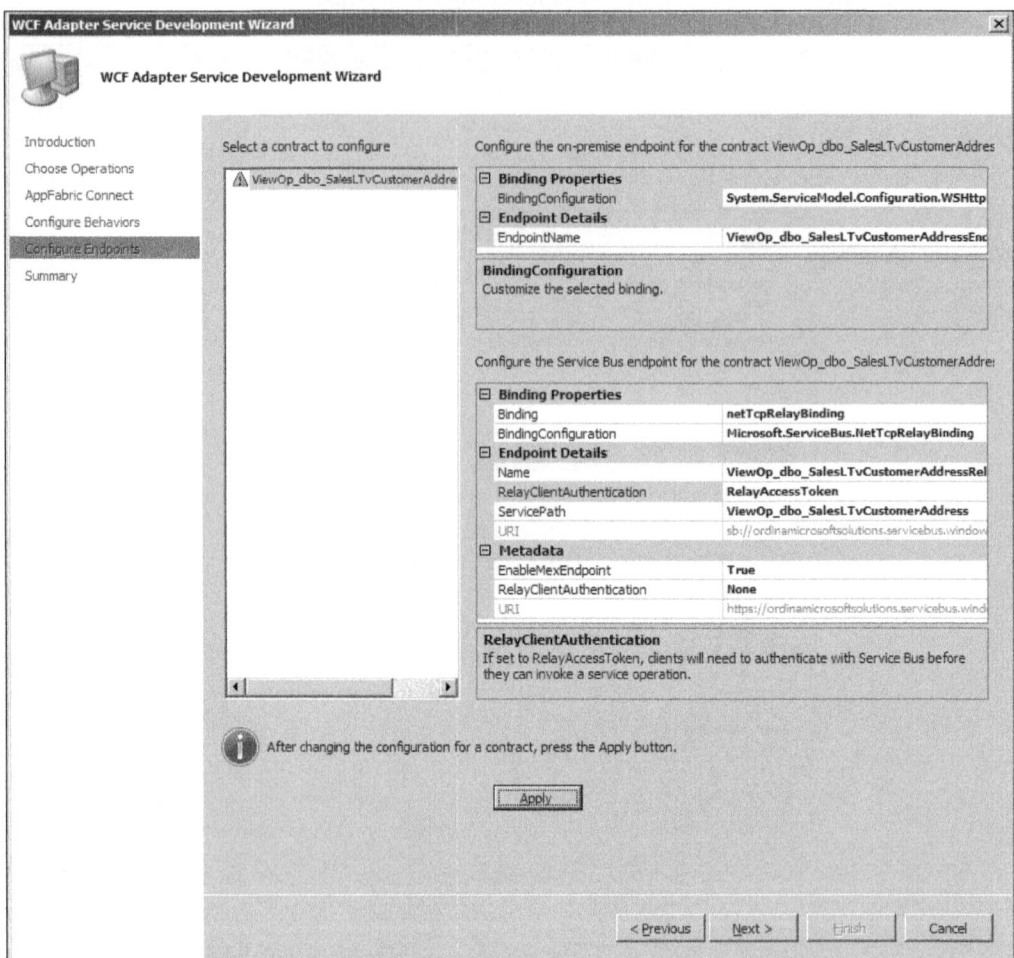

9. Click on **Apply** and then click on **Next**.

10. In the Summary page, review the summary and click on **Finish**. The wizard creates the WCF Service (.svc) and a web configuration for the service and adds it to the Visual Studio project.

11. The on-premise endpoint only supports wsHttp binding and has to be hosted locally, which can only have an https scheme. Hence, to ensure that the local endpoint is hosted successfully, you must add https to the list of supported bindings. Now, open the IIS Manager.

12. Navigate to sites in the left pane called **Connections**, expand and right-click on **Default Web Site** and select **Edit Bindings....**

13. In the **Site Binding** dialog, click on **Add**.

14. Choose **Select Type** as **https**, IP **unassigned**, and port **443**.

15. Select the appropriate **Certificate**.

16. Click on **Ok**.

17. Now you can publish the service locally. In the Visual Studio project for the service, right-click on the project in **Solution Explorer** and click on **Properties**.

18. On the **Properties** page, in the **Web** tab, under the **Servers** category, select the **Use Local IIS Web Server** option.

19. The **Project URL** text box is automatically populated. Specify a different URL if you want and then click on **Create Virtual Directory**.

20. In **Solution Explorer**, right-click on the project again and then click on **Build**.

21. Open the IIS Manager and verify whether a site directory is created.

22. In the IIS Manager, expand **Default Web Sites** and then click on the service **CustomerAddress_Service**.

23. In the **Actions** pane, under the **Manage WCF and WF Services** section, click on **Configure**.

24. In the **Configure WCF and WF for Application** dialog box, from the left pane, click on **Auto-Start** and in the right pane, select **Enabled**.

25. In the dialog box informing that all the services will be recycled, click on **Yes**.

26. To verify if the service is published, go to the URL `https://namespace.servicebus.windows.net`. In this case,

    `https://ordinamicrosoftsolutions.servicebus.windows.net/`.

27. To invoke the service, you will need a client application.

28. In Visual Studio, add a new project to the existing solution. Choose a new console application. Give it an appropriate name (for example, **CustomerAddress_Service_TestConsole**).

29. In **Solution Explorer**, right-click on **References**, and select **Add Service Reference**.

30. In the **Add Service Reference** dialog box, do the following:

    a. In the **Address** text box, enter the URL for the Service Bus metadata exchange endpoint for the WCF Service you hosted on the Service Bus. You can get the URL from the Service Bus ATOM feed page that listed all the publicly discoverable endpoints (`https://ordinamicrosoftsolutions.servicebus.windows.net/`). Right-click on the metadata exchange endpoint, select **Copy Shortcut**, and paste it in the **Address** text box in the **Add Service Reference** dialog box.

a. Specify the namespace.

c. Click on **OK**.

31. In this recipe, the **RelayClientAuthentication** property for the relay service endpoint is set to **RelayAccessToken**, the client will need to pass the authentication token to authenticate itself to the Service Bus. Provide the client authentication token by modifying app.config in the following manner:

    a. Open app.config for the client and add the following code within the system.serviceModel element:

    ```
    <behaviors>
      <endpointBehaviors>
        <behavior name="secureService">
          <transportClientEndpointBehavior
          credentialType="SharedSecret">
            <clientCredentials>
              <sharedSecret issuerName="<name>"
              issuerSecret="<value>" />
            </clientCredentials>
          </transportClientEndpointBehavior>
        </behavior>
      </endpointBehaviors>
    </behaviors>
    ```

    b. In app.config, add the behaviorConfiguration property to the client/endpoint element for the relay service endpoint. You must set the behaviorConfiguration property to the value you specified for the behavior name. So, if you set the behavior name to **secureService**, you must set the behaviorConfiguration property as behaviorConfiguration ="secureService" and the endpoint will look similar to the following:

    ```
    <endpoint
    address="sb://ordinamicrosoftsolutions.
    servicebus.windows.net/ViewOp_dbo_
    SalesLTvCustomerAddress/"
      binding="netTcpRelayBinding"
      bindingConfiguration="ViewOp_dbo_
      SalesLTvCustomerAddressRelayEndpoint"
      contract="SRCustomerAddressService.ViewOp_dbo_
      SalesLTvCustomerAddress"
      name="ViewOp_dbo_SalesLTvCustomerAddressRelayEndpoint"
      behaviorConfiguration="secureService"/>
    ```

    c. Save and close app.config.

32. Open `Program.cs` for the application and do the following:

   a. Add the Service Reference namespace.

   b. Create a client as described in the following code snippet:

```
ViewOp_dbo_SalesLTvCustomerAddressClient client = new
ViewOp_dbo_SalesLTvCustomerAddressClient("ViewOp_dbo_
SalesLTvCustomerAddressRelayEndpoint");
```

   c. Specify the username and password to connect to the SQL Server database. This is required to authenticate the client against the backend LOB systems, in this case, the SQL Server:

```
client.ClientCredentials.UserName.UserName = "<username>";
client.ClientCredentials.UserName.Password = "<password>";
```

   d. Open the client as described in the following code snippet:

```
try
  {
    Console.WriteLine("Opening client...");
    Console.WriteLine();
    client.Open();
  }
catch (Exception ex)
  {
    Console.WriteLine("Exception: " + ex.Message);
    throw;
  }
```

   e. Take the last name as the user input:

```
string lastname;
Console.Write("Enter the Last name for which you want to
retrieve the Customer Adresses: ");
lastname = Console.ReadLine();
Console.WriteLine();
```

   f. Retrieve the records from the `CustomerAddress` view based on the last name provided by the user:

```
SalesLTvCustomerAddress[] records = client.Select("*",
"WHERE [LastName]=" + lastname);
```

g. For the last name that is specified, present the data from the `CustomerAddress` view back to the client:

```
Console.WriteLine("****************************************
*****************");
  Console.WriteLine("FirstName           :" +
  records[0].FirstName);
  Console.WriteLine("MiddelName          :" +
  records[0].MiddleName);
  Console.WriteLine("LastName            :" +
  records[0].LastName);
  Console.WriteLine("AddressLine1        :" +
  records[0].AddressLine1);
  Console.WriteLine("PostalCode          :" +
  records[0].PostalCode);
  Console.WriteLine("City                :" + records[0].
City);
  Console.WriteLine("StateProvince       :" +
  records[0].StateProvince);
  Console.WriteLine("CountryRegion       :" +
  records[0].CountryRegion);
Console.WriteLine("****************************************
*****************");
```

h. Close the client and exit the application, as shown in the following code snippet:

```
client.Close();
  Console.WriteLine("Press any key to exit...");
  Console.ReadLine();
  Console.ReadLine();
```

i. Build the solution and then press *F5* to run the application.

How it works...

To expose on-premise data, you can use the WCF Adapter Service Development Wizard, which essentially exposes the operations on the LOB applications as WCF services. Through these services, you can pull data from an on-premise database or delete, update, and insert data. In this recipe, on-premise data is pulled from a database view. The wizard enables you to select the operations that you want to expose as services and then creates the following:

▶ An on-premise endpoint for the WCF Service

▶ A Service Bus endpoint for the WCF Service

▶ A Service Bus endpoint for exchanging metadata pertinent to the WCF Service

While running the wizard, you should configure a connection to the SQL Server database first and then select the operation you want to expose as the WCF Service. In subsequent steps, after selecting the operation(s), you can configure the service behaviou, the Service Bus endpoint behavior, and the endpoints (deployment).

The service behaviour configuration is based on the set of properties that you define. These concern whether or not to enable message-level security using certificates, exchanging metadata, and to include exception information in SOAP headers. In this recipe, message-level security is not enabled. EnableMetadataExchange is set to True, meaning that the service metadata is available using standardized protocols, such as the WS-Metadata Exchange (MEX).

The service bus endpoint behavior you define, can be discovered through the EndpointDiscovery property. This is set to True meaning that the endpoints are publicly discoverable and listed on the Service Bus ATOM Feed. With the other two properties, IssuerName and IssuerKey, you can enter authentication information required to authenticate the identity of the service namespace owner to the Service Bus.

The final step is to configure endpoints by specifying properties for both on-premises and the Service Bus endpoint configuration. The on-premise endpoints are defined for you, BindingConfiguration is wsHttp as the WCF Adapter Service Development Wizard only supports WSHttpBindingElement for the on-premise endpoint and EndPointName is generated for you. For the service bus endpoint, you can specify the binding, details, and metadata. Binding is netTcpRelayBinding as the wizard will then generate a relay service endpoint, which is necessary to forward a call to operating, on-premise service. BindingConfiguration is generated for you based on binding.

The EndPoint detail enables you to specify the RelayClientAuthentication property; this determines whether the Service Bus authenticates the client before routing the message from the client to the service. It is set to RelayAccessToken for the service endpoint, which is recommended by Microsoft so that only authenticated clients can traverse through the relay service. The ServicePath property is filled in for you, as, by default, it is the contract name. The URI property is also filled in for you and resembles the relay service endpoint. The values you entered for the service namespace and the ServicePath properties are used to create the URI.

The last part of the endpoint behavior configuration is the Metadata part. The EnableMexEndpoint properly is set to True, to enable the relay metadata exchange endpoint on the Service Bus. The next property RelayClientAuthentication is set to None, disabling the fact that the Service Bus authenticates the client before routing the request to the metadata exchange endpoint. The other option is to set the property to RelayAccessToken, which would mean you have to add a behaviors element which will contain the token credentials for accessing the relay metadata exchange endpoint. The last property that the URI displays, is the URI for the relay metadata exchange endpoint.

After going through all the steps in the wizard, it will create the WCF Service (`.svc`) and a `web.config` for the service and add both to the Visual Studio projects. By defining in-project web properties using a local IIS and publishing it, the workflow service is deployed locally in IIS. Then you can configure the service and set it to autostart. By starting the service locally, the corresponding relay service endpoint will be registered on the Service Bus.

To access the service, a client application can be built to consume the WCF Service for which a relay service was created and hosted on the Service Bus. The client will take a last name as input and will present customer address details for that last name.

There's more...

On the BizTalk Server Team blog, you will find a general article called **BizTalk Server 2010 AppFabric Connect for Services** (`http://blogs.msdn.com/b/biztalk_server_team_blog/archive/2010/10/21/biztalk-server-appfabric-connect-for-services.aspx`) on AppFabric Connect for services.

There is a wiki article called **Expose LOB Services on the Cloud Using AppFabric Connect for Services** (`http://social.technet.microsoft.com/wiki/contents/articles/expose-lob-services-on-the-cloud-using-appfabric-connect-for-services.aspx`) which served as a base for this recipe.

See also

▸   Refer to the *Installing AppFabric Connect and AppFabric Connect for Services* recipe discussed earlier in this chapter

Exposing BizTalk applications in the cloud using AppFabric Connect for Services

The ability of BizTalk to connect to the cloud through the AppFabric Connect for Services feature opens the door for hybrid solutions. The BizTalk application can be exposed as WCF Services on the cloud, by adding Windows Azure AppFabric Service Bus endpoints. These endpoints can be consumed by clients residing outside the enterprise's organizational firewall enabling them, for instance, to easily invoke a process. Clients can connect through the Windows Azure AppFabric Service Bus to on-premise applications or services through a relay service. This service can listen to external clients on behalf of the on-premise web service at a given public address and relay messages between both parties. In this recipe, you see how to use the BizTalk WCF Service Publishing Wizard to expose orchestration to the cloud.

Getting ready

Before you can try and use this recipe, you must have a registered service namespace with the Windows Azure AppFabric Service Bus. Go to the Windows Azure AppFabric portal (`http://www.microsoft.com/windowsazure/appfabric/`) to register a service namespace with the Service Bus. You must also have Windows Azure AppFabric SDK version 1.0 (September update or later) and the BizTalk Server 2010 Feature Pack installed. Also, refer to the *Installing AppFabric Connect and AppFabric Connect for Services* recipe discussed earlier in this chapter. Finally, you need a BizTalk Application with an orchestration to publish in the cloud. The code accompanied by this book provides one you can use, see `BTS.Cookbook.Orchestration.Cloud`.

How to do it...

You have to perform the following steps to expose the orchestration as a service on the cloud using the BizTalk WCF Service Publishing wizard:

1. Open the BizTalk Server Administration Console by clicking on **Start | BizTalk Server 2010 | BizTalk Server Administration**.

2. In **Administration Console,** navigate to **Application**. Right-click on the application and select **New | Application...**.

3. Give it an appropriate name and click on **OK**.

4. Run the BizTalk WCF Service Publishing Wizard by clicking on **Start | Microsoft BizTalk Server 2010 | BizTalk WCF Service Publishing Wizard**. Click on **Next** on the welcome screen of the wizard.

5. The wizard will prompt for the configuration of the type of service endpoints which you will create. The service has an on-premise metadata endpoint for on-premise testing purposes. Check the **Enable on-premise metadata exchange** checkbox and the option **Create BizTalk receive locations in the following application**. Select the BizTalk application you previously created and click on **Next**.

6. The next screen will prompt you to decide if the reach of the WCF Service will be extended to the cloud. In order to extend the reach of the WCF Service to the cloud, click on the **Add a Service Bus endpoint** checkbox. Then click on **Next**:

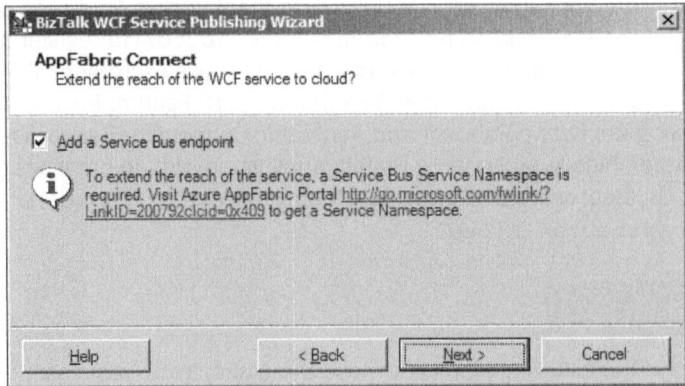

7. Now, you will have to specify which BizTalk artefacts are to be exposed as a service. Choose **Publish BizTalk orchestration as WCF service** and then click on **Next**.

8. In the next screen, you have to select **BizTalk Assembly** which contains the orchestrations on which the WCF Service will be based. Browse to the correct assembly, and click on **Next**.

9. The next screen will allow you to configure the namespace for the WCF Service. In this case, accept the default and click on **Next**.

10. In the next screen, accept the default location and allow anonymous access to the WCF Service by clicking on **Allow anonymous access to the WCF service**. Then click on **Next**.

11. The next screen is an important one. Here, you can configure the Service Bus endpoint relay bindings. Depending on which namespace you choose, select the options, as shown in the following screenshot and fill in your own namespace:

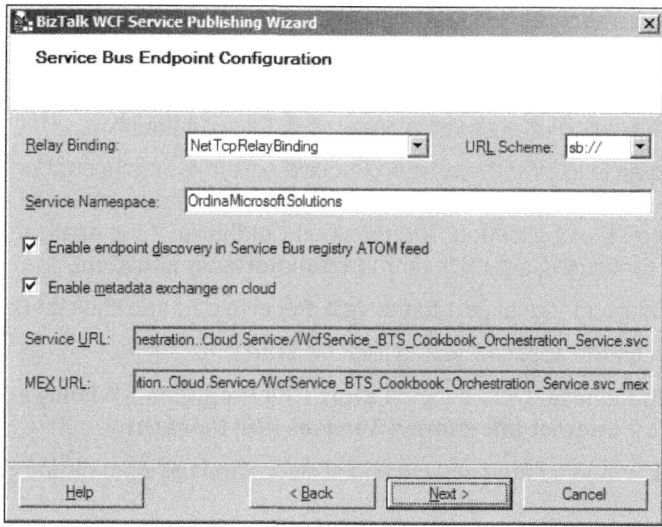

12. In the next screen, you have to fill in the authentication information for the previously configured Azure AppFabric Service Bus namespace. Make the selections, as shown in the following screenshot, and click on **Next**:

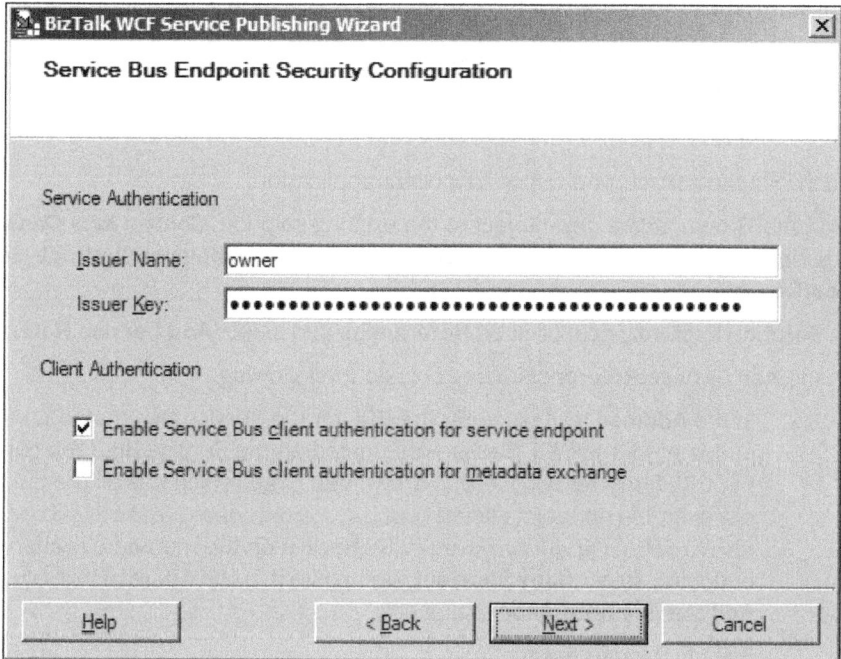

13. In the next screen, you will see a summary of the configurations allowing you to verify all the configurations. Click on **Create**.

14. When the WCF Service has been successfully created along with the Azure AppFabric Service Bus endpoint, a report is generated. Click on **Finish**.

15. The next step is to bind the created Receive port to the orchestration. In the BizTalk Administration Console, navigate to the application that has the orchestration and right-click on the application. Then click on **Configure**. If the application's host has not been configured, set the host to **BizTalkServerApplication**.

16. Bind the inbound logical port to the WCF Receive port and click on **OK**.

17. Right-click on the application and click on **Start**.

18. Run the IIS Manager by clicking on **Start | All Programs | Windows Server AppFabric | Internet Information Services (IIS) Manager**.

19. Right-click on the created service and click on **Manage Application | Advanced Settings**.

20. Set the **Application Pool** setting to an Application Pool which supports the .Net Framework version 4.0 and the Integrated managed pipeline mode. Click on **OK**.

21. Right-click on the created service in IIS and click on **Configure** under **Manage WCF and WF Services**.

22. Set **Auto-Start** to **Enabled** for the service and click on **OK**.

23. To verify if the service is published, go to the URL `https://namespace.servicebus.windows.net`. In this case,

    `https://ordinamicrosoftsolutions.servicebus.windows.net/`.

24. To invoke the service, you will need a client application.

25. In Visual Studio, add a new project to the existing solution. Choose **New Console Application**. Give it an appropriate name (for example, **EmployeeContract_Service_TestConsole**).

26. In **Solution Explorer**, right-click on **References** and select **Add Service Reference**.

27. In the **Add Service Reference** dialog box, do the following:

    1. In the **Address** textbox, enter the URL for the Service Bus metadata exchange endpoint for the WCF Service you hosted on the Service Bus. You can get the URL from the Service Bus ATOM feed page, which has all the publicly discoverable endpoints listed (`https://ordinamicrosoftsolutions.servicebus.windows.net/`). Right-click on the metadata exchange endpoint, select **Copy Shortcut**, and paste it in the **Address** text box in the **Add Service Reference** dialog box.

    2. Specify the namespace.

    3. Click on **OK**.

28. In case, the Service Bus client authentication for the service endpoint is enabled, the client will need to pass an authentication token to authenticate with the Service Bus. Provide the client authentication token by modifying the `app.config` file for the client application in the following manner:

    a. Open `app.config` for the client and add the following within the `system.serviceModel` element:

    ```
    <behaviors>
      <endpointBehaviors>
        <behavior name="sharedSecretClientCredentials">
          transportClientEndpointBehavior
          credentialType="SharedSecret">
            <clientCredentials>
              <sharedSecret issuerName="owner"
              issuerSecret="issuerkey" />
            </clientCredentials>
          </transportClientEndpointBehavior>
        </behavior>
      </endpointBehaviors>
    </behaviors>
    ```

    b. In `app.config`, add the `behaviorConfiguration` property to the client/endpoint element for the Service Bus endpoint named `RelayEndpoint`. You must set the `behaviorConfiguration` property to the same value you specified for the behavior name:

    ```
    <endpoint address="sb://ordinamicrosoftsolutions.servicebus.
    windows.net/BTS.Cookbook.Orchestration.Cloud.Orchestration/
    WcfService_BTS_Cookbook_Orchestration_Cloud_Orchestration.
    svc"
      binding="netTcpRelayBinding"
      bindingConfiguration="RelayEndpoint"
      contract="SREmployeeContract.
      WcfService_BTS_Cookbook_Orchestration_Cloud_Orchestration"
      name="RelayEndpoint"
      behaviorConfiguration="sharedSecretClientCredentials"/>
    ```

    c. Save and close `app.config`.

29. Open `Program.cs` for the application and add the following code:

    ```
    WcfService_BTS_Cookbook_Orchestration_Cloud_
    OrchestrationClient client = new WcfService_BTS_Cookbook_
    Orchestration_Cloud_OrchestrationClient
    ("WSHttpBinding_ITwoWayAsync");
    Console.WriteLine("\
    n\n*******************************************");
      Console.WriteLine("*** Request using Service Bus Endpoint
      ***");
    ```

```
Console.WriteLine("*********************************************\n");
  Request request = new Request();
  request.FullName = "JanJanssen";
  request.SocialSecurityNumber = "123456789";
  Response response = new Response();
  response = client.EmployeeContractDetails(request);
Console.WriteLine("********************************");
              Console.WriteLine("*** Employee Contract Result
***");
              Console.WriteLine("*******************************
*\n");
  Console.WriteLine("ContractType  :\t" + response.Type);
  Console.WriteLine("Function      :\t" + response.Function);
  Console.WriteLine("Salary        :\t" +
  response.Salary.ToString());
  Console.WriteLine("Pension       :\t" +
  response.Pension.ToString());
  Console.WriteLine("Benefits      :\t" +
  response.Benefits.ToString() + "\n");
  Console.WriteLine("Press any key to exit...");
Console.ReadLine();
```

30. Save `Program.cs` and build the solution. Now, press *F5* to run the application.

How it works...

The BizTalk WCF Service Publishing Wizard aids in having an endpoint in the cloud to access a process (orchestration) running on-premise. The first step in the wizard is choosing a binding (WCF-BasicHttp, WCF-WSHttp, or WCF-CustomIsolated), and WCF-WSHttp is chosen as it is the only binding that supports `WSHttpBindingElement` for the on-premise endpoint. By checking the **Enable on-premise metadata exchange** checkbox, you can test the service on-premise and with the **Create BizTalk receive locations in the following application** option, the Receive port is created in the desired application. In the subsequent page, the **Add a Service Bus endpoint** option is checked as the reach of the orchestration is extended to the cloud. By checking this option, all selected ports will be merged into a single WCF Service (this is the reason that the merge option is disabled). Since a process (orchestration) is going to be accessed through the cloud, the **Publish BizTalk orchestrations as WCF service** option is chosen in the **Create WCF services** page. Then, you are prompted to select the appropriate assembly containing the orchestration you want to be accessed through the cloud. Two subsequent pages involve the location of the on-premise service (`http://host[:port]/path`) and determine security (that is, allow anonymous or not). Other security details of the service are set in IIS while configuring the application pool.

After configuring the on-premise part of the service, you will have to configure the Service Bus endpoint and configuration. In the Service Bus Configuration page, you choose **Relay Binding** as **NetTcpRelayBinding**, fill in **Service Namespace** as a namespace associated with an enabled Azure AppFabric Service Bus account, if the Service Bus endpoints are to be publicly discoverable in an ATOM feed page and if metadata is exchanged in the cloud. Here, choices can be based on whether or not you want your service to be discovered in the cloud by clients.

The last stage, before creating the endpoint locally and the ability to have it extended to the cloud, involves security. Similar to when exposing on-premise data to the cloud, you need to provide an issuer name associated with the Azure account and issuer key. On this page, you can also decide on the client authentication. By enabling Service Bus client authentication for the service endpoint, you can force the client consuming the service to present an authentication token to the relay service. This helps preventing unauthorized client access and charges against the Service Namespace. Setting the Service Bus client authentication for the metadata exchange is disabled as this forces the client to present an authentication token to relay the service before it can retrieve the metadata. It depends whether or not you want your clients to be able to discover your service in the cloud.

Once the service has been created, you can bind a psychical port to the orchestration and configure the application pool service which is running under IIS and set it on Auto-Start. Once it has started, the Service Bus endpoints are established and an external client can access the service.

To access the service, a client application can be built to consume the WCF Service for which a relay service was created and hosted on the Service Bus. The client sends a request to the service request contract detail based on the name and social security number.

There's more...

Microsoft has provided a wiki explaining how to expose the BizTalk application to the cloud, including details about how to consume the application in a document called **Expose BizTalk Applications on the Cloud Using AppFabric Connect for Services** at `http://social.technet.microsoft.com/wiki/contents/articles/expose-biztalk-applications-on-the-cloud-using-appfabric-connect-for-services.aspx`.

There is a blog post called **Metadata Handling in BizTalk Server 2010 AppFabric Connect for Services** (`http://seroter.wordpress.com/2010/10/28/metadata-handling-in-biztalk-server-2010-appfabric-connect-for-services/`) by Richard Seroter that details metadata handling for AppFabric Connect for services.

See also

▸ Refer to the *Installing AppFabric Connect and AppFabric Connect for Services* recipe discussed earlier in this chapter

Performing table operations in SQL Azure

AppFabric Connect for Services also offers the possibility of connecting BizTalk with the cloud. It is possible to get connected with SQL Azure and call a stored procedure or perform a table operation. SQL Azure delivers cloud database services which are built on SQL Server technologies and is a component of the Windows Azure platform. Instead of storing or retrieving data from the on-premise SQL Server database, you can do it in the cloud. Benefits of SQL Azure are scalability and high availability because of elasticity to the cloud. With AppFabric Connect for Services, you are able to develop a hybrid BizTalk solution connecting with the cloud and on-premise systems.

Getting ready

Before you can try with use this recipe, you must have an account on Windows Azure and the SQL Azure database. Go to the SQL Azure Portal (`http://www.microsoft.com/windowsazure/sqlazure/`) to get a SQL Azure database. You must also have Windows Azure AppFabric SDK version 1.0 (September update or later) and the BizTalk Server 2010 Feature Pack installed. Also, see the Installing the AppFabric Connect Feature and AppFabric Connect for Services recipe discussed earlier in this chapter. You will find SQL the Script for the SQL Azure Database and table and the BizTalk project (`BTS.Cookbook.SQLAzure.TableOps`), which you can use for reference, accompanied with this book.

How to do it...

You have to perform the following steps to be able to perform table operations in SQL Azure:

1. Open Visual Studio.

2. Create a **New Project** dialog box, select **BizTalk Projects** and in the middle pane, click to select **Empty BizTalk Server Project**. Give it a descriptive name and click on **OK**.

3. Click to select the project in **Solution Explorer**, right-click to display the context menu and click to select **Add | Generated Items...** to display the **Add Generated Items** dialog box. Select **Consume Adapter Service** and click on **Add**:

   a. Choose **sqlBinding** in the **Select a binding** section.

   b. Click on **Configure** and then click on the **Security** tab. In **Client Credential Type,** select **UserName**.

   c. Fill in the credentials for the account which has access to the SQL Azure database.

   d. Select the **URI Properties** tab and fill in the Server name as **Initial Catalog**.

e. On the **Binding** tab, set **UseAmbientTransaction** to **False**. Setting it to **True** will elevate the transaction to MSDTC. This is not supported in SQL Azure yet (`http://msdn.microsoft.com/en-us/library/ee336250.aspx`).

f. Click on **OK** and you will see a URI, as shown in the following screenshot:

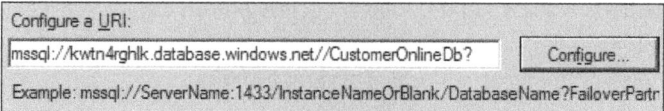

4. Click on **Connect**.

5. Verify that the **Consume Adapter Service** dialog box is populated with the values, as shown in the following screenshot, and click on the **OK** button:

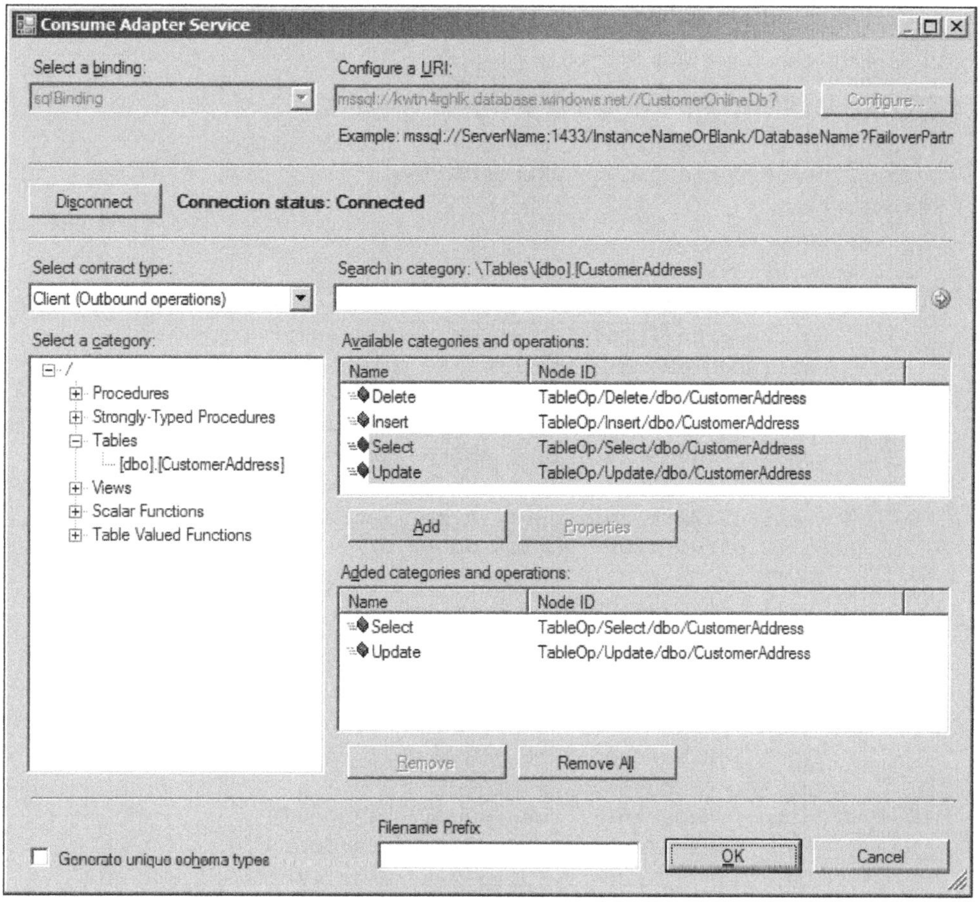

6. The schemas and a custom binding file will be created.

7. Right-click on the schema which has a name similar to **TableOperation.dbo. CustomerAddress.xsd** and click **Generate Instance**.

8. Save the generated XML to the file.

9. Modify the file, as shown in the following code snippet:

```
<ns0:Select xmlns:ns0="http://schemas.microsoft.com
/Sql/2008/05/TableOp/dbo/CustomerAddress">
  <ns0:Columns>*</ns0:Columns>
  <ns0:Query></ns0:Query>
</ns0:Select>
```

10. Move the **Update** node in the schema above **Select**.

11. Right-click on the schema which has a name similar to **TableOperation.dbo. CustomerAddress.xsd** and click on **Generate Instance**.

12. Save the generated XML to the file.

13. Modify the file, as shown in the following code snippet:

```
<ns0:Update xmlns:ns0="http://schemas.microsoft.com/
Sql/2008/05/TableOp/dbo/CustomerAddress">
<ns0:Rows>
  <ns0:RowPair>
    <ns0:After>
      <ns1:FirstName xmlns:ns1="http://schemas.microsoft.com/
      Sql/2008/05/Types/Tables/dbo">Jay</ns1:FirstName>
      <ns1:MiddleName xmlns:ns1=
      "http://schemas.microsoft.com/Sql/
      2008/05/Types/Tables/dbo">K.</ns1:MiddleName>
      <ns1:LastName xmlns:ns1="http://schemas.microsoft.com/
      Sql/2008/05/Types/Tables/dbo">Adams</ns1:LastName>
      <ns1:FullName xmlns:ns1="http://schemas.microsoft.com/
      Sql/2008/05/Types/Tables/dbo">
      Jay K.Adams</ns1:FullName>
      <ns1:CompanyName xmlns:ns1=
      "http://schemas.microsoft.com/Sql/2008/05/
      Types/Tables/dbo">Bicycle Specialists</ns1:CompanyName>
      <ns1:FullAddress xmlns:ns1=
      "http://schemas.microsoft.com/Sql/2008/05/
      Types/Tables/dbo">Blue Ridge Mall</ns1:FullAddress>
      <ns1:PostalCode xmlns:ns1=
      "http://schemas.microsoft.com/Sql/2008/05/
      Types/Tables/dbo">64106</ns1:PostalCode>
      <ns1:City xmlns:ns1="http://schemas.microsoft.com/Sql/
      2008/05/Types/Tables/dbo">Kansas City</ns1:City>
      <ns1:StateProvince xmlns:ns1=
      "http://schemas.microsoft.com/Sql/2008/05/
```

```
            Types/Tables/dbo">Missouri</ns1:StateProvince>
            <ns1:Country xmlns:ns1=
            "http://schemas.microsoft.com/Sql/2008/05/
            Types/Tables/dbo">United States</ns1:Country>
        </ns0:After>
        <ns0:Before>
            <ns1:FirstName xmlns:ns1=
            "http://schemas.microsoft.com/Sql/2008/05/
            Types/Tables/dbo">Jay</ns1:FirstName>
            <ns1:MiddleName xmlns:ns1=
            "http://schemas.microsoft.com/Sql/2008/05/
            Types/Tables/dbo">K.</ns1:MiddleName>
            <ns1:LastName xmlns:ns1=
            "http://schemas.microsoft.com/Sql/2008/05/
            Types/Tables/dbo">Adams</ns1:LastName>
            <ns1:FullName xmlns:ns1=
            "http://schemas.microsoft.com/Sql/2008/05/
            Types/Tables/dbo">Jay K. Adamns</ns1:FullName>
            <ns1:CompanyName xmlns:ns1=
            "http://schemas.microsoft.com/Sql/2008/05/
            Types/Tables/dbo">Bicycle Specialists</ns1:CompanyName>
            <ns1:FullAddress xmlns:ns1=
            "http://schemas.microsoft.com/Sql/2008/05/
            Types/Tables/dbo">Blue Ridge Mall</ns1:FullAddress>
            <ns1:PostalCode xmlns:ns1=
            "http://schemas.microsoft.com/Sql/2008/05/
            Types/Tables/dbo">64106</ns1:PostalCode>
            <ns1:City xmlns:ns1=
            "http://schemas.microsoft.com/Sql/2008/05/
            Types/Tables/dbo">Kansas City</ns1:City>
            <ns1:StateProvince xmlns:ns1=
            "http://schemas.microsoft.com/Sql/2008/05/
            Types/Tables/dbo">Missouri</ns1:StateProvince>
            <ns1:Country xmlns:ns1=
            "http://schemas.microsoft.com/Sql/2008/05/
            Types/Tables/dbo">United States</ns1:Country>
        </ns0:Before>
      </ns0:RowPair>
    </ns0:Rows>
```

14. Move the **Update** node back to its original place in the schema.

15. Sign the solution and give it an appropriate application name.

16. Build and deploy the solution.

17. Open the BizTalk Administration Console and navigate to the application you just deployed.

18. Right-click on the application and then select **Import | Bindings...**.

19. Go to the created binding file and click on **Open**.

20. Navigate to the Send ports in **Application** and you will see a newly created Send port.

21. Double-click on the Send port and then click on **Configure**.

22. In the **General** tab, remove **Update Operation in SOAP Action Header**.

23. In the **Credentials** tab, fill in the credentials for the account which has access to the SQL Azure database.

24. Click on **OK**.

25. Select **Filters** in the left pane of the Send port.

26. Create the following filter:

```
BTS.MessageType == http://schemas.microsoft.com/Sql/
2008/05/TableOp/dbo/CustomerAddress#Select
```

27. Click on **OK**.

28. Create a new Send port similar to the created Send port from the imported binding file.

29. In the **General** tab, put the following as a SOAP action header:

```
<BtsActionMapping xmlns:xsi="http://www.w3.org/2001/XMLSchema-
instance" xmlns:xsd="http://www.w3.org/2001/XMLSchema">
  <Operation Name="Update"
  Action="TableOp/Update/dbo/CustomerAddress" />
</BtsActionMapping>
```

30. In the **General** tab, fill in the same URI as in the other Send port.

31. In the **Credentials** tab, fill in the credentials for the account that has access to the SQL Azure database.

32. Click on **OK**.

33. Create the following filter:

```
BTS.MessageType == http://schemas.microsoft.com/Sql/2008/05/
TableOp/dbo/CustomerAddress#Update
```

34. Navigate to the Receive ports and create a new Receive port. Give it an appropriate name.

35. Create a new receive location, select the **File** adapter and give it an appropriate name, and point to the folder from where it can pick up XML messages.

36. Navigate to the Send ports and create a new Send port. Give it an appropriate name.

37. Select the **File** adapter for this port and point to the folder where messages can be dropped.

38. Add one of the following filters to this port:

    ```
    BTS.MessageType == http://schemas.microsoft.com/Sql/2008/05/
    TableOp/dbo/CustomerAddress#SelectResponse
    ```

    Or

    ```
    BTS.MessageType == http://schemas.microsoft.com/Sql/2008/05/
    TableOp/dbo/CustomerAddress#UpdateResponse
    ```

39. Right-click on the application and click on **Start**.

40. Drop a message for the selected operation in the folder and check the other folder for the result.

41. You can do the same for the update operation message.

How it works...

The Consume Adapter Service is a metadata generation tool included in the WCF LOB Adapter SDK for using with BizTalk Projects. This tool can be used by adapter consumers in Visual Studio 2010 to browse (and search) metadata from the adapter and then generate XML Schemas for selected operations. Once you have started this tool, you can configure security, LOB connection strings, and adapter binding properties. To connect with SQL Azure, you have to choose sqlBinding, hence, SQL Azure is built on SQL Server technologies. You can choose to use an inbound or outbound contract type and select one or more operations. Based on your choice, you will see that the tool will generate schemas and either a WCF-Custom Send port binding information XML or a WCF-Custom Receive port binding information XML. In this recipe, you have created an XML schema for the Select and Update operation on the table in SQL Azure. The generated WCF-Custom Send port binding is imported to create a Send port for communication with SQL Azure. You have to create a Send port for each operation unfortunately, because multiple SOAP header actions result in a BizTalk runtime and not understanding which one to choose.

In the schema, as shown in the following screenshot, you can see how messages with certain operations (Select, Update) are routed by BizTalk to SQL Azure and the results of the operations are routed back and end up as messages in the file folder:

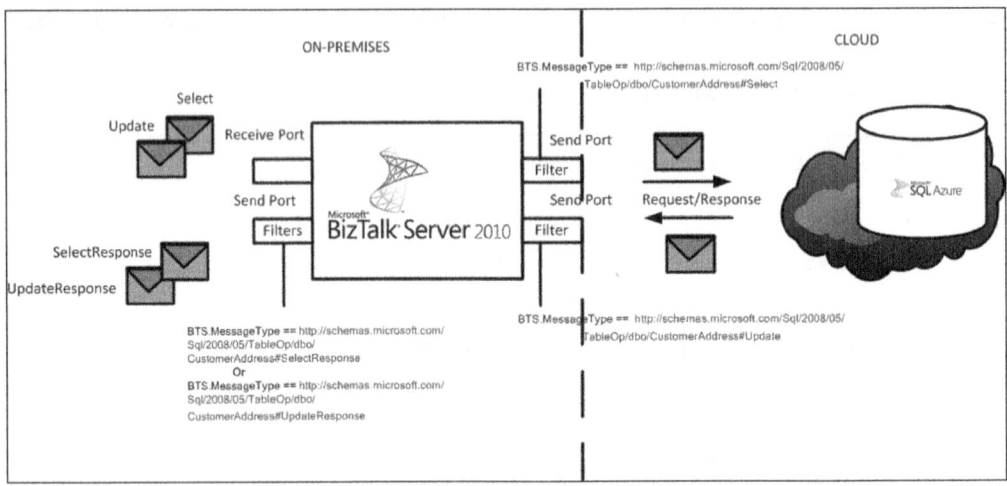

There's more...

Besides operations performed directly on the table, it is also possible for instance, to call a stored-procedure in SQL Azure. It is explained in the document called **BizTalk AppFabric Connect: WCF-Adapter Service Stored Procedure** at http://soa-thoughts.blogspot. com/2011/03/biztalk-appfabric-connect-wcf-adapter.html.

You can find a lot of information online for SQL Azure and a quick start to have some basic understanding is the wiki page called **SQL Azure FAQ** at http://social.technet. microsoft.com/wiki/contents/articles/sql-azure-faq.aspx.

See also

▶   Refer to the *Installing AppFabric Connect and AppFabric Connect for Services* recipe discussed earlier in this chapter

7
Monitoring and Maintenance

In this chapter, we will cover:

- ▶ Importing the BizTalk Management Pack in SCOM
- ▶ Using the BizTalk Administration Console
- ▶ Alternative BizTalk monitoring solution: BizTalk360
- ▶ Configuring the BizTalk database jobs
- ▶ Leveraging the BizTalk monitoring job
- ▶ Identifying bottlenecks with the Performance Monitor
- ▶ Using the BizTalk Message Box Viewer

Introduction

This chapter will provide some recipes for monitoring and maintaining BizTalk. To fully describe BizTalk operations, it would require a book by itself. Here, focus lies on some important aspects of operating BizTalk, keeping it healthy, troubleshooting, and monitoring. The recipes in this book can help you as an administrator to do day-to-day operations, help in diagnosing issues, and thinking about the best fit tool for monitoring your BizTalk environment.

Monitoring BizTalk can primarily be done with the out of the box Administration Console, but the focus is mainly BizTalk itself, managing applications, adapters, and so on, and for troubleshooting purposes. Microsoft offers the System Center Operation Manager to enable overall end-to-end monitoring of your entire enterprise IT infrastructure and its applications (that is, other server products such as BizTalk, Exchange, and third-party software).

To use SCOM solely for BizTalk would use too much overhead, require training for BizTalk administrators, and can be costly. However, SCOM can be a valuable asset, yet it requires an investment from IT. There are third-party products available which can provide a monitoring solution for the BizTalk environment. For instance, BizTalk360 can serve as a great alternative and delivers a web-based UI, which has been a long demanded feature by administrators. BizTalk360 also addresses some of the issues one may have with the BizTalk Administration Console.

The BizTalk Administration Console is a very useful tool with multiple purposes such as maintaining a BizTalk group, configuring applications, adapters, and so on. It is one tool provided by Microsoft to target audiences, such as developers, IT professionals, performance experts, and operators, but for instance, it is not web based and it lacks fine grained authorization, auditing, and governance. The *Alternative BizTalk monitoring solution: BizTalk360* recipe will reveal more of BizTalk360's capabilities and the *Using the BizTalk Administration Console* recipe will show some of its capabilities. Besides BizTalk360, there are other third-party monitoring solutions such as Minotaur, IPM, FRENDS Helium, and Moesioen.

The BizTalk Server delivers jobs for its databases. These jobs are important to keep BizTalk healthy and running smoothly. Some of the jobs are not configured after installation and configuration of the BizTalk environment. Two of the following jobs, you need to configure by yourself:

- ▶ Backup BizTalk Server (`BizTalkMgmtDb`)
- ▶ DTA Purge Archive (`BizTalkDTADb`)

The *Configuring the BizTalk database jobs* recipe will detail how to do this for your environment. Then, there is a new job called the BizTalk monitoring job, which enables you to identify any known issues in the Management, Message Box, or DTA databases. The *Leveraging BizTalk monitoring job* recipe will tell you how to leverage this job for altering purposes.

The final two recipes in this chapter will aid you in troubleshooting your BizTalk environment when it comes to performance or other issues. The Performance Monitor, which is included with the Windows operating system, can be of tremendous value when it comes to identifying performance bottlenecks in your BizTalk environment. The Message Box Viewer can be a very useful tool to retrieve information from a BizTalk group and identifying all possible issues, which could be critical or need attention. The tool offers capabilities to present them in a user friendly format.

Importing the BizTalk Management Pack in SCOM

Microsoft **System Center Operation Manager** (**SCOM**) is a component which belongs to the System Center Suite. It can be installed as a standalone product. The latest version is SCOM 2007 R2 and it enables you to do end-to-end service management, meaning that you can monitor your entire Microsoft infrastructure from the Windows Server (OS), application servers to the Microsoft Exchange. Through a single UI, an administrator and/or engineer can monitor the health, performance, and availability of data-center environments across applications, operating systems, hypervisors, and even hardware.

What happens when you use SCOM is described in this section. Each machine which needs to be monitored has an agent (that is, opsmgr healthservice) running. This agent watches several sources on that computer, including the Windows Event Log, for specific events or alerts generated by the applications executing on the monitored computer. When a specific event or alert occurs, the agent will detect it and forward it to a SCOM Server. The SCOM application maintains a database that includes a history of alerts and events and applies filtering rules to alerts/events as they arrive. Each rule can trigger some sort of notification, like an email to be sent to the operator or start a workflow intended to correct the cause of the alert in an appropriate manner.

SCOM uses the term management pack to refer to a set of filtering rules specific to some monitored applications such as the BizTalk Server. Microsoft and other software vendors make management packages available for their products, SCOM also provides for authoring custom management packs. Microsoft and other software vendors make these management packages available through the System Center Marketplace.

Getting ready

The SCOM instance needs to be installed on a machine. An administrator role is needed to install agents, configure monitored computers, and create management packs. It should also have rights to simply view the list of recent alerts which can be given to any valid user account.

How to do it...

As an administrator, you can log in to the machine with SCOM running on it. Then the following steps need to be performed to import the management pack for the BizTalk Server:

1. Open the Operations Console by navigating from the start menu to **System Center Operation Manager 2007 R2**.

2. In the SCOM Operation Console, select **Administration Pane**.

3. In **Administration Overview,** select **Actions** and then select **Import Management Pack**.

4. Then, the **Import Management Packs** dialog window will appear.

5. Select **Add | Add from catalog...**:

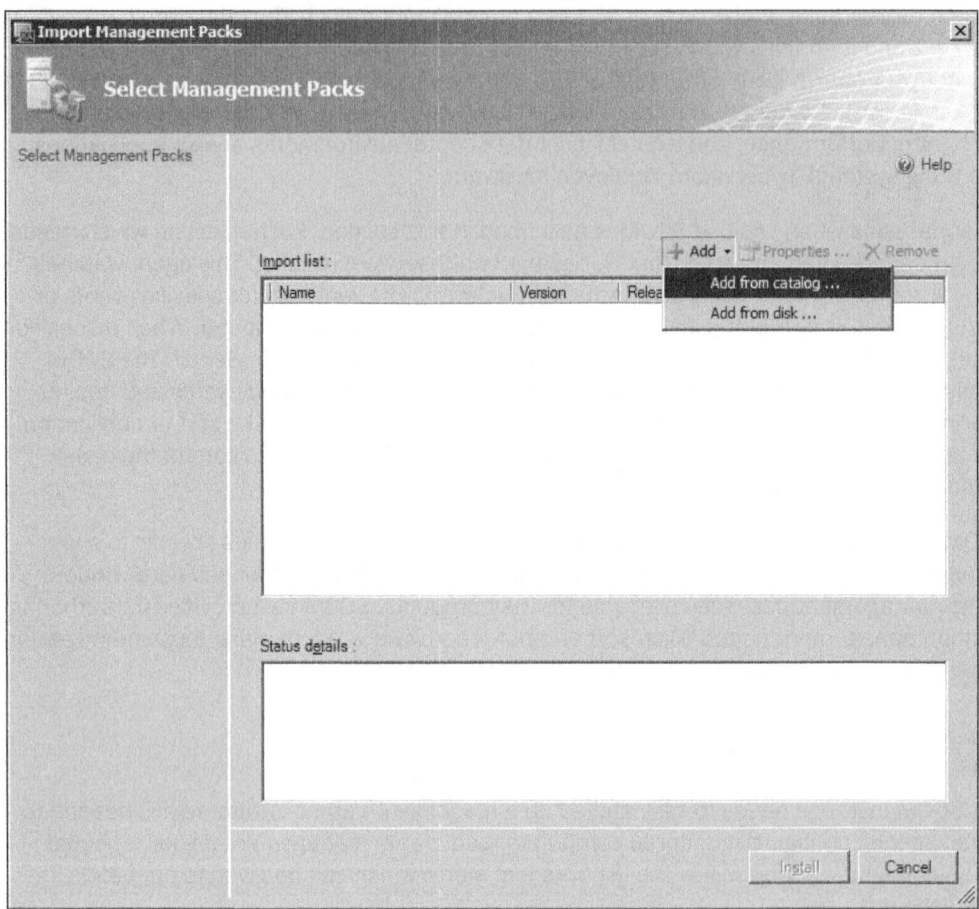

6. A connection will be made to the internet.

7. In the **Select Management Packs from Catalog** dialog, fill in **BizTalk** in the **Find** textbox and click on **Search**.

8. In **Management packs in the catalog**, select **BizTalk 2010** and click on **Add**:

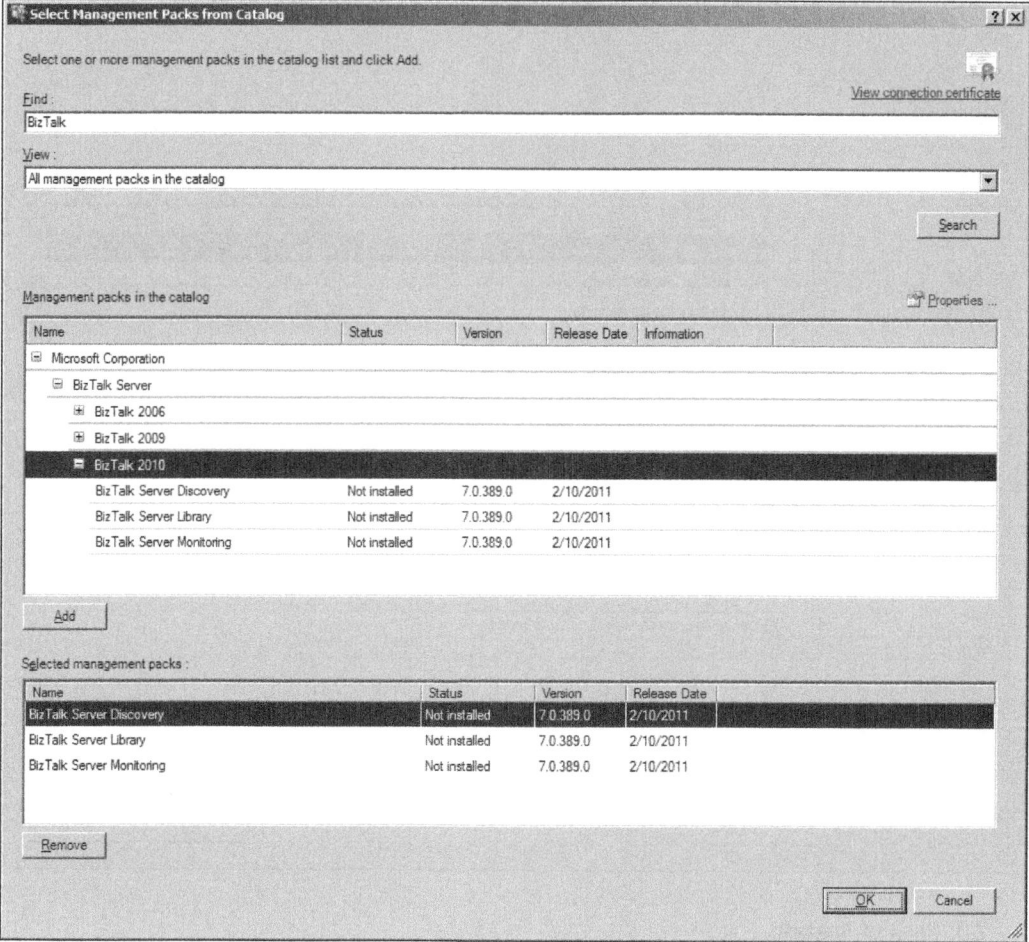

9. Click on **OK** and a new **Import Management Packs** dialog will appear:

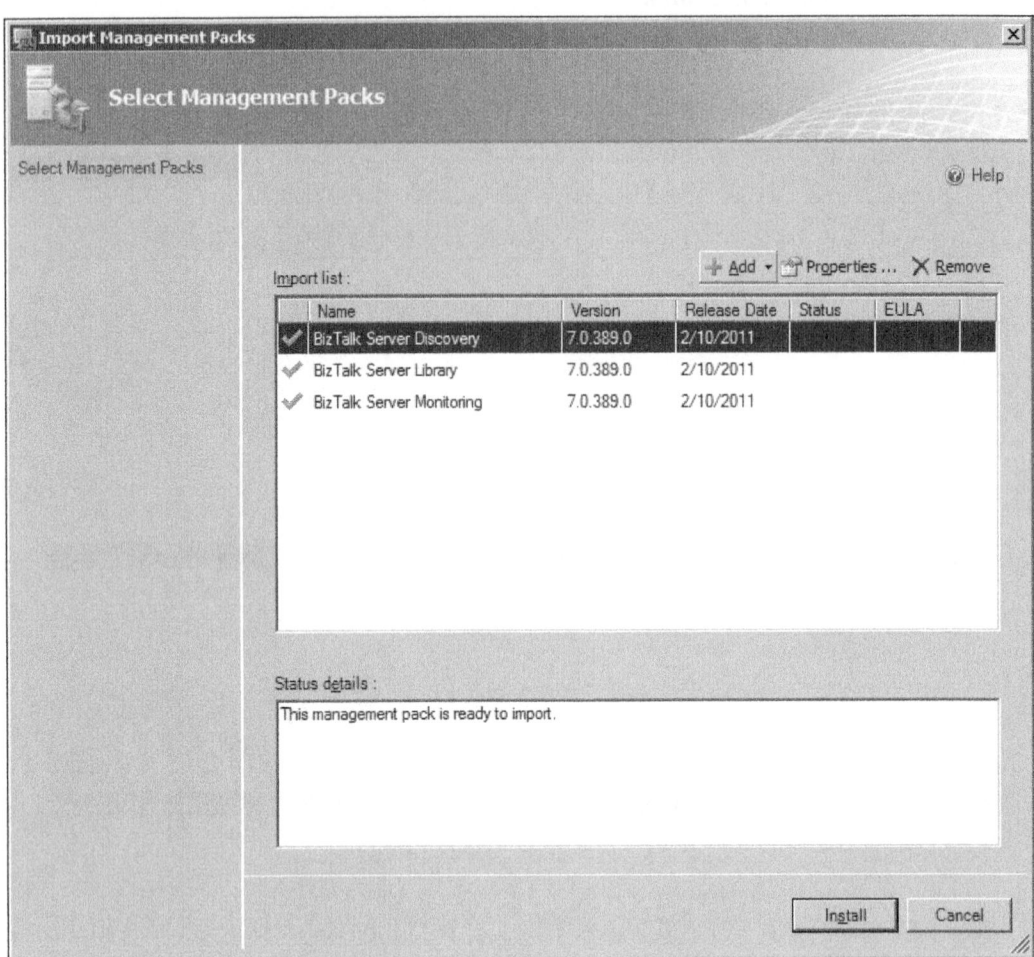

10. Click on **Install**.

11. The management packs will be downloaded and imported:

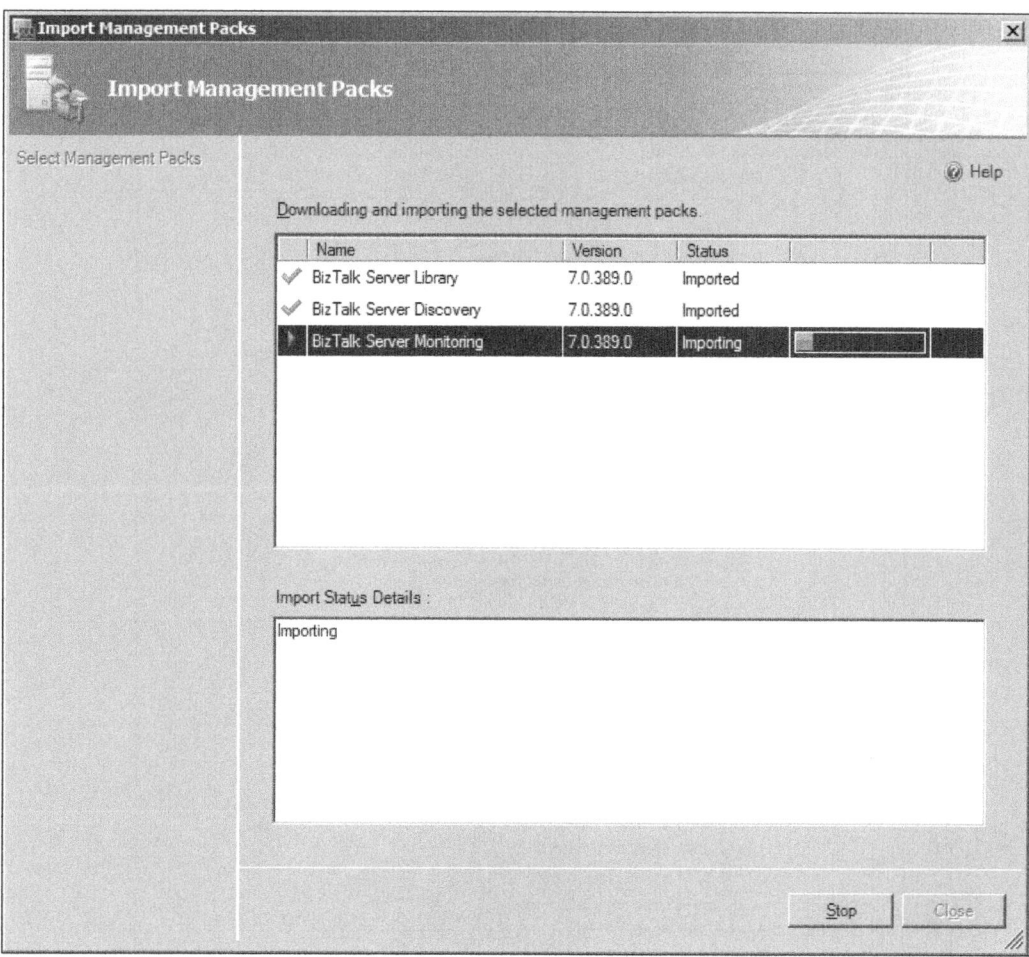

12. When each pack is imported, click on **Close**.

13. Go to the **Monitoring** pane.

14. Press *F5* to refresh and you will see that there is a folder called **Microsoft BizTalk Server 2010**:

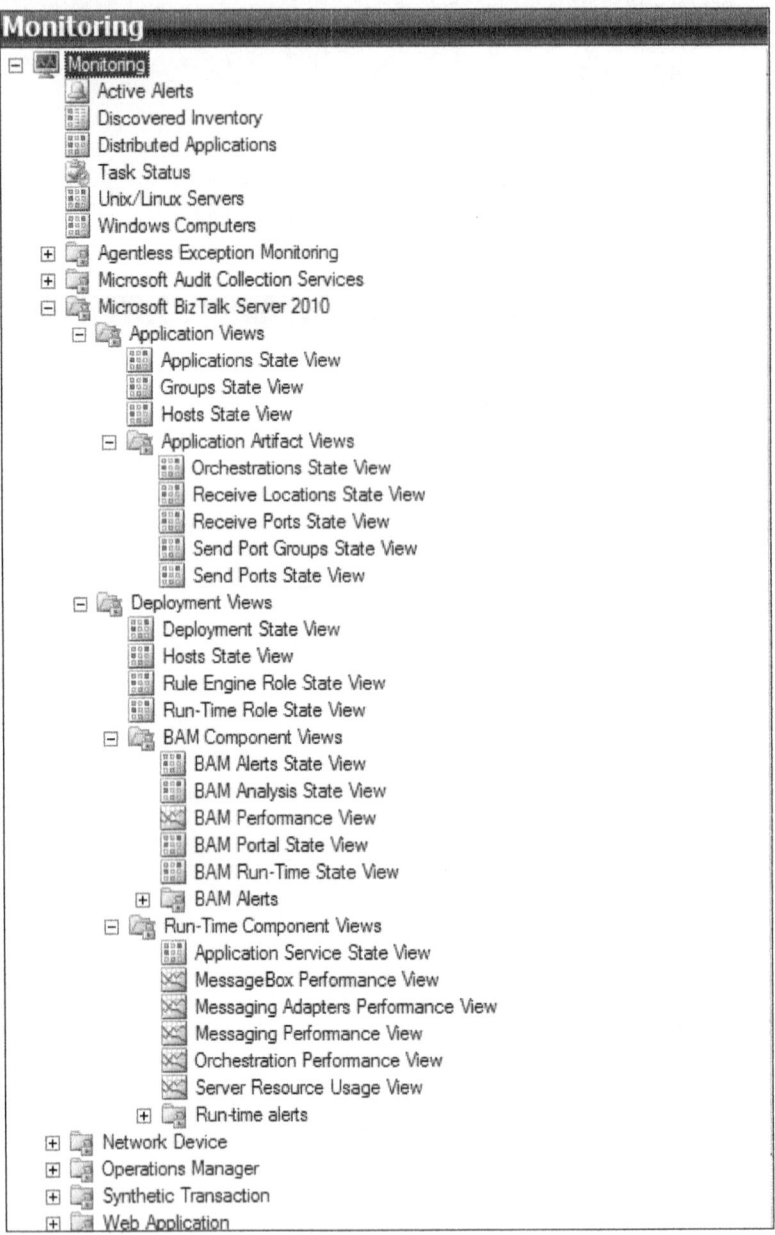

How it works...

The management packs can be imported through the online catalog which connects with Microsoft from the disk after downloading the packs manually through the System Center Marketplace. The best option is to collect them through the online catalog, so you will always have the latest version of the management pack. With connection to the online catalog, you can search for the BizTalk Management Packs. The management packs are offered for BizTalk 2006 (R2), 2009, and 2010. For each version there are three packs:

- ▸ Discovery
- ▸ Library
- ▸ Monitoring

Each pack will be downloaded from the catalog and installed. This process is an automated process. The following table shows what each management pack contains:

File name	Display name	Description	Purpose
Microsoft. BizTalkServer2010. Library.mp	BizTalk Server Library	Contains generic classes, relationships, and other management pack building blocks which are used by other management packs to provide monitoring for all BizTalk applications	To provide one profile for association with all discoveries and one for all monitors and tasks
Microsoft.BizTalk. Server.2010. Monitoring.mp	BizTalk Server Monitoring	Contains monitors, rules, and views which provide an extensible way to control all BizTalk applications	To understand the current availability, configuration, health, and performance of your BizTalk Server environment
Microsoft.BizTalk. Server.2010. Discovery.mp	BizTalk Server Discovery	Contains discoveries that are used for finding the various components of BizTalk applications	To enable discovery of the object types such as the BizTalk Group, BizTalk Host, BizTalk Application, and so on

After installation of the packs, the following views are listed directly under the **BizTalk Server 2010** node in the **Monitoring** pane of the Operations Console (see the previous screenshot). There are two views, one intended for the BizTalk administrator/operator and one for the enterprise IT administrator:

▶ **Application views**: With these views, a BizTalk administrator or operator is able to monitor the state and health of various BizTalk Server artefacts and applications such as orchestrations, Send ports, receive locations, and so on.

▶ **Deployment views**: An enterprise IT administrator is able to monitor the state and health of the various enterprise deployments such as the machines hosting the SQL Server databases, machines hosting the SSO service, host instance machines, IIS, network services, and so on.

There's more...

You can learn how to work with SCOM through the administration course which Microsoft has made available. There is a document called **BizTalk Server 2010 Administrator Training Kit** at `http://www.microsoft.com/download/en/details.aspx?id=27148`.

If you need to plan, deploy, operate, and maintain the Operations Manager 2007 R2, you can find the guidance in a documentation called **System Center Operations Manager 2007 R2 Product Documentation** at `http://technet.microsoft.com/en-us/systemcenter/om/bb498235`.

Specific documentation for the BizTalk Management Pack is available at the following links, The pack itself can be downloaded through the Microsoft Download Center:

▶ **BizTalk Server 2010 Management Pack Documentation**: `http://www.microsoft.com/download/en/details.aspx?displaylang=en&id=21232`

▶ **BizTalk Server 2010 Monitoring Management Pack**: `http://www.microsoft.com/download/en/details.aspx?id=14897`

See also

▶ Refer to the *Alternative BizTalk monitoring solution: BizTalk360* recipe discussed later in this chapter.

Using the BizTalk Administration Console

The BizTalk Server Administration Console is a **Microsoft Management Console** (**MMC**) which you can use to manage and monitor the BizTalk Server, and which you can use to deploy and manage your BizTalk Server applications. Administrators and/or BizTalk operators will use this tool for numerous tasks as all the settings in the BizTalk group can be controlled in a single user-interface common such as other MMC snap-ins and IIS.

Often the BizTalk Administration Console is the first place the administrator will look to identifying errors or issues in BizTalk and determine how to resolve them. Other tools which can aid, or are better suited to do so, are the Windows Event Log (that is also accessible through the BizTalk Administration Console), SQL Server, and other external applications. The SCOM Event Viewer can give a first indication about an error that has occurred in BizTalk. The BizTalk Server writes errors to the application event log each time an error occurs. Error information in the event log contains information on when, why, and where the fault happened. Through the BizTalk Administration Console, the event log can be viewed and the administrator or operator can start investigating the problem within the same snap-in using the console's Group Hub page.

Getting ready

For this recipe, you will need access to the BizTalk Server Administration Console and the appropriate rights to be able to operate it. In this recipe, a sample solution called `BTS.Cookbook.Calculator` is used. You can find it with the code belonging to this book.

How to do it...

In this recipe, you will identify an error in an orchestration using the Administration Console and you will learn how to perform custom queries.

You need to perform the following steps to troubleshoot a suspended orchestration:

1. Drop a message called `DivideCalOperation` in the folder called **In** from the sample solution.
2. Open the BizTalk Administration Console.

3. Expand the **Event Viewer** folder in the left pane, click on **Windows Logs**, and select **Application**. You should see an error event relating to the service instance that was suspended. This event is flagged with a BizTalk-related source, such as **BizTalk Server** or **XLANG/s**:

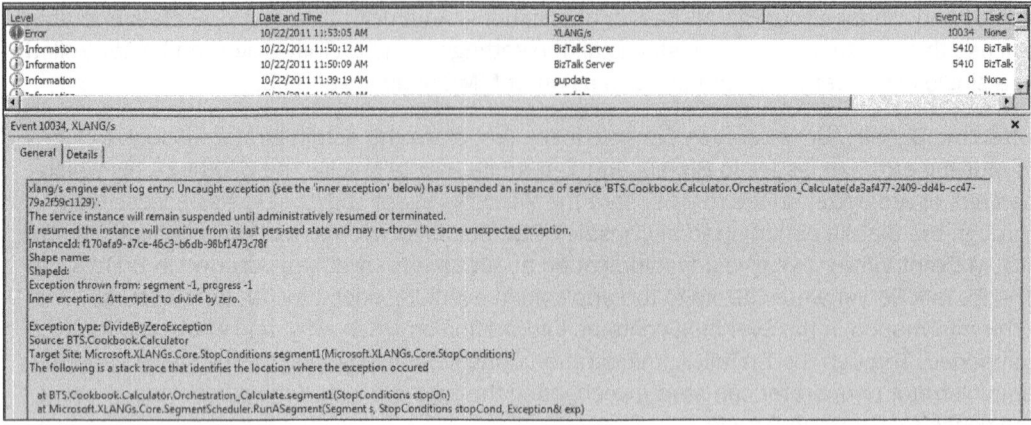

4. To obtain more detailed information about this event, you can expand the **BizTalk Server Administration** folder in the left pane, and select your BizTalk group. This opens the **Group Hub** page. Press *F5* to refresh. This page is divided into four sections that provide an overall view of the health of your BizTalk Server system:

   ❑ **Configuration Overview**: This section is located in the upper part of the **Group Hub** page. It indicates the overall health of the BizTalk group by displaying the state of the applications, host instances, and adapter handlers configured in this group.

   ❑ **Work in Progress** and **Suspended Items**: These sections are located in the middle of the **Group Hub** page. The **Work in Progress** section displays running service instances, dehydrated orchestrations, retrying and idle ports, ready service instances, and scheduled service instances. The **Suspended Items** section displays the number of suspended service instances, resumable and non-resumable instances, and suspended MSMQT messages.

   ❑ **Grouped Suspended Service Instances**: This section is also located in the middle part of the **Group Hub** page and it displays suspended service instances grouped by application, service name, error code, and URI.

   ❑ **Tracked Service Instances** and **Tracked Message Event**: These sections are located in the lower part of the **Group Hub** page and they display tracked service instances and tracked messages:

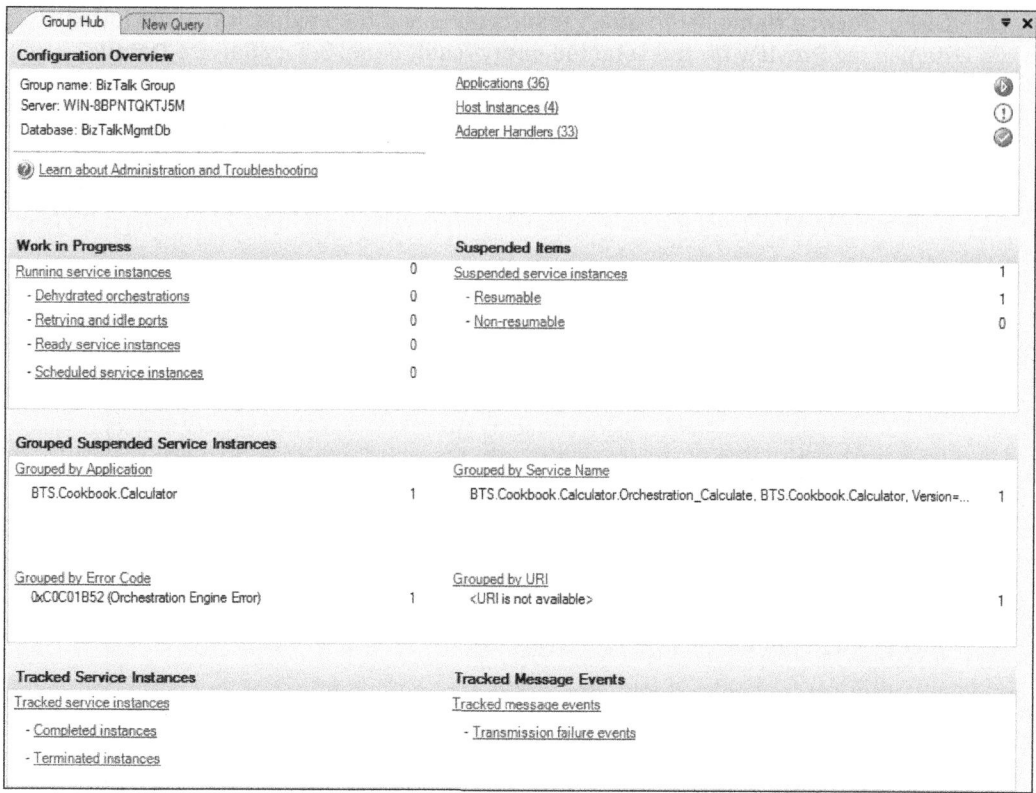

5. In **Grouped Suspended Service Instances,** click on the link in the **Grouped by Service Name** section, as shown in the previous screenshot. Clicking on this link launches a query window, as shown in the following screenshot:

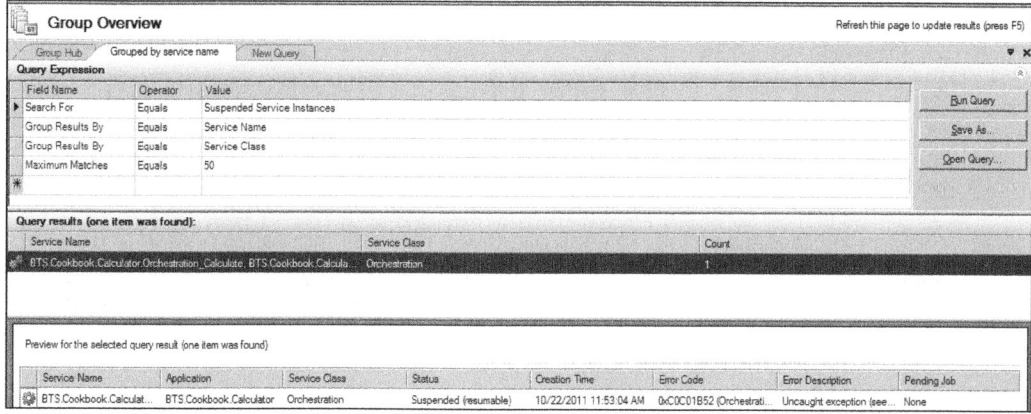

6. Select **Service Name** in the **Query results** pane and then right-click on the found item in the **Preview for the selected query result** pane. Select **Service Details** and a dialog will appear.

7. Click on the **Error Information** tab. This tab displays the text of the exception which the suspended service instance encountered, which is the same as what is written to the application event log. The error text usually includes key stack information, indicating at what level the fault occurred and how it was bubbled up through BizTalk:

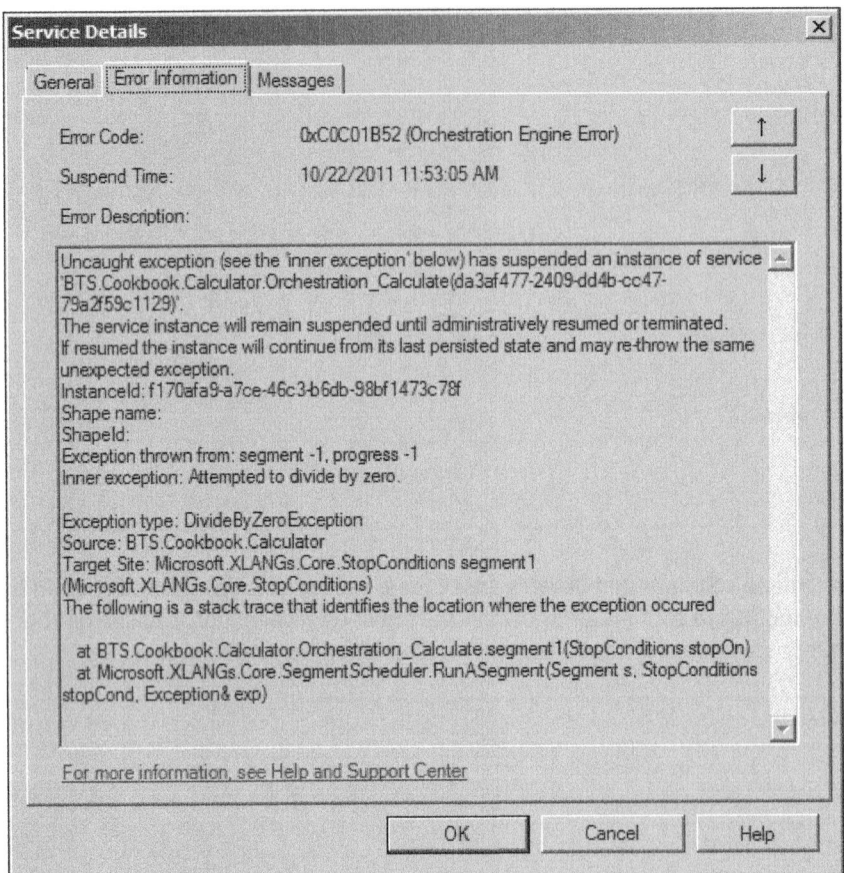

8. Click on the **Messages** tab. This tab displays a list of all messages related to the suspended service instance. From this tab, you can save the suspended message to a file for further inspection, turn on tracking for the message, or view additional details of the message (right-click on the message for these capabilities):

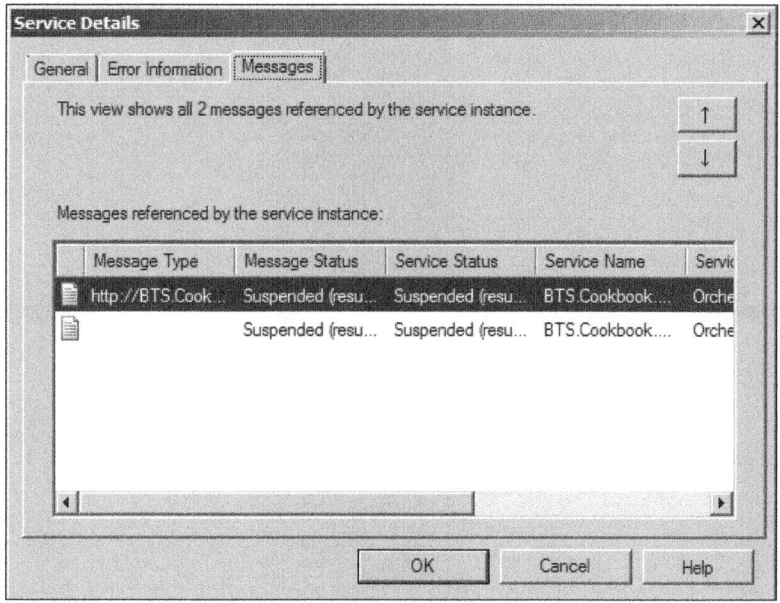

9. Double-click on one of the messages and select the **body** section of **Message Parts** to investigate the message:

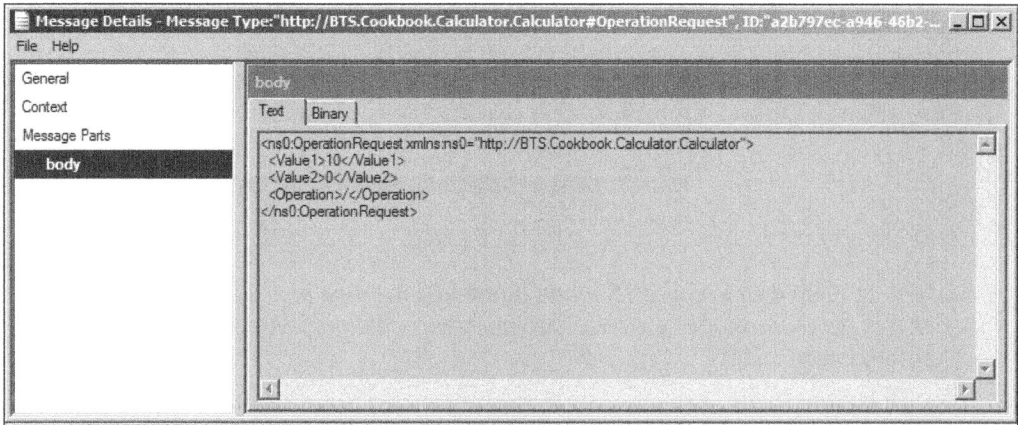

10. It will show that the second value is **0** and is the cause of the error.

To perform a custom query you need to perform the following steps:

1. In the **Group Hub** page of **Group Overview**, click on **New Query**.

2. **Query Expression** will appear and choose **Suspended Service Instances** for the column **Value**.

3. Click on **Run Query**:

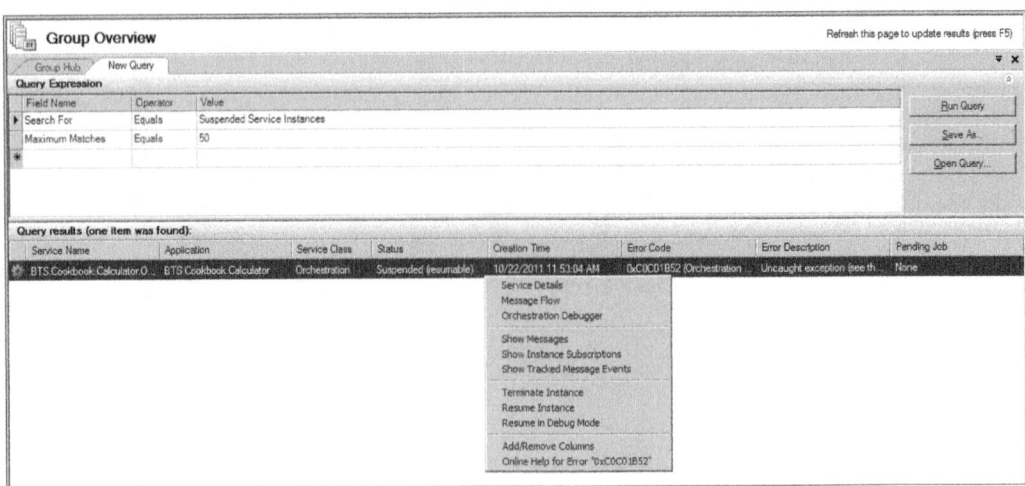

4. In the previous screenshot, you can see that you can drill down into **Service Details**, **Message Flow**, and so on.

5. In **New Query**, under **Value**, select **Subscriptions**:

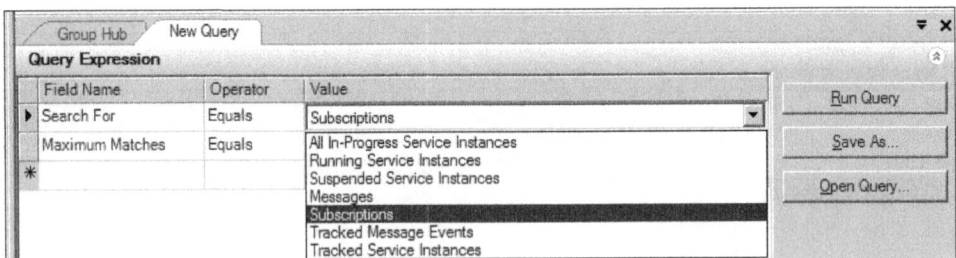

6. Next, in **Field Name**, choose **Service Name** and in **Value** select an application (that is, BTS.Cookbook.Calculator, which is a sample orchestration provided by the accompanied code).

7. Click on **Run Query**:

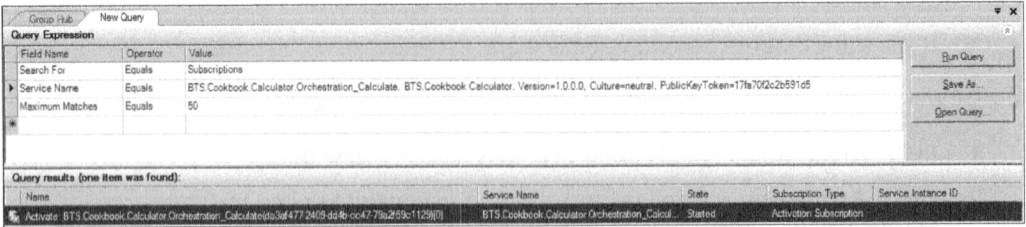

In certain scenarios, especially those using orchestrations, we can also make a visual debug into the orchestration process in order to visualize where the error occurred. To perform **Orchestration Debugger**, you need to perform the following steps:

1. Perform the same first four steps described in the steps to troubleshoot a suspended orchestration.

2. In the fifth step, instead of selecting **Service Details**, choose the **Orchestration Debugger** option:

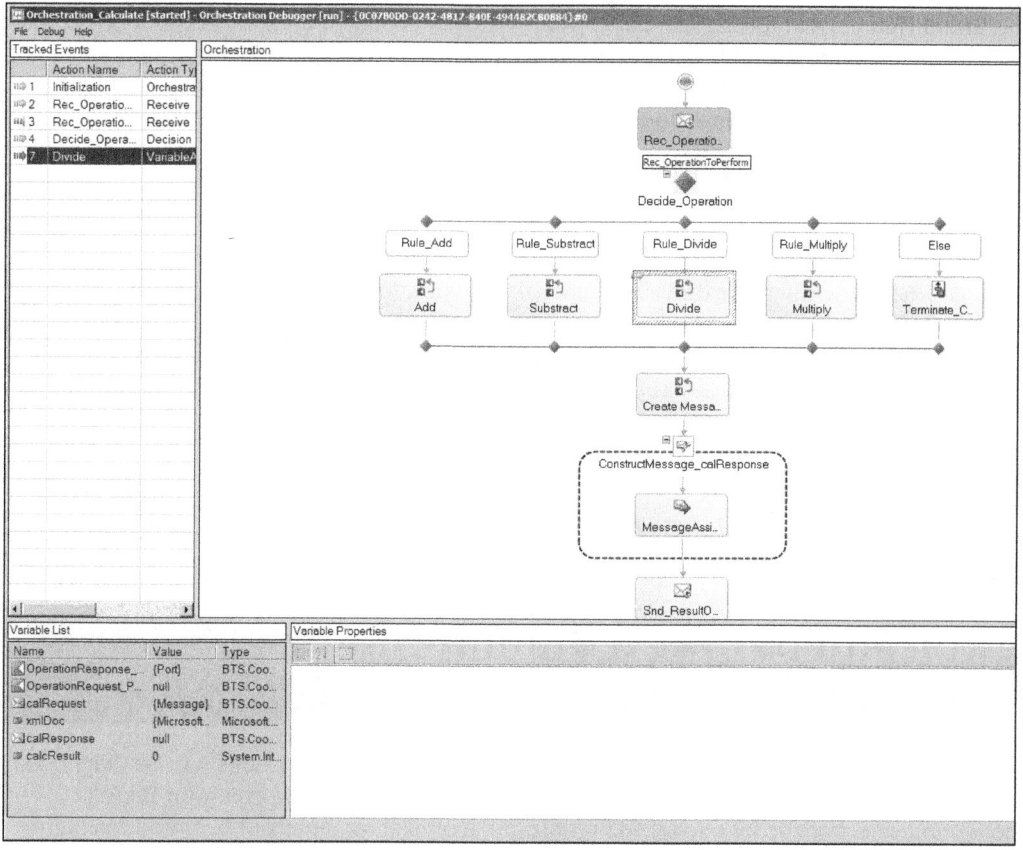

You can find more details at http://msdn.microsoft.com/en-us/library/ aa953746%28v=bts.20%29.aspx.

How it works...

This recipe showed some of the capabilities of the BizTalk Administration Console. When an error occurs in your solution, BizTalk will typically suspend the service instance encountering the error, when it is not gracefully handled. A service in this context is a generic term to describe a part of BizTalk processing such as the orchestration, messaging, or adapter. A service instance refers to a specific instance of the orchestration, messaging, or adapter component. An operator can drill down into the service instance and view the details. Messages referenced by an instance can be viewed that is, context, parts, and body. Through the **Group Hub** page in the BizTalk Server Administration Console an administrator or operator can find specific running and suspended service instances, messages, or subscriptions by performing queries. These queries will search through active items, which are stored in the `MessageBox` database. A **New Query** tab will appear each time you run a new query.

There's more...

This recipe scratches the surface on capabilities of the BizTalk Administration Console. Through MSDN you will find extensive information on how to use the BizTalk Server Administration Console, and where you can read more about the capabilities. For more deatils, see the **Using the BizTalk Administration Console** document at `http://msdn.microsoft.com/en-us/library/aa578089%28v=bts.70%29.aspx`.

See also

▸ Refer to the *Alternative BizTalk monitoring solution: BizTalk360* recipe, discussed later in this chapter.

Alternative BizTalk monitoring solution—BizTalk360

Monitoring BizTalk can be done using SCOM by administrators and issues can be diagnosed and resolved using the BizTalk Administration Console. To use SCOM solely for BizTalk monitoring, is too costly for mid-sized organizations or even an enterprise. It requires highly skilled people as learning to operate SCOM is a steep learning curve. Besides the skill set, it also requires an investment in hardware and software. Since SCOM can monitor any Microsoft product, Azure, and third-party products, it would be a waste of resources to just use SCOM for monitoring BizTalk.

The BizTalk Administration Console is a very useful tool with multiple purposes, such as maintaining a BizTalk group, configuring applications, adapters, and so on. It is one tool provided by Microsoft to target all audiences such as developers, IT professionals, performance experts, and operators. Due to these characteristics, there are two major drawbacks:

- It is too powerful for day-to-day support/monitoring operations
- There are some gaps in the product when it comes to operations, such as fine grained authorization (for example, read-only access, restricting operators to certain applications, and so on), governance/auditing (for example, who did what), and so on.

Another important limitation of the BizTalk Administration Console is that it is not web-based.

BizTalk360 (`http://www.biztalk360.com`) is the first product which is targeted to address these challenges. It comes with the in-built proactive alerting/notification capability targeted towards BizTalk administrators. So, there is no steep learning curve similar to SCOM. It also addresses the majority of the gaps in the BizTalk Administration Console when it comes to day-to-day support/operation.

The other key capabilities of BizTalk360 are:

- Web-based (**Rich Internet Application—RIA**) application
- Advanced authorization
- Governance/auditing
- Proactive alerting
- Various dashboards
- Integrated **Business Activity Monitoring** (**BAM**) portal
- Integrated Message Box Viewer
- Multi-environment support
- Knowledge-based repository
- Advanced Event Viewer

You can take a quick tour to understand all the capabilities at `http://www.biztalk360.com/Content/Tour.aspx?q=uap`.

Getting ready

Download the tool from `http://www.biztalk360.com/` and install it on the developer's virtual machine.

How to do it...

Let us see how we can use some of the core functionalities of BizTalk360:

- ▸ Providing read-only access to operators
- ▸ Setting up alerts for applications
- ▸ How to use the Advanced Event Viewer

Providing read-only access to operators

One of the common challenges organizations face while monitoring/supporting the BizTalk Server environment is to provide read-only access to certain people (such as first-level support). By giving read-only access, companies can be confident that no one can modify things in a production environment. Let us take a look at how BizTalk360 can be configured to do this:

1. Click on the **Settings** link at the top right-hand corner, which will bring the admin UI.
2. Under the **User Access Policy** section, click on **Add New**.
3. Supply the domain name and user name or NT role name for whom you need to provide the read-only access.
4. Select the BizTalk applications for which you need to provide access.
5. Do not select the following options:
   - ❑ **Operate on Host Instances**
   - ❑ **Operate on Service Instances**
   - ❑ **Operate on Application**
6. Click on **Save**.

BizTalk360 allows controlling read-only access at the Application, Service Instances, and Host Instances levels. Based on your requirements you can choose the appropriate options:

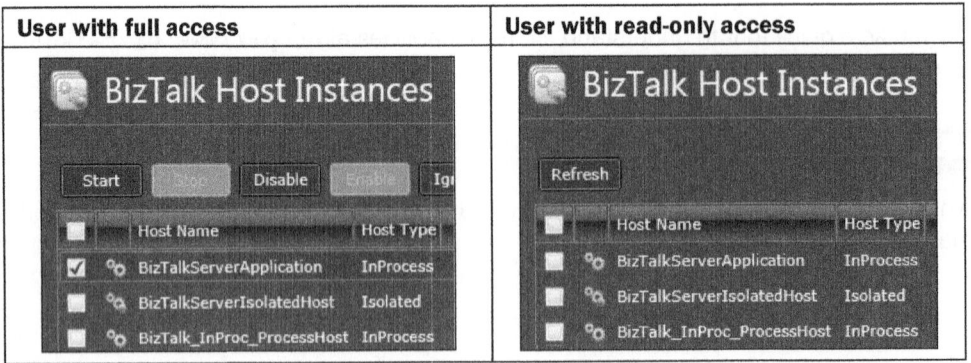

You will notice, there are no options to start, stop, disable, enable the host instances for the user with only read-only access.

 The user should not have the BizTalk operator or BizTalk administrator's role and access to the BizTalk Administration Console; otherwise he is able to do the above actions.

Setting up alerts for applications

In this section, we will take a look at how you can configure BizTalk360's notification capabilities to monitor the health of your environment:

1. Click on the **Alert Settings** link on the top right-hand corner.

2. Create an **Alarm**:

    a. Provide a friendly **Alarm Name** (for example, **Weekdays**).

    b. Provide an e-mail address in the **Email** section (multiple e-mail addresses can be provided).

    c. Set the regular alarm timings, and also set your error threshold settings.

    d. Click on **Save**:

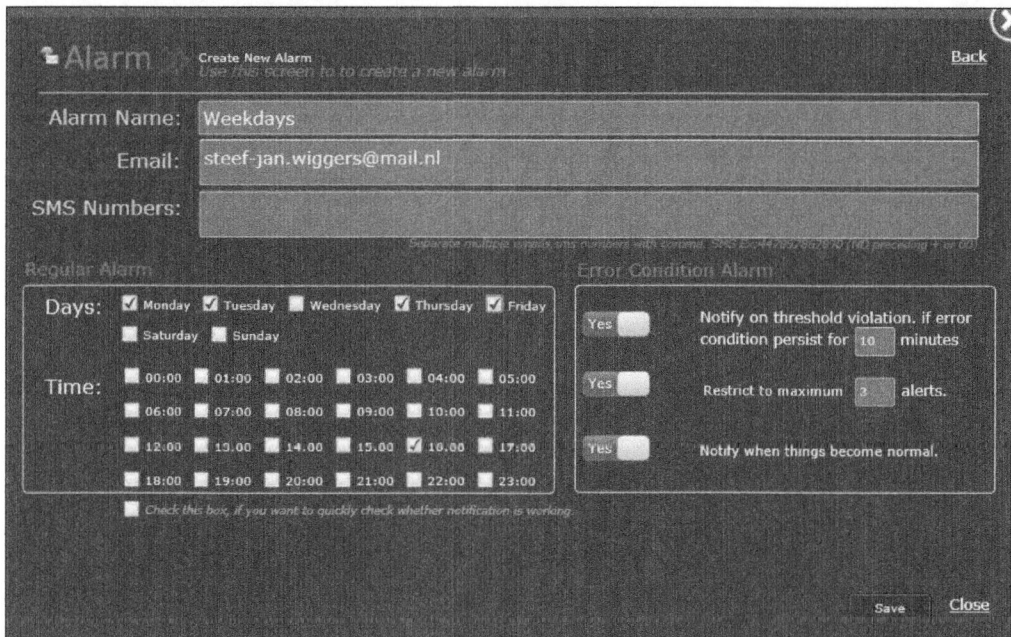

3. Map the applications to the alarm:

    a. On the alert settings home screen, under the **Applications** sections click on **Add applications for notification**.

    b. Choose the alarm we created in step 2.

    c. Choose the environment (BizTalk360 supports configuring multiple environments).

    d. Choose the applications you want to monitor.

    e. Configure the threshold settings appropriate for you.

    f. Click on **Save**:

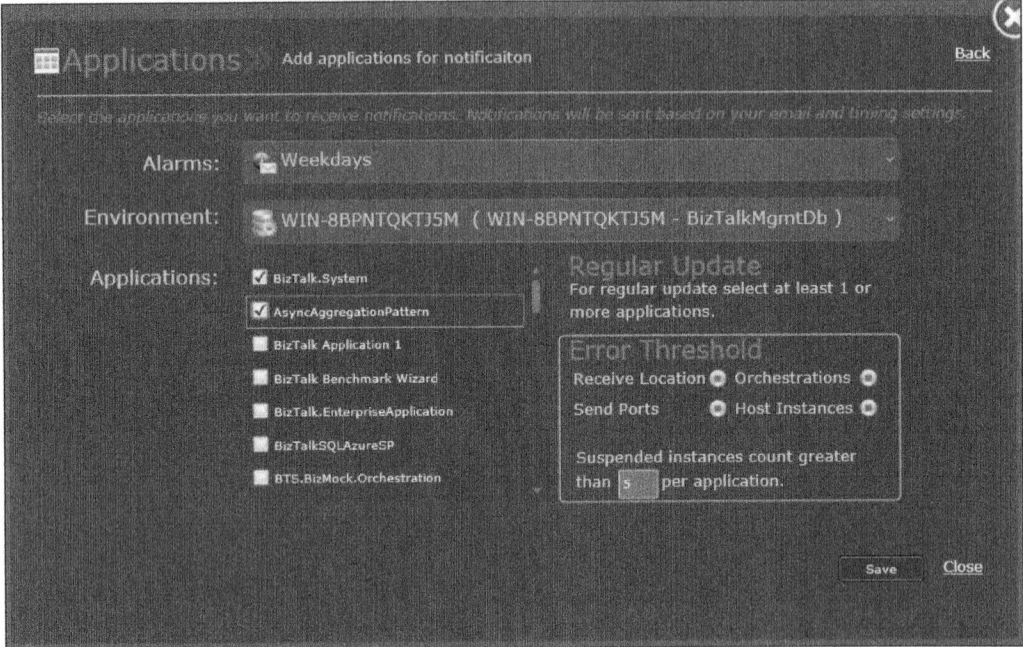

Based on your regular alarm timings or threshold violation, you will start receiving e-mails, as shown in the following screenshot:

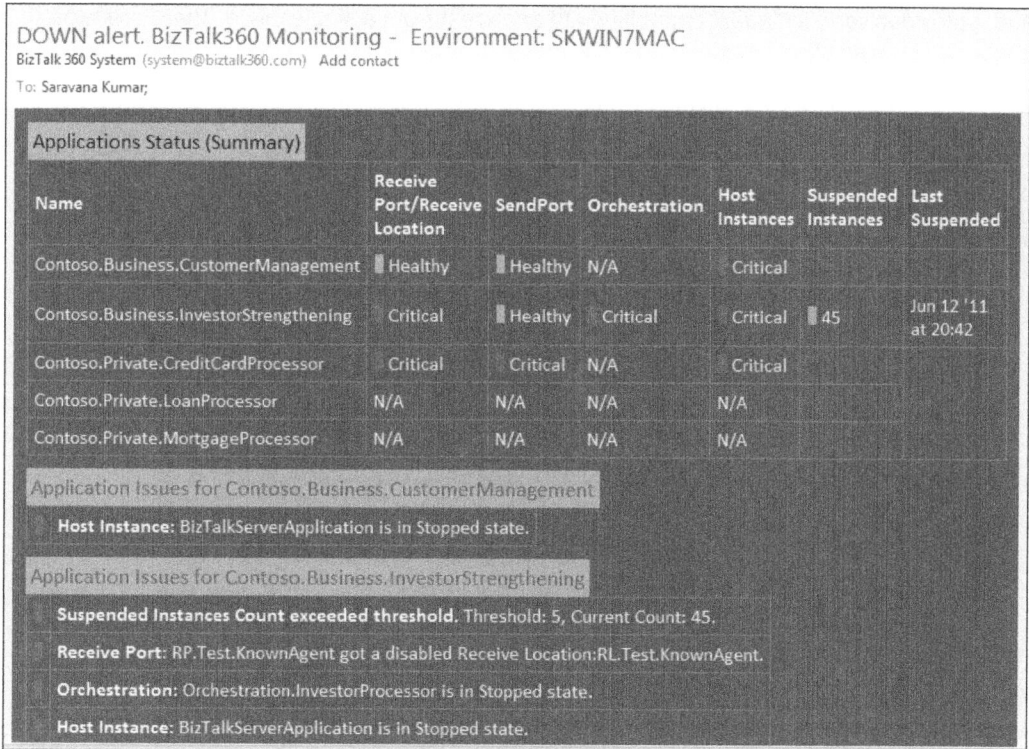

The e-mail will contain a summary section of all the chosen applications with the status highlighted in red/green/yellow format and a detailed error section for each application at the bottom.

How to use the Advanced Event Viewer

The Advanced Event Viewer module is especially useful for technical support people working on BizTalk environments. A typical enterprise BizTalk environment will have at least two or more BizTalk servers and two or more SQL Servers. The first source of information for resolving BizTalk exceptions will be the Event Viewer in the servers.

The support person may need some time to resolve an issue to look into all the Event Viewers in the BizTalk environment. It is a time consuming process. The BizTalk360 Advanced Event Viewer module resolves this issue by bringing all the Event Viewer data to a single location, and it provides very rich query capabilities to analyze it from a single place. There are two major advantages of this module:

▸ Security because the support people are not required to login to physical servers

▸ It increases the speed at which problems can be resolved

The following screenshot shows the rich query interface of the Advanced Event Viewer, the values are pre-populated so the users not required to type it and can get quality results:

How it works...

The following screenshot shows the high level technical architecture of BizTalk360, there are three core components involved in BizTalk360:

▸ A Silverlight application and set of WCF Services hosted on an ASP.NET application

▸ Monitoring Windows NT Services

▸ A SQL Server database

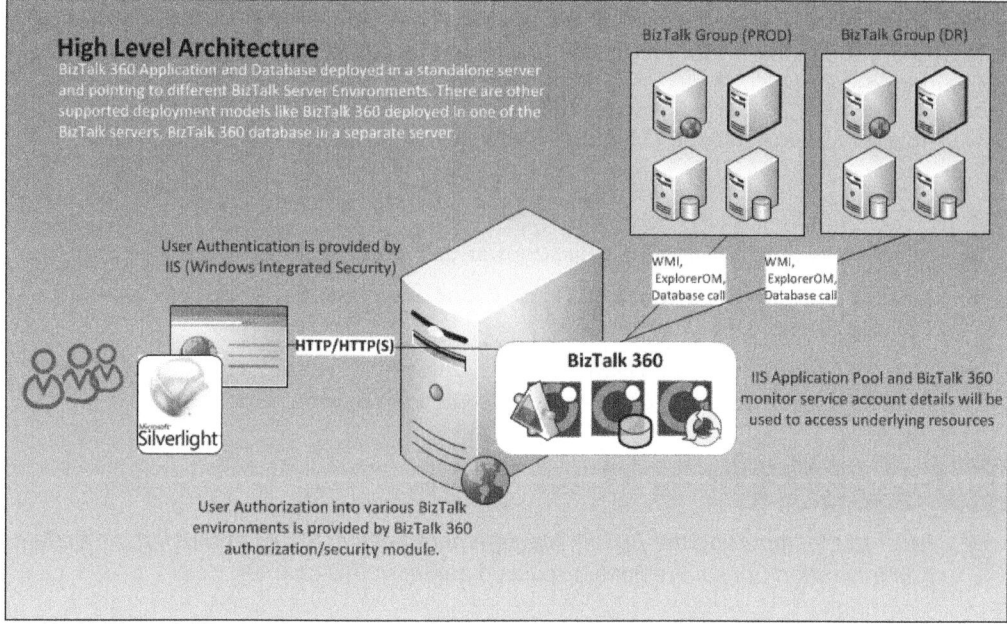

BizTalk360 utilizes the administration APIs such as ExplorerOM and WMI provided by the Microsoft BizTalk Server to access the underlying BizTalk Server environments. BizTalk360 is capable of working with any BizTalk environment configurations such as single-server or multi-server configurations. It has also got the ability to connect to multiple remote environments from a single installation, as shown in the previous screenshot. The user can either install BizTalk360 on one of their existing BizTalk Servers or they can just install the BizTalk administration components on a separate machine, install BizTalk360, and start pointing to various environments in the organization.

The background Windows NT Service is responsible for alerting, notifications, scheduled execution of the Message Box Viewer, collecting event log data from the configured server for the Advanced Event Viewer , and so on.

The frontend part is a rich internet application built using Microsoft Silverlight. One of the restrictions (security) of Silverlight is, it can not directly access underlying stores, such as filesystem, WMI, database, and so on. It will always communicate to a web service. So BizTalk360 comes with eight WCF Services and around 80 operations to support the frontend Silverlight UI.

There's more...

We have covered only a few scenarios of BizTalk360, there are many options which will help you to support and monitor your production environments efficiently. The following links provide more details:

- `http://blogs.digitaldeposit.net/saravana/category/BizTalk-360.aspx`
- `http://support.biztalk360.com/`
- `http://www.biztalk360.com/Content/Tour.aspx`
- `http://support.biztalk360.com/customer/portal/topics/92108-videos/articles`
- `http://support.biztalk360.com/customer/portal/articles/265487-biztalk36-biztalk-admin-console-feature-mapping`

See also

- Refer to the *Importing the BizTalk Management Pack in SCOM* and *Using the BizTalk Administration Console* recipes discussed earlier in this chapter.

Configuring the BizTalk database jobs

BizTalk Server database jobs are required to keep BizTalk healthy. The jobs are important for preventing the database from becoming too large and cripple BizTalk's performance. The following table lists the BizTalk Server and SQL Server Agent jobs with a description of their responsibilities:

Job name	Description
Backup BizTalk Server	It consists of several steps to perform full database backups of the BizTalk Server databases and logs. It also specifies a retention period of the backup history.
CleanupBTFExpiredEntriesJob_BizTalkMgmtDb	It deletes expired BizTalk Framework entries from the BizTalk Management (BizTalkMgmtDb) database.
DTA Purge and Archive	It automates the archiving of tracked messages and the purging of the BizTalk Tracking database to maintain a healthy system and to keep the tracking data archived for future use.

Job name	Description
`MessageBox_DeadProcesses_ Cleanup_BizTalkMsgBoxDb`	It detects when a BizTalk Server host instance (BTSNTSvc.exe) has stopped responding. Then, the job releases the work from the host instance, so a different host instance can finish the tasks.
`MessageBox_Message_Cleanup_ BizTalkMsgBoxDb`	It removes all messages which are not referenced by any subscribers in the BizTalkMsgBoxDb database tables.
`MessageBox_Message_ ManageRefCountLog_ BizTalkMsgBoxDb`	It starts the MessageBox_Message_Cleanup_ BizTalkMsgBoxDb job and runs in an infinite loop. It deletes the entries from the two individual message reference count logs. It manages the reference count logs for messages and determines when a message is no longer referenced by a subscriber.
`MessageBox_Parts_Cleanup_ BizTalkMsgBoxDb`	It removes all message parts which are no longer referenced by a message in the BizTalkMsgBoxDb database tables. All messages are composed of one or more message parts that contain the message data.
`MessageBox_UpdateStats_ BizTalkMsgBoxDb`	It updates the statistics for the BizTalkMsgBoxDb database.
Monitor BizTalk Server	It scans for any known issues with the BizTalkMgmtDb, BizTalkMsgBoxDb, and BizTalkDTADb databases. This includes orphaned instances.
`Operations_ OperateOnInstances_OnMaster_ BizTalkMsgBoxDb`	It is used for multiple BizTalkMsgBoxDb database deployments. It asynchronously performs operational actions.
`PurgeSubscriptionsJob_ BizTalkMsgBoxDb`	It purges unused subscription predicates from the BizTalkMsgBoxDb database.
`Rules_Database_Cleanup_ BizTalkRuleEngineDb`	It purges old audit data from the Rule Engine (BizTalkRuleEngineDb) database every 90 days. This job also purges old history data (deploy/ undeploy notifications) from the Rule Engine (BizTalkRuleEngineDb) database every three days.
`TrackedMessages_Copy_ BizTalkMsgBoxDb`	It copies the message bodies of tracked messages from the BizTalkMsgBoxDb database to the Tracking (BizTalkDTADb) database.
`TrackingSpool_Cleanup_ BizTalkMsgBoxDb`	It purges inactive tracking spool tables to free database space.

By default, some of the jobs are not configured and are scheduled after installation and configuration of the BizTalk environment. These jobs are:

- Backup BizTalk Server (`BizTalkMgmtDb`)
- DTA Purge and Archive (`BizTalkDTADb`)
- `MessageBox_Message_Cleanup_BizTalkMsgBoxDb`

 There are other means of backing up the BizTalk Server databases, yet the Backup BizTalk Server job is the only one supported by Microsoft.

In this recipe, the first two jobs will be configured and the last one can be left disabled, as this job is also started by the `MessageBox_Message_ManageRefCountLog_BizTalkMsgBoxDb` job. It is recommended that you disable the `MessageBox_Message_Cleanup_BizTalkMsgBoxDb` job. If you run the BizTalk Server Best Practices Analyzer, you may see that two of the SQL Server Agent jobs that BizTalk relies on are not running successfully (as those are not configured).

Getting ready

For this recipe, you will need access to the SQL Server database through the SQL Management Studio and the appropriate rights to be able to operate it.

How to do it...

You need to perform the following steps to configure the Backup BizTalk Server (`BizTalkMgmtDb`) job:

1. Open the SQL Management Studio.
2. Connect to the SQL Server instance which contains the BizTalk Server databases.
3. Navigate to **SQL Server Agent**.
4. Expand **SQL Server Agent** and navigate to **Jobs**.
5. Expand **Jobs**.
6. Select the **Backup BizTalk Server (BizTalkMgmtDb)** job and right-click. Select **Properties**.

7. In the **Select a page** pane on the left, choose **Steps**. You will see four steps, as shown in the following screenshot:

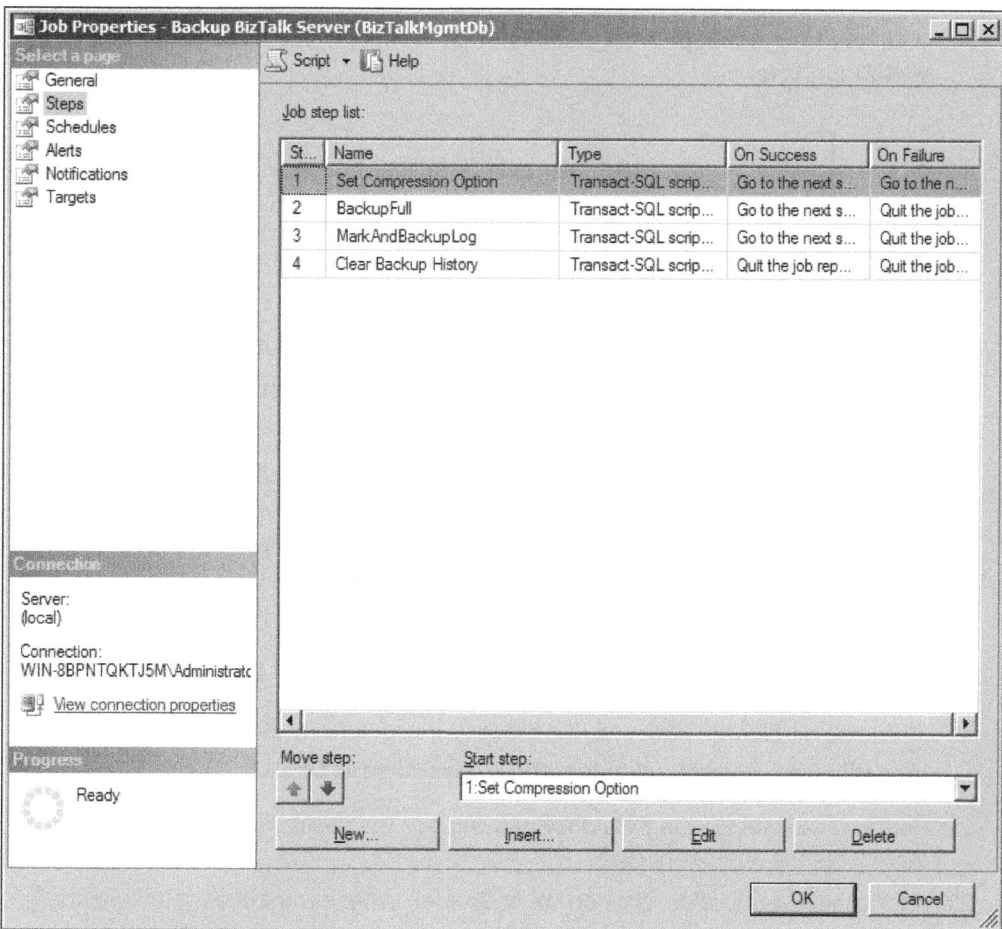

8. Double-click on the first step named **Set Compression Option**.

9. You will see the following procedure in the Command box:

    exec [dbo].[sp_SetBackupCompression] @bCompression = 0 /*0 - Do not use Compression, 1 - Use Compression */

10. Change **@bCompression** to **1** if you need compression. Click on either **OK** or **Cancel**.

11. Double-click on the step named **BackupFull**.

12. In the command box, you will find the following procedure:

    exec [dbo].[sp_BackupAllFull_Schedule] 'd' /* Frequency */, 'BTS' /* Name */, '<destination path>' /* location of backup files */

13. Change **Frequency** to the desired value, where **d** (daily) is the default name of your backup, and the location of the backup path (destination path). You can have something similar to the following:

    exec [dbo].[sp_BackupAllFull_Schedule] 'd', 'BTS_Test_Machine_X012', 'D:\ MyBizTalkServer'

 Backups must never be on the same disks!

14. After changing the procedure, click on **OK**.

15. Double-click on the step named **MarkandBackupLog**.

16. Here you will find the following procedure in the command box:

    exec [dbo].[sp_MarkAll] 'BTS' /* Log mark name */, '<destination path>' /* location of backup files */

17. Change the log mark name and destination path to your requirements. You could have something as follows:

    exec [dbo].[sp_MarkAll] 'BTS_Test_Machine_X012_Logs', 'C:\ MyBizTalkServerDbLogs'

18. After changing the procedure, click on **OK**.

19. Finally you can double-click on the last step named as **Clear Back Up History**.

20. Here you will find the following procedure in the command box:

    exec [dbo].[sp_DeleteBackupHistory] @DaysToKeep=14

21. Here you can change the **@DaysToKeep** value to the desired value. This value represents the number of days.

22. After changing the value, click on **OK** or **Cancel**, in case you will want to keep the default.

23. Click on **OK** again to save job.

24. Right-click on the job and choose **Enable**.

You need to perform the following steps to configure the DTA Purge and Archive (BizTalkDTADb):

1. Open the SQL Management Studio.

2. Connect to the SQL Server instance that contains the BizTalk Server databases.

3. Navigate to **SQL Server Agent**.

4. Expand **SQL Server Agent** and navigate to **Jobs**.

5. Expand **Jobs**.

6. Select the **DTA Purge and Archive (BizTalkDTADb)** job and right-click on it. Select **Properties**.

7. In the **Select a page** pane on the left, choose **Steps**. You will see one step in **Job step list**:

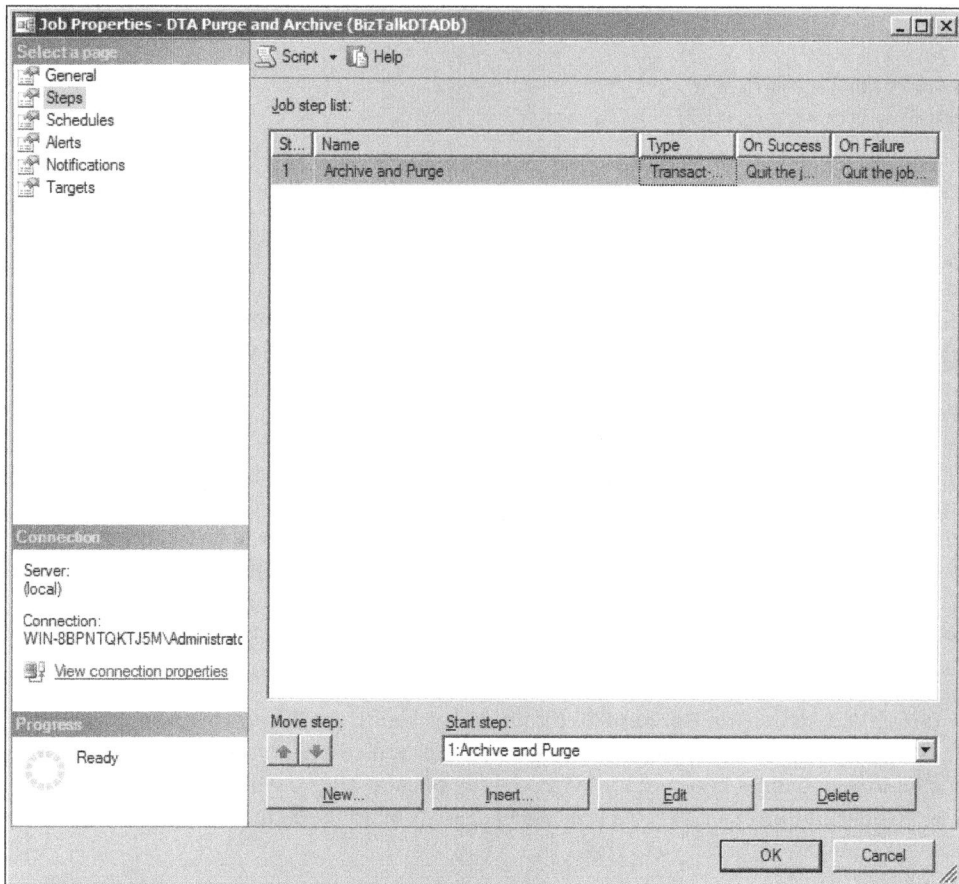

8. Double-click on the step named **Archive and Purge**.

9. You will see the following procedure in the command box:

    exec dtasp_BackupAndPurgeTrackingDatabase 0, --@nLiveHours tinyint, 1, --@ nLiveDays tinyint = 0, 30, --@nHardDeleteDays tinyint = 0, null, --@nvcFolder nvarchar(1024) = null, null, --@nvcValidatingServer sysname = null, 0 --@ fForceBackup int = 0

10. Change **@nLiveHours**.

11. Eventually you have a procedure as follows:

    exec dtasp_BackupAndPurgeTrackingDatabase 1, 0, 1, '\\WIN-8BPNTQKTJ5M\ MyBizTalkServer', null, 0

12. Click on **OK** after changing the procedure.

13. Click on **OK** again to save the job.

14. Right-click on the job and select **Enable**.

How it works...

Both jobs are essential for running BizTalk successfully. The backup job runs as scheduled by the SQL Server Agent service and create synchronized backups of all BizTalk Server databases by using full database backups and transaction log backups, in conjunction with a type of transaction known as a marked transaction. The latter are transactions that place a mark into the transaction log of all databases participating in the transaction. This transaction blocks new distributed transactions from starting, waits for the distributed transactions which are currently running to complete, and then executes to place the mark. The mark represents a transaction point which is consistent across all databases, you can use the mark with subsequent log backups to restore your databases to that point.

The job consists of four steps, each responsible for completion of the job. The first step is **Set Compression Option** which is an option not present in previous BizTalk versions. This step enables you to set compression to on or off. Enabling compression will give you benefits, such as less space needed for the backup files, fewer I/O operations for the backup and restore, faster backup and restore, and less network usage to transfer the files to your disaster recovery site. The drawback is that it requires more CPU utilization and with today's hardware that can be a real problem.

The subsequent step is the **BackupFull** that requires you to set a few parameters, such as frequency, name, and location of the backup. You can also provide values for three optional parameters to force a full backup after partial backups (`ForceFullBackupAfterPartialSetFailure`), time for backup to run (`BackUpHour`), and to use local time (`UseLocalTime`).

The subsequent step is **MarkAndBackUpLog**. Here, you again have to provide values for two parameters. You should provide a name and backup path (location). You can also provide a value for `timestamp` (that is, local time) which is optional.

The final step is **Clear Backup History**. Here, you provide value for the `DaysToKeep` parameter to determine after how many days the backup log has to be removed. Again, there is an optional parameter for using local time (`UseLocalTime`). This job step does not provide functionality for deleting backup files which have been accumulated over time (see the blog post at `http://sandroaspbiztalkblog.wordpress.com/2011/01/27/biztalk-2010-installation-and-configuration-configure-biztalk-server-sql-jobs-part-11/` by Sandro Pereira to circumvent this issue).

DTA Purge and Archive is a job you configure to keep BizTalk healthy and to bloat the archive database until a point when there is no disk space left, or overall performance can be crippled. It also enables archiving of tracked data. The job consists of one step, where six parameters have to be configured. You configure the parameters such as `nLiveHours`, `nLiveDay`, and `nHardDeleteDays` for setting the time-frame for deletion of the tracked data. Configure the `nvcFolder` parameter for determining the location of the backup file. With the `nvcValidatingServer` parameter, you can provide a value to optionally set up a secondary database server to validate the archives as they are created. The last parameter, `fForceBackup`, is used to determine whether or not to force a backup.

There's more...

For a complete overview of backing up and restoring BizTalk databases in context of the BizTalk Backup job see MSDN:

- **Backing Up and Restoring the BizTalk Server Databases**: `http://msdn.microsoft.com/en-us/library/aa560972%28v=BTS.70%29.aspx`
- **Backing Up and Restoring BizTalk Server**: `http://msdn.microsoft.com/en-us/library/aa562140%28v=BTS.70%29.aspx`

The backup of BizTalk databases is one part of backup and recovery in case of disaster recovery. To have a full disaster recovery in place, the following resources can be of use:

- **PowerShell cmdlet for BizTalk db restore**: `http://blogical.se/blogs/mikael/archive/2011/02/22/powershell-cmdlet-for-biztalk-db-restore.aspx`
- **Backing Up and Restoring BizTalk Server**: `http://msdn.microsoft.com/en-us/library/aa562140.aspx`

With regards to the DTA Purge and Archive job, refer to the document called **Archiving and Purging the BizTalk Tracking Database** (`http://msdn.microsoft.com/en-us/library/aa560754%28v=BTS.70%29.aspx`) on MSDN.

The BizTalk Database Server job is part of the overall strategy to maintain and troubleshoot the BizTalk Server databases. You can read more on it in the document called **How to maintain and troubleshoot BizTalk Server** databases at `http://support.microsoft.com/kb/952555`.

See also

- Refer to the *Leveraging the BizTalk monitoring job* recipe discussed later in this chapter

Leveraging the BizTalk monitoring job

A new feature in the BizTalk Server 2010 is a new SQL job that enables you to identify any known issues in the Management, Message Box, or DTA databases. This job and other database jobs are created when you configure a BizTalk group. It scans for issues, but does not fix them for you. The job scans for the following issues in the Management, Message Box, and DTA databases:

- Messages without any references
- Messages without reference counts
- Messages with reference counts less than zero
- Message references without spool rows
- Message references without instances
- Instance states without instances
- Instance subscriptions without corresponding instances
- Orphaned DTA service instances
- Orphaned DTA service instance exceptions
- **Tracking Data Decode Service** (**TDDS**) is not running on any host instance when global tracking option is enabled

 By default, the Monitor BizTalk Server job is configured and automated to run once a week and requires a lot of computational (that is, processing) power. It is best to schedule it during downtime/low traffic.

Although this job does not fix any issues, you can leverage this job by creating a monitoring solution or altering mechanism for the administrator. So, they can act on the issues at hand.

Getting ready

You need to have sufficient rights in the SQL Server database. You should have SMTP and Database Mail configured.

How to do it...

To configure the BizTalk monitoring job to send an email notifying a BizTalk operator, you need to follow these steps:

1. Navigate to the SQL Server Management Studio. Click on **SQL Server Management Studio**.

2. Connect with the appropriate credentials to **Database Engine**.

3. In **Object Explorer**, navigate to Jobs and expand by clicking on **[+]**. Then select **SQL Server Agent**.

4. Navigate to **Operators**.

5. Right-click on **Operators** and select **New Operator...**.

6. Fill in **Name** and **Email Name**.

7. Next, select **Notifications**:

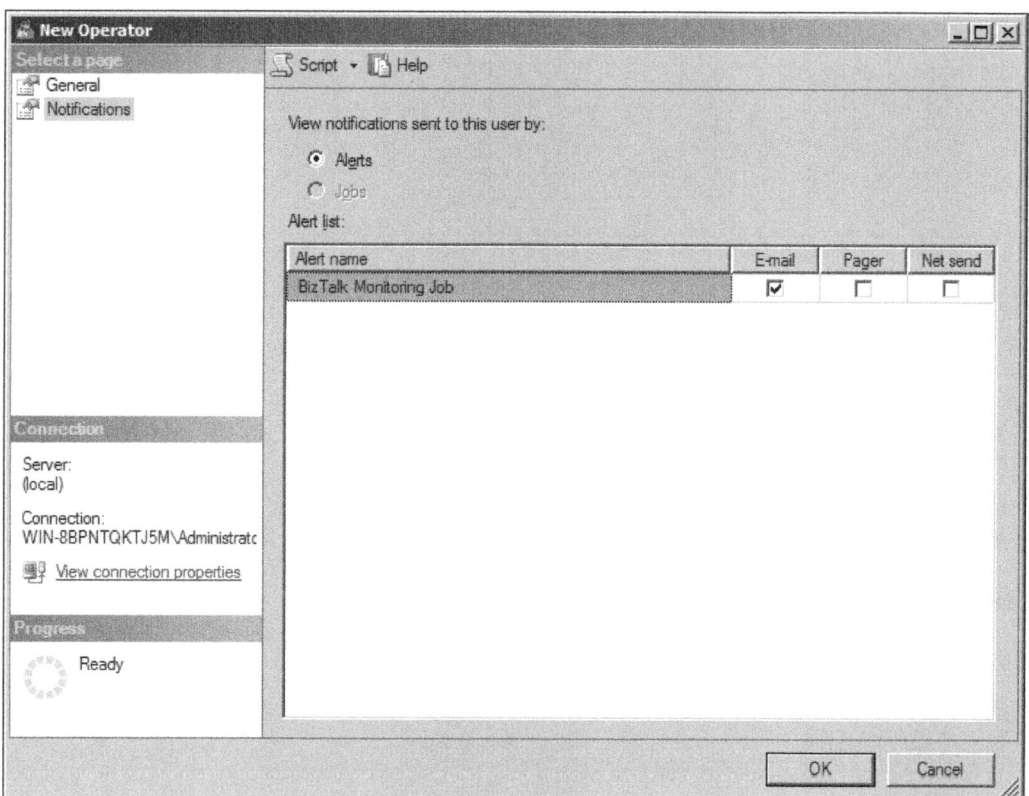

8. Check the **E-mail** checkbox next to **Alert name** and select **BizTalk Monitoring Job**.

9. Click on **OK**.

10. Expand **Jobs** by clicking on **[+]**.

11. Navigate to the **Monitor BizTalk Server (BizTalkMgmtDb)** job and right-click on it. Then, select **Properties**.

12. In **Select a page,** select **Notifications**.

13. In the **Actions to perform when the job completes** section, select the newly created operator and in the next combo box select **When the job fails** (see the following screenshot):

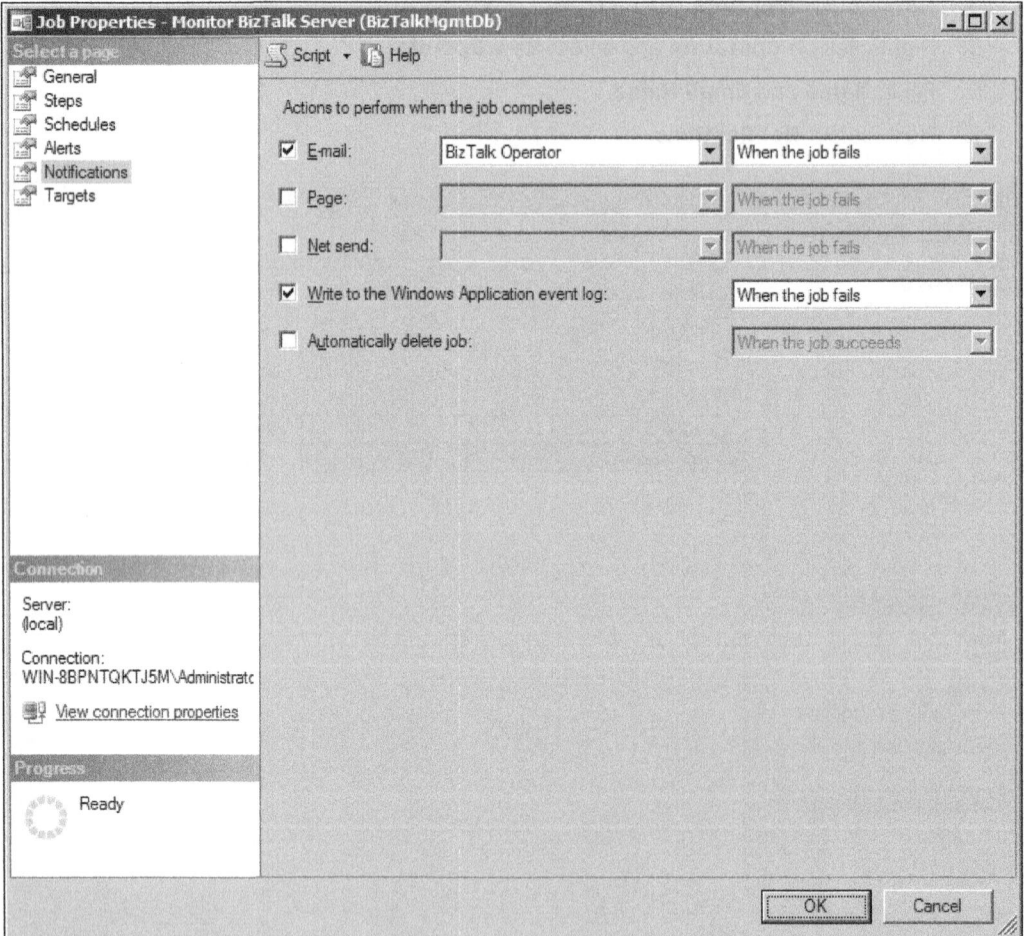

14. Click on **OK**.

How it works...

BizTalk Monitoring consists of two steps:

- ▸ Check issues in all Message Box and DTA databases
- ▸ Generate error strings in case of any issue

The first step will execute a procedure called `[dbo].[btsmon_Inconsistent]` in the BizTalk Management database. On its turn, this procedure will call other procedures in the Message Box, Management, and Tracking database to collect error data (such as messages without references). The second step calls the procedure `[dbo].[btsmon_GenerateErrorString]` in the Management database, which involves a query of two tables—`[btsmon_Inconsistancies]` and `[dbo].[btsmon_Issues]`.

If this job encounters any issues it will fail and return a string containing the number of issues found (that is, the result of the second step). By default, this string will be logged to the Event Viewer and is also visible in the Job History. In case a notification is configured with the job, a notification in the form of an e-mail can be sent to an operator. By creating an operator in the SQL Server Agent and configuring it with appropriate e-mail address, a notification will be sent to the operator if the job fails and the operator can investigate the issue at hand.

There's more...

There are not many resources found for this job, besides the Microsoft documentation. Randal van Splunteren has written an excellent blog post about it. The subsequent post explains how to handle issues found by the job:

- ▸ **Monitor BizTalk Server Job in BizTalk 2010**: `http://biztalkmessages.vansplunteren.net/2010/10/19/monitor-biztalk-server-job-in-biztalk-2010/`
- ▸ **Using BizTalk Terminator to resolve issues identified by BizTalk MsgBoxViewer and the BizTalk 2010 Monitor BizTalk Server Job**: `http://blogs.msdn.com/b/biztalkcpr/archive/2009/05/06/using-biztalk-terminator-to-resolve-issues-identified-by-biztalk-msgboxviewer.aspx`

See also

- ▸ Refer to the *Configuring the BizTalk database jobs* recipe discussed earlier in this chapter

Identifying bottlenecks with the Performance Monitor

There are different tools to monitor the BizTalk Server using SCOM or BizTalk360. Both are excellent tools, but are not suitable to measure performance or to examine how a program such as BizTalk affects a machine's performance, both in real time and by collecting log data for later analysis. You can use the Windows Performance Monitor for this task. The Windows Performance Monitor is an MMC snap-in that combines the functionality of previous standalone tools including performance logs and alerts, the Server Performance Advisor, and the System Monitor. It provides a graphical interface for customizing data collector sets and event trace sessions.

In case an administrator is facing several potential bottlenecks such as the BizTalk databases, adapters, pipelines, the filesystem, and the orchestration, the performance monitor can be a useful tool to use instead of reading the BizTalk performance optimization guide on finding and eliminating bottlenecks. An administrator can monitor performance by focusing on the performance counters. BizTalk provides performance counters to monitor the individual components such as the message box, orchestration, and adapters (refer to the document called **Performance Counters** at `http://msdn.microsoft.com/en-us/library/aa578394%28BTS.70%29.aspx`).

Getting ready

Identify which potential bottlenecks you expect with BizTalk, or which part of the BizTalk runtime you suspect is causing performance issues.

How to do it...

To monitor the performance counter, you first need to create a data collector set:

1. Navigate in the start menu to the administrative tools and click on **Performance Monitor**.
2. Expand **Data Collecter Sets**.
3. Right-click on **User Defined** and select **New**, click on **Data Collector Set**.
4. Provide a descriptive name in the **Name** text box.
5. Select **Create manually (Advanced)**.
6. Click on **Next**.

7. In the next dialog, check the options **Create data logs** and **Performance counter**:

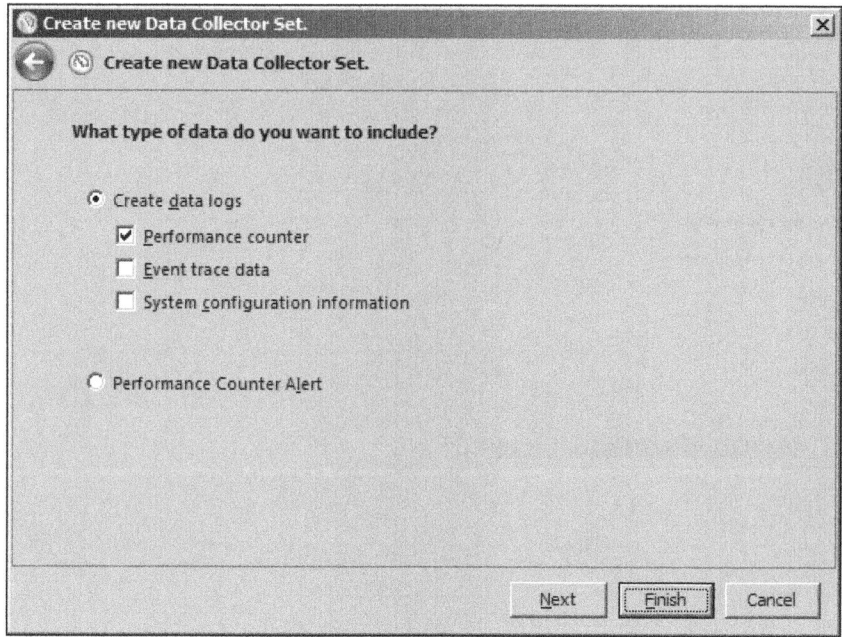

8. Click on **Finish**.

9. Now a new **Data Collector Set** is created and you will see this in the right-hand-side pane.

10. Select the newly created data collector set and right-click on it. Select **New** and then click on **Data Collector**.

11. A new dialog will appear.

12. Provide a descriptive name in the **Name** text box.

13. Leave the option on the Performance counter data collector.

14. Click on **Next**.

15. In the next dialog, click on **Add** to add performance counters.

16. A new dialog will appear.

17. The counter for the local machine will be loaded and you will see them below **Select counters from computer**:

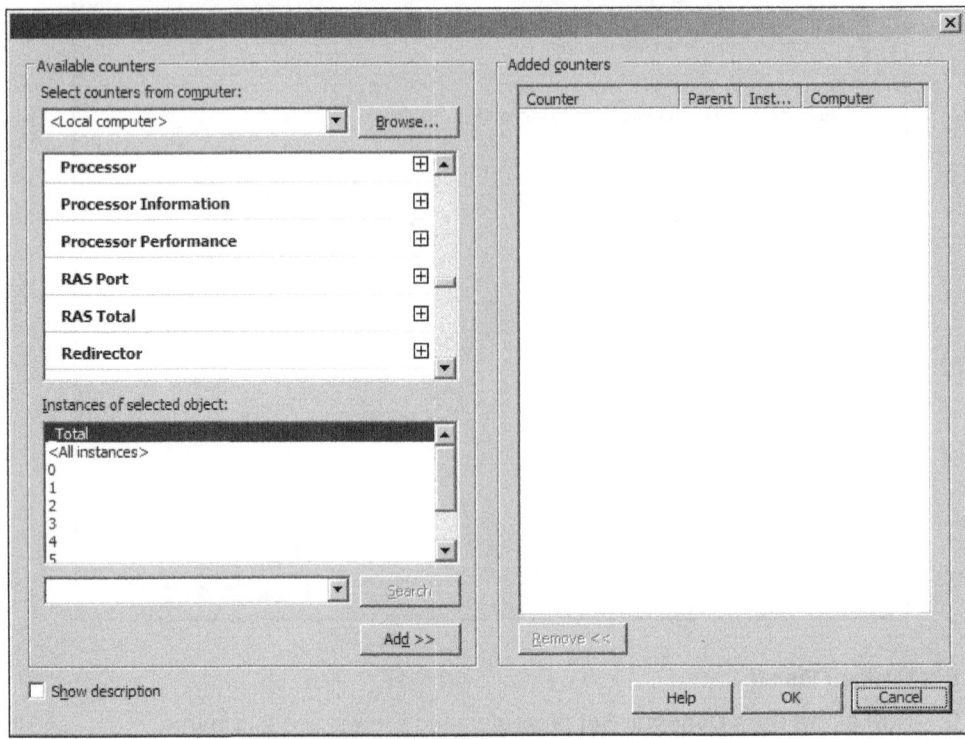

18. Scroll down to find counter **BizTalk:Messaging**.

19. Select the **Documents Processed/sec** counter and click on **Add**.

20. Select the **Documents Received/sec** counter and click on **Add**.

21. From the **Performance Object** drop-down list, select **SQL Server:Buffer Manager**.

22. Select the **Page reads/sec** counter and click on **Add**.

23. Select the **Page writes/sec** counter and click on **Add**.

24. Click on **OK**:

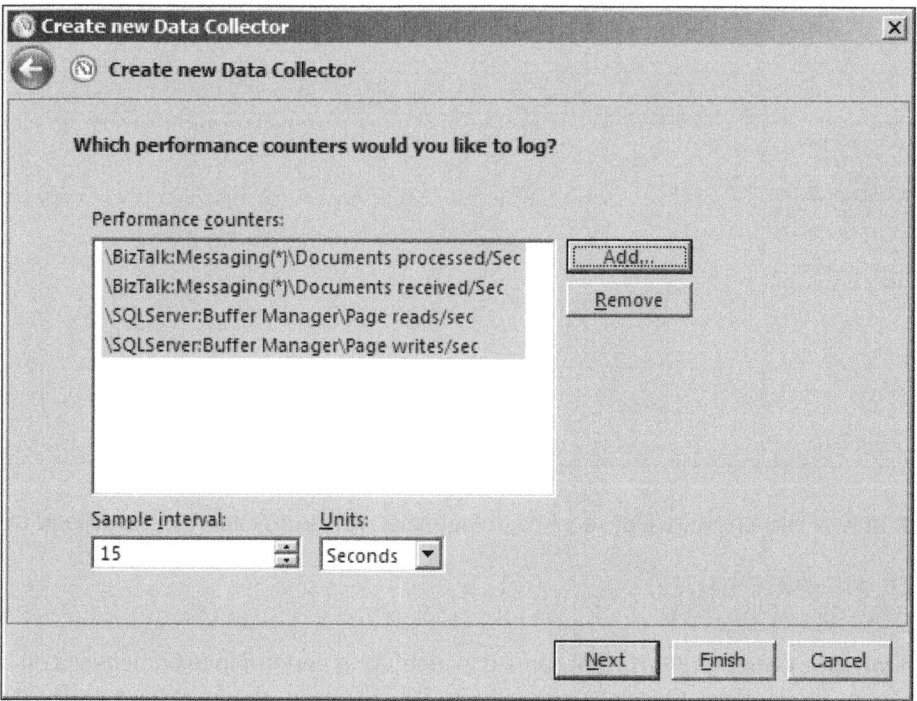

25. Change the sample interval to your desire or leave it as it is.

26. Click on **Finish**.

27. In the left pane, select **User Defined**.

28. In the right pane, select **Data Collector Set**.

29. Right-click on it and click on **Start**:

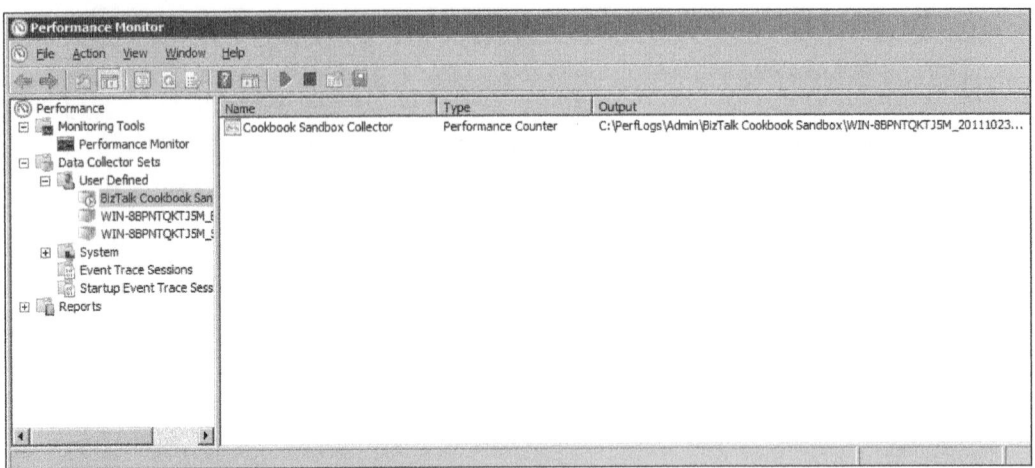

30. After a certain interval of seconds, minutes, or hours you can stop the collector.

How it works...

The **Performance Monitor** (**PerfMon**) can aid in identifying performance bottlenecks on your system. This includes the system running BizTalk. For instance, if you have a very low percentage of CPU idle, it could mean that you may have too many host instances running or custom pipelines which are improperly implemented. This kind of situation calls for using PerfMon. You first create a data collector set which will act as a container for the performance counters.

Once you have created a data collector set, you can create one or more data collectors. A data collector contains the performance counters you want to monitor. The counters are selected and added manually. The counters are chosen in a way that provides you with meaningful information about your system performance. The data collected from the counters are stored as logs to be used for later review.

There's more...

The administrator can also choose to use the PAL tool. This tool can be used to create a Microsoft Performance Monitor template file from the PAL threshold files. After collecting the counters, the created log file can be fed into the PAL tool for analysis. You can find more about it in the document called **How to use the PAL Tool for BizTalk Performance Analysis** at http://blogs.technet.com/b/clint_huffman/archive/2008/09/02/how-to-use-the-pal-tool-for-biztalk-performance-analysis.aspx.

More details on PerfMon can be found on MSDN in the document called **Windows Performance Monitor** at `http://technet.microsoft.com/en-us/library/cc749249.aspx`.

On performance optimization of the BizTalk Server, you can read in more detail in the document called **Microsoft BizTalk Server 2010 Performance Optimization Guide** at `http://msdn.microsoft.com/en-us/library/ee377064%28v=bts.70%29.aspx`.

See also

 ▸ Refer to the *Importing the BizTalk Management Pack in SCOM* and *An alternative BizTalk monitoring solution: BizTalk360* recipes discussed earlier in this chapter

 ▸ Refer to the *Automating performance analysis by using the PAL tool* recipe in *Chapter 1, Setting up a BizTalk Server Environment*

Using the BizTalk Message Box Viewer

The BizTalk Message Box Viewer, also known as the **Message Box Viewer** (**MBV**), was created by Jean-Pierre Auconie. The MBV tool retrieves information from a BizTalk System and identifies many possible issues, which could be critical or need attention, and presents them in a user friendly format. This tool is like the **BizTalk Best Practices Analyzer** (**BPA**) which is a health check tool that generates reports of a BizTalk System. Both the BPA and MBV are complementary to each other. The MBV can help administrators in acquiring information of a production the system very fast, with hardly any impact on running environment. It can help administrators to identify possible issues, which could be critical or need attention.

The MBV has two executables; one to fire up a console application and another to the Windows Form application. Both use the same engine by reading only in the BizTalk databases and Server's registry to retrieve useful lists of information. Both console applications, as they are Windows Form applications can produce three types of reports:

 ▸ **HTML report**: This is the first file to open. It shows a well formatted result of the health check.

 ▸ **History log file**: It contains the history of all reports in a textual format.

 ▸ **Status log file**: It contains a detailed status of each query execution and possibly errors met. The status log file is important to read if some errors were met during the collect process. It displays the start time of each query.

Both tools also offer the option to generate an XML report.

Getting ready

Download the latest version of BizTalk Message Box Viewer Version 11 (`http://blogs.technet.com/b/jpierauc/archive/2007/12/18/msgboxviewer.aspx`). Unzip the file to a folder.

How to do it...

The following steps need to be performed to obtain results from the BizTalk Message Box Viewer to investigate the health of the BizTalk system or for troubleshooting purposes:

1. Open the `MsgBoxViewer` application.

2. In the **Global Properties** tab, you can set properties according to your requirements, for instance, changing the format of the output file; for example, you might want the output in an HTML file:

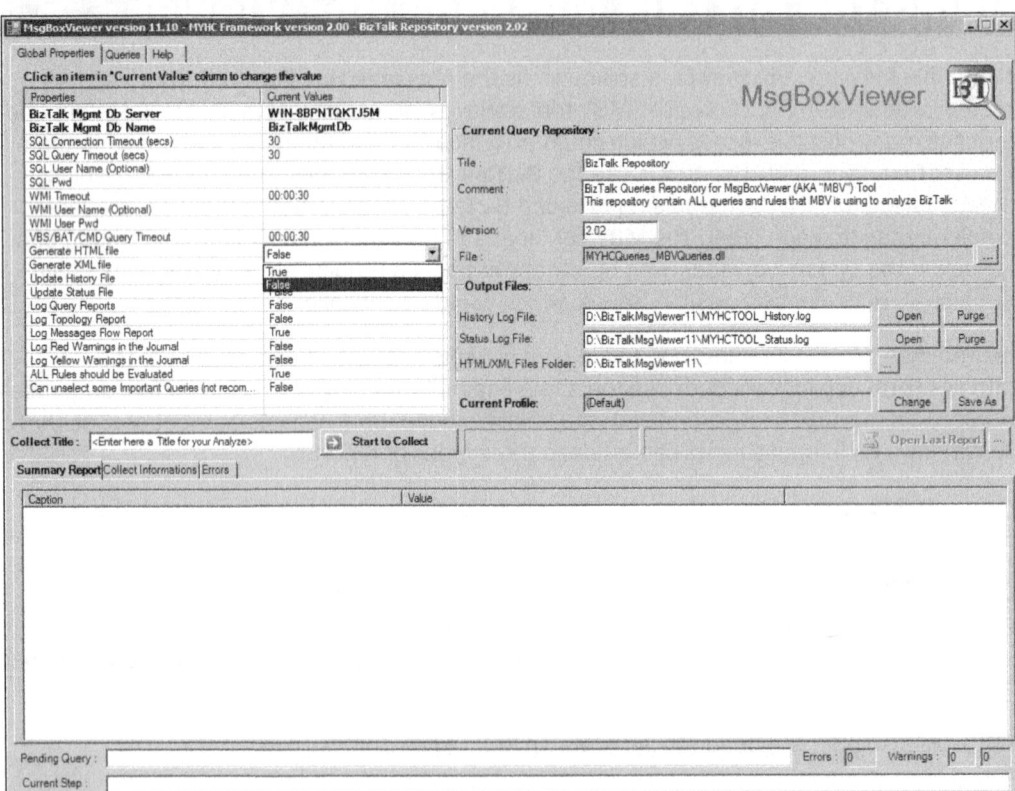

3. In the **Queries** tab, you can change different settings on the queries.

4. Click on the **Help** tab if you require more information on the tool.

5. Click on the **General** tab and change the setting to an output file location if you desire so.

6. Next in **Collect Title**, fill in a descriptive name.

7. Click on **Start to Collect**:

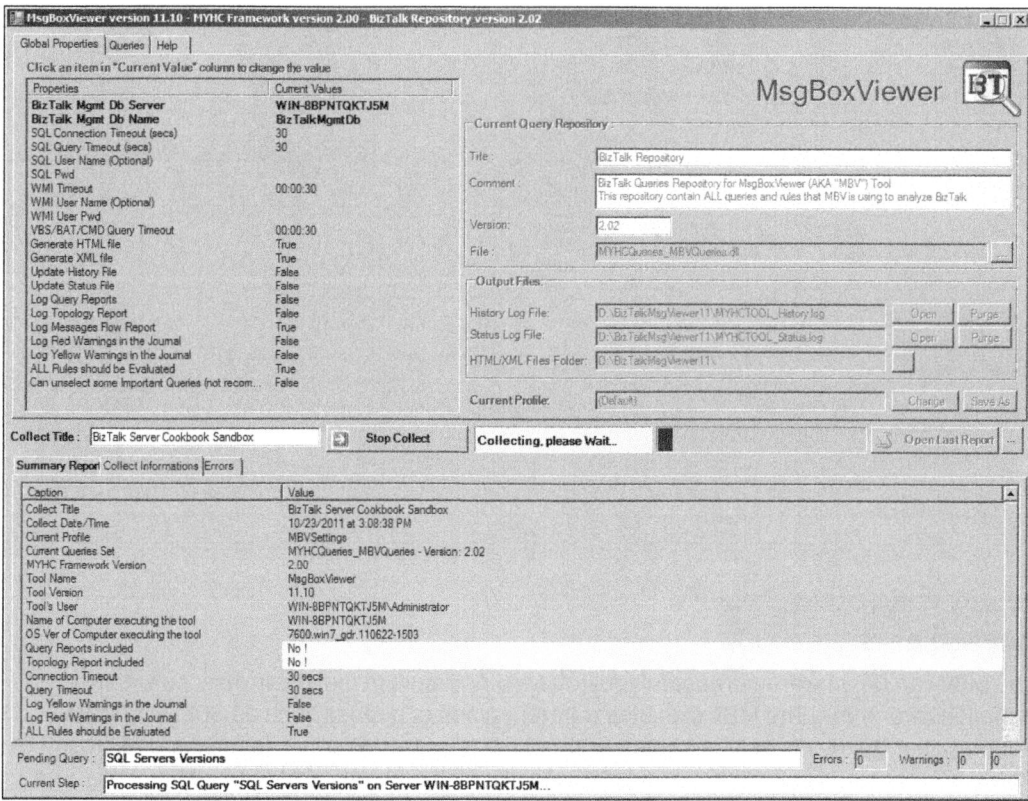

8. When the collection is done, a dialog will appear asking if you want to see the HTML report.

9. Click on **OK**.

10. An HTML report will appear:

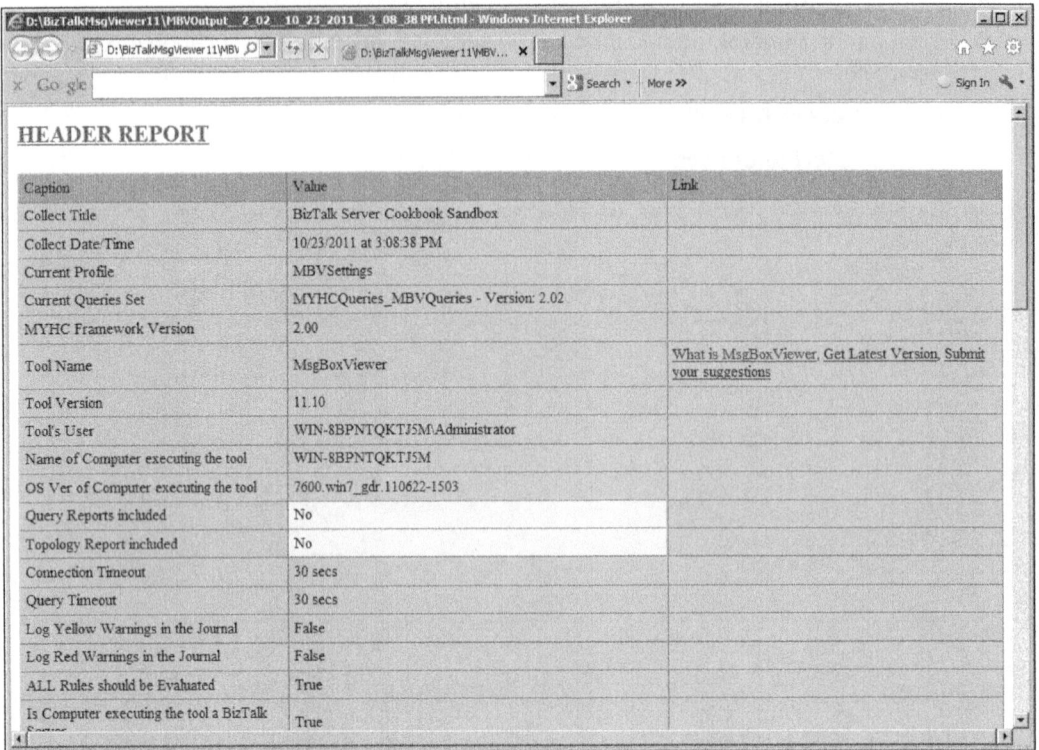

How it works...

The MBV can be an extremely useful tool for administrators in diagnosing issues within a BizTalk environment. The MBV executes different types of queries such as SQL, File, WMI, and Registry. Queries have been obtained from the Microsoft Product Teams, and Microsoft Product Support Services (the author of this tool is also currently working for Microsoft). The following diagram shows the architecture of the MBV:

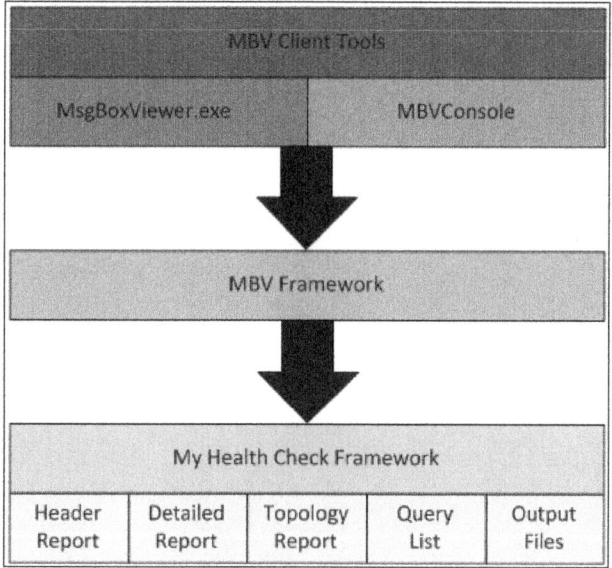

As you can see in the architecture, both the console and Windows Form tools rely on the MBV Framework, which in turn rely on the **My Health Check Framework** (**MYHC**). The latter is represented by two assemblies (MYHCQueries_MBVQueries.dll and MYHC.dll) that reside in the same folder as the executables. These assemblies contain the logic to perform the different type of queries and output of information to different file types (XML, HTML, and Text).

There's more...

The BizTalk Terminator was created by the BizTalk support team to resolve common database integrity issues typically found in the BizTalk Message Box Viewer output. Common tasks include removing instances and purging large tables. You can find the BizTalk Terminator tool through the Microsoft download center (http://www.microsoft.com/download/en/details.aspx?id=2846).

See also

▶ Refer to the _Alternative BizTalk monitoring solution: BizTalk360_ recipe discussed earlier in this chapter

8
Applying Rules

In this chapter, we will cover:

- ▸ Calling rules in an orchestration
- ▸ Using the BRE outside of BizTalk
- ▸ Using the BRE with a database

Introduction

The **Business Rule Engine** (**BRE**) is a software system that executes one or more business rules in a runtime production environment. Oracle, for instance, has Oracle Business Rules and IBM has the iLog **Business Rule Management System** (**BRMS**). Microsoft has their own rule engine that is shipped with the BizTalk Server and is also called the Business Rule Engine or the BRE for short. But, not only BizTalk has a rule engine, there is also the **Windows Workflow Foundation** (**WF**) that has rule engine capabilities.

The BRE enables users, often referred to as business analysts, to directly create and modify sets of business rules. These rules are typically authored in the Business Rules Composer. With this tool, users can define a vocabulary for specifying the rules. A vocabulary is a collection of definitions consisting of friendly names for the facts used in rule conditions and actions. These definitions make the rules easier for users to read and understand. The vocabularies are stored in a shared rule store (that is, the BizTalk Rule Engine Database—`BizTalkRuleEngineDb`). Another important container in the Business Rules Engine is the rule policy, which is a logical collection of business rules.

The BRE implements the Rete algorithm, which is an efficient pattern matching algorithm for implementing production rule systems, and provides forward chaining execution. You will find more about this algorithm at `http://en.wikipedia.org/wiki/Rete_algorithm`. Forward chaining is one of the two main methods of reasoning when using inference rules (in artificial intelligence) and more can be found in wiki pages on forward chaining at `http://en.wikipedia.org/wiki/Forward_chaining` and inference rules at `http://en.wikipedia.org/wiki/Inference_rules`.

A characteristic of the business policies, which you will build, is that they are updatable. This means that you do not have to shut down BizTalk processes to update the necessary components. When a new business rule is deployed, BizTalk will recognize that a new version has been implemented and it will pick up the new data. Using rules that change constantly rather than code, allows you to avoid having to redo their applications systematically.

In this chapter, we will scratch the surface of possibilities of the BRE. In many situations, this is an overlooked feature and not widely used. Recipes in this chapter will show ease of using BizTalk BRE with or without using BizTalk's runtime.

Calling rules in an orchestration

A rule set (policy) can be called inside an orchestration by using the Call Rules shape. Within an orchestration, you can use the Call Rules shape to invoke a policy. The policy on its turn, invokes the rule engine which operates on the rules in the policy. The rules engine can also be programmatically called from the expression code, for example, in an Expression or Message Assignment shape. The following diagram illustrates an orchestration calling the rule engine:

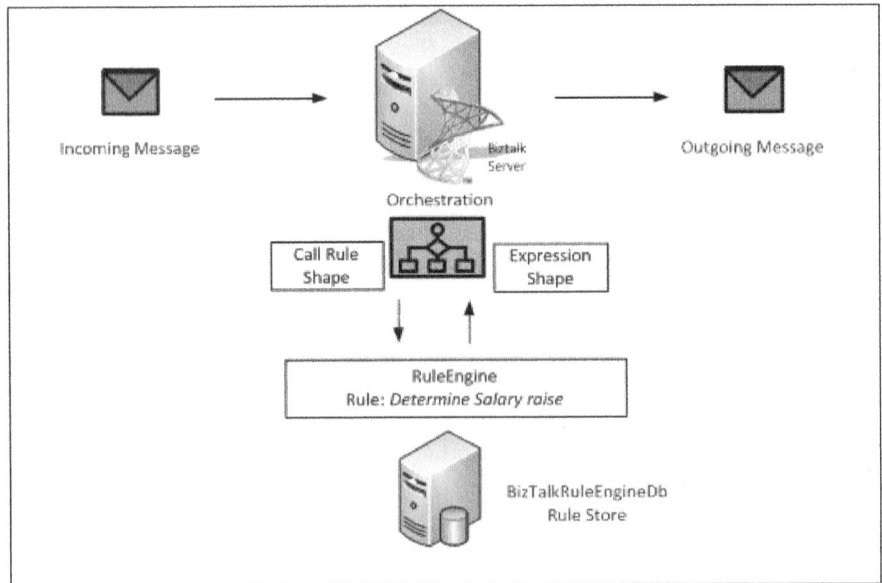

The difference between calling rules from the Call Rules shape and calling rules from the Expression shape is that with the Call Rules shape the latest version will always be called, while with the Expression shape older versions will be called. The Expression shape offers more flexibility when it comes to calling rules. However, the Call Rules shape is the most common and recommended way to invoke a policy from an orchestration.

In this recipe, you will:

- ▶ Create an XML schema
- ▶ Create a policy using the Business Rule Composer
- ▶ Create an orchestration calling a BRE

This recipe will illustrate how you can use a policy to calculate salaries based upon a certain set of facts. You will also see how you can test the policy within the Business Rule Composer.

Getting ready

To run this sample, Business Rules Engine components must be installed. You can download the code accompanied with this book regarding this recipe.

How to do it...

The following steps illustrate how to create an XML schema:

1. Open Visual Studio 2010.
2. In the **New Project** dialog box, from the list of installed templates, click on **BizTalk Projects**. In the right pane, select **Empty BizTalk Server Project**. For the project name, enter an appropriate name and then click on **OK**.
3. Right-click on **Solution** and select **New Item...**.
4. A new dialog will appear and select **Schema**.
5. Provide an appropriate name for the schema for example, **Employee**.
6. Rename the root node to **Employee**.
7. Right-click on **Employee**. Then select **Insert Schema Node | Child record** and name it as **Detail**.
8. Create the following elements:
   - ❑ **FirstName** (data type – xs:string)
   - ❑ **LastName** (data type – xs:string)
   - ❑ **FullName** (data type – xs:string)
   - ❑ **EmployeeNumber** (data type – xs:string)

<ul>
<li>❑   **SocialSecurityNumber** (data type – xs:string)</li>
<li>❑   **Contract** (data type – xs:string)</li>
<li>❑   **Department** (data type – xs:string)</li>
<li>❑   **Manager** (data type – xs:string)</li>
</ul>

9. Right-click on **Employee** and select **Insert Schema Node**. Then select **Child record** and name it as **Salary**.

10. Create the following elements:

<ul>
<li>❑   **CurrentSalary** (data type – xs:int)</li>
<li>❑   **SalaryUpgrade** (data type – xs:boolean)</li>
<li>❑   **Amount** (data type – xs:int)</li>
<li>❑   **NewSalary** (data type – xs:int)</li>
</ul>

11. Sign the project with a strong name. Then build it and deploy the BizTalk project.

12. See to it that the assembly is in the GAC:

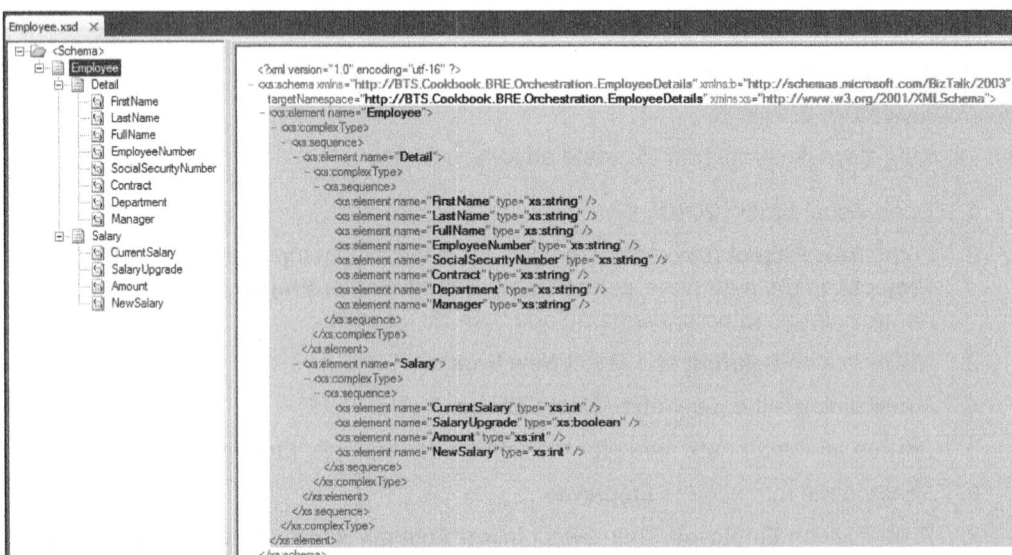

The following steps illustrate how to create a new policy from an orchestration:

1. Open the Business Rule Composer by navigating to the BizTalk Server 2010 and then selecting **Business Rule Composer**.

2. Within **Policy Explorer**, right-click on the **Policies** node. Then, click on **Add New Policy** and give the policy a descriptive name that is, in the sample code it is **Assess Salary Raise**.

3. By default, version 1.0 of the policy is created. You may change the version number if you want by selecting the version, navigating to the **Properties** window, and setting the **Version** property.

4. In **Facts Explorer**, select the **XML Schemas** tab.

5. Select the **Schema** node and right-click on it. Click on **Browse...**.

6. Navigate to the **Employee** schema and click on **Open**.

7. Now, you will see the **Employee** schema in **Facts Explorer**:

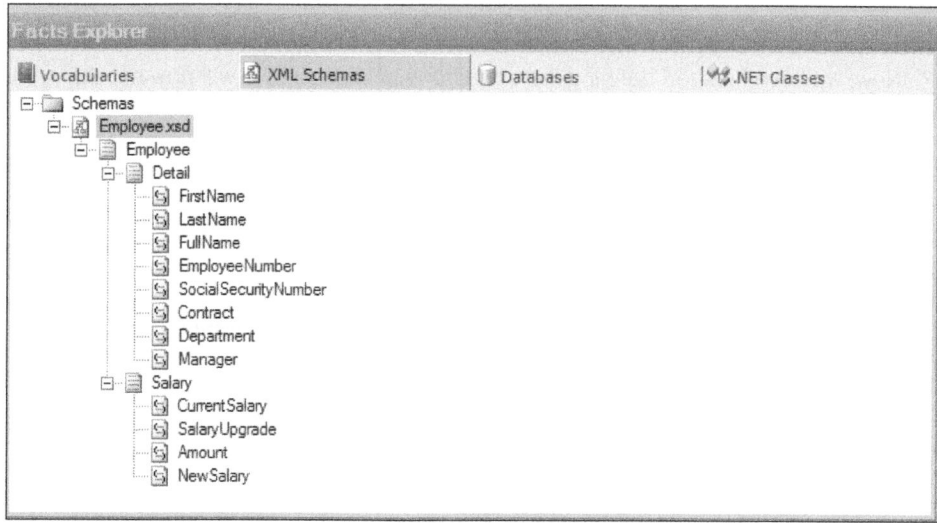

8. In **Policy Explorer**, right-click on **Version 1.0** and select **Add New Rule**.

9. Name it with a descriptive name, in the sample it is **Salary Upgrade Rule**.

10. In the **Conditions** pane, right-click and select **Add Logical AND**.

11. In the **Conditions** pane, right-click and select **Predicates | Less Than**.

12. From **Facts Explorer** select the **Employee** Schema, drag the **CurrentSalary** element to **argument1**.

13. Select **argument1** and enter **50000**.

14. In the **Conditions** pane, right-click and select **Predicates | Equal**.

15. From **Facts Explorer** select the **Employee** schema, drag the **SalaryUpgrade** element to **argument2**.

16. Select **argument2** and enter **True**:

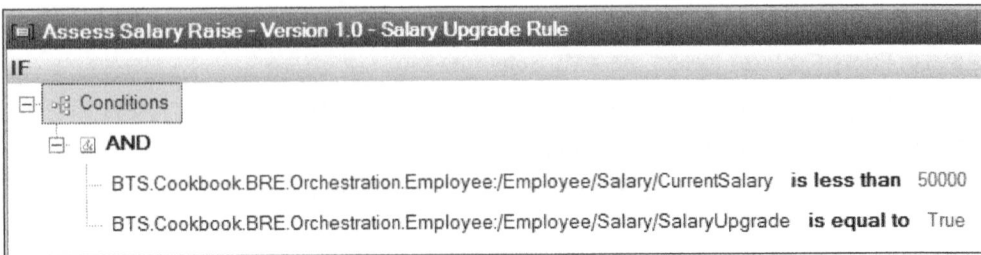

17. Now, we have finished defining the conditions of the rule, we will now set the result. In the **Then** pane, drag the **Amount** element and set the value to **1000**.

18. Drag **Holidays** below the **Bonus** element and set the value to **1**.

19. Drag **SalaryUpgrade** below the **Holidays** element and set the value to **True**.

20. In the **Then** (actions) pane, drag the **NewSalary** element onto the canvas.

21. Right-click on the new value and select **Functions Add**.

22. In **argument1**, drag the **CurrentSalary** element and in **argument2**, drag the **Amount** element:

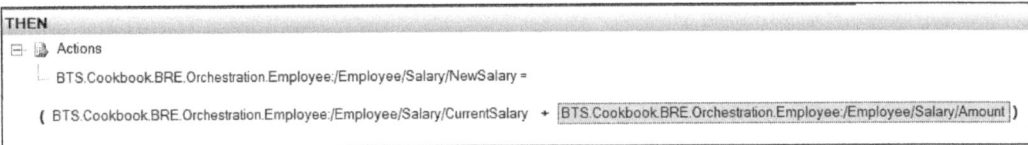

23. Right-click on **Version 1.0** and click on **Save**.

24. Right-click on **Version 1.0** and click on **Publish**.

25. Right-click on **Version 1.0** and click on **Deploy**.

The following steps illustrate how to call a policy from an orchestration:

1. In the BizTalk project, right-click and select **Add | New Item...**.

2. In the dialog that appears, select **Orchestration** and give it a descriptive name.

3. Click on **OK**.

4. Select **Orchestration View**.

5. Right-click on **Message** and click on **New Message**.

6. Give a descriptive name to the message and select the created schema as the message type.

7. From the toolbox, drag the following onto the design surface in top-down order, as shown in the following screenshot:

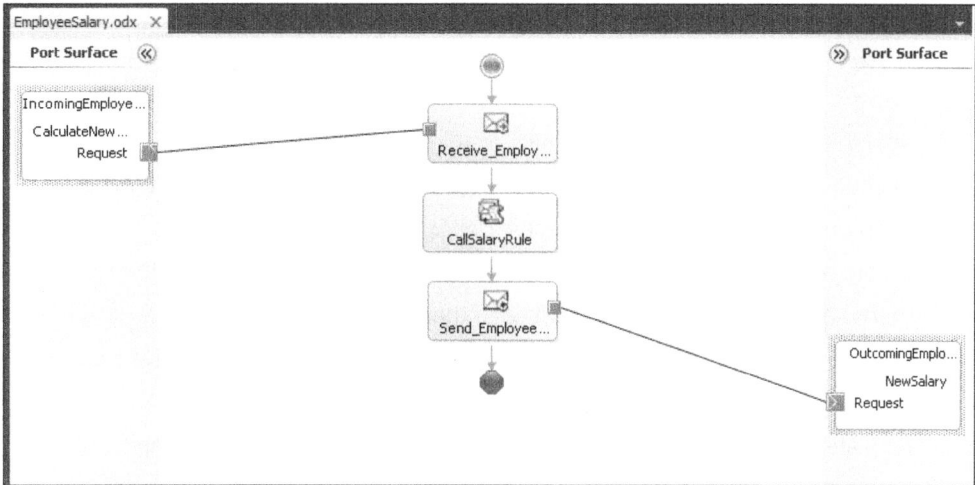

a. Drag the **Receive** shape to receive the initial message. Configure this shape to use the message created earlier, activate the orchestration to use an orchestration Receive port.

b. Drag the **Call Rules** shape and give it a descriptive name.

c. In properties of this shape, click on **Configure Policy...**.

d. In the dialog that appears, select the business policy you wish to call, from the combobox.

e. In **Parameter Name**, select the message:

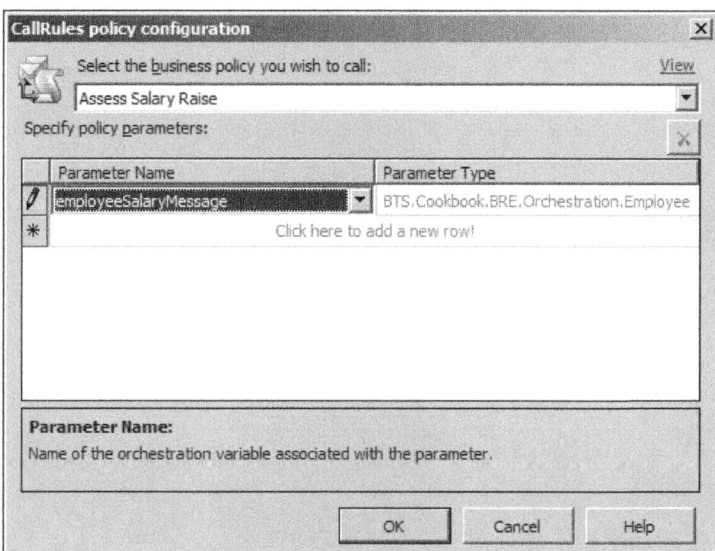

f. Click on **OK**.

g. Drag the **Send** shape. This delivers the message to the destination system. Configure this shape to use an orchestration Send port.

8. Sign the project with a strong name.

9. Subsequently go to the deployment and give it an appropriate application name.

10. Build and deploy the BizTalk project.

11. Create a Receive port and receive location to receive messages from the file system.

12. Create a Send port to send messages to the file. Start the application.

13. Test the solution by dropping a message in the folder, where the receive location is listening.

The following steps illustrate how to test a policy within the Business Rule Composer:

1. Right-click on **Version 1.0** of the created policy and select **Test Policy**.

2. You will be asked to assign a test instance for the fact(s) being used by the rule, as shown in the following screenshot:

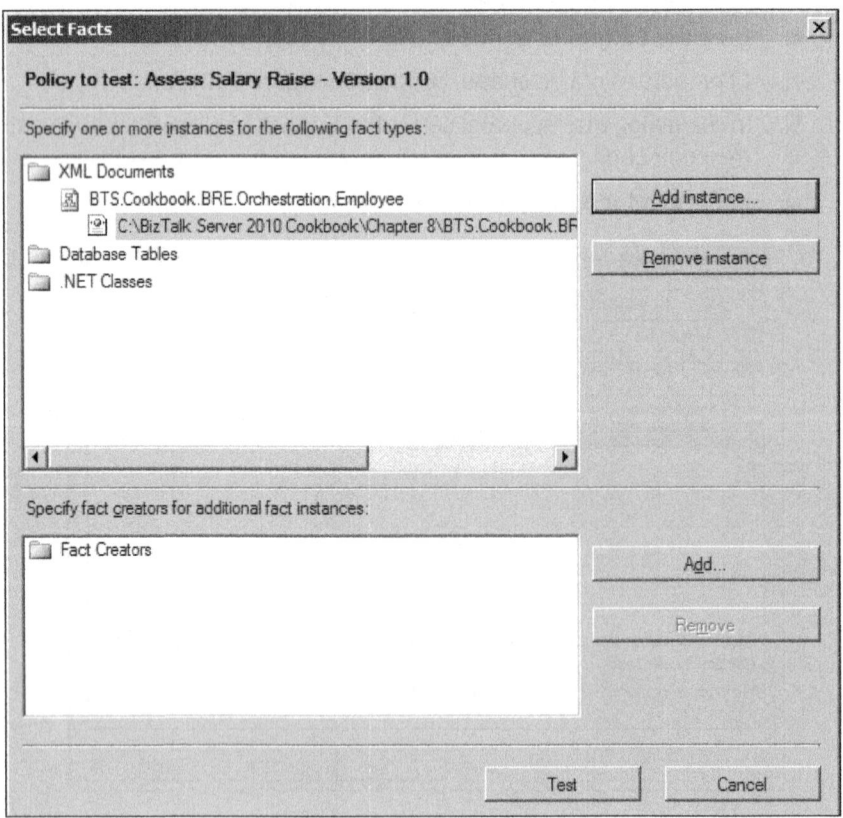

3. Add the test instance (that is, an instance of the schema created earlier), and then click on **Test:**

```
Assess Salary Raise - Version 1.0

Output

RULE ENGINE TRACE for RULESET: Assess Salary Raise 11/25/2011 3:15:58 PM

FACT ACTIVITY 11/25/2011 3:15:58 PM
Rule Engine Instance Identifier: 1a79f097-81f1-4408-b123-26e81c6a8430
Ruleset Name: Assess Salary Raise
Operation: Assert
Object Type: TypedXmlDocument:BTS.Cookbook.BRE.Orchestration.Employee
Object Instance Identifier: 37685299

FACT ACTIVITY 11/25/2011 3:15:58 PM
Rule Engine Instance Identifier: 1a79f097-81f1-4408-b123-26e81c6a8430
Ruleset Name: Assess Salary Raise
Operation: Assert
Object Type: TypedXmlDocument:BTS.Cookbook.BRE.Orchestration.Employee:/Employee/Salary
Object Instance Identifier: 3623379

CONDITION EVALUATION TEST (MATCH) 11/25/2011 3:15:58 PM
Rule Engine Instance Identifier: 1a79f097-81f1-4408-b123-26e81c6a8430
Ruleset Name: Assess Salary Raise
Test Expression: TypedXmlDocument:BTS.Cookbook.BRE.Orchestration.Employee:/Employee/Salary.CurrentSalary < 50000
Left Operand Value: 40000
Right Operand Value: 50000
Test Result: True

CONDITION EVALUATION TEST (MATCH) 11/25/2011 3:15:58 PM
Rule Engine Instance Identifier: 1a79f097-81f1-4408-b123-26e81c6a8430
Ruleset Name: Assess Salary Raise
Test Expression: TypedXmlDocument:BTS.Cookbook.BRE.Orchestration.Employee:/Employee/Salary.SalaryUpgrade == True
Left Operand Value: True
Right Operand Value: True
Test Result: True

AGENDA UPDATE 11/25/2011 3:15:58 PM
Rule Engine Instance Identifier: 1a79f097-81f1-4408-b123-26e81c6a8430
Ruleset Name: Assess Salary Raise
Operation: Add
Rule Name: Salary Upgrade Rule
Conflict Resolution Criteria: 0

RULE FIRED 11/25/2011 3:15:58 PM
Rule Engine Instance Identifier: 1a79f097-81f1-4408-b123-26e81c6a8430
Ruleset Name: Assess Salary Raise
Rule Name: Salary Upgrade Rule
Conflict Resolution Criteria: 0

FACT ACTIVITY 11/25/2011 3:15:58 PM
Rule Engine Instance Identifier: 1a79f097-81f1-4408-b123-26e81c6a8430
Ruleset Name: Assess Salary Raise
Operation: Retract
Object Type: TypedXmlDocument:BTS.Cookbook.BRE.Orchestration.Employee
Object Instance Identifier: 37685299

FACT ACTIVITY 11/25/2011 3:15:58 PM
Rule Engine Instance Identifier: 1a79f097-81f1-4408-b123-26e81c6a8430
Ruleset Name: Assess Salary Raise
Operation: Retract
Object Type: TypedXmlDocument:BTS.Cookbook.BRE.Orchestration.Employee:/Employee/Salary
Object Instance Identifier: 3623379

----------------------------------------------------
```

How it works...

A message is offered to the BizTalk orchestration and passed within the orchestration to Call Rules shape. The BRE captured the XML message as a parameter, evaluated it, and then modified the `NewSalary` value. The modified message is then sent to its destination folder.

When you work with rules, it is possible that one rule may invoke another rule of logic. As you see in this recipe, a rule evaluates the values in `SalaryUpgrade` and `CurrentSalary`. This is called a **forward-chaining**.process, because the events considered are all linked together.

When you test the policy within the Business Rule Composer, the BRE will process your rule(s) and you will see a report on the various rules and processes which were fired during the execution of your instance (see previous screenshot).

There's more...

General information about the BRE and creating rules can be found on MSDN and the BizTalk website:

- **Creating and Using Business Rules**: `http://msdn.microsoft.com/en-us/library/aa577691.aspx`

- **The Business Rules Framework**: `http://www.microsoft.com/biztalk/en/us/business-rule-framework.aspx`

The BizTalk documentation on MSDN provides a couple of walkthroughs for using the Business Rules Framework for the BRE. One of them is a document called **Business Rules Framework Walkthroughs** at `http://msdn.microsoft.com/en-us/library/aa995562%28v=BTS.70%29.aspx`.

The Microsoft BizTalk Server includes several business rules samples in its **Software Development Kit** (**SDK**). These rules are explained in a document called **Business Rules** (**BizTalk Server Samples Folder**), found at `http://msdn.microsoft.com/en-us/library/aa578627.aspx`.

See also

- The BRE can also be used without the BizTalk runtime. For this, refer to the *Using the BRE outside of BizTalk* recipe discussed later in this chapter.

Using the BRE outside of BizTalk

Out of the box, BizTalk Server offers the BRE and it can be installed with or without the BizTalk Server runtime. It can be used separately, but you will still need a BizTalk license (similar to the scenario using the AppFabric Connect feature explained in *Chapter 6, BizTalk AppFabric Connect*). The BRE is essentially an independent product which can be accessed by its own APIs and tools. Through the .NET application, you can use the engine with no need for orchestrations or other BizTalk objects.

In this recipe, you will create:

- ▸ A schema that will provide information on an employee, an instance of a schema will serve as input for the application
- ▸ A policy that will determine employee benefits
- ▸ A .NET application calling the policy

Although the business rules engine comes as part of the BizTalk Server, this recipe will show that .NET assemblies outside the BizTalk environment can call into it. The created external application is allowed to use the same rule framework that BizTalk uses. It will show that organizations can consolidate their business rules functionality onto one platform.

Getting ready

To run this, the sample Business Rule Engine component must be installed. You can download the code accompanied with this book regarding this recipe.

How to do it...

The following steps illustrate how to create an XML schema:

1. Open Visual Studio 2010.
2. In the **New Project** dialog box, from the list of installed templates, click on **BizTalk Projects**. In the right pane, select **Empty BizTalk Server Project**. For the project name, enter an appropriate name and then click on **OK**.
3. Right-click on **Solution** and select **New Item...**.
4. A new dialog will appear and select **Schema**.
5. Provide an appropriate name for the schema for example, **Employee**.
6. Rename the root node to **Employee**.

7. Right-click on **Employee**, and select **Insert Schema Node**. Then select **Child record** and name it as **Detail**.

8. Create the following elements:
   - ❏ **FirstName** (data type – xs:string)
   - ❏ **LastName** (data type – xs:string)
   - ❏ **FullName** (data type – xs:string)
   - ❏ **EmployeeNumber** (data type – xs:string)
   - ❏ **SocialSecurityNumber** (data type – xs:string)
   - ❏ **Contract** (data type – xs:string)
   - ❏ **Department** (data type – xs:string)
   - ❏ **Manager** (data type – xs:string)

9. Right-click on **Employee** and select **Insert Schema Node**. Then select **Child record** and name it as **Benefits**.

10. Create the following elements:
   - ❏ **Rating** (data type – xs:string)
   - ❏ **Bonus** (data type – xs:int)
   - ❏ **Holidays** (data type – xs:int)
   - ❏ **SalaryUpgrade** (data type – xs:boolean)

11. Refer to the following screenshot:

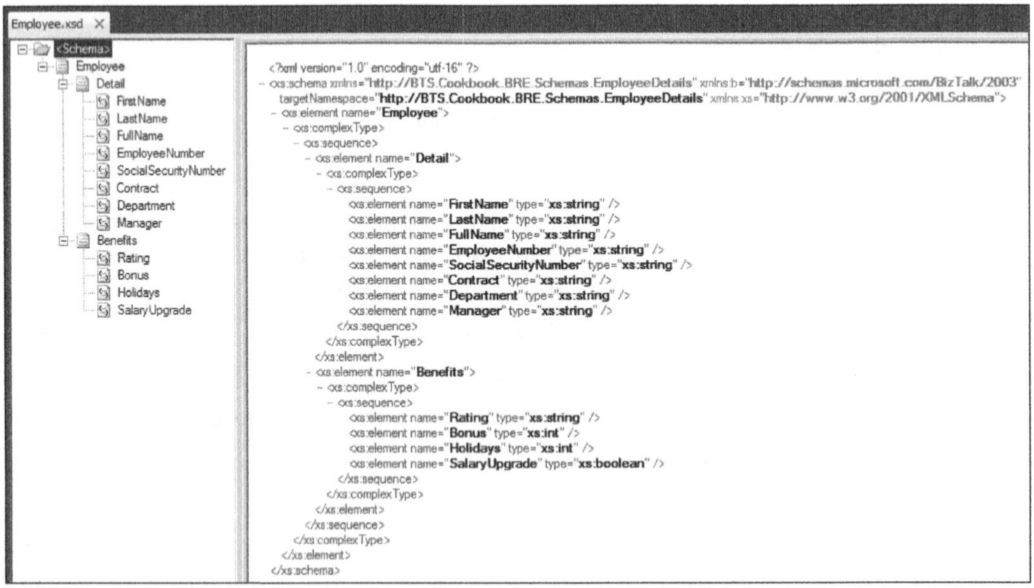

12. Sign the project with a strong name. Build and deploy the BizTalk project.

13. See to it that the assembly is in the GAC.

Now you have your schema ready, you can create a policy using the Business Rule Composer:

1. Open the Business Rule Composer.

2. Right-click on **Policies** in the **Policy Explorer** pane and click on **Add New Policy**.

3. Name it as **Assess Benefits**.

4. In **Facts Explorer**, select the **XML Schemas** tab.

5. Select the **Schemas** node and right-click on it. Then click on **Browse....**

6. Navigate to the **Employee** schema and click on **Open**.

7. You will now see the **Employee** schema in **Facts Explorer**:

8. In **Policy Explorer**, right-click on **Version 1.0** and select **Add New Rule**.

9. Name it as **Bonus Rule**.

10. In the **Conditions** pane, right-click and select **Predicates | Equal**.

11. From **Facts Explorer** select the **Employee** schema, drag the Rating element to **argument1**.

12. Select **argument2** and enter **A**.

13. In the **Then** pane, drag the **Bonus** element and set the value to **1000**.

14. Drag **Holidays** below the **Bonus** element and set the value to **1**.

15. Drag **SalaryUpgrade** below the **Holidays** element and set the value to **True**:

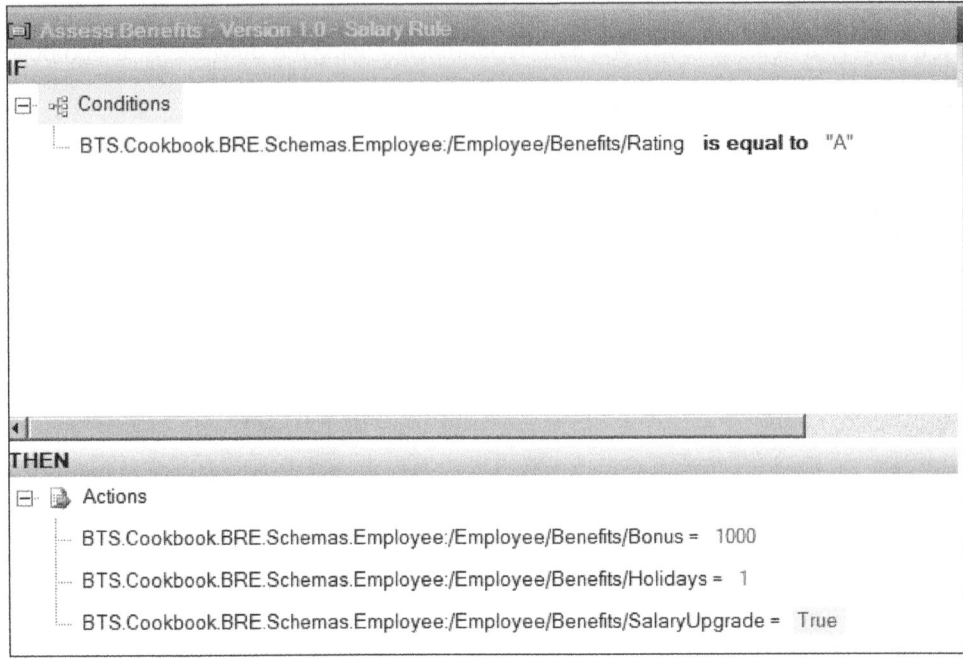

16. Right-click on **Version 1.0** and click on **Save**.

17. Right-click on **Version 1.0** and click on **Publish**.

18. Right-click on **Version 1.0** and click on **Deploy**.

Now you have your policy ready and published in the rule store:

1. Right-click on **Solution** in Visual Studio and select **Add | New Project**.

2. In the **New Project** dialog box, from the list of installed templates, click on **Visual C#**. In the right pane, select **Windows Form Application**. For the project name, enter an appropriate name and then click on **OK**.

3. Drag a button to the form and name it as **Request**.

4. Drag a text below button, name it appropriately, and set the **Multiline** property to **True**.

5. Double-click on the **Request** button and the **Code Behind** pane will appear in Visual Studio.

6. Add a project reference to the **Microsoft.RuleEngine.dll** assembly, which contains the classes required to call the BRE. This assembly can be found in $\Program Files\Common Files\Microsoft BizTalk.

7. Add the following to the using statement above the namespace:

```
//To use the XmlDocument class
using System.Xml;
//To use the TypedXmlDocument and Policy classes
using Microsoft.RuleEngine;
```

8. Add the following code below the button and click on **Event**:

```
// Create instance xmldocument object
XmlDocument xmlDoc = new XmlDocument();
  //Load xml file
  xmlDoc.Load(@"C:\BizTalk Server 2010 Cookbook\Chapter8\
  BTS.Cookbook.BRE.Schemas\Xml File\Employee Dan Janssen.xml");
    // Create the input parameter for the Assess Benefits policy
    based   on a typed BizTalk schema (fully qualified .NET type)
    TypedXmlDocument typedXmlDoc = new TypedXmlDocument
    ("BTS.Cookbook.BRE.Schemas.Employee", xmlDoc);
    // Create the Assess Benefits policy object
    Policy policy = new Policy("Assess Benefits");
      //Call Policy
      policy.Execute(typedXmlDoc);
      //Show results
      txtResult.Text = typedXmlDoc.Document.OuterXml;
```

9. The location of your input XML may vary from the above code snippet.

10. Now, you can run the .NET application by right-clicking on the project, selecting **Debug**, and then selecting **Start New Instance**.

How it works...

To be able to call into the rules engine, you need to reference the Microsoft.RuleEngine.dll assembly, which contains classes used to access the rules framework, including those to execute policies as you can see in the code sample. In this recipe, you created a schema which imported into the Business Rule Composer as facts to work with the composing rules.

An Assess Benefits policy was created which contains one rule. The rule evaluates one condition which has to be met to fire off actions that sets values in the elements in the Benefits. This policy is saved, published in the rule store, and deployed. In the .NET application, a message is loaded into the `XmlDocument` instance. Subsequently, a `Microsoft.RuleEngine.TypedXmlDocument` instance is created specifying the document type (the fully qualified .NET type name) and the XML document instance. The message in a single fact is going to be offered to the policy and be evaluated.

An instance of the policy object is created with the name of the policy created in the Business Rule Composer. Policy is executed with the `Microsoft.RuleEngine.TypedXmlDocument` instance and the outcome is shown in the .NET application. It is also possible to use code to call the policy in .NET in the Expression shape in an orchestration.

There's more...

On the DevX website you will find an extensive article, **Programming with the Microsoft Business Rules Framework** (`http://www.devx.com/codemag/Article/40489/1763/page/1`), by Rick Garibay. It explains about programming with Microsoft Business Rules.

Another good resource is the blog by Charles Young, a BizTalk MVP, that has a lot of content on the BRE. You can find it at `http://geekswithblogs.net/cyoung/category/2771.aspx`.

See also

▶ This recipe is an alternative way of using the BRE, while the BRE can be used from the BizTalk runtime. For this you can refer to the *Calling rules in an orchestration* recipe discussed earlier in this chapter.

Using the BRE with a database

Business rules are stored in a rule store, which is basically a SQL Server database. When you configure the BRE with the BizTalk Server Configuration tool, you deploy a database called `BizTalkRuleEngineDb`. With the Business Rule Composer, you can create policies containing rules and vocabularies. These are stored in the rule store. The interactions with the rule store are depicted in the following diagram. Rules can be applied on a message provided through an orchestration or .NET application, as shown in the previous recipe. The BRE separates rules from your orchestration or .NET program:

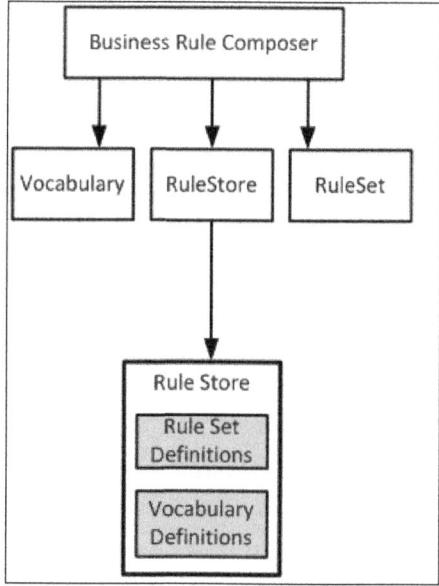

Besides the rule store you can use another database that could contain data for rules. Data that can be used to evaluate with facts, which are delivered to a policy through a Rule shape in an orchestration. Business users can change this data instead of the rule itself and prevent updating the rules. With an update of rules, you have to go through steps in the Business Rule Composer—undeploy, version, publish, and redeployment process. This way you can separate the data from the rules in just about the same way as the BRE separates the rules from the orchestration.

In this recipe, we will build a schema first and then:

- Create a database with a table and fill it with data
- Create a new vocabulary with definitions
- Create a new policy with a rule
- Create a BizTalk process that will call the rule in the policy

Getting ready

To run this sample, the Business Rules Engine components must be installed. You can download the code accompanied with this book regarding this recipe.

How to do it...

The following steps illustrate how to create an XML schema:

1. Open Visual Studio 2010.

2. In the **New Project** dialog box, from the list of installed templates, click on **BizTalk Projects**. In the right pane, select **Empty BizTalk Server Project**. For the project name, enter an appropriate name and then click on **OK**.

3. Right-click on **Project** and select **New Item...**.

4. A new dialog will appear and select **Schema**.

5. Provide an appropriate name for the schema for example, **Employee**.

6. Rename the root node to **Employee**.

7. Right-click on **Employee** and select **Insert Schema Node**. Then select **Child record** and name it as **Detail**.

8. Create the following elements:

   - **FirstName** (data type – xs:string)
   - **LastName** (data type – xs:string)
   - **FullName** (data type – xs:string)
   - **EmployeeNumber** (data type – xs:string)
   - **SocialSecurityNumber** (data type – xs:string)
   - **Contract** (data type – xs:string)
   - **Department** (data type – xs:string)
   - **Manager** (data type – xs:string)

9. Right-click on **Employee** and select **Insert Schema Node**. Then select **Child record** and name it as **Salary**.

10. Create the following elements:

    - **CurrentSalary** (data type – xs:int)
    - **SalaryUpgrade** (data type – xs:boolean)
    - **Rating** (data type – xs:string)
    - **Amount** (data type – xs:int)
    - **NewSalary** (data type – xs:int)

Now, you can create a new database with a table and fill it with data:

1. Open the SQL Server Management Studio 2008 (R2).

2. Connect to the database.

3. In **Object Explorer**, right-click on **Database** and select **New Database...**.

4. Name the database as **SalaryDb**.

5. Open **New Query** for the created database.

6. Paste following code for creating the table and execute:

```
CREATE TABLE [dbo].[SalaryRaise](
   [Rating] [varchar](1) NOT NULL,
   [SalaryLimit] [numeric](18, 0) NOT NULL,
   [LastUpdatedBy] [varchar](50) NOT NULL,
   [LastUpdated] [datetime] NOT NULL
) ON [PRIMARY]
```

7. Paste the following code for inserting data into the table and execute:

```
Insert into SalaryRaise VALUES ('A', 5000, 'SMacDonalds',
GetDate()) -- A Rating Salary Raise
Insert into SalaryRaise VALUES ('B', 1000, 'SMacDonalds',
GetDate()) -- B Rating Salary Raise
Insert into SalaryRaise VALUES ('C', 500,  'SMacDonalds',
GetDate()) -- C Rating Salary Raise
Insert into SalaryRaise VALUES ('D', 100,  'SMacDonalds',
GetDate()) -- D Rating Salary Raise
```

Now, you have your database with a table and filled it with data, you can create a new vocabulary with definitions.

In these steps we will create a vocabulary of facts which we can use in the rule conditions and actions:

1. Open the Business Rule Composer.

2. In the **Facts Explorer** window, right-click on **Vocabulary**. Then select **Add New Vocabulary** and name it as **SalaryLimit**.

3. Right-click on **Version 1.0 (not saved)** and select **Add New Definition**. Click on the last radio button **Database Table or Column**. Put **SalaryType** in the **Definition Name**, click on the **Browse** button (select Windows authentication for convenience). Select the **SalaryRaise** table and the **Rating** column.

4. Select the **Perform Get Operation** radio button and click on **Finish**.

5. Repeat the steps for **SalaryLimit**. Right-click on **Version 1.0 (not saved)** and select **Add New Definition**. Click on the last radio button **Database Table or Column**. Put **SalaryLimit** in **Definition Name**, click on the **Browse** button (select Windows authentication for convenience). Select the **SalaryRaise** table and the **SalaryLimit** column. Select the **Perform Get Operation** radio button and click on **Finish**.

6. Repeat the steps for **Amount**. Right-click on **Version 1.0 (not saved)** and select **Add New Definition**. Click on the last radio button **XML Document Element or Attribute**. Put **Amount** in **Definition Name**, click on the **Browse** button (select your **Employee** schema). Select the **Amount** field in the schema. Select the **Perform Get Operation** radio button and click on **Finish**.

7. Repeat the steps for **Rating**. Right click on **Version 1.0 (not saved)** and select **Add New Definition**. Click on the last radio button **XML Document Element or Attribute**. Put **Rating** in **Definition Name**, click on the **Browse** button (select your **Employee** schema). Select the **Rating** field in the schema. Select the **Perform Get Operation** radio button and click on **Finish**.

8. Repeat the steps for **SalaryUpgrade**. Right-click on **Version 1.0 (not saved)** and select **Add New Definition.** Click on the last radio button **XML Document Element or Attribute**. Put **SalaryUpgrade** in **Definition Name**, click on the **Browse** button (select your **Employee** schema). Select the **SalaryUpgrade** field in the schema. Select the **Perform Set Operation** radio button and click on **Next**. Then click on **Finish**.

9. Now you have the vocabulary created, right-click on **Version 1.0 (not saved)** and select **Publish**:

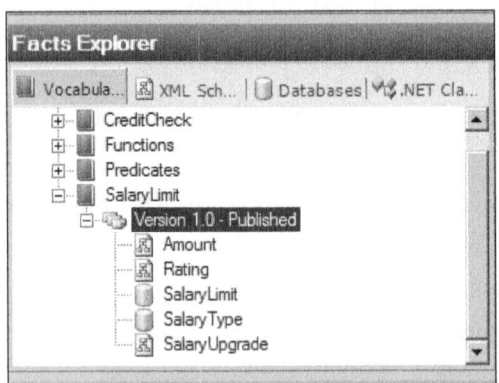

Now, you have your vocabulary, you need to create a new policy with a rule:

1. Go to **Policies Explorer** and right-click on **Policies.** Select **Add New Policy**, name it as **SalaryRaisePolicy**.

2. Right-click on **Version 1.0 (not saved)** and select **Add New Rule**. Name it as **SalaryUpgrade**.

3. Right-click on the **Conditions** text and select **Add logical AND**.

4. Right-click on **AND** and select **Predicates | Equal**. Add **2** fields from the Vocabulary so it reads:

   IF Rating Equals SalaryType.

5. Right-click on **AND** again and select **Predicates | Less than Equal**. Add the fields **Amount** and **SalaryLimit**.

6. Next, in the **Actions** pane drag-and-drop **SalaryUpgrade** to **True**. So, the whole rule reads as shown in the following screenshot:

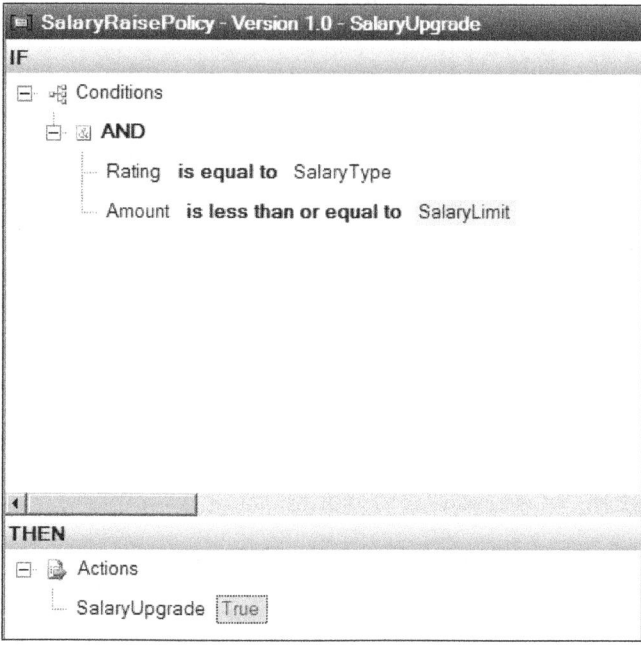

7. Right-click on **Version 1.0 - Publish** and select **Deploy**.

Now you have to create a BizTalk process which will call the rule in the policy:

1. Go to your Visual Studio BizTalk project.

2. Right-click on **Project** and select **New Item...**.

3. A new dialog will appear and select **Orchestration**.

4. Name the orchestration as **SalaryUpgradeCheck.odx** and click on **OK**.

5. Right-click in the canvas and select **Properties Window**.

6. In **Transaction Type**, select **Long Running**.

7. Change the name of **TransactionIdentifier** to **Transaction_SalaryUpgradeCheck**.

8. On the project reference, select the following three DLLs:
   - **System.Transactions**
   - **System.Data**
   - **Microsoft.RuleEngine.dll**

9. Drop a Receive port called **SalaryUpgardeCheckPort** of type `SalaryUpgardeCheckPortType` and select **Always receive message on this port**.

10. Drop the **Receive** shape and set **Activate** to **True**.

11. In the **Orchestration** pane on the studio, right-click on **Message** and select **New Message** and name it as **MsgSalaryUpgradeCheck** of type `Employee.xsd`.

12. Assign the message to the Receive shape and connect it with the port. Click on the empty space in the orchestration and make the transaction type as long running.

13. Now drag the **Scope** shape from the toolbox and set the transaction type of this scope shape as **Atomic**. Name the shape as **CallRulesEngine**.

14. In the **CallRulesEngine** scope, create two new variables:

    ❑ **SQLConn** of type `System.Data.SqlClient.SqlConnection`

    ❑ **RulesDataConn** of type `Microsoft.RuleEngine.DataConnection`

15. In the **Scope** shape, drag-and-drop the **Expression** shape and paste the following code:

    ```
    SQLConn = new System.Data.SqlClient.SqlConnection("Initial
    Catalog=SalaryDb;Data Source=(local);Integrated Security=SSPI;");
    RulesDataConn = new Microsoft.RuleEngine.DataConnection
    ("SalaryDb", "SalaryRaise", SQLConn);
    ```

16. Just below the **Expression** shape, drag the **Call Rules** shape and configure it to use **SalaryRaisePolicy**. You will get two parameters automatically— **MsgSalaryUpgradeCheck** and **RulesDataConn**. So, configure them and click on **OK**:

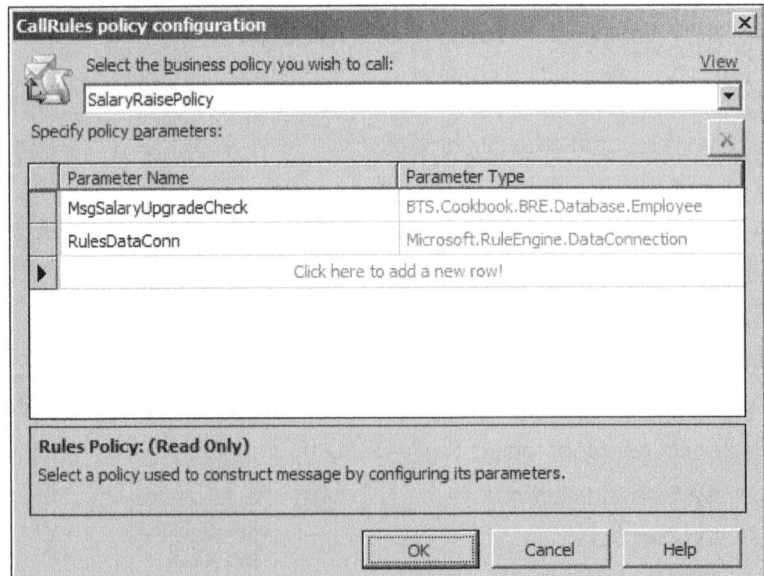

17. Drop the **Send** shape from the toolbox below the **Scope** shape and configure it to send the **MsgSalaryUpgradeCheck**.

18. Drop a Send port called **SalaryUpgardeCheckSendPort** of type `SalaryUpgardeCheckSendPortType` and select **Always send messages on this port**.

19. Sign the project with a strong name and give it an appropriate application name.

20. Right-click on the project and click on **Deploy**. Then, configure the Send and Receive ports from the BizTalk Admin Console and test them with a test message.

How it works...

This recipe showed you how to separate the data from the rules and provide a different paradigm for applying rules to a process. Instead of changing rules, you can change the data applied to the rules. The vocabulary built in this recipe is used to apply facts from messages provided through an orchestration to rule and compare them with facts from the database table column. Vocabularies are user-defined names for the facts that you use in rule conditions and actions. Their definitions can make rules easier to read and understand within particular business domains. The vocabulary created in this recipe is for a human resource domain for salary upgrades. Facts are created to be obtained from messages (that is, an XML schema) and database. Subsequently, a policy with a rule is created, where these facts are going to be used.

The orchestration (process) is going to provide a message, where the rule of `SalaryUpgradeCheck` is to be applied. The Rule shape is placed in the Scope shape with an atomic transaction type to facilitate connection with the database containing the rule data. The connection is assigned to the variable that is to be provided to the Call Rules shape along with the message. To be able to do so, a reference is required to the `System.Transaction`, `System.Data` assemblies, and the `Microsoft.RuleEngine.dll`. `Microsoft.RuleEngine.DataConnection` class has a `DataConnection` object which is required to get facts from the database. `DataConnection` is provided through `System.Data.SqlClient.SqlConnection`. The rule engine will be provided with facts through the message and can get facts from the database through the `DataConnection` object. A rule can be executed with these facts and the result is passed back to the orchestration.

There's more...

This recipe is based on an MSDN blog post called **Simple example of using the BizTalk Business Rules Engine (BRE)** with Database (`http://blogs.msdn.com/b/rgarg/archive/2009/04/23/using-biztalk-business-rules-engine-bre-with-database.aspx`) and I found it interesting that with usage of a database you could separate rule data from rules.

On MSDN, you can also find information on passing database facts to the BRE in the document called **Passing Database Facts to the Business Rule Engine** (http://msdn.microsoft.com/en-us/library/aa951249.aspx).

See also

▸ Refer to the *Using the BRE outside of BizTalk* and *Calling rules in an orchestration* recipes discussed earlier in this chapter

9
Testing BizTalk Artifacts

In this chapter, we will cover:

- ▶ Testing BizTalk artifacts inside Visual Studio
- ▶ Unit testing a BizTalk solution with BizUnit
- ▶ Applying code coverage to a BizTalk orchestration
- ▶ Testing BizTalk solutions with BizMock
- ▶ Using the BizTalk Map Test Framework
- ▶ Testing pipelines and pipeline components

Introduction

Testing is an important part when you are developing BizTalk solutions. Before deploying your solution into production, you need to be confident that it will perform, and do the job it is intended to do. A developer is responsible for creating robust and solid BizTalk solutions. He/she needs to test the BizTalk solutions with its artifacts before it is deploy to a test environment, where integration and other tests will be performed.

With the BizTalk Server 2009, the unit test feature was introduced, which offered built-in developer support for testing schemas, maps, and pipelines. This was a great enhancement for developers. Before that, developers had to rely on frameworks such as BizUnit. Now, the developer has one IDE for developing and testing the BizTalk solutions. Yet, the frameworks such as BizUnit or BizMock still have their value as they provide a rich API. They also offer great flexibility and control over your tests.

For last couple of years, people in the community have built frameworks to support developers in testing. Frameworks such as BizUnit, BizMock, and the BizTalk Map Test Framework are all available through CodePlex and support the BizTalk Server 2010. Another useful tool for testing is the Pipeline Testing Library made by Tomas Restrepo.

How to use these frameworks and the test library will be discussed in the recipes which you will find in this chapter. The focus in this chapter is on testing artifacts during development and not integration, load, or performance testing. You will find recipes to test the following artifacts:

- Document schemas
- Orchestrations
- Pipelines
- Pipeline components
- Maps

Testing BizTalk artifacts inside Visual Studio

During development of your BizTalk solution, you can do some of the testing before you even deploy your solution. You can leverage the capabilities of testing in Visual Studio using, for instance, the **Test Map** menu item for testing a map. Besides that you can use the Unit Test functionality offered by Visual Studio. The Unit Testing Framework (`http://msdn.microsoft.com/en-us/library/ms243147(v=VS.90).aspx`) supports unit testing in Visual Studio and allows you to create unit tests (`http://msdn.microsoft.com/en-us/library/ms182517.aspx`). In this recipe, you will learn the test capabilities offered by Visual Studio in BizTalk projects. The following tasks will be shown in this recipe:

- Validating an XML document instance
- Testing a map
- Unit test a schema

Getting ready

Download the code (`BTS.Cookbook.Test.SchemaAndMap`) belonging to this book from the Packt website or use your own BizTalk project.

How to do it...

Performing the following steps will enable you to test an instance of a document schema:

1. Navigate to a schema you want to test in your BizTalk project.

2. In **Properties**, select **Input Instance Filename**, as shown in the following screenshot, and click on ellipsis (**...**):

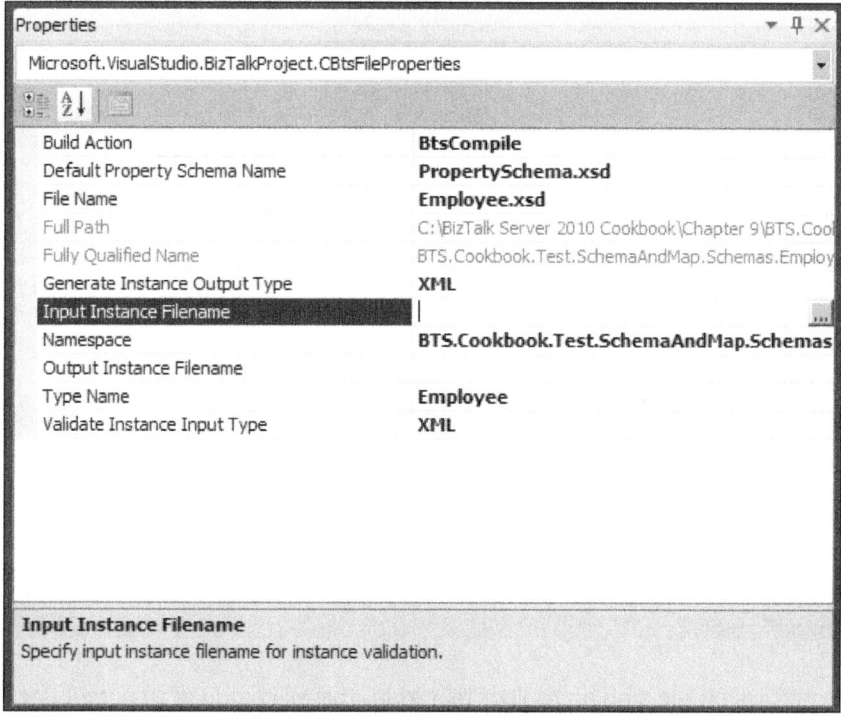

3. Navigate to the XML file you want to validate (that is, test).

4. Click on **Open**.

5. Right-click on the schema and select **Validate Instance**.

6. In the **Output** window, you will see the result, as depicted in the following screenshot:

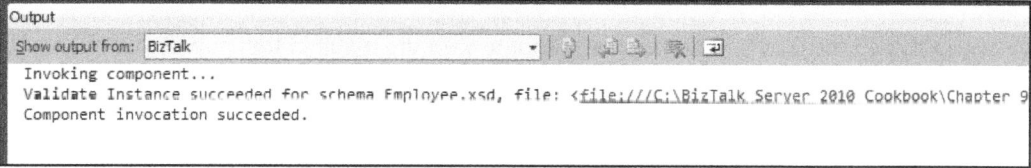

Performing the following steps will enable you to test a map:

1. In **Solution Explorer**, right-click on the map to test and select **Properties**.

2. Set **TestMap Input** and **TestMap Output** to **XML**.

3. Set the **TestMap Input Instance** property to the path of the instance you want to use as input to test the map:

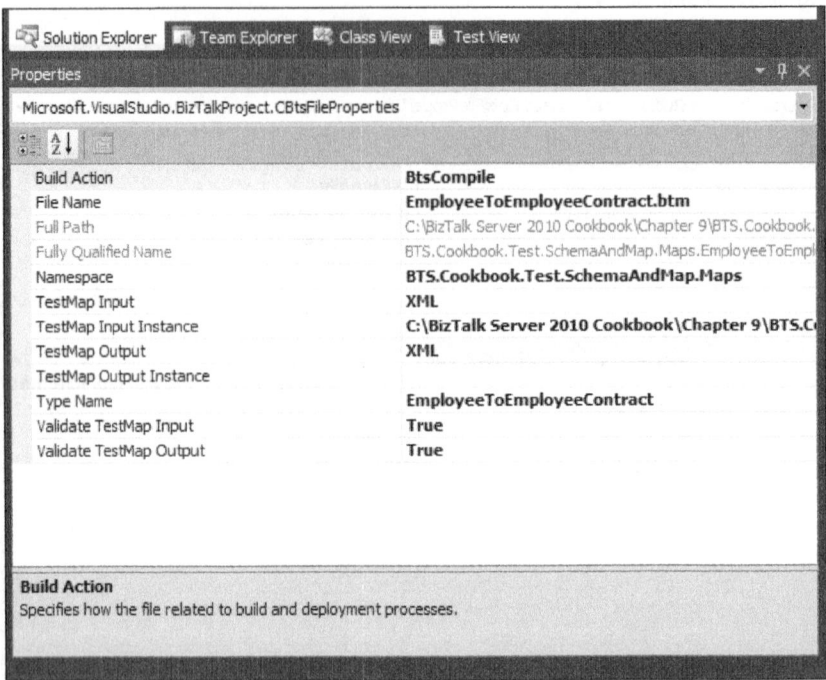

4. Right-click on the map and select **Test Map**. This will produce an output document that can be validated for accuracy. Check the **Output** window in Visual Studio for details in case of a failure:

5. Click on the provided link for the output to view the result of the map.

Performing the following steps will enable you to unit test your BizTalk project containing schema(s), map(s), or pipeline(s). Here, the unit test of a map and schema will be outlined:

1. Right-click on the BizTalk project containing the schemas.

2. Select the **Deployment** tab and set the **Enable Unit Testing** property to **True**. This will modify the BizTalk artifacts so that they inherit from `TestableSchemaBase`, `TestableMapBase`, or `TestablePipelineBase`:

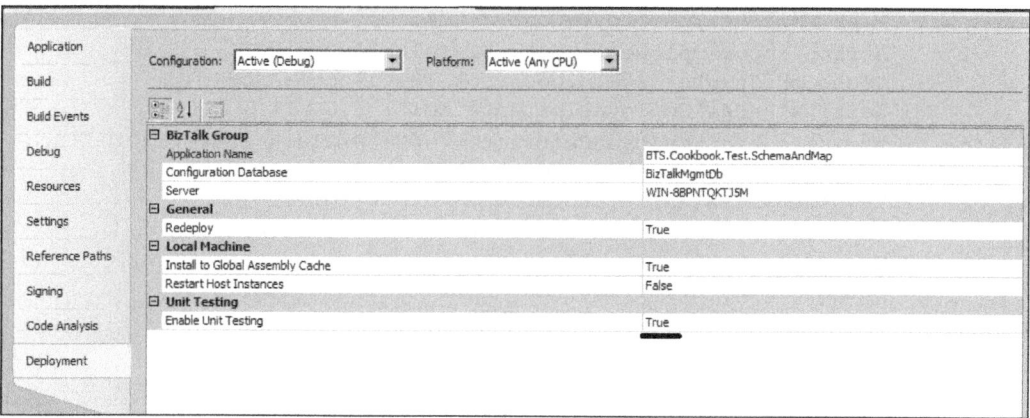

3. Build the project and then click on **Rebuild Solution**.

4. You can repeat these steps for other BizTalk projects which you want to unit test.

5. The next step is to build a unit test applicable for BizTalk projects.

6. Add a test project to your solution and give it an appropriate name.

7. Within the test project, set references to your BizTalk projects on which you wish to perform the unit test.

8. Set the reference to `Microsoft.BizTalk.TestTools.dll` and `Microsoft.XLANGs.BaseTypes.dll`.

9. In **Unit Test Class**, you can test methods, as shown in the following code snippet for validating an XML document instance and/or test map:

```
[TestMethod]
  public void ValidateEmployeeInstanceTest()
  {
    BTS.Cookbook.Test.SchemaAndMap.Schemas.Employee emp = new
    Schemas.Employee();
    bool success = false;
    success = emp.ValidateInstance(@"C:\BizTalk Server 2010
    Cookbook\Chapter 9\BTS.Cookbook.Test.SchemaAndMap\
    TestInstances\EmployeeInstance.xml",
    Microsoft.BizTalk.TestTools.Schema.OutputInstanceType.XML);
    Assert.IsTrue(success);
  }
[TestMethod()]
```

```
public void MapOutputEmployeeToEmployeeContractTest()
{
  BTS.Cookbook.Test.SchemaAndMap.Maps.
  EmployeeToEmployeeContract emp2empcon = new
  Maps.EmployeeToEmployeeContract();
  string inputEmployee = @"C:\BizTalk Server 2010
  Cookbook\Chapter 9\BTS.Cookbook.Test.SchemaAndMap\
  TestInstances\EmployeeInstance.xml";
  string outputEmployeeContract = @"C:\BizTalk Server 2010
  Cookbook\Chapter 9\BTS.Cookbook.Test.SchemaAndMap\
  TestInstances\EmployeeContract_Output.xml";
  emp2empcon.TestMap(inputEmployee, Microsoft.BizTalk.
  TestTools.Schema.InputInstanceType.Xml,
  outputEmployeeContract, Microsoft.BizTalk.TestTools.
  Schema.OutputInstanceType.XML);
  Assert.IsTrue(File.Exists(outputEmployeeContract));
}
```

10. You can test the methods by clicking on **Run all Tests in Solution**.

How it works...

Testing of schemas can be done within a BizTalk project by validating an instance of that schema. You provide the location of the instance in the schema file property **Input Instance Filename**. The other schema file property which needs to be set is **Validate Instance Input Type** to configure the format of the instance message identified by the **Input Instance Filename** property. By choosing **Validate Instance**, the specified document instance will be loaded and validated to the selected schema.

Testing of maps can also be done within a BizTalk project containing them. Again, you have to set some properties. These involve properties of the map you select. You will find all the properties that need to be set when testing a map in the following table:

Property	Description
Validate TestMap Input	It is a Boolean value indicating whether the source document will be validated against the source schema or not.
Validate TestMap Output	It is a Boolean value indicating whether the output document should be validated against the destination schema or not.
TestMap Input Instance	It is a path to the file which contains an instance of the source schema. It is used when the TestMap Input property is not set to the Generate Instance.

Property	Description
TestMap Input	It indicates the origin of the source document. If it is set to the Generate Instance, BizTalk will generate an instance in its memory that contains values for all attributes and elements in the source schema. If it is set to XML or Native, BizTalk will look for an instance of the document in the location specified in the TestMap Input Instance property. Native indicates a non-XML file such as a flat file.
TestMap Output	It indicates the format of the output document. The document will be output to a file stored in a temporary directory on Windows and accessible through Visual Studio.

By choosing **Test Map**, the specified source document will be loaded and the mapping will occur. The output of the mapping will be either stored in a location that has been provided or to a temporary directory provided through a link in the output window of Visual Studio.

Unit testing a schema means the `ValidateInstance` method is used, which is similar to choosing **Validate Instance** on a schema in a BizTalk project. The `ValidateInstance` method is a member of the `TestableSchemaBase` class belonging to the namespace `Microsoft.XLANGs.BaseTypes`. While calling this method you have to provide the path to the document and the output instance type. This method will return a Boolean value indicating whether validation was successful (`true`) or not (`false`).

Unit testing a map means that the `TestMap` method is used, which is similar to choosing **Test Map** on a map in a BizTalk project. The `TestMap` method is a member of the `TestableMapBase` class belonging also to the namespace `Microsoft.XLANGs.BaseTypes`. While calling this method you have to provide the path to a source document (instance), type of the instance, the path to the location for the output document (instance), and the type of output instance. This method will not return anything (that is, void method). The way to validate that the map has been executed successfully, is to validate that the output was created.

There's more...

On the TechNet Wiki, you can find an article called **Load Testing BizTalk Server Solutions with Visual Studio 2010** (`http://social.technet.microsoft.com/wiki/contents/articles/load-testing-biztalk-server-solutions-with-visual-studio-2010.aspx`). This article shows how to use Visual Studio test projects for the purpose of load testing a BizTalk Server application including how to create unit tests, how to create load tests, and how to configure load tests to capture the performance counter data required to determine the **Maximum Sustainable Throughput** (**MST**) of a BizTalk Server application:

Michael Stephenson has written an extensive series of blog post on testing in the BizTalk Server (targeted on BizTalk 2009). You can find that post in the document called **BizTalk Testing Guidance – Revisited** at `http://geekswithblogs.net/michaelstephenson/archive/2008/12/12/127828.aspx`.

See also

▸ Refer to the *Unit testing a BizTalk solution with BizUnit*, *Testing BizTalk solutions with BizMock*, and *Using the BizTalk Map Test Framework* recipes discussed later in this chapter

Unit testing a BizTalk solution with BizUnit

BizUnit is a framework for testing BizTalk artifacts. It offers a flexible and extensible declarative test framework. The BizUnit framework has no dependency on Visual Studio unit testing. Yet, you can leverage the framework in the Visual Studio Test Project.

A developer authors the BizUnit test case(s) in XML or code (BizUnit object model), and by doing so he/she configures how the test framework should execute the case(s). A test case is made up of three stages:

▸ Test setup

▸ Test execution

▸ Test cleanup

Each stage in a test case can have zero or more test steps, and these test steps are, in general, autonomous. This means that the state can be flowed between each state if required by using the `context` object which is passed to each test step by the framework.

Currently, BizUnit is at its fourth version supporting BizTalk 2010 (.NET 4.0) and this recipe will show how to use BizUnit 4.0 to unit test an orchestration in BizTalk 2010. The test case demonstrated in this recipe will execute a test case through code.

Getting ready

Download BizUnit from CodePlex (`http://bizunit.codeplex.com/releases/view/66850`). Install BizUnit on your machine. For reference, you can download the sample solution belonging to this chapter from the Packt website.

How to do it...

The following steps will show how to perform automated tests with BizUnit:

1. Open the solution you want to test in Visual Studio 2010.

2. Add a test project to the solution:

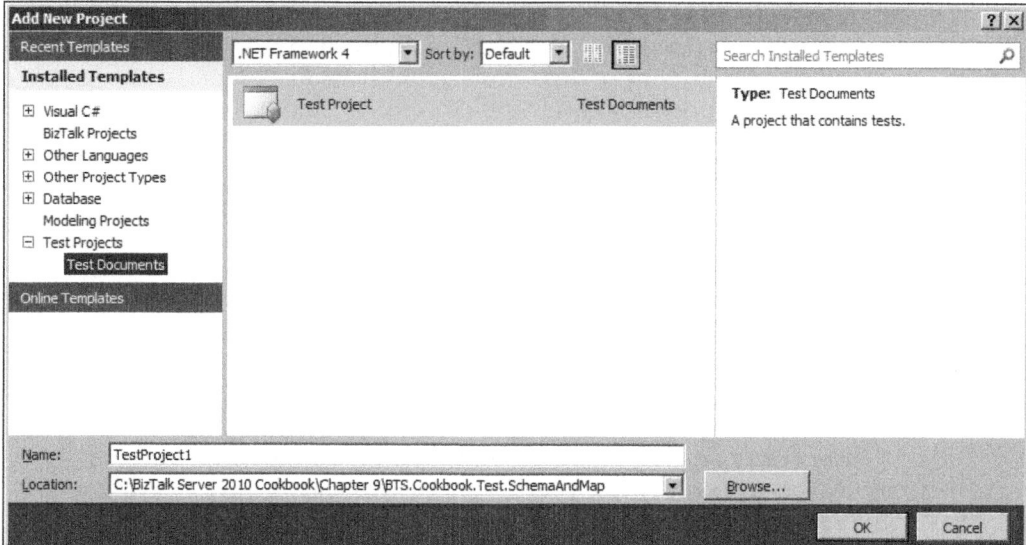

3. Give the project an appropriate name.

4. Click on **OK**.

5. Next, you need to add the BizUnit references to the test project. You will find them at `<install path>\BizUnit\BizUnit 4.0\Bins`. Reference to the following assemblies needs to be added:

   ❑ `BizUnit.dll`

   ❑ `BizUnit.TestSteps.dll`

   ❑ `BizUnit.TestSteps.BizTalk.dll`

6. Now you can create your test methods. Rename `UnitTest1.cs` to an appropriate name if you desire.

7. Add the appropriate `using` statements to the `test` class.

8. Create a test method and add the following code snippet:

```
[TestMethod]
  public void TestEmployeeContractOrchestration()
  {
    var employeeContractTest = new TestCase { Name = "Test
    EmployeeContract Orchestration" };
    //Delete of any files that are already there
    DeleteStep deleteStep = new DeleteStep();
    var filePathsToDelete = new Collection<string>
    { @"C:\BizTalk Server 2010 Cookbook\Chapter
    9\BTS.BizUnit.Sample\Out\*.xml" };
    deleteStep.FilePathsToDelete = filePathsToDelete;
    employeeContractTest.SetupSteps.Add(deleteStep);
    //Create the test step
    var testStep = new CreateStep();
    //Where are we going to create the file
    //Change directory to your own requirement
    testStep.CreationPath = @"C:\BizTalk Server 2010
    Cookbook\Chapter 9\BTS.BizUnit.Sample\
    In\EmployeeInstance.xml";
    var dataLoader = new FileDataLoader();
    //Where are we getting the file from
    //Change directory to your own requirement
    dataLoader.FilePath = @"C:\BizTalk Server 2010
    Cookbook\Chapter 9\BTS.BizUnit.Sample\TestInstances\
    EmployeeInstance.xml";
    testStep.DataSource = dataLoader;
    employeeContractTest.ExecutionSteps.Add(testStep);
    //Create a validating read step
    //We should only have one file in the directory
    var validatingFileReadStep = new FileReadMultipleStep
    {
      DirectoryPath = @"C:\BizTalk Server 2010 Cookbook\Chapter
      9\BTS.BizUnit.Sample\Out\",
      SearchPattern = "*.xml",
      ExpectedNumberOfFiles = 1,
      Timeout = 3000,
      DeleteFiles = true
    };
    //Create an XML Validation step
    //This will check the result against the XSD for the Employee
    document
    var validation = new XmlValidationStep();
    var employeeSchema = new SchemaDefinition
```

```
    {
      XmlSchemaPath =
      @"C:\BizTalk Server 2010 Cookbook\Chapter
      9\BTS.BizUnit.Sample\BTS.BizUnit.Sample.Schemas\
      EmployeeContract.xsd",
      XmlSchemaNameSpace =
      "http://BTS.BizUnit.Sample.Schemas.EmployeeContract"
    };
    validation.XmlSchemas.Add(employeeSchema);
    validatingFileReadStep.SubSteps.Add(validation);
    employeeContractTest.ExecutionSteps.
    Add(validatingFileReadStep);
    //Execute Tests
    var bizUnit = new BizUnit.BizUnit(employeeContractTest);
    bizUnit.RunTest();
}
```

9. Build the test project.

10. Test the project by clicking on **Run Tests in Current Context** (refer to the following screenshot) or **Run all Tests in Solution**:

```
namespace Sample.Tests
{
    [TestClass]
    public class UnitTestEmployeeContract
    {
        [TestMethod]
        public void TestEmployeeContractOrchestration()
        {
            var employeeContractTest = new TestCase { Name = "Test EmployeeContract Orchestration" };

            //Delete of any files that are already there
            DeleteStep deleteStep = new DeleteStep();

            var filePathsToDelete = new Collection<string> { @"C:\BizTalk Server 2010 Cookbook\Chapter 9\BTS.BizUnit.Sample\Out\*.xml" };

            deleteStep.FilePathsToDelete = filePathsToDelete;

            employeeContractTest.SetupSteps.Add(deleteStep);
```

11. Check if the test has run successfully:

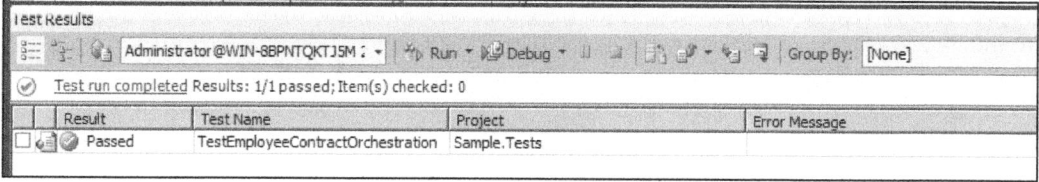

How it works...

A BizUnit test case in this recipe is created through code. First a `TestCase` is instantiated and then the first step is to delete any files in the location, where the bound port will send its messages to. This is necessary to bring the status to its original state, where no processing of messages has taken place. The first stage of the test case is to put it up-front, but you can choose to have this stage at the end.

The next step is to define the test step(s) for the unit test to execute. The `TestStep` object has a `CreationPath` property that defines the path (directory and filename) that BizTalk should be watching with a Receive port. A `FileLoader` object is instantiated to enable to assign the `FilePath` property. This property contains the location to the XML message which is going to be offered to the orchestration. Now, this step is fully configured and added to the `TestCase` object:

```
employeeContractTest.ExecutionSteps.Add(testStep)
```

The following steps involve checking the execution of the orchestration. Does the file exist in the output directory (has the orchestration processed the incoming message and sent it to the `out` folder), and does the message in the output directory adhere to the schema (for example, `EmployeeContract`)? A `FileReadMultiStep` object is created and a few properties are set:

- The `DirectoryPath` property which defines the directory to read
- The `SearchPattern` property for the type of file
- `ExpectedNumberOfFiles` to define the number of files to be expected
- `TimeOut` to define the time (milliseconds) when timeout will occur
- The `DeleteFiles` property to determine whether or not to delete the file

To determine if the output message adheres to the schema a `ValidationStep` object and a `SchemaDefinition` object are instantiated. Then, for the next steps two more properties are set:

- `XmlSchemaPath` to determine the location of the schema
- `XmlSchemaNamespace` to set the namespace (that is, `targetNamespace`)

To the `validation.XmlSchemas.Add` method, the instance of the `SchemaDefinition` object is offered. The instance of the `ValidationStep` object is added to `FileReadMultiStep` as a substep. Finally, the instance of this object is added to an instance of the `TestCase` object (that is, `employeeContractTest`). Now the test setup stage is complete.

To execute the test case a `BizUnit` object is instantiated with reference to the `TestCase` object (that is, `employeeContractTest`). Then the `Run` method is called. This concludes the test execution stage. As the complete test case is coded in a `test` class of a test project in Visual Studio, you can execute the test within Visual Studio and view the result.

There's more...

You will find more background information on BizUnit itself on MSDN and CodePlex:

- **Using BizUnit for Automated Testing**: `http://msdn.microsoft.com/en-us/library/cc594538(v=BTS.10).aspx`

- **BizUnit - Framework for Automated Testing of Distributed Systems**: `http://bizunit.codeplex.com/`

On CodeProject, you will find an article called **BizUnit 4.0 and BizTalk 2010** (`http://www.codeproject.com/KB/biztalk/BizUnit4BTS2010.aspx`). This article explains about BizUnit 4.0 and BizTalk 2010 in more detail.

See also

- Refer to the *Testing BizTalk artifacts inside Visual Studio* recipe discussed earlier in this chapter

Applying code coverage to a BizTalk orchestration

Code coverage (`http://en.wikipedia.org/wiki/Code_coverage`) describes the degree to which a source code of a certain program has been tested. In the BizTalk context this means how much of the orchestration flow has been covered based on the tracked data. The code coverage is measured through a community tool called the **Orchestration Profiler**. This tool queries the BizTalk databases and creates CHM (compiled help) report files illustrating the level of coverage for specified BizTalk orchestrations. In this recipe, we will apply code coverage for an orchestration used in *Chapter 7, Monitoring and Maintenance*. You can also apply code coverage to orchestration(s) of your own choice.

Getting ready

Download the Orchestration Profiler v1.2 from CodePlex (`http://biztalkorcprofiler.codeplex.com/releases/view/42777`). Extract the files and run the `.msi` file. Finally, make the following adjustments to the `config` file in folder, where the profiler is installed:

```
<add key="HelpCompilerLocation" value="C:\Program Files (x86)\HTML
Help Workshop\hhc.exe" />
<codeBase version="3.0.1.0" href="C:\Program Files (x86)\Microsoft
BizTalk Server 2010\Tracking\Microsoft.BizTalk.XLangView.dll"/>
```

Try adding the following at the end of the `config` file (but before the `</configuration>` tag):

```
<startup useLegacyV2RuntimeActivationPolicy="true"><supportedRuntime
version="v4.0" sku=".NETFramework,Version=v4.0"/></startup>
```

How to do it...

The following steps will show you how to work with the Orchestration Profiler:

1. Open the Orchestration Profiler.

2. Click on **List Orchestrations**:

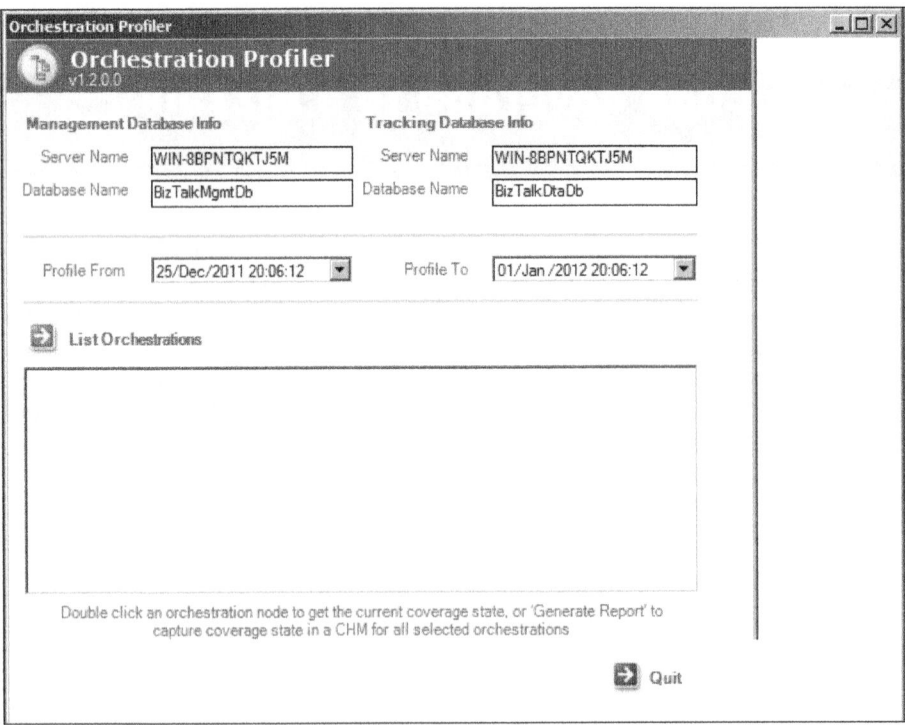

3. Select the orchestration(s) for which you want to generate a report to obtain a view of the coverage:

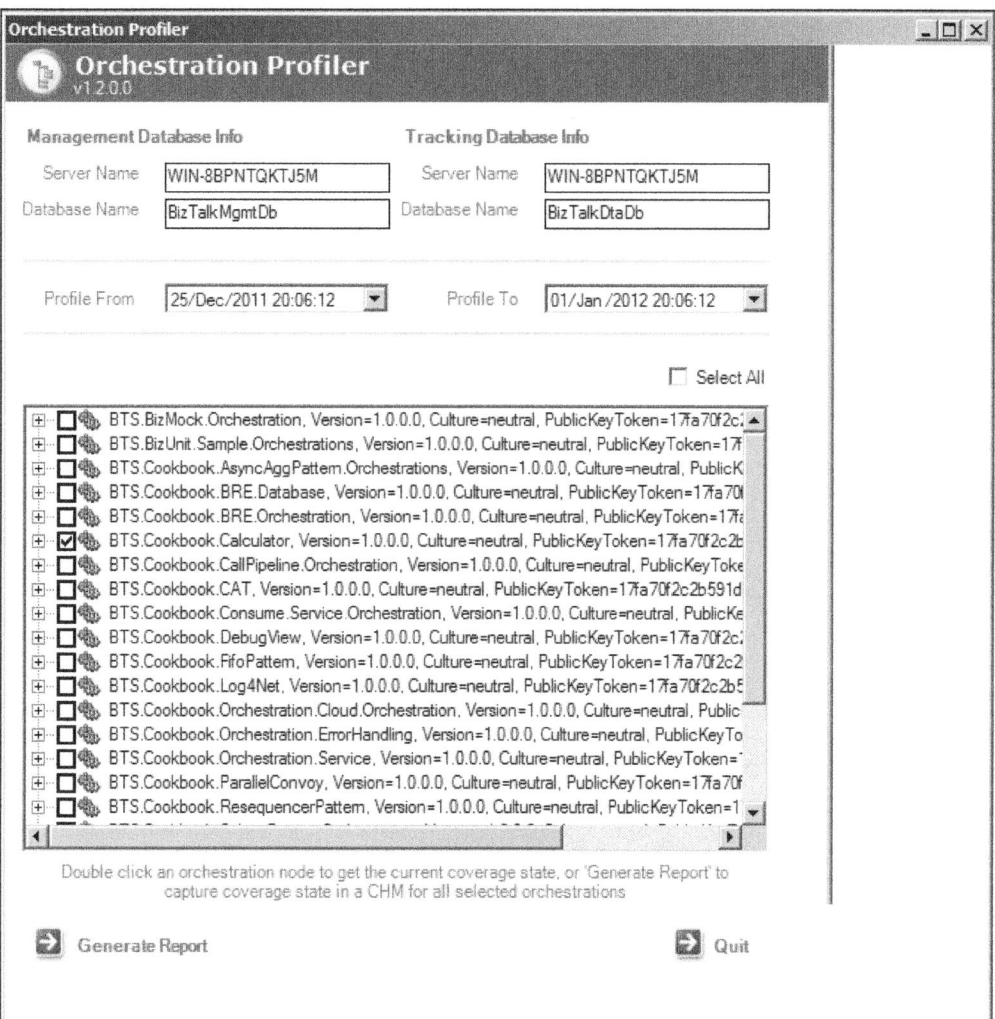

4. When you clicked on **Generate Report**, you have to choose a location for the report and click on **OK**:

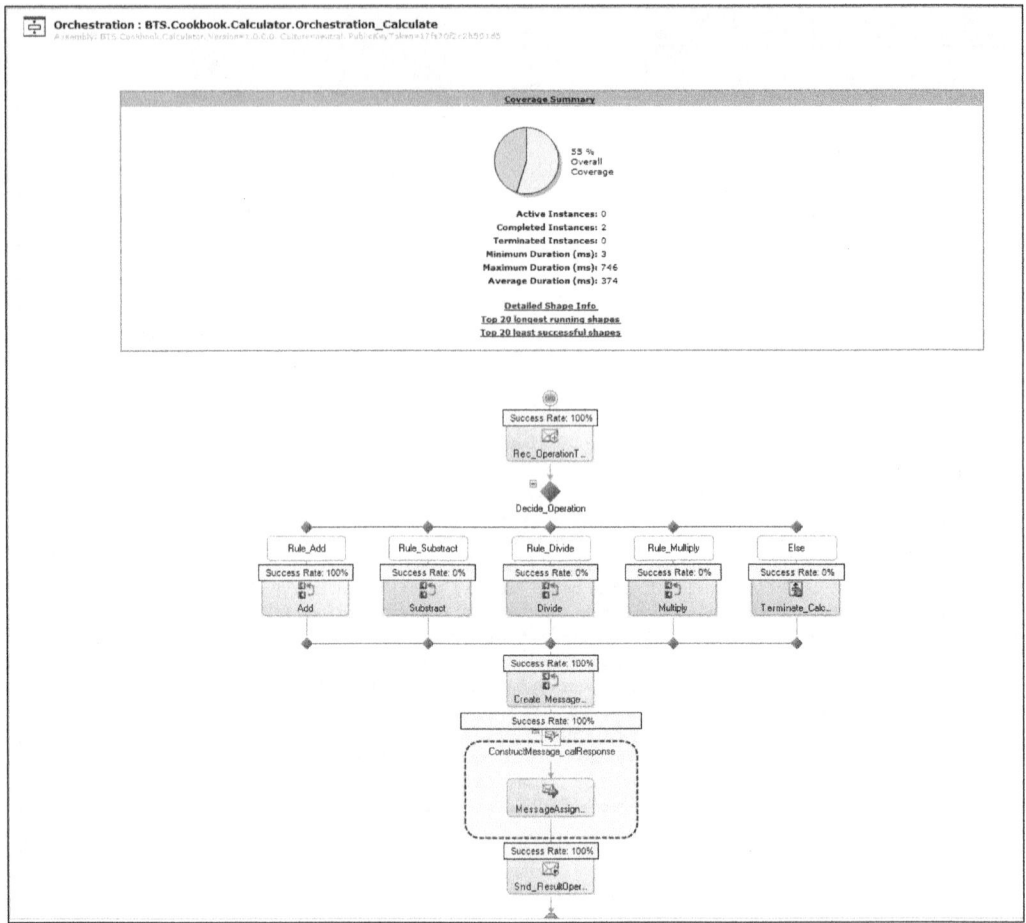

5. You can click on one of the following links in the report:

   ❑ **Detailed Shape Info**

   ❑ **Top 20 longest running shapes**

   ❑ **Top 20 least successful shapes**

How it works...

This tool generates a CHM report file illustrating the level of coverage for the specified BizTalk orchestrations. It is important that in the configuration the `HelperCompilerLocation` property is set to the folder containing the `hhc.exe` file.

While running the Orchestration Profiler, you can select one or more orchestrations and then choose **Generate Report**. The profiler will then query the BizTalk databases and execute `hhc.exe`. Subsequently, a consolidated view of the orchestration tracking data for a specified period of time will be produced. A developer will then see how the orchestrations are running and how much coverage they get. In addition to the simple coverage information, the data presented helps to identify latency and code path exceptions by highlighting long running and error prone orchestration shapes, which are key to effective performance testing.

There's more...

The Orchestration Profiler is a pretty straightforward tool you can use to measure code coverage. There is, unfortunately, not much documentation to be found on the Orchestration Profiler. The following are the resources related to this tool:

▸ **BizTalk Orchestration Profiler v1.2**: `http://santoshbenjamin.wordpress.com/2010/03/29/biztalk-orchestration-profiler-v1-2/`

▸ **Performance Tools**: `http://msdn.microsoft.com/en-us/library/ee377051%28v=bts.70%29.aspx`

▸ **BizTalk Server 2006 Orchestration Profiler**: `http://biztalkorcprofiler.codeplex.com/`

See also

▸ Refer to the *Testing BizTalk artifacts inside Visual Studio* recipe discussed earlier in this chapter

Testing BizTalk solutions with BizMock

BizMock is a framework for testing BizTalk solutions. It has been developed by Pierre Milet Llobet. It is available through CodePlex. BizMock uses a **Domain Driven Design** (**DDD**) approach, fluent interface API, and has mocking capabilities. The latter means you do not need to depend on an infrastructure, such as a database, as you isolate the tests on the developer machine or build server.

The tests you write are executed with Visual Studio using its regular tests and C# code. With BizMock, you can quickly test your orchestrations, schemas, maps, and pipelines by writing unit tests that can emulate the messages received at the Receive ports and validate messages sent from the Send ports.

In this recipe, we will follow the typical steps for the BizMock test project:

1. Deploy your BizTalk orchestration, pipeline, or map.

2. Create a test project and add the BizMock assembly references.

3. Add the `artifacts.tt` and `artifacts.xml` file to the test project.

4. Modify `artifacts.xml` declaring your artifacts definitions.

5. Write the test methods that use the generated artifacts and run it.

Getting ready

Download BizMock2010 from CodePlex (`http://bizmock.codeplex.com/`). Extract the files, and then go to `.\src\BizMockSetup\Debug` and execute `BizMockSetup.msi`. Finally, register the BizMock adapter from the BizTalk Administration Console. For a reference project (`BTS.BizMock.Orchestration`), you can download the source code belonging to this chapter.

How to do it...

The following steps describe how to test an orchestration using BizMock:

1. Build and deploy the solution containing the orchestration, pipeline, map, and/ or other artifacts (with the sample belonging to the book you can deploy `BTS.BizMock.Orchestration`).

2. Open Visual Studio 2010.

3. In the **New Project** dialog box, from the list of installed templates, click on **Visual C#**. In the right pane, select **Test** and choose **Test Project**. For the project name, enter an appropriate name and then click on **OK**.

4. Add the following references to the project:

   - `Microsoft.Biztalk.Adapter.Framework.dll`
   - `Microsoft.BizTalk.ApplicationDeployment.Engine.dll`
   - `Microsoft.BizTalk.ExplorerOM.dll`
   - `Microsoft.BizTalk.GlobalPropertySchemas.dll`
   - `Microsoft.BizTalk.Interop.TransportProxy.dll`
   - `Microsoft.BizTalk.Operations.dll`

- Microsoft.BizTalk.Pipeline.dll
- Microsoft.BizTalk.Streaming.dll
- Microsoft.Samples.BizTalk.Adapter.Common.dll
- Microsoft.XLANGs.BaseTypes.dll
- BizMockAdapterManagement.dll
- BizMockArtifactsSchema.dll
- BizMockery.dll
- BizMockMessaging.dll
- BizMockReceiveAdapter.dll
- BizMockTransmitAdapter.dll
- System.Xml.dll
- Reference to your orchestration (that is, BTS.BizMock.Orchestration)

5. Rename UnitTest1.cs to ArtifactsTests.cs.

6. This class needs to contain the following assemblies:

```
using BizMock;
using BizMock.Tools;
using System.Xml.Serialization;
using BTS.BizMock.Orchestration;
```

7. Copy the Artifacts.tt and Artifacts.xml files from <install directory>\ Install older \BizMock 2010\BizMock 2010\src\BizMockTest\ Artifacts.tt to your project.

8. Add the Artifacts.tt and Artifacts.xml files to your project.

9. Modify both files to your requirements (for example, artifacts), see the sample part of the artefact definition in the following code snippet:

```
<MessageInstanceArtifacts>
  <MessageInstance>
    <Name>Msg_Simple</Name>
    <Type>SimpleMessageType</Type>
    <Filco>
      <File>C:\\BizTalk Server 2010 Cookbook\\Chapter
      9\\BTS.BizMock.Test\\BTS.BizMock.Test\\MessageInstances
      \\simpleschema_input.xml</File>
    </Files>
  </MessageInstance>
  <MessageInstance>
    <Name>Msg_Simple2</Name>
    <Type>SimpleMessageType2</Type>
```

```
      <Files>
        <File>C:\\BizTalk Server 2010 Cookbook\Chapter
        9\BTS.BizMock.Test\\BTS.BizMock.Test\\MessageInstances\\
        simpleschema2_input.xml</File>
      </Files>
    </MessageInstance>
    <MessageInstance>
      <Name>Msg_MultiPart</Name>
      <Type>MultiPartMessageType</Type>
      <Files>
        <File>C:\\BizTalk Server 2010 Cookbook\\Chapter
        9\BTS.BizMock.Test\\BTS.BizMock.Test\MessageInstances\\
        simpleschema_input.xml</File>
        <File>C:\\BizTalk Server 2010 Cookbook\\Chapter
        9\BTS.BizMock.Test\\BTS.BizMock.Test\MessageInstances\\
        simpleschema2_input.xml</File>
      </Files>
    </MessageInstance>
  </MessageInstanceArtifacts>
  <MessageVerifierArtifacts>
```

10. In `ArtifactsTests.cs` you can create the test methods with artifacts and use the code shown, as follows (that is, you will find the complete code with the source code):

```
[TestMethod]
  [DeploymentItem("MessageInstances")]
  //testing an orchestration that receives a multipart message and
  return 2 multipart messages
  public void MultipartWithLoopDirectTest()
    {
      Expect.TIMEOUT = 6000;
      Expect.DELAY = 5000;
      artifacts.MultipartWithLoopOrchestration.Start();
        artifacts.Msg_MultiPart.InterchangeID = "X";
        artifacts.Vrf_Multipart.MultiPart1.Field = "Y";
        artifacts.Vrf_Multipart.MultiPart2.Field = "Y";
      Submit.Request(artifacts.Msg_MultiPart).
      To(artifacts.OneWayDirect);
      Expect.AtLeast(2).Request.At(artifacts.OWPort_2).
      Verify(artifacts.Vrf_Multipart);
    }
```

11. Create a new `test` class and name it as `BizMockeryTests.cs`.

12. This class can contain one or more test methods to all kinds of test regarding the artifacts you are using for your mock test.

13. With the samples provided with BizTalk, you can pick any tests you want, or create them by yourself as the following code:

```
[TestMethod]
  [DeploymentItem("MessageInstances")]
  public void VerifyFileInstance()
  {
    //Change directory to your requirement
    BizMockMessage msg = new BizMockMessage(@"C:\BizTalk Server
    2010 Cookbook\Chapter 9\BTS.BizMock.Test\BTS.BizMock.Test\
    MessageInstances\simpleschema_input.xml");
    XmlMessageVerifier msgVrf = new XmlMessageVerifier();
    msgVrf.ExpectedValue("/*[local-name()='Root' and namespace-
    uri()='http://BTS.BizMock.Orchestration.SimpleSchema']/
    *[local-name()='Field' and namespace-uri()='']", "X");
    Expect.Message(msg).Verify(msgVrf);
  }
```

14. Once you are done with building your test methods, you can build and run the tests.

How it works...

As a developer you do not have to configure the BizTalk solution you build. You can deploy the solution and then setup a test project. To the test project, a `T4-template` (http://msdn.microsoft.com/en-us/library/bb126445.aspx) file (`artifcats.tt`) is added which is used to convert the XML file to a class that can be used in the tests. The XML file contains references to all artifacts used in the test, such as messages, ports, maps, and so on. The artifacts are required to be able to run a test that is defined in a class module within a `test` method. In this recipe, a test is run for an orchestration using the artifacts orchestration object start method:

```
artifacts.MultipartWithLoopOrchestration.Start();
```

A multipart message is constructed with the artifacts `MsgMultipart` object assigning values to the `InterchangeID`, and `Multipart Field` properties. Then, this is submitted to BizTalk. The `Expect` object method `RequestAtInfo` will be called to verify the result.

Another class is created in this recipe that contains the test methods for the messages themselves, such as `verify` if the message exists and if the accepted results are in the message itself. An instance of the `BizMockMessage` object is created with a reference to the location of the input message and then an instance of the `XMLMessageVerifier` object is created. The `ExpectedValue` method of the `XMLMessageVerifier` object is called with an XPath query to the field element in the message with the expected value as the parameters.

When running the test, the artifacts such as ports are created, enlisted, and started. The same counts for the orchestration. A message is picked up through a Receive port configured with the BizMock adapter. Furthermore, the location of the input message and its expected values are verified.

There's more...

There is little documentation on BizMock itself, other than what is offered through CodePlex. For more details refer to the **BizMock** documentation at `http://bizmock.codeplex.com/documentation`.

There are a few blog posts on using the BizMock, where people share their experiences:

- ▶ **BizMock using it for orchestration unit testing**: `http://snefs.blogspot.com/2011/08/bizmock-using-it-for-orchestration-unit.html`
- ▶ **Introduction to BizMock**: `http://talentedmonkeys.wordpress.com/2011/08/29/introduction-to-bizmock/ (with reference to PowerPoint presentation)`

See also

- ▶ Refer to the *Testing BizTalk artifacts inside Visual Studio* and *Unit Testing a BizTalk solution with BizUnit* recipes discussed earlier in this chapter

Using the BizTalk Map Test Framework

The BizTalk Map Test Framework has been developed by Maurice den Heijer. It enables developers to perform tests on their maps using template files and XPath queries. The framework offers a great deal of extensibility when using it within a Visual Studio Test Project.

A developer can define a large number of test cases to be applied upon the map and these test cases are run within a single method call. Hence, the productivity of testing a map is enhanced significantly. Also, the developer only needs to maintain two XML files (one source XML (that is, the input file) and a result XML (that is, the output file)). Both files are basically instances of a source schema and a destination schema of the map to be tested.

In this recipe, a BizTalk map will be tested through using the BizTalk Map Test Framework in the Visual Studio Test Project (that is, unit testing).

Getting ready

Download the BizTalk Map Test Framework 1.0 from CodePlex (`http://mtf.codeplex.com/releases/view/58330`). Unzip it and place the content in a folder. In the folder, you will have three assemblies—`MapTestFramework.Common.dll`, `nunit.framework.dll`, and `xmlunit.dll`. To use this recipe, you can use your own mapping or one provided through the code accompanying this book.

How to do it...

The following steps describe the process to test a BizTalk map using the BizTalk Map Test Framework:

1. Open your BizTalk solution that contains the map(s) you want to test.

2. Right-click on the BizTalk project containing the maps and click on **Properties**.

3. Select the **Deployment** tab and set the **Enable Unit Testing** property to **True**.

4. Build/rebuild your project.

5. Right-click on your solution, select **Add**, and choose **New Project...**.

6. Select the **Test Projects** templates.

7. Expand the node and choose **Test Document**. Click on the **Test Project** template.

8. Give it an appropriate name and click on **OK**.

9. Add a reference to `MapTestFramework.Common.dll`, `Microsoft.BizTalk.TestTools.dll`, `Microsoft.XLANGs.BaseTypes.dll`, and the assembly that contains the map(s) you want to test.

10. Inherit from the `MappingFixture` class:

    ```
    public class UnitTests : MappingFixture
    ```

11. Implement the `CreateMap` method and return an instance of the `TestableMapBaseMapExecuter` class. Pass an instance of the map as a parameter to the constructor of the class:

    ```
    protected override IMapExecuter CreateMap()
    {
      return new TestableMapBaseMapExecuter(new
      EmployeeToEmployeeContract());
    }
    ```

12. The next step is to add the `SourceBasePath` and the `ExpectedBasePath` properties and return your template files:

    ```
    protected override string ExpectedPathBase
    {
      get { return @"C:\BizTalk Server 2010 Cookbook\Chapter
      9\BTS.Cookbook.Map.Test.Framework\TestInstances\Output.xml";
      }
    }
    protected override string SourcePathBase
    {
      get { return @"C:\BizTalk Server 2010 Cookbook\Chapter
      9\BTS.Cookbook.Map.Test.Framework\TestInstances\
      TestInstance.xml"; }
    }
    ```

13. Now implement the `base` test:

```
[TestMethod]
  public void TestBase()
  {
    base.ExecuteBaseTest();
    return;
  }
```

14. Determine which elements participate in your test and instantiate your `MapTestCases` (this depends, of course, on your schemas, the following code illustrates the XPath queries belonging to the code sample):

```
MapTestCases collection = new MapTestCases(
  new string[] {
    "/*[local-name()='Employee' and namespace-
    uri()='http://BTS.Cookbook.Map.Test.Framework.
    Schemas.Employee']/*[local-name()='Salary' and namespace-
    uri()='']",
    "/*[local-name()='Employee' and namespace-
    uri()='http://BTS.Cookbook.Map.Test.Framework.Schemas.
    Employee']/*[local-name()='Bonus' and namespace-uri()='']"
  },
  new string[] {
    "/*[local-name()='Employee' and namespace-
    uri()='http://BTS.Cookbook.Map.Test.Framework.Schemas.
    EmployeeContract']/*[local-name()='Contract' and namespace-
    uri()='']/*[local-name()='Salary' and namespace-uri()='']"
  }
);
```

15. Add the test cases by specifying values for the source and the expected files based on the XPath queries of the previous step:

```
collection.AddTestCase(
  new string[] { "10000","1000" },
  new string[] { "$11000" }
);
base.ExecuteMapTest(collection);
return;
```

16. You can test the methods by clicking on **Run all Tests in Solution**.

How it works...

To test a map leveraging the BizTalk Test Map Framework, you will need to enable unit testing in the BizTalk project that contains the map(s). Similar to BizUnit, you setup a test case(s) and then execute the test case(s).

Setup involves building the project with the map(s). The created assembly is referenced in the test project, together with references to `Microsoft.BizTalk.TestTools.dll`, `MapTestFramework.Common.dll`, and `Microsoft.XLANGs.BaseTypes.dll`. In the test project you set up the test by implementing a class that inherits from the `MappingFixture` class. In this class, a `CreateMap` method is implemented that returns a `TestableMapBaseMapExecuter` instance with reference to a map (that is, a map called `EmployeeToEmployeeContract`). The next two properties, `SourceBasePath` and `ExpectedBasePath` are set with locations to the path where the input message (that is, the instance of the source schema) and output message (that is, instance of destination schema) reside. Then the `TestBase` method is created that will test whether the source schema instance correctly maps into the expected destination schema instance. Finally, you determine which elements in the source schema instance participate in the test cases. A `MapTestCases` object is instantiated with XPath queries to elements in source schema which will be involved in the test cases. Subsequently, a collection of test cases is built and executed. Each test case uses separate files which are generated by the `ExecuteMapTest` method.

When the test is run, you will see the files, as depicted in the following screenshot, and you can compare the actual and expected files, and investigate the map to determine if the test has failed or succeeded:

Name ↑	Date modified	Type	Size
Output	12/29/2011 12:10 PM	XML Document	1 KB
OutputTestBase_Actual	1/1/2012 6:17 PM	XML Document	1 KB
OutputTestBase_Expected	1/1/2012 6:17 PM	XML Document	1 KB
OutputTestFieldValues_Actual	1/1/2012 6:17 PM	XML Document	1 KB
OutputTestFieldValues_Expected	1/1/2012 6:17 PM	XML Document	1 KB
TestInstance	12/29/2011 11:04 AM	XML Document	1 KB
TestInstanceTestBase	1/1/2012 6:17 PM	XML Document	1 KB
TestInstanceTestFieldValues	1/1/2012 6:17 PM	XML Document	1 KB

There's more...

You can find more information on the BizTalk Map Test Framework at CodePlex in the document called the **BizTalk Map** Test Framework (`http://mtf.codeplex.com/`).

See also

  ▸ Refer to the *Testing BizTalk artifacts inside Visual Studio* and *Unit testing a BizTalk solution with BizUnit* recipes discussed earlier in this chapter

Testing pipelines and pipeline components

The testing of pipelines and pipeline components can be done through the Visual Studio unit tests. Similar to the unit testing of the schemas and maps described in the first recipe. The unit testing of the pipelines within Visual Studio is similar to the `Pipeline.exe` tool (for more information on the `Pipeline.exe` tool, see `http://msdn.microsoft.com/en-us/library/aa547988.aspx`.

Besides unit testing of pipelines through Visual Studio, you can also opt for testing a pipeline and its components using the Pipeline Testing Library created by Tomas Restrepo. This library allows developers to programmatically create pipelines, create instances of components, and assign them to their respective stages (including their own custom components and the familiar out of the box components), or load an existing BizTalk pipeline without the need to deploy the supporting BizTalk project.

In this recipe, you will see two possible ways to test pipeline components. One is using Visual Studio's capability of running tests and the other is using a test library in a Visual Studio unit test.

Getting ready

To use this recipe, you can use your pipeline component(s) or use the one provided through the code accompanied by this book. The code belonging to `BTS.Cookbook.Pipeline.Test` solution also has a reference to the Pipeline Testing Library, which you need to download (the library can be downloaded from this location: `http://winterdom.com/2007/08/pipelinetesting11released`) and build on your own machine.

How to do it...

The following steps involve setting up a test, to test a custom pipeline through Visual Studio 2010:

1. In Visual Studio 2010, open the solution containing the custom pipeline(s).

2. In **Solution Explorer**, right-click on the project and then click on **Properties**.

3. In **Project Designer**, click on the **Deployment property page** tab and set **Enable Unit Testing** to **True**.

4. Close the **Project Properties** page after saving the changes.

5. On the main menu, click on **Build** and then click on **Rebuild Solution**.

6. On the main menu, click on **Test** and then click on **New Test**.

7. In the **Add New Test** dialog box, select **Create a new Visual C# test project** for the **Add to Test Project** field. Select **Unit Test Wizard** in the **Templates** list, and then click on **OK**:

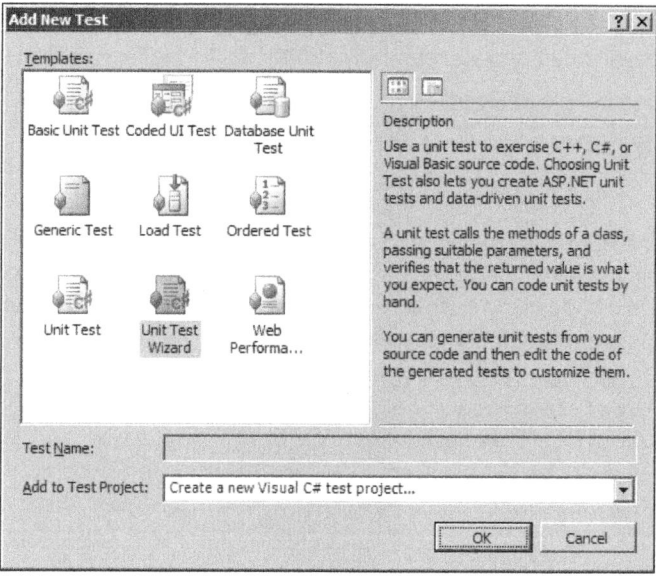

8. In the **New Test Project** dialog box, give the project an appropriate name and click on **Create**.

9. In the **Create Unit Tests** dialog box, expand **Types** and select the pipelines and/or components' node(s) and select the constructor(s). For the sample provided by this recipe, the `ReceivePipelineCurrencySymbol` constructor is selected:

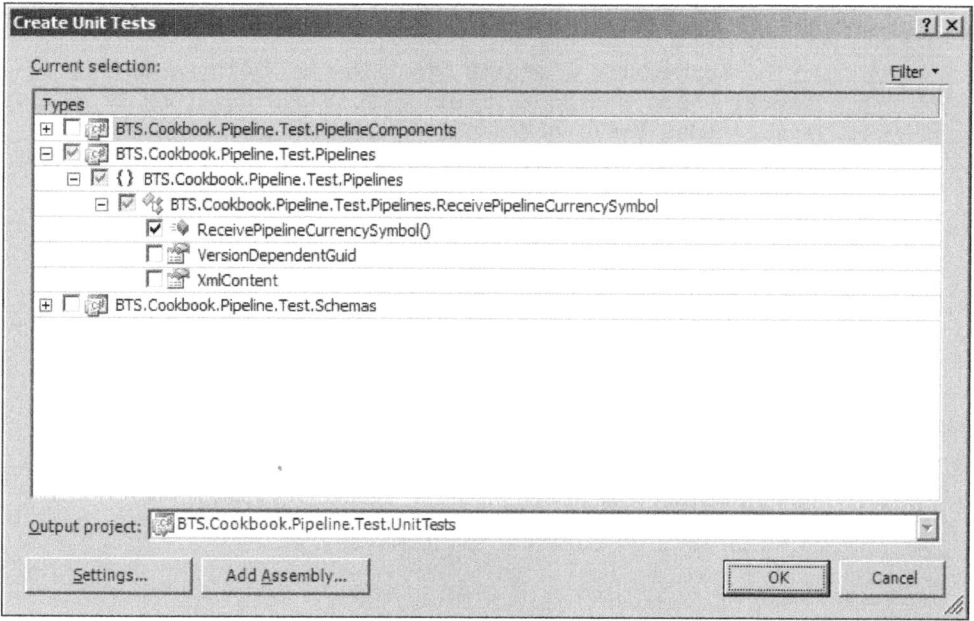

10. Click on **OK**.

11. A class file will open and you can now add the following `using` statements:

- ❑ using System.IO
- ❑ using System.Collection.Specialized
- ❑ using System.Collection.Generic

12. Scroll to the bottom of the file and replace your `ConstructorTest` method with the following code which verifies that the pipeline inputs exist before testing the pipeline. This code also verifies that a message conforming to the **Employee** schema is generated (the code reflects the sample belonging to this recipe):

```
ReceivePipelineCurrencySymbol target = new
ReceivePipelineCurrencySymbol();
  //Collection of messages to test the pipeline
  StringCollection documents = new StringCollection();
    string strSourceEmployee_XML = @"C:\BizTalk Server 2010
    Cookbook\Chapter 9\BTS.Cookbook.Pipeline.Test\TestInstance\
    EmployeeInstance.xml";
      Assert.IsTrue(File.Exists(strSourceEmployee_XML));
      documents.Add(strSourceEmployee_XML);
      // Only a body part for this test message so an empty
      // collection will be passed.
      StringCollection parts = new StringCollection();
      // Dictionary mapping the schema to the namespace and type
      // as displayed in the properties window for the *.xsd
      Dictionary<string, string> schemas = new Dictionary<string,
      string>();
      string SchemaFile = @"C:\BizTalk Server 2010 Cookbook\
      Chapter 9\BTS.Cookbook.Pipeline.Test\BTS.Cookbook.Pipeline.
      Test.Schemas\Employee.xsd";
      Assert.IsTrue(File.Exists(SchemaFile));
      schemas.Add("BTS.Cookbook.Pipeline.Test.Schemas.Employee",
      SchemaFile);
      // Test the execution of the pipeline using the inputs
      target.TestPipeline(documents, parts, schemas);
      // Validate that the pipeline test produced the message
      // which conforms to the schema.
      string[] strMessages = Directory.
      GetFiles(testContextInstance.TestDir +
      "\\out", "Message*.out");
      Assert.IsTrue(strMessages.Length > 0);
      Schemas.Employee employee = new Schemas.Employee();
      foreach (string outFile in strMessages)
```

```
{
  Assert.IsTrue(employee.ValidateInstance(outFile,
  Microsoft.BizTalk.TestTools.Schema.
  OutputInstanceType.XML));
}
```

13. In **Solution Explorer**, right-click on **Test Project** and then click on **Build**.

14. On the main menu, click on **Test** and then in the **Windows** list, click on **Test View**.

15. In the **Test View** window, right-click on your pipeline unit test, and then click on **Run Selection**. Verify that you see **Passed** in the **Test Results** window:

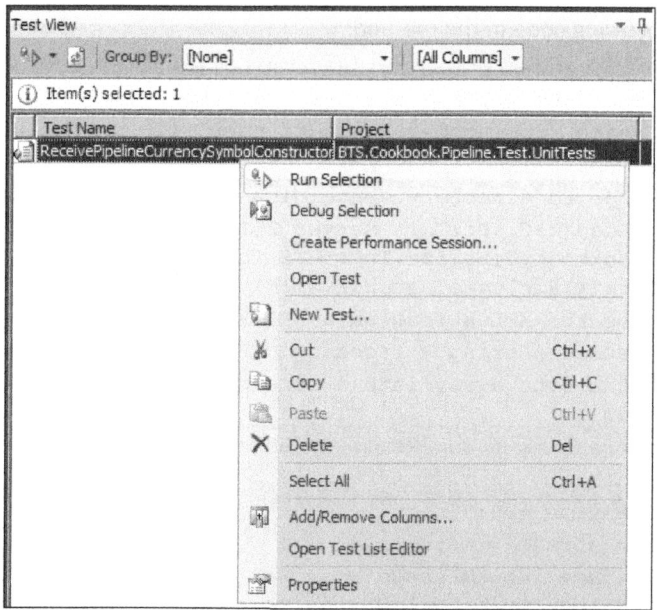

16. If any test fails, you can double-click on the test in the **Test Results** window to see the assert or exception that caused the test failure.

The following steps involve setting up a test for testing a custom pipeline using the Test Library:

1. Right-click on your solution and select **Add**, choose **New Project...**.

2. Select the **Test Projects** templates.

3. Expand **Node** and choose **Test Document**. Click on the **Test Project** template.

4. Give it an appropriate name and click on **OK**.

5. Add a reference to the following assemblies:

    ❑ `Winterdom.BizTalk.PipelineTesting.dll`

    ❑ `Microsoft.BizTalk.Pipeline.dll`

    ❑ `Microsoft.BizTalk.TestTools.dll`

    ❑ `Microsoft.XLANGs.BaseTypes.dll`

    ❑ `Assembly containing your pipeline component(s)`

    ❑ `Assembly containing your pipeline(s)`

6. Create a `test` method in the **Unit Test Class**.

7. Add the following code in the method:

```
ReceivePipelineWrapper pipeline = PipelineFactory.CreateReceivePip
eline(typeof(ReceivePipelineCurrencySymbol));
  //// Create the input message to pass through the pipeline
  XmlDocument xmlDoc = new XmlDocument();
  ////Change to directory containing the file you use as resource
  xmlDoc.Load(@"C:\BizTalk Server 2010 Cookbook\Chapter
  9\BTS.Cookbook.Pipeline.Test\BTS.Cookbook.Pipeline.Test.
  TestLibrary\EmployeeInstance.xml");
  // Encode the XML string in a UTF-8 byte array
  byte[] encodedString = Encoding.UTF8.GetBytes(xmlDoc.InnerXml);
  // Put the byte array into a stream and rewind it to the
  beginning
  MemoryStream ms = new MemoryStream(encodedString);
    ms.Flush();
    ms.Position = 0;
    Stream stream = ms;
  IBaseMessage inputMessage =
  MessageHelper.CreateFromStream(stream);
  //// Add the necessary schemas to the pipeline, so that
  //// disassembling works
  pipeline.AddDocSpec(typeof(Schemas.Employee));
  //// Execute the pipeline, and check the output
  MessageCollection outputMessages =
  pipeline.Execute(inputMessage);
  //// Assert if outputMessage exists
  Assert.IsNotNull(outputMessages);
  Assert.IsTrue(outputMessages.Count > 0);
  //// Create output message
  if (outputMessages.Count > 0)
  {
    Stream outStream =
    outputMessages[0].BodyPart.GetOriginalDataStream();
```

```
xmlDoc.Load(outStream);
xmlDoc.Save(@"C:\BizTalk Server 2010 Cookbook\Chapter
9\BTS.Cookbook.Pipeline.Test\BTS.Cookbook.Pipeline.
Test.TestLibrary\OutEmployeeInstance.xml");
}
```

8. In **Solution Explorer**, right-click on **Test Project** and then click on **Build**.

9. On the main menu, click on **Test**, and then in the **Windows** list, click on **Test View**.

10. In the **Test View** window, right-click on your pipeline unit test, and then click on **Run Selection**. Verify that you see **Passed** in the **Test Results** window.

How it works...

This recipe showed two possible ways to test pipelines and pipeline components by either unit testing them with or without using the Pipeline Testing Library. In case you do not use the Test Library you can enable unit testing in the BizTalk project containing the pipeline(s). The `pipeline` class in your project is derived from the `Microsoft.BizTalk.TestTools.Pipeline.TestableReceivePipeline` class, which models some of the same functionality exposed by the `Pipeline.exe` tool. With the Unit Test Wizard, you can implement the code to the constructor of this class. Within the constructor you can implement the code to set up a test with the pipeline by assigning one or more test documents (path with a file name) to a string collection and a dictionary mapping to the schema and its namespace and type. Next, the `TestPipeline` method with parameters, string collection of test documents, and the dictionary is created. Finally, within the constructor you can put asserts to the test to check if, for instance, there are any output files created.

With the test library you can basically do the same thing as with the Visual Studio unit test. First, an instance to a pipeline that has been referenced in the test project is created. Next, you configure the pipeline by providing a message by loading a test document and a document specification (that is, the schema that the message needs to adhere to). Finally, you assign the result of the execution of the pipeline to a `MessageCollection` object. You can, again, put asserts to the test to check if, for instance, there is any output and stream output of the file.

There's more...

On MSDN, you can find more on unit testing:

▶ **Unit Testing with BizTalk Server Projects**: http://msdn.microsoft.com/en-us/library/dd257907.aspx

▶ **Using the Unit Testing Feature with Pipelines**: http://msdn.microsoft.com/en-us/library/dd792682.aspx

Besides the MSDN resource, BizTalk MVP Michael Stephenson has written an excellent series of blog posts on BizTalk Testing. One of his posts, **BizTalk Testing Series - Testing Pipeline Components** (`http://geekswithblogs.net/michaelstephenson/archive/2008/03/30/120852.aspx`), details the possibilities with testing pipeline components:

You can find information about the Pipeline Testing Library through the following posts:

> ▸ **PipelineTesting 1.1 Released**: `http://winterdom.com/2007/08/pipelinetesting11released`

> ▸ **Testing Pipeline Components**: `http://winterdom.com/2006/04/testingpipelinecomponents`

See also

> ▸ Refer to the *Testing BizTalk artifacts inside Visual Studio* and *Unit testing a BizTalk solution with BizUnit* recipes discussed earlier in this chapter

Index

Thank you for buying
BizTalk Server 2010 Cookbook

About Packt Publishing

Packt, pronounced 'packed', published its first book "*Mastering phpMyAdmin for Effective MySQL Management*" in April 2004 and subsequently continued to specialize in publishing highly focused books on specific technologies and solutions.

Our books and publications share the experiences of your fellow IT professionals in adapting and customizing today's systems, applications, and frameworks. Our solution-based books give you the knowledge and power to customize the software and technologies you're using to get the job done. Packt books are more specific and less general than the IT books you have seen in the past. Our unique business model allows us to bring you more focused information, giving you more of what you need to know, and less of what you don't.

Packt is a modern, yet unique publishing company, which focuses on producing quality, cutting-edge books for communities of developers, administrators, and newbies alike. For more information, please visit our website: www.PacktPub.com.

About Packt Enterprise

In 2010, Packt launched two new brands, Packt Enterprise and Packt Open Source, in order to continue its focus on specialization. This book is part of the Packt Enterprise brand, home to books published on enterprise software – software created by major vendors, including (but not limited to) IBM, Microsoft and Oracle, often for use in other corporations. Its titles will offer information relevant to a range of users of this software, including administrators, developers, architects, and end users.

Writing for Packt

We welcome all inquiries from people who are interested in authoring. Book proposals should be sent to author@packtpub.com. If your book idea is still at an early stage and you would like to discuss it first before writing a formal book proposal, contact us; one of our commissioning editors will get in touch with you.

We're not just looking for published authors; if you have strong technical skills but no writing experience, our experienced editors can help you develop a writing career, or simply get some additional reward for your expertise.

Microsoft BizTalk 2010: Line of Business Systems Integration

ISBN: 978-1-84968-190-2   Paperback: 536 pages

A practical guide to integrating Line of Business systems with BizTalk Server 2010

1. Deliver integrated Line of Business solutions more efficiently with BizTalk Server 2010

2. Obtain pre-requisite ERP and CRM knowledge that will make your integration project successful

3. Examine ways to integrate with leading Enterprise Resource Planning (ERP) systems like SAP and Microsoft Dynamics AX 2009

Microsoft BizTalk Server 2010 Patterns

ISBN: 978-1-84968-460-6   Paperback: 396 pages

Create effective, scalable solutions with Microsoft BizTalk, Server 2010

1. How BizTalk Server 2010 works and appropriate topologies for different scenarios

2. Structure and unit test BizTalk Server 2010 solutions

3. Build BizTalk Server 2010 solutions that are easy to modify and expand

4. Create compelling Business Activity Monitoring

Please check **www.PacktPub.com** for information on our titles

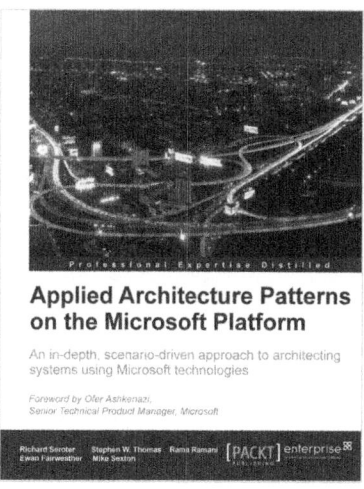

**Applied Architecture Patterns
on the Microsoft Platform**

An in-depth, scenario-driven approach to architecting
systems using Microsoft technologies

Foreword by Ofer Ashkenazi,
Senior Technical Product Manager, Microsoft

Richard Seroter Stephen W. Thomas Rama Ramani [PACKT] enterprise
Ewan Fairweather Mike Sexton

Applied Architecture Patterns on the Microsoft Platform

ISBN: 978-1-849680-54-7   Paperback: 544 pages

An in-depth, scenario-driven approach to architecting
systems using Microsoft technologies

1. Provides an architectural methodology for
   choosing Microsoft application platform
   technologies to meet the requirements of
   your solution

2. Examines new technologies such as Windows
   Server AppFabric, StreamInsight, and Windows
   Azure Platform and provides examples of how they
   can be used in real-world solutions

3. Considers solutions for messaging, workflow, data
   processing, and performance scenarios

**SOA Patterns with
BizTalk Server 2009**

Implement SOA strategies for BizTalk Server solutions

Richard Seroter   PACKT

SOA Patterns with BizTalk Server 2009

ISBN: 978-1-847195-00-5   Paperback: 400 pages

Implement SOA strategies for BizTalk Server solutions

1. Discusses core principles of SOA and shows them
   applied to BizTalk solutions

2. The most thorough examination of BizTalk and
   WCF integration in any available book

3. Leading insight into the new WCF SQL Server
   Adapter, UDDI Services version 3, and ESB
   Guidance 2.0

Please check **www.PacktPub.com** for information on our titles

Lightning Source UK Ltd.
Milton Keynes UK
UKOW06f1055111013

218905UK00003B/104/P